Malaysia in the World Economy (1824–2011)

Malaysia in the World Economy (1824–2011)

Capitalism, Ethnic Divisions, and "Managed" Democracy

Azlan Tajuddin

LEXINGTON BOOKS
Lanham • Boulder • New York • Toronto • Plymouth, UK

Published by Lexington Books
A wholly owned subsidiary of The Rowman & Littlefield Publishing Group, Inc.
4501 Forbes Boulevard, Suite 200, Lanham, Maryland 20706
www.rowman.com

10 Thornbury Road, Plymouth PL6 7PP, United Kingdom

British Library Cataloguing in Publication Information Available

Library of Congress Cataloging-in-Publication Data
Tajuddin, Azlan, 1961–
Malaysia in the world economy, 1824–2011 : capitalism, ethnic divisions, and "managed" democracy / Azlan Tajuddin.
p. cm.
Includes bibliographical references and index.
Summary: "From colonialism to independent statehood, the extent of Malaysia's capitalist development has been significantly limited by its peripheral position in the world economy. As a result, the fruits of economic growth have not been equally shared among its citizens and neither has economic prosperity done much to foster greater multiculturalism or democracy in the country"—Publisher's description.
ISBN 978-0-7391-7196-7 (cloth : alk. paper)—ISBN 978-0-7391-7197-4 (electronic)
1. Economic development—Political aspects—Malaysia—History. 2. Malaysia—Ethnic relations—Economic aspects. 3. Malaysia—Economic conditions. 4. Malaysia—History. I. Title.
HC445.5.T336 2012
330.9595—dc23 2012012408

The paper used in this publication meets the minimum requirements of American National Standard for Information Sciences—Permanence of Paper for Printed Library Materials, ANSI/NISO Z39.48-1992.

Printed in the United States of America

Contents

Figures

Tables

Abbreviations

AMCJA	All-Malaya Council of Joint Action
ASEAN	Association of Southeast Asian Nations
BA	*Barisan Alternatif* (Alternative Front)
BBC	British Broadcasting Corporation
BEIC	British East India Company
BMA	British Military Administration
BNBCC	British North Borneo Chartered Company
CCP	Communist Party of China
CIAM	Central Indian Association of Malaya
COMINTERN	Communist International
DAP	Democratic Action Party
EC	Elections Commission
EEZ	Exclusive Economic Zone
EIU	Economist Intelligence Unit
EPZ	Export Processing Zone
FDI	Foreign Direct Investments
FMS	Federated Malay States (encompassing the states of Perak, Selangor, Negeri Sembilan, and Pahang from 1895-1946)
FMSR	Federated Malay States Railways
GDP	Gross Domestic Product
GERAK	Social Justice Movement of Malaysia
HICOM	Heavy Industries Corporation of Malaysia
ICA	Industrial Coordination Act
IMP	Independence of Malaya Party
IPP	Independent Power Providers
ISA	Internal Security Act
JI	*Jemaah Islamiyah* (alleged terrorist group)
KMM	*Kesatuan Melayu Muda* (Young Malays' Union)
KMT	*Kuomintang* (Chinese Nationalist Party)
MARA	*Majlis Amanah Rakyat* (Citizens' Trust Council)
MAS	Malaysia Airlines
MCA	Malayan/Malaysian Chinese Association
MCP	Malayan Communist Party
MDU	Malayan Democratic Union
MIC	Malayan/Malaysian Indian Congress
MNLA	Malayan National Liberation Army
MNP	Malay Nationalist Party
MPAJA	Malayan Peoples' Anti-Japanese Army
NATO	North Atlantic Treaty Organization
NDP	National Development Policy
NEAC	National Economic Advisory Council

NEM	New Economic Model
NEP	New Economic Policy
NIE	Newly Industrializing Economies
NGO	Non-Government Organization
NOC	National Operations Council
OCA	Overseas Chinese Association
OSA	Official Secrets Act
Pakatan	*Pakatan Rakyat* (Malaysia's main opposition front, the People's Alliance)
PAP	People's Action Party (Singapore)
PAS	*Parti Islam Se-Malaysia* (Pan-Malayan Islamic Party)
PBS	*Partai Bersatu Sabah* (United Sabah Party)
PDRM	*Polis Di Raja Malaysia* (Royal Malaysian Police Force)
PETA	*Pembela Tanah Air* (Defenders of the Motherland)
Petronas	*Petrolium Nasional* (National Petroleum Corporation of Malaysia)
PKFZ	Port Klang Free Trade Zone
PKI	*Partai Komunis Indonesia* (Communist Party of Indonesia)
PKR	*Parti Keadilan Rakyat* (People's Justice Party)
PMFTU	Pan-Malayan Federation of Trades Union
PNB	*Permodalan Nasional Berhad* (National Equity Corporation of Malaysia)
PRB	*Partai Rakyat Brunei* (Brunei Peoples' Party)
PUTERA	*Pusat Tenaga Rakyat* (Peoples' Labor Center)
RHB	Rashid Hussain Bank
RIDA	Rural Industrial Development Authority
RM	Ringgit Malaysia (Malaysian national currency)
RTM	Radio Television Malaysia
SEATO	Southeast Asia Treaty Organization
SFTU	Singapore Federation of Trades Union
SNAP	Sarawak National Party
SUPP	Sarawak United People's Party
TNB	*Tenaga Nasional Berhad* (National Power Company, Malaysia)
TNC	Transnational Corporation
UFMS	Unfederated Malay States (designation for Kedah, Kelantan, Perlis, Terengganu, and Johor from 1895-1946)
UMNO	United Malays National Organisation
VOC	*Vereenigde Oost-Indische Compagnie* (Dutch United East India Company)

Preface

There are few things one is able to remember from childhood, but one particular incident in my first grade class stands out vividly in my mind. My school was located within the city of Kuala Lumpur, and my class comprised mainly of ethnic Chinese students, with a sprinkling of some Malays and Indians. During a class session—and I cannot remember what the exercise was for—our teacher, an ethnic Chinese lady, asked students to choose the person they admired most in class. Almost everyone pointed out to this Chinese boy, who happened to be the smartest one in class. When prompted why he was singled out, some said that he was "clever," while others said he was "handsome" and "rich." A few also referred to his skin as "very fair." When asked by the teacher who they felt should be voted the worst in class, the majority of students called out to a particular Malay boy—Jazmi—of whom I vaguely remember as being the slowest in class and also perhaps suffering from various mental challenges. When asked to justify their choice, many students mentioned that he was "stupid," "lazy," and "ugly." Then someone shouted that he also had "dark skin and full of black spots." Everyone laughed, including Jazmi, who appeared to be flattered by the sudden showering of attention centered upon him.

This was in 1968. A year later, Malaysia's worst ethnic riots tragically occurred in Kuala Lumpur. I am not about to amplify the above classroom incident as representative of what had taken place in every school in Malaysia. But ethnic prejudices and antagonisms were definitely rife during that period. Such tensions may have reduced over the years, but the ethnic divisions and distances are still glaringly evident. This, unfortunately, forms part of the major theme of the book—that ethnic suspicions and hostilities have in fact, become the basis for the kind of politics that have thus far kept the ruling elites in power in Malaysia.

I would like to start by very briefly introducing Malaysia as a country. Malaysia lies geographically at the heart of Southeast Asia, located at 2°30 N 112°30 E, with its capital in Kuala Lumpur (metro area pop. 8,500,000). The South China Sea separates the two main geographical regions of west Malaysia (formerly referred to as Malaya) and the northern Borneo states of Sabah and Sarawak (please refer to map on page xix). Malay is the official language, although other languages such as English and the various Chinese dialects are widely spoken and extensively used in business, media, and social events. With a population of approximately 29 million in 2010, the country is made up of three major ethnic categories. Bumiputera, the term designated for Malaysia's indigenous groups, consist the majority with around 67 percent of the total population. From this group, Malays constitute the largest (approximately 17 million), followed by Kadazans (800,000), and Ibans (750,000). The other ethnic groups comprise the economically successful ethnic Chinese, which portioned at about 25 percent of the population, ethnic Indians at 7 percent, and other smaller non-Bumiputera ethnic communities at less than 1 percent.

With the fall of the Berlin Wall in 1989, there had been high expectations that the democratization of Eastern Europe would rapidly spread to the developing world. However, fully inclusive and free political systems have been slow to emerge, and where democracy does exist as a formal system, the extent and nature of its implementation has yet to be entirely complete or consistent. Even in the developed capitalist states of the west, the general practice of democracy has often been confined to civic freedoms that are obtrusively non-threatening to the political economic interests of the elites. Here, policies involving immigration, labor, and education have often been unfair and biased against minorities and other affected groups.

Malaysia represents one of many developing capitalist states, whose appearance as a modern political system seems to qualify it as a free country, There is freedom to practice one's religion and culture here, while an operational electoral system serves as the primary conduit for holding public office. Malaysia has also been undoubtedly blessed with economic success. Its rapid industrial growth has unmistakably elevated the quality of life of many Malaysians, bringing global recognition and prestige to the Malaysian state and its leaders. However, practices in civil and human rights have fallen far short of what can be considered democratic. For example, there have always been constraints placed on Malaysians, inhibiting them from publicly making anti-government statements or joining associations regarded as "radical." Censuring of information on state policy weaknesses, problems, and failures has also been widely practiced by the ruling alliance of parties, who has been in power since the country's independence in 1957.

As my birthplace and original home, Malaysia will always be cherished however, for its unique multi-religious co-existence, blending of cultures, and extremely hospitable people. These are the country's most treasured attributes that must be celebrated and preserved for posterity, and never allowed to dissipate under the weight of industrial modernization. Unfortunately, there have instead been signs that the country may be heading toward impending social and political troubles. For one, there has been increased ethnic polarization, particularly between the indigenous Malays and the ethnic Chinese and Indians. This is easily noticeable in schools, social events, political memberships, and other forms of associational and organizational affiliations. More unsettling have been the continuing disparity gaps between and within all ethnic groups, even as the country as a whole has enjoyed tremendous economic progress. As of late, there have been unparalleled incidences of corruption involving high-profiled public officials, state dignitaries, and corporate executives, some of whom have yet to receive the appropriate punishment for their respective crimes or misconducts.

It has often been assumed, quite contentiously, that as developing countries attained increased levels of industrialization, their political democratization process becomes more pronounced. The growth of an educated and powerful middle class, whose desire for greater shares of opportunities, participation, and rewards, it seems, would have entailed demands for greater involvement in decision-making and higher standards of public scrutiny of state actions. For a long time however, Malaysians have only silently complained about their inability to publicly express critical opinions on various political matters. Fewer still have openly criticized the lack of transparency that has allowed the state to abuse its power for the benefit of the ruling elites. A sound reason for this can perhaps be attributed to the state's frequent pre-emptive and repressive actions against organized dissent and public criticism. These have included the existence and enforcement of many of the state's "emergency regulations" that have served to restrict, circumvent, and suppress fundamental civil liberties in Malaysia. Those who have incurred the wrath of the ruling elites have often been labeled as national security risks, while others have found their way to indefinite detentions without trial in the country's infamous *Kamunting* center.

How did Malaysia get to this point and why hasn't economic prosperity moved the country toward a more progressive and liberal brand of politics? I believe that any investigation into a country's social and political problems requires a comprehensive historical approach. It is never sufficient to lay focus on parts of a system without looking at the system in totality. For example, when discussing American racial and ethnic inequalities in educational achievement in my *Education and Society* class, I am always confronted by a persistent question from my students; why do minority children, despite advances made in civil rights and educational equality, still suffered from disproportionately low test scores and poor overall academic achievement when compared to whites? Such an inquiry could only be addressed through a historical and comprehensive study of the political economic development of the United States within the larger world economy. By doing this, students are better able to recognize the severe limitations of current American policies aimed at equalizing life-chances of minorities and the poorer classes, especially African-Americans, when these groups continue to be politically and economically handicapped by world economic transformations that have mainly served the interests of the white upper class in the United States. This is further reinforced by non-commitments on the part of the influential classes within the dominant group to fully support policies that could truly empower the underprivileged classes, and which have instead seriously reproduced the debilitating effects of sustained poverty and disenfranchisement among minorities in the country.

Similarly, it would be a mistake to analyze specific problems or issues within Malaysia's democratization process, or lack of, without understanding the historical-world systemic framework within which they exist or occur. In the context of this research, this framework refers largely to the capitalist world economy. Unlike the European experience or that of Japan or even China, Malaysia's incorporation into the capitalist world economy was through the exploitative and dehumanizing process of colonialism. It is not accidental therefore that critical discussions of colonial rule and colonialism are brought back into the discourse of Malaysian development. Far too often, many critics and scholars have discounted this period in any country's history as irrelevant to its current social problems, resulting in those analyses being incomplete or inadequate. It is an indisputable fact however, that colonial rule had molded in Malaysia, political economic structures and practices that were unjust and highly unequal. Thus despite political independence, the legacy of colonialism in the form of state exploitation, inequities, and wide social distances, has remained entrenched within the country's current social system. This is further strengthened by Malaysia's marginal position within the world system that subjects it to various forms of neo-colonial dependency in the world economy, and which compels it to survive as a capitalist democracy with inherently volatile and state-centric political system.

Since Malaysia's capitalist democracy has historically been shaped and catered to specific class and ruling elite interests, any prospective development in the extension of greater civil rights for all Malaysians becomes problematic for the state. This is especially so when increased citizen empowerment may come at the expense of reducing existing elite class privileges, including the dilution of state monopoly of power. It is not surprising then that past efforts to further widen democratic processes in the country have often been ideologically dismissed by the state as "destabilizing," or even "culturally alien." Such a worldview has been extensively ingrained in Malaysian political life ever since colonial rule that for a long time, Malaysians have accepted state patronization to be an inevitable prerequisite for national peace and stability.

As a result, many Malaysians have come to support instead, state-led industrial development as the only logical path toward the pursuit of happiness. At the core of this ideology has been the central role of the state in providing stable, paternalistic governance for its citizens. This has made any struggle for democratization in Malaysia subordinated to a larger *weltanshauung*—the belief that the state's delivery of strong economic performance benefiting its citizens would ultimately justify the means of undemocratic processes. Such concept, however, rarely takes into account the fact that economic benefits are never equally distributed to all citizens. Neither has the capitalist state been equal and just in its relationship with its all of its citizens, since the state's whole creation has been borne out of political-systemic processes specifically serving the class-related interests of the ruling and economic elites.

Hence, "rehabilitating" such a system in Malaysia can only be done through a concerted will of citizens under a broad, cross-class, and multiethnic front for equality and justice for all. Given the pervasive ethnic-class divisions in Malaysia however, the question arises as to whether the struggle for greater democracy in this country can ever be successful. Instead, would higher levels of political contestation end up in prolonged civil and ethnic unrests, thus furnishing the state with stronger justifications for an authoritarian-type rule to ensure political stability?

It is the opinion of this author that while human agency is extremely critical in initiating social changes, solutions to social problems cannot be successfully achieved inside a political economic vacuum or in a climate not conducive to reforms. Unless structural and paradigmatic shifts are operatively and mutually realigned, neither a systemic nor individual policy approach to solving any social problem can ever be entirely successful. This does not mean in any way that this research portrays a fatalistic outlook on the current problems in Malaysia. It asks that we begin with the awareness that social efforts to improve on or change the existing system must first require a clear ideological understanding of the larger political economic structure, within and with which critical components of the system interact, and out of which the present problems have emerged. Second, in order to examine and propose solutions to the injustices and structural weaknesses of the system, we have to address them as a force transcending the widest political spectrum and social divisions in order to target for goals that are collectively rewarding and socially just. In this respect, there definitely is hope and possibility for a freer and more equal Malaysia, provided that an all-encompassing approach to social justice and political economic equality becomes the higher goal for social change, and therefore serves as the unconditional premise for rectifying the many ills of the present capitalist democracy.

As we enter the second decade of the new millennium, we also witness the almost sudden and unexpected civil uprisings in a number of countries in the Middle-East, many of whose political histories for the last fifty years or so have been marked by stubbornly static authoritarian systems. While the final outcomes of these revolutions have yet to be discernible, this latest wave of globalization-led democratization, together with this research on Malaysia, should provide renewed attention on the subject of democracy in the developing world.

I conclude by extending my heartfelt gratitude to those with whom I have engaged in endless discussions relating to this project. I am also particularly indebted to Darrin Palilla for helping me produce "presentable-looking" maps for this book. Last but not least, my immeasurable appreciation goes to my wife Noor, and children Dan, Sarah, Hannah, and Adam for their patience and support for my work.

Azlan Tajuddin PhD
Pittsburgh, PA

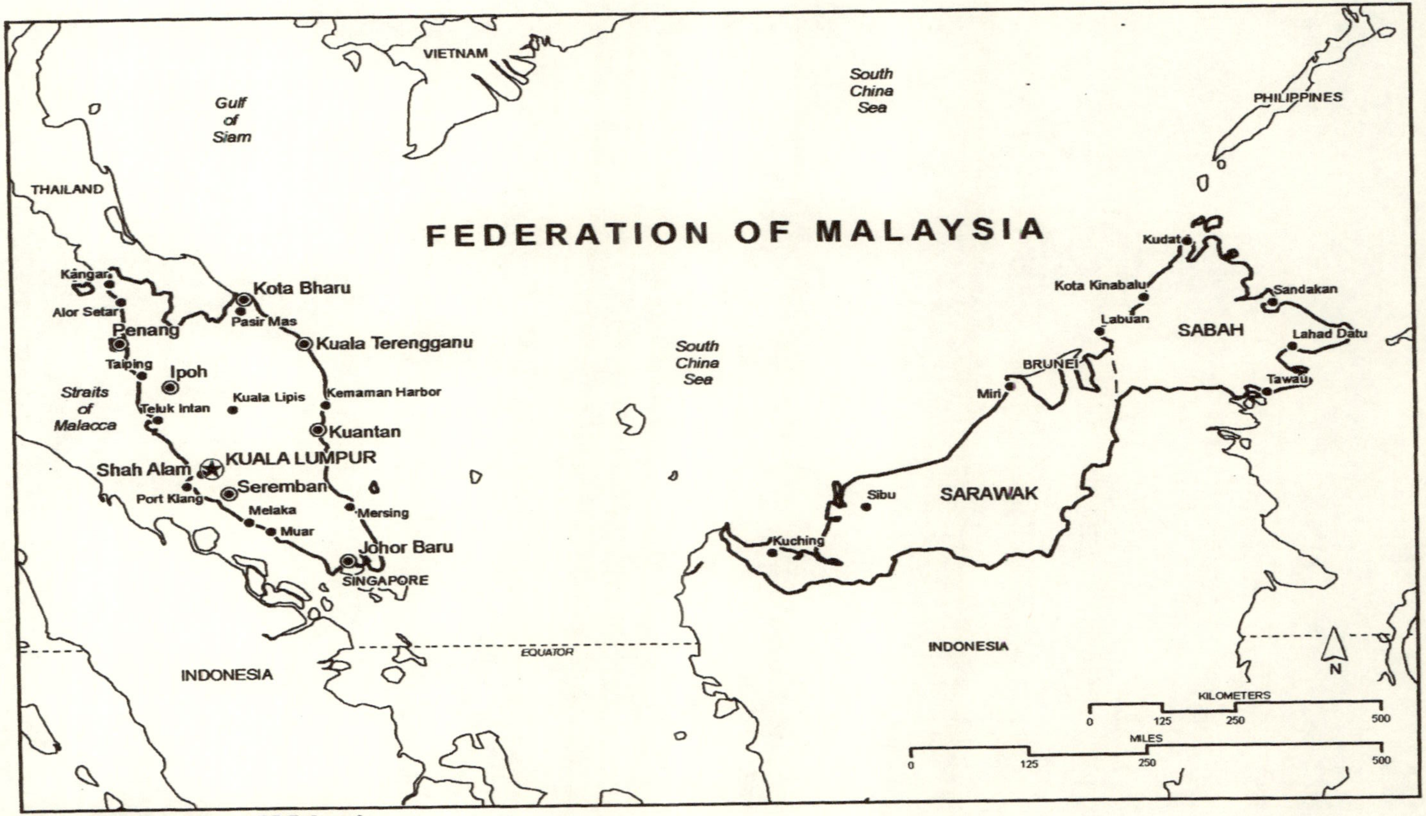

Map of Federation of Malaysia

Chapter 1
World Systemic Context of Capitalist and Democratic Development

There is often a presumption that a country's capitalist development would naturally entail or coincide with a liberalization of its political system. Hence, when Malaysia entered the league of newly industrializing economies (NIE) with double-digit economic growths in the 1990s, there had been high optimism surrounding the country's improved quality of life being complemented by a significant degree of political democratization.

However, despite economic prosperity, Malaysia's formal democratic institutions have become inwardly dysfunctional and their freedoms increasingly regulated by the overarching powers of the state. Indeed, there is increasing anxiety among many that the state has tightened its grip on the country's politics, leaving few avenues for dissension and opposition from citizens. There is also concern that the Malaysian state's hesitance in fully relinquishing its "emergency" powers over fundamental individual liberties such as freedom of expression, right to peaceful assembly, or due process for political detentions, would further propel the country closer to authoritarianism. Additionally, the tightening of state powers over citizens has exacerbated the latent tensions emanating from the country's wide and persistent ethnic-class inequalities and distances.

There have been many books written on the political economic history of Malaysia. The difference between this book and many others lies in its analytical approach, which focuses on the dynamic interplays between world systemic forces and internal-cultural factors that have also shaped the direction and character of Malaysia's political system to where it is today. In this, I am compelled to mention the great American sociologist C. Wright Mills and his narration of the *sociological imagination*, in which he explained that discussions of individual and social experiences, the formation of social-institutional structures, along with the problems that accompany them, cannot be detached from the analyses of the larger historical system within which they occur.[1] Similarly, any analytical discourse of state, ethnic relations, civil society, and democracy of a particular country should be carried out within the context of larger world historical forces, which for the last two hundred years have been notably shaped and dictated by developments within the capitalist world economy.

From this, the foundational argument posited in this research is that the explanation of the relationship between economic growth and the institutional provision of civil liberties and political freedom in Malaysia is best taken through a comprehensive and comparative-historical perspective. The aim of this approach is to enable a broader understanding of the historical sources of present political problems in Malaysia as part of larger global-systemic developments. This is especially useful when narrow approaches to social analyses are often likely to risk being inaccurate or misleading. This means that problems relating to democratic development in Malaysia should not be articulated in simplified and reductive terms such as third world culture, authoritarian leadership, or ethnic discrimination alone—Malaysia's political economic development has never been an autonomous process involving single dimensional actors or institutions.

In other words, the trajectory of Malaysia's political economy and the sources of its accompanying problems are generally systemic in origin. Here, the content and scope of Malaysia's capitalist development have been very much influenced by the interplays between the country's historical position in the world economy and the development of its local-cultural institutions, out of which comes the fusion of political economic problems unique to Malaysia. This requires the examination and analysis of social and political issues to go beyond issue-specific perspectives. Thus, students, scholars, and general readers, especially those who have little knowledge of Malaysia or the developing world, need to look at the country's ongoing social problems as products of its relationship with the capitalist world economy. Such a comprehensive approach to analysis will help uncover the historical totality of Malaysia's development process, making it easier to identify the systemic sources of the country's political economic problems, including the lack of democratization.

It is for this reason that the study of democratic development in Malaysia requires the critical analyses of the country's political economic history, beginning with British colonial rule in 1824 and concluding with the current phase of industrialization in 2011. The capitalist world economy provides the structural-contextual analysis of this research primarily because of its systemic shaping of inequities between the industrialized western countries and the developing world. Throughout the history of capitalist development, the more advanced countries have amassed tremendous amounts of wealth from their plundering of labor and resources in the world's peripheral societies. This has resulted in poorer countries being rendered impoverished and dependent on western countries for their own economic development and survival. The history of Malaysia's dependent capitalist development, which began with colonial rule and continues today with its relatively subordinate position in the larger world economy, is reflective of this relationship.

Hence, the discussion of colonialism as a starting point assumes a crucial component of this research. As an invasive historical process, British colonial rule had been responsible for the founding of Malaysia's current political economy, out of which problems pertaining to democracy have also emerged. A brief discussion on the origins of capitalist democracy in Europe would serve helpful at this juncture, since it highlights the political-historical factors surrounding the emergence of capitalism and capitalist democracy in Malaysia, which forms part of the central theme of the book.

Capitalist Democracy and Colonialism

The history of the modern world began with the conflation of capitalist development and the formation of distinct nation-states in Western Europe. As a consequence of class struggles that eventually brought the capitalist bourgeoisie to power, a gradual institutionalization of greater individual rights, upheld and guarded by an all-encompassing rule of law, eventually became the transformative hallmark of newly-emergent capitalist states throughout Western Europe.

However, this political liberalization also served to protect the system's elites and their economic interests over that of other social classes. While greater civil liberties were eventually extended to all citizens, it was membership in the ruling bourgeoisie or capitalist elite that allowed for unrestricted access to economic resources as well as the necessary qualifications to hold public office. In a somewhat vicious cycle, it was this disproportionate distribution of privileges that enabled the elites and their future generations to consolidate their monopoly of social, political, and economic resources through the capitalist system.

The growth of Europe as an "enlightened" society saw the need to institute civil reforms through a generally passive but an increasingly visible non-state sector, or civil society. This concept was first discussed by G.W.F. Hegel, and revitalized by Antonio Gramsci, to denote national-institutional areas of education, labor, churches, and other civil organizations that provided a political sphere for non-state actors in a capitalist society.[2] Through civil society, these organizations were eventually able to obtain some political reforms, namely those pertaining to particular group and communal interests, despite the prevailing hegemony of the ruling class. Nevertheless, a major outcome of this struggle includes the significant advancement of basic civil liberties, including the principle that no institution is considered above the law and that every citizen is entitled to seek redress for any maltreatment or harm done against him or her by the state or any other party. Within the current modern democratic state structure, the realm of civil society comprising of non-government bodies has also often provided the political space for citizens to initiate social changes.

Hence, the development of democracy in European capitalist societies would eventually involve the formulations and liberal interpretations of laws that were increasingly favorable to the protection of citizens. For the state, meeting the demands for the expansion of the voting franchise, wider political participation, and greater labor rights became increasingly essential for its political legitimacy, especially among male members of the dominant group, to whom these rights were initially confined. Through the years however, many states in western countries have exhibited some reluctance or lethargy in the effective extension of these privileges to "others," especially certain religious groups, ethnic minorities, and women. Even as these countries reached high levels of capitalist development, the total conferment of equal social economic opportunities to marginal groups has been less than convincing.

The hypocrisy of European capitalist democracy was even more glaring when capitalism spread to Africa and Asia through the confrontational and exploitative process of annexation and colonialism. Marxist theorists asserted that colonialism, which facilitated the growth of the capitalist world economy, had been a rationalizing process in the search for lower market and labor costs as a way to overcome falling rates of profits in the industrializing countries of Western Europe.[3] Colonial expansion brought the world's peripheral regions into an intensifying and unequal political economic relationship with their European colonial masters, ensuring that the provision of cheaply expropriated raw materials for European capitalist production and consumption markets remained uninterrupted.[4] Colonial rule therefore greatly benefited Europe's wealthy classes at the expense of local populations, especially when colonial policies and legislations would serve to socially and politically subjugate colonial subjects under European hegemony. In this respect, native populations under colonial rule were never held in equal terms to Europeans where political rights, economic opportunities, and social status were concerned.

It was during the early part of the nineteenth century that the British began its formal colonization of Malaysia through the institutionalization of a visibly modern political administrative structure. British colonialism began with a gradual process of one-sided negotiations and treaties between the British East India Company (BEIC) and the various Malay rulers. As the colonial venture became more complex and expensive however, the governing task was taken over by the Crown in London. This was particularly so when the use of state violence increasingly became an inevitable means to fully control the Malay states.

In view of the multifaceted character of colonial societies as well as the vastness of their territories, legitimizing colonial rule often required the assistance of marginal political centers outside the colonial administration.[5] In many cases, the colonial state would retain various aspects of indigenous pre-capitalist power structures to indirectly constrict its colonial subjects from accessing or acquiring positions of power. The colonial state performed this task by formally recognizing and endorsing a particular indigenous ruler's absolute sovereignty over his people or by preserving salient aspects of feudal life that would continually preclude the local population from any opportunity to challenge the authorities of both the traditional ruler and the state.[6]

In Malaysia too, colonialism became impossible without the agency of Malay sultans, whose cultural preeminence over their subjects was indispensable in strengthening British colonial rule. Taking advantage of their super-ordinate relationship with the respective Malay rulers, the British were able to establish hegemony over the indigenous Malay populations as well. As the British colonial state consolidated its hold on the political economy of the Malay states, it began to centralize the various territories of its new colonies through a federated system, enabling it to cater to the demands of the world economy.

A visible feature of British colonial rule in British Malaya (the political term for colonial Malaysia then) was the gradual introduction of modern administrative structures in the form of legislative assemblies, modern state bureaucracies and an English judicial-legal system. One can be forgiven to mistake the introduction of these institutions for efforts at providing the preparatory framework for democracy in European colonies. Indeed, various branches of the modernization and social-evolutionary theoretical schools have, in one way or another, implied that the development of democracy in "oriental" societies hinged considerably on the effective infusion and influences of modern European culture. Some even went as a far as to suggest that the legacy of British colonialism in particular, was inherently conducive to the development of democracy in former British colonies.[7] Not much has been said however, on whether these crude and superficial versions of representative governance ever intended to facilitate any active political participation, especially against the backdrop of rising European capitalist class interests.

Among the transformative features of colonization, including those in colonial Malaysia, was the introduction of wage labor. As the capitalist economy expanded globally toward the end of the nineteenth century, specialized labor for particular tasks along the industrial production chains were introduced in the colonial periphery. In Malaya, this came in the form of mass arrivals of low-waged ethnic Chinese and Indian workers into the increasingly lucrative tin and rubber industries, which not only helped spur the growth of Britain's imperious economy during that period, but also radically transformed Malaya into an increasingly multicultural capitalist society. With native Malays residing in the rural areas and engaged in subsistence agriculture, the stationing of migrant communities in their respective industry-related geo-economic zones would soon produce distinct associations between the various capitalist occupations and their respective ethnicity. However, as these foreign workers became permanent immigrant communities, the general demography of Malaya began taking on a segregated multiethnic landscape, with a majority of Malays subsumed into perpetual marginality and poverty in the countryside.

The prioritization of specific economic activities over others resulted in certain geographical zones to experience much higher development rates than other areas, bringing about clear social-economic disparities between the various ethnic communities living in these different geo-economic regions. Since different tasks under the new division of labor also dispensed a different range of remunerations and incomes, the new ethnic stratification structure of colonial Malaysia would soon confer on each racial-ethnic group, varying degrees of social economic importance and status along an emergent economic hierarchy.

In explaining the world systemic context within which ethnicization of labor takes place, world systems theory pioneer Immanuel Wallerstein asserted that "...at all times there has existed an occupational-reward hierarchy that has tended to be correlated with some so-called social criteria."[8] Indeed, the rationalization for the unequal ethno-occupational structure in the new capitalist society was often based on what can be categorized today as racist colonial discourse. Under capitalism, these so-called social criteria were in fact laid out by the biased reasoning of Orientalist scholars and racial scientists, who attributed the low status of non-European peoples to the biology, collective character, and cultural values of their respective communities.[9] Some of the more popular narratives of indigenous cultures explained these societies' economic backwardness as inherent outcomes of their relatively inferior intellect and naturally-occurring degenerative behaviors.[10] Such theories were used to justify the prevalence of non-Europeans in the lower rungs of the social-economic ladder. Conversely, the "naturally superior" intellect, dexterity, diligence, and brevity of the Europeans were highlighted to justify their eminent standing in the social, political, and economic hierarchies, wherever they lived.

However, there was conviction among some proponents of colonialism that although the lowly positions of Eastern peoples within the capitalist-colonial hierarchy were "natural," these peoples' overall social-economic capacity could be somewhat enhanced through increased exposure to enlightened western-capitalist traditions and principles. Here, colonial rule was often portrayed as an onerous but moral duty to transform "backward" societies into modern communities. Colonialism was therefore also seen as an obligatory calling or a "Christian mission" for Europeans to spread the enlightenment of Western-Christian civilization to as many "heathen" populations around the world as possible.[11]

In such light however, the transformative role of colonialism became contradictory. On one hand, colonial rule purportedly functioned as a benevolent instrument of civilizational expansion. On the other, the same so-called honorable establishment systematically inflicted varying degrees of mistreatments and repression against the people it ruled over. Particularly apparent was the deprivation of European civil rights and liberties, despite many local natives already having converted to Christianity or accepted the fundamental tenets of colonial rule and values. When few groups of colonial subjects did eventually initiate demands for greater political autonomy, the colonial state often reacted with substantial levels of discrimination and violence.

In reconciling this paradox, the colonial state and its apologists often explained that the use of coercion in dealing with local populations was deemed necessary and unavoidable. The argument goes that since non-European populations were predisposed to primitive child-like, or even sub-human characteristics, the patronizing role of the state often required the use of considerable force to stabilize the often chaotic and unruly nature of these communities.[12] Since the learning process of colonial subjects are not "well-adapted" to the complexities of modernity, the burdens of civilization were manifested in the difficulties of the mission itself, which can only be made expedient through punitive discipline.

As the low status of non-Europeans was considered natural and necessary by mainstream western logic of the time, the entailing rank-ordered hierarchies, more than anything else, served to mark the paramount position and prestige of

Europeans over non-Europeans as an accepted fact of life. Furthermore, the social-hierarchical rankings between colonial populations and the ethnogeographic segregation that resulted from capitalist development performed a colonial utility function for the colonial state in places such as Malaya. The emergent ethnic stratification structure would often pre-empt any form of civic association or collective consciousness among colonized subjects, which could perceivably have led to serious concerted challenges against colonial rule.

Here is an important point—that colonialism's existence pivoted primarily on the suppression of local populations. With their social and political institutions weakened by a powerful external force, many of these populations found it extremely difficult to contest colonial authority. Even if there was relative freedom for colonial subjects to voice and carry out resistance against the colonial state, the vast majority of colonial communities remained divided along class and cultural lines, restricting their ability to further mobilize as a united force.

For popular and grassroots actions to achieve political effectiveness, they must operate on the principle of civic virtue and in the spirit of moral collaboration.[13] Unfortunately, Malaya's multiethnic capitalist society, like many others, virtually developed from colonialism's ethnicized labor structure that prevented a unified and cooperative civil society from emerging. The prevalence of ethnic inequalities, divisions, and prejudices as inexorable outcomes of British colonization had also made it extremely difficult for a common and overarching national aspiration, or *nationalism*, to materialize among its culturally diverse ethnic Malay, Chinese, and Indian populations.

Anthropologist Ernest Gellner asserted that in principle, nationalism is from which nations and states are created, and with which the state maintains the conformity and unison between national and local units.[14] Additionally, famed political scholar Benedict Anderson argued that a national consciousness precedes any notion of nationalism because the concept of a nation is an "imagined" political community, entrenched in the common historical bonds of language, culture, or territorial origin.[15] When politically suppressed, many ethnic groups often seek to turn such imagination into national political reality, usually manifested through the formation of a culturally unique and sovereign nation-state.

However, in an unequal and culturally differentiated Malaya, each ethnic group came to develop its own perception or "imagination" of a nation-state shaped by the respective group's internal articulation of ethnic sentiments or *ethnonationalism*. A group's ethnonationalism is often generated and formed by distinct ethnic experiences of oppression, and becomes a means through which the advancement and protection of ethnic interests could be pursued.[16] It is not uncommon therefore that in a multiethnic society like Malaysia, there is a multitude of ethnonationalisms that co-exist within an environment of competing ethnic interests and aims.

Hence, ethnic divisions have remained a persistent obstacle to civil society mobilization in Malaysia. On this premise, this book will closely examine the historical development of each ethnic group's concepts of nation, state, and citizenship as a consequence of their differentiated formations under colonialism's highly stratified and segregated social system. It will also look at the history and extent of conflicting ethnonational interests and deep-rooted prejudices among Malaysians, whose parochial loyalties had automatically defined their respective political affiliations, and which made it difficult for cross-ethnic anti-state alliances to emerge or coalesce.

This is particularly significant considering that for genuine democracy to develop within a framework of broad popular objectives, formal democratic institutions must be pillared by commitments to soften particularistic, ethnic and class-related demands.[17] Under colonial rule, the construction of dichotomous "us and them" social boundaries had not only been the very premise upon which relationships between Europeans and locals were expressed, but it also served to delineate the social worlds of the various local groups. Under an oppressive colonial setting, each ethnic group felt threats coming not only from the colonial state but also from the rivaling interests of other ethnic groups.

Additionally, discussions of class are also relevant since the idea of nation and the propagation of nationalism as mobilization apparatuses have often been influenced by and contingent on elite manipulation. Rosa Luxemburg had posed a pertinent question: "The nation should have the right to self-determination. But who is that nation and who has the authority and the right to speak for the nation and express its will?"[18] In most instances, political economic aspirations of the elite class have run counter to that of the working and peasant classes, giving rise to paradigmatic inconsistencies within independence movements. Often, these class-related conflicts would also likely be carried over to the newly independent state, in which case the elite class would often have the superior resources at their disposal to promulgate the brand of nationalism as well as construct the type of national identity that is favorable to the advancements of its future political interests and goals.[19]

In many ways, nationalism and national identity in a majority of former colonies were partly shaped by events taking place after the Second World War. This war produced contrasting outcomes for its victors—Western Europe and the United States. It left the former virtually bankrupt, weakening their capacity to effectively maintain their territorial possessions in the periphery. The United States, on the other hand, emerged triumphant from the war and quickly assumed world leadership role. To sustain its primary position in the capitalist world economy, and in the face of competing interests from the Soviet Union and its communist allies, the United States sought to protect American leadership abroad through a supra-national structure of the United Nations. This international body was established to shape a new global order. In effect however, the newly-independent countries were expected to pledge to the ideals of western capitalist democracy and with it, American global leadership. The somewhat unequal relations formalized between countries within this body definitely favored the United States and its allies.

Hence, it was for this reason that when pressing for rapid decolonization of European colonies, the United States also stipulated that national independence in the periphery should ease in pro-western regimes with capitalist democratic systems.[20] In Malaya, there was pressure on the British to follow this lead and recruit local candidates for a leadership they saw as suitable and reliable in safeguarding the capitalist system. This was especially urgent in view of the growing influence of communist and left-wing revolutionary movements across the region that threatened to displace colonialism with socialist rule.

Thus under the "cold war" political environment, the form of nationalism that eventually prevailed in most of these post-colonial states, including Malaya, was often connected to local elite aspirations for leaderships in capitalist democratic systems. The catalytic rise of Malaya's English-educated Malay elite through the United Malays National Organisation (UMNO) exemplified this. The British were initially wary of UMNO for its anti-colonial stance. However, the British realized that the organization's aristocratic leadership and anti-communist leaning appeared to be the most relevant political attributes in developing and preserving a capitalist democracy after Malaya's independence, which was attained in 1957.

Emulating what the British had skillfully shown to be efficacious in sustaining its power and legitimacy during colonial rule, the UMNO elite carried on their former master's ability to manipulate and secure the political allegiance of the indigenous Malay population through the sultans. At the same time however, there was also the imperative of sustaining the country's continued prosperity through the stability of the capitalist system, within which British and local elite interests could continue to flourish in the new Malaya. For this reason, the Malay ruling elite was also compelled to incorporate their economically influential Chinese and Indian counterparts into an ethnic power-sharing governing structure in the form of the National Alliance.[21]

Hence a collaborative multiethnic elite class was formed. To the present day in 2011, these ruling elites, along with their circle of family members and associate entrepreneurs, have gained enormous social and economic privileges from their links with the ruling political parties. While consecutive generations of Malay political elites have generally assumed a *primus inter pares* position in this political partnership, succeeding generations of ethnic Chinese and Indian elites have preserved their foothold on the country's commercial sectors.

Importantly, the period immediately following the end of the Second World War also saw the rise in left-wing anti-systemic struggles across many parts of the global periphery.[22] Prior to the war, major leftist groups in Vietnam, Indonesia, and the Philippines had already assumed a significant role in the fight for national liberation against western colonization. In their struggle for a socialist political system, these organizations often advocated for political economic parity between all cultural groups and all classes of people. Like elsewhere in the periphery, these left-wing groups were able to appeal to a huge following among the working classes and peasants, especially in the delivery of equal distribution of benefits and resources through a centralized national economy.[23]

As the book examines such efforts by left-wing movements in Malaya to inspire broad cross-ethnic coalitions against the colonial state, relevant points of discussion will be raised as to whether the transcendent approach of socialism could have provided the essential ingredient for Malayans to overcome the distances and prejudices that existed between the various ethnic groups. It will also critically discuss the ensuing efforts by the Malayan state, with the support of the United States and Britain, to systemically eliminate left-wing threats to the country, and ensure capitalism's enduring dominance in the region. The crafting of Malaya, Singapore, and the northern Borneo states of Sabah and Sarawak into the *Federation of Malaysia* in 1963 was a culmination of this effort.

Dependent Capitalist Development and "Managed" Democracy

A major part of the Malaysian state's success in sustaining its political legitimacy has come from its use of a highly effective form of elite-driven nationalism—*economic nationalism.* This form of nationalism takes on an added dimension in economic development, in which national pride and prestige is measured by the extent of industrial growth a particular country experiences. In many countries, economic nationalism has become an effective political tool for legitimizing repressive state actions and policies, which are often deemed necessary by the state in sustaining the twin pillars of national development—economic growth and political stability.[24] Hence, it is not unusual for the ruling elites of countries with generous economic resources such as Malaysia to take advantage of industrial growth to unite their populations behind the state and its policies. Historically, economic nationalism has been particularly rife in East and Southeast Asian countries, where cultural and geopolitical factors have been said to contribute to the social elevation of national economic goals over other policy objectives. Promises of increased life chances and higher quality living have rendered state-led industrial development as the most valuable and overriding national aspiration.[25] As long as the state is given credence for its role in the country's high-performing economy, it will also be able to legitimize its patronizing role over society.

In this respect, economic growth has also served to strengthen state power over civil society and other political-oppositional forces. This is especially so when there is tendency to interpret political activism against the state as politically destabilizing and abortive of industrial development. When the legitimacy of the state is deeply embedded in the pursuit of industrialization goals, economic growth serves to keep political competitors and civil society at bay since there would be little with which to confront the state when standards of living are on the rise.[26] Thus when the state is applauded for bringing wealth and economic prosperity to its people, there would be few on the side of those critical of the state and its policies. It is for this reason that post-colonial economic nationalism quickly became a persistent feature in newly-independent countries with relatively strong economic potentials.[27] The ruling elites in these countries have become truly cognizant of the legitimacy derived from industrialization and have thus exploited economic growth to their advantage.

For economic nationalism to be truly effective in Malaysia, its propagation must also be seen to prioritize the numerically dominant Malay ethnic group, which constitutes the core support for UMNO and the ruling National Front. The state has sought to achieve this through preferential policies catering to Malays and other historically-disadvantaged indigenous groups, or *Bumiputeras*, especially in the access of valuable economic resources and opportunities. Politically, such a move has benefited the state since it has effectively entered Malays into a highly dependent relationship with UMNO, which has long been held as these groups' indisputable economic provider. Here, the prioritization of ethnic Malay economic goals by the state, which at times may seem to assume precedence over the *immediate* interests of the ethnic Chinese and foreign capitalist classes, becomes necessary in sustaining the ruling coalition's long-term survival. This is not surprising, since according to structural and state-centered theorists, states sometimes act autonomously of their relationships with other social forces, including its capitalist class, in order to sustain the legitimacy of its authority and that of the political system under which it operates.[28]

In this respect, Malaysia's economic nationalism also contains an inherent contradiction in terms of its implementation. This is expressed in the state's pursuit of industrialization that requires full utilization of resources on one hand, and the prioritization of affirmative-action policies that seek to section off certain exclusive opportunities for Malays on the other. The question remains as to whether this political paradox will pose considerable difficulty for the state in its ability to maintain its political legitimacy among Malays through its state-led industrialization efforts, the attainment of which, ironically, would also necessitate the full participation of other ethnic communities in the country.

Through a Habermasian analytical lens, the book looks at the contradictions of economic nationalism in terms of cultural-ideological legitimations concocted by the ruling elites to sustain support for the existing system, and along with it, the authority of the state.[29] An illusory side to economic nationalism often lies in the misleading presumption that the state has full control of the development process, especially in producing its desired results. While during boom times the state may be able to project its image behind the country's rising economic indicators, in periods of downturns however, the state becomes more susceptible to criticisms of its "poor performance" in the economy. Here, the state often manipulates information in order to conceal its weaknesses in resolving economic problems.

In other words, legitimacy derived from economic nationalism becomes difficult to sustain without continuous industrial growth. In Malaysia, the ruling elites persist in maintaining full control of economic development, especially in projecting a positive picture of growth and in channeling resources toward political benefits. This has been done through the nurturing of a stable pool of state-linked entrepreneurs and crony capitalists. This has been particularly significant for UMNO, which needed the services of its own reliable and well-resourced

Malay capitalist class to secure the party's financial lifeline and reduce its dependence on other sources of funding.

State-capitalist collaborations have been prominently inseparable features throughout the developing world, especially where governments aspire to modernize their economies as a means to consolidate their power base. In any case, the ruling elites in Malaysia, like in other developing countries, must also take into account the crucial role foreign capitalists and their investments play in the country's economic development. This explains why the main strategy for industrialization in Malaysia has been premised on the enticement and solicitation of massive amounts of foreign investments, which have often been successfully obtained through the accommodation and servicing of foreign capitalists' needs.

At the global level, the United States have always advocated modernization-oriented national policies for newly-established postwar regimes and other developing countries as a way to keep their economies open to international capital, which would culminate into the strengthening of the capitalist world economy. Scholars from the modernization school especially, often assert the criticalness of this political strategy in "helping" the less resourceful countries of the world to rapidly progress toward industrial development.[30] According to these theorists, infusions of western, namely American, funds and investments into developing countries could expedite these countries' transformation into fully-industrialized societies, notwithstanding the gradual and evolutionary nature of capitalist development.[31]

Furthermore, according to the modernization and other liberal schools of thoughts, such "assistance" would not be effective or complete without serious efforts to inculcate in these societies western organizational standards in governance and business. Such process was thought critical in supplanting any "obsolete" traditional practices considered extraneous to or inhibitive of capitalist development.[32] In other words, the western work ethic and cultural values must be adopted as part of these societies' mainstream values in order for them to successfully attain modern capitalist development. This rather Eurocentric prescription to development continues to be welcomed by many pro-capitalist and western-educated leaders in the developing world, who often perceive themselves as the vanguards of modernization in their respective societies.

In many ways however, the relationship between local elites and foreign capitalists in the industrialization process of developing countries has often been corrupt and mainly beneficent to the wealthy and politically-connected classes. As world-systems scholar Thomas Shannon puts it, "each member of the alliance stands to benefit from a policy and needs the other members to implement the rapid industrialization strategy."[33] For the ruling elites in developing countries, economic alliances with foreign capitalists serve to strengthen the state by enhancing their accessibility to generous influxes of investments into the country, especially in periods of growth.[34]

Nevertheless, state-capitalist alliances in the developing world tend to advantage the foreign investing parties even more. Since the terms of international exchanges have always favored the developed countries, the larger returns on investments often head toward the accounts of these foreign capitalists. In many instances, state-capitalist alliances ultimately reproduce the larger dependency of poorer countries upon the investing countries for their sources of funds. This is especially so when a serious lack of domestic technological capability subjects many less-developed countries to the lifeline of foreign capital for internal industrial production.[35] As it stands, very little of the foreign investments made in peripheral countries has substantially earned toward these countries' own industrial capacity or economic independence. For that matter, even "foreign aid" meant to help developing countries overcome their economic distress has actually adversely impacted many of these countries' economies. This is especially so when these assistances are often tied to stringent conditions imposed upon the recipient countries in the form of public spending reductions.[36]

Caught in a vicious cycle, developing countries are often confronted with the inability to manage their own economies, forcing them to borrow even more heavily from international financial institutions just to stay afloat. The exceptionally high financial liabilities incurred upon these countries serves to further entrap them in perpetual debt peonage. Such fragile dependence upon the developed world often fastens them into permanently disadvantaged positions in the capitalist world economy, and instead of attaining industrialization many have experienced what dependency theorists call, greater *underdevelopment.*[37]

However, throughout the last two decades of the twentieth century, Malaysia, along with a few other developing countries, recorded a significantly high level of industrial development, marked by impressive annual growth rates. Many of these countries such as Singapore, Chile, and South Korea also displayed an outwardly pro-capitalist political orientation. Neo-classical liberals, inspiring the resuscitation of modernization theories, heralded these countries' economic growth as symptomatic of future development trends.[38] The principle of equating modernization and capitalist growth with democratic development among other things, was once again revisited and rejuvenated. In their research, Ronald Inglehart and Christian Wenzel reiterated strong proportionate correlations between economic development, culture, and modern values, especially those pertaining to democratic principles of civility, freedom, and equality.[39]

In contrast, Neo-Marxists in the tradition of the world system perspective have always maintained that only a handful among these states would be able to successfully industrialize, namely those located in the northeastern Asia region where US political interests had been highly prioritized. The argument made here rests on the premise that the United States was determined to ensure that capitalist growth in this part of the world functioned to offset potential Soviet and Chinese penetrations.[40] Thus direct capital assistance and substantial technological transfer from the United States into South Korea and Taiwan in the 1960s were unique transformational events relating solely to American hegemonic power interests in terms of geo-economic strategy. Economic and technological aid as well as market accessibility was generously given to these countries, which then enabled them to develop their own export-based technologies and direct much of their goods toward American consumer markets.[41] To solidify its political influence in these countries, the Americans actually endorsed and aided authoritarian leaderships to power.

An area in which neo-Marxist theorists have perhaps concurred with modernization theorists with regards to development has been on the crucial role of the all-powerful and global-reaching transnational corporation (TNC). They both agree that TNCs' quests for cheap production and labor costs have gravitated many of their lower-level production processes toward the shores of the world's peripheral regions. As TNCs seek to enhance their global market competitiveness by exploiting cheaper factors of production in these countries, they also tend to provide industrial jobs and manufacturing-related occupational exposure for local populations. This often serves as a catalyst for substantial industrial growths in what had previously been agrarian economies.[42]

In East Asia, TNC investments followed a similar regional technical flow that was accelerated by close geographical proximity between countries. As Northeast Asian countries of South Korea and Taiwan reached a cyclical maturation point in production, in which real wages rose and competitive export rates fell, these "second tier Asian countries" then embarked on higher technological and capital-intensive production processes.[43] As a result, assembly and lower level technological investments gradually moved to other parts of Asia, where labor skills have become relatively high but labor costs remained low.[44]

Hence, "third tier countries" in Southeast Asia, especially Malaysia, received fresh penetrations of low capital and technological flows associated with higher-end labor-intensive production.[45] Absorptions of surplus capital and some limited technology from Northeast Asia into Malaysia during the 1980s greatly enhanced the country's industrialization capacity in low-technology production. In the short term, this transplantation of low-cost production undoubtedly benefited Malaysia since it sparked rapid growths in exports.

In the longer term however, according to world system theorists, industrialization in these lower-end countries has been limited to their roles as production or financial intermediaries between the rich nations of the north and less-developed countries of the global south. Much of their exports have also been in the form of intra-corporation trades, in which industrial sales were mainly confined to semi-manufactured goods re-exported to the parent country for completion of assembly or final production. This also meant that these countries still lacked accessibility to higher-end capital, technology, and intellectual property rights, which have continued to prevent them from moving beyond a level presently described as newly-industrializing economy (NIE) or "middle income." The world system theorists refer to such countries, which include Malaysia, as *semi-peripheral* countries.[46]

Herein lies another misleading assumption with regards to the end product of economic nationalism—that the rewards of industrial growth would benefit every citizen proportionately. In countries like Malaysia, one of the more obvious social consequences of this dependent and limited industrial development has been the continuing social inequalities.[47] The persistence of these inequalities is explained by the fact that in many NIEs, only a few among the local population could profitably reap the benefits from the industrial investments and manufacturing processes outsourced into that country by foreign capitalists. The social economic gains derived from the internal monopoly of resources would further engender high cultural and social capitals for these privileged classes, thereby enhancing the life chances of their successive generations. In comparison, the rest of the population would either remain untouched by industrial growth or confined to low-level economic involvement.

The repercussions of social inequalities have intensified the existing cultural resentments and ethnic suspicions that characterize the dynamics of a multicultural society such as Malaysia, especially between the wealthier non-Malays and the relatively poorer Malays. However, the nurturing of a privileged class through nepotism, cronyism, and corruption, which are inherent feature of elite-centered economic development, has also given rise to deeper inequalities within each ethnic group. This means that intra-ethnic disparities have also begun to occur alongside the long-established inter-ethnic income and wealth gaps.

However, as a growing middle class emerges, there would be among this class who would be willful and passionate in publicly highlighting these problems and in advancing their political interests.[48] In fact, there have actually been increasingly vigorous demands among civil society groups in Malaysia for fairer economic terms and greater political reform. The ruling elites' usual response to these impending challenges however is by portraying these demands as subversive, thereby often justifying its efforts to limit, manage, or suspend existing democratic institutions in order to further deflect public contestations against the state. The callousness shown by the state in enforcing these restrictions as well as in determining the form of castigatory measures imposed on its detractors, usually in the name of preserving "political stability," reflects the extent to which it is able to exert tremendous discretionary powers over society.

Interestingly, the United States and other western countries have often shown to prioritize capitalist systems maintenance over political democratization when their extensive commercial and investment interests in developing countries are at stake.[49] This is not surprising since despite the Americans' fierce propagation of democracy throughout the world, their true policy aim has often focused instead on preserving a compliant and abiding ruling elite in those countries, whose primary role has been to safeguard US and western economic interests in the region.[50] Thus, there have been continuous anxiety on the part of the United States with regards to mass popular demands for greater political freedom and economic rights in developing countries. This is especially so when these challenges become increasingly militant or nationalistic in character, and as such, is often seen as potentially destabilizing the capitalist system, and therefore undermining American influence in the region.

Hence, during the cold war era, governments were quick to impose the "radical" and "extremist" labels on left-wing movements, many of whom were plainly fighting against the tyranny of the capitalist state. However, in the post-September 11, 2001, "war on terror," the list of anti-systemic elements has been enlarged to incorporate mainly Muslim and other oppositional groups, a majority of whom has been struggling against the injustices of western-backed capitalist regimes. It is not unusual then that many western countries have turned a blind eye on the oppressive treatments of political opposition groups, minorities, and grassroots movements in the developing world since it would be to their own interests not to intervene on behalf of the oppressed.[51]

Thus instead of condemnation, many western nations and leaders have often conferred recognition and praises on these states, whose constitutional democratic features are applauded or whose commitment to combat terrorism touted as models for other countries to emulate. If there were any public criticism or official reprimand aired by western countries regarding major human rights infringements in these countries, it has rarely been followed up by any effective punitive actions or economic sanctions. This lack of serious reprove from powerful western governments has encouraged many relatively free countries like Malaysia to continue discreet forms of suppression against political opposition.

According to political analyst Fareed Zakaria, many such states, which he terms "illiberal democracies," exhibit their superficial commitment to democracy by the mere existence of formal democratic institutions, but whose democratic processes have remained non-transient and even edged closer to authoritarianism.[52] The appeal of these "managed" systems for the ruling elite has been in the way they are able to strengthen as well as widen the elites' policing capacities behind a façade of a seemingly democratic appearance. Since any further liberalization of the political system may become detrimental to its monopoly of political economic power, the ruling elite in many of these supposedly "democratic" countries have often made this type of system its deliberate policy choice.[53]

Hence, while constitutional provisions in these "managed" democracies do accord some space for political contestations, any demand for greater empowerment that may perceivably cross the accommodative threshold of elite class interests would likely be repressed by the state in the name of public safety or national security.[54] Similarly in Malaysia, which possesses structural flexibility for civil society groups to operate, the extent to which these groups, along with the political opposition, could freely function or exert their influence on society is contingent upon the political limits imposed by the state.

Globalization and Democratization

There has been a proliferation of emerging literature touching on the various relational dimensions of democracy and globalization.[55] In the period of unprecedented deepening of the capitalist world economy through economic globalization, an important point of attention has been directed toward the notion that an increasingly globalized world may evoke authoritarian responses from various states in the developing world. On the other hand, there is also high possibility that globalization brought on by information and communication technology may instead widen the prospects for democratization in those states.

Indeed, an unmistakable feature of the world economy affecting the community of nations today has been the process of globalization through informational accessibility and exchange. Technological convergences in computer and telecommunications since the 1990s have paved the way for revolutionary information flows, providing citizens all over the world with instant, extensive, and valuable knowledge-based resources. An important outcome of this has been in the way rapid, multilateral, and voluminous information exchanges have led to more effective citizen mobilization and greater public confidence in democratization across the globe.[56] A myriad of networks established through these new information superhighways have also made idea exchanges and opinion gathering more readily available to a huge portion of previously closed groups.

Over the years, a multiplicity of affiliations to international social and civil organizations has mushroomed throughout every continent, enabling the recruitment of new members and leaders for social-political struggles across many countries. As a result, an increasing number of civil society and political groups have gained inspiration and support from other global organizations and movements to effectively pursue their social-organizational missions within the countries they reside.[57] Thus a global civil society has surfaced, whose social movements and non-governmental organizations (NGOs) have been vigorously advocating and pursuing global-oriented solutions to a host of global and local issues relating to environmental and economic decline, labor exploitation, and persecution of minority groups, among many others.[58]

The larger focus of these civil society organizations, of course, has been the liberalization of their countries' political system, without which the attainment of their organizational objectives and future ambitions become difficult to realize. Importantly, the emergence of WEB 2.0 social media in the form of the internet, e-mail, cellular phones, text messaging, and more recently Facebook, and Twitter has provided an unprecedented and effective mobilization strategy for civil society and political opposition groups in their effort to exert effective challenges against the state. In a broader sense, these seemingly unstoppable influxes of instantaneous cross-border information flows available through various provider networks have undermined traditional patterns of state management of information primarily used for ideology-building strategies or censorship of state abuses and misconducts. Consequently, the state is confronted with immense public pressure created by unremitting demands for more extensive civil liberties as well as greater state transparency and accountability for decision-making and policy implementations.

In recent years, the influence of various informational resources on civil society mobilization as well as citizen empowerment has had successes especially in the way of incremental state concessions to popular demands for greater civil liberties.[59] Most states negotiate with civil society organizations out of survival. Those obstinately refusing to institute any reform have ultimately paid a heavy price. The 1997 overthrow of President Suharto in Indonesia and the 2011 popular uprisings in the Middle East for example, have reinforced optimisms regarding effective grassroots "cyberspace mobilization" as an effective and viable avenue for greater democratization in previously authoritarian regimes.

In Malaysia, there has been a series of unprecedented public rallies by various social groups calling for major political and electoral reforms since the late 1990s. The ruling elites, which for decades had been impervious to overt public expressions and criticisms, have become increasingly aware and perturbed by the Malaysian civil society's ability to mobilize and organize more efficiently through the use of social media. In most instances, these public demonstrations were met with the only way with which the state has known to deal—harsh reprisals and arrests.

However, an increasing number of Malaysians today have been emboldened by the provision of a forum for dissent found in the various alternative media, which have proliferated throughout the country since the year 2000. A report by *The Star* newspaper dated May 20, 2011, also mentioned that a survey carried by an international group, International TNS, revealed that Malaysians lead the world in the highest average number of friends per person on Facebook.[60] Such social networking can and has developed into vitally important support bases for groups critical of the state especially from those sympathetic to the cause and struggle for democracy. In this respect, cyber networking could turn out to be among the most important mobilizing force in the quest for advancing and widening civil liberties in Malaysia. Thus an important issue discussed in this book will be to what extent the availability and accessibility of this communicative space among Malaysians could ultimately lead to a greater and more extensive multiethnic democracy in the country.

Interestingly, both neo-Marxist and liberal theoretical paradigms may parallel each other on the correlations between communication technological development and democracy. Neo-Marxists often argue that the effect of *economic* globalization on developing countries, especially those with vulnerable democratic systems, may be detrimental to any further democratization. However, they might just agree with the postulations of liberal and modernization theorists that communications-centered globalization might help cultivate the "appropriate values" or "consciousness" needed for greater and more effective democratization. The accumulated awareness of existing social injustices, strengthened by the knowledge of options in proposed remedies, would provide the preparatory framework ripe for public action. Renowned scholar Amartya Sen says it best when he asserted that a culture of apathy persists in societies where freedom and political alternatives are absent.[61] Conversely, a more visible activism would emerge when informed choices are availed to them.

Plan of Book

It is hoped that this study on Malaysia would help pull together the relevant theoretical perspectives into a more comprehensive dialogue on the relationship between capitalist development and democracy in developing countries. Each chapter of the book will illustrate the interplays between structural-global factors and cultural-domestic forces that serve to strengthen the state as well as help the ruling elites maintain political power through social and ethnic divisions in the country. The following chapter, "Transplanting the Old World: British Colonial State in Malaya, 1824-1942," takes the reader to the historical origins of capitalist development in Malaya and northern Borneo under British colonialism. The chapter will critically examine the formative political processes of capitalist development introduced through the colonial state, and how they provided the foundational framework for Malaysia's modern state structure that has thus far catered favorably to capitalist elite class interests.

In chapter 3, "The Making of an Unequal Multiethnic Society, 1850-1957," the book continues to examine the effects of the capitalist world economy on the structure of colonial Malaysia's newly-emerging modern society. Here, the chapter will discuss the surfacing of a highly stratified multiethnic social structure in colonial Malaysia as a product of worldwide capitalist labor migrations and ethnic labor division formations. The uneven and disproportionate pace of capitalist development would also contribute to greater ethno-regional disparities, which have significantly enhanced the social-economic distances between the various culturally-distinct ethnic groups.

The effects of these differentiated experiences under colonialism on each of Malaya's major ethnic groups, the Malays, Chinese, and Indians, are further analyzed in chapter 4, "Fragmented Identities and the Rise of Pro-Western Elites, 1918-1963." World systemic changes occurring after the Second World War in the form of the decolonization in Africa and Asia would also eventually pave the way for the eventual political independence of Malaya. Here, the book will examine the development of each ethnic group's conceptual approach to nation, state, and citizenship, as embodied within each of these groups' ethnonationalism. The conflicting and divergent nature of these ethnonationalisms would make it very difficult for a broad and popular democratic movement for independence to emerge. Instead, this lack of a cogent Malayan vision would allow for the emergence of a group of pro-western multiethnic elite, tied by class interests, to eventually hold power through the National Alliance led by the United Malay Nationalist Organisation (UMNO).

The eventual support given by the British to this westernized multiethnic elite was further strengthened by a worldwide American-led effort to eliminate any potentiality of leftist or other anti-systemic governments coming to power in the developing world. This is discussed in chapter 5 "The Leftists in Malaya, 1945-1963." This chapter analyzes whether a leftist approach to political independence, one which challenges elite class interests, could have stimulated a more conducive environment for popular democracy to emerge in colonial Malaysia.

Table 1.1: Formal Historical Names for Malaysia, 1824-2011

Political entity	Type of state	Territories/states	Political Period
British Straits Settlements	Colonial possessions of the East India Company (EIC), and later, as Crown colonies of the Colonial Office in London	Penang, Dindings, and Malacca in the western coast of the Malay Peninsula, and Singapore	1824 to 1867 (EIC)/1867 to 1946 (London)
Federated Malay States[a]	Federated British protectorates	Perak, Selangor, Negeri Sembilan, Pahang	1896 to 1946
Unfederated Malay States[a]	Separate British protectorates	Kedah, Terengganu, Kelantan, Johor	1909 to 1946
Malayan Union	Centralized British Protectorate	All Malay states except Singapore	1946-1948
Federation of Malaya	Federated British protectorate/independent state	All Malay states except Singapore	1948-1957 / 1957 to 1963 as independent state
Federation of Malaysia	Independent federation inclusive of Singapore	All Malay states in the Malay Peninsula, Sabah, Sarawak, and Singapore	1963 to 1965
Federation of Malaysia	Independent federation excluding Singapore	All Malay states in the Malay Peninsula, Sabah and Sarawak (Singapore expelled in 1965)	1965 to present

[a] The combined name for the Federated Malay States and the Unfederated Malay States was British Malaya.

From here, the proceeding chapters of the book will then examine efforts by the new western-educated elites to sustain their political power through the state. This is done in two ways. One is by displaying the state's ability to plan and realize the country's national economic development. This is discussed in chapter 6, "Dependent Development and State-Capital Alliance, 1957-2011." To encourage continuous investments in the economy, the state forges close alliances with both local and foreign capitalists, which have enabled the ruling elite full accessibility to valued resources and political economic power. However, the dependent and increasingly globalized nature of capitalist industrialization would restrict the full extent of Malaysia's economic development, resulting in increased social inequalities in the country. The group most affected by any economic imbalances has been Malays, whose electoral franchise has ironically been crucial to the ruling alliance. Thus the state has worked hard in instituting policies to avert any opportunity for Malay political challenge against the ruling elites, whether unilaterally or through alliances with other ethnic groups.

Another way in which the state sustains the country's ethnic power-sharing system, which ensures the ruling elites of the National Front (new name for National Alliance) maintain their political hegemony, is by regularly tightening ideological and political control over its citizens. In chapter 7 "Sustaining Elite Dominance: Economic Nationalism and Institutional Control, 1980-2011," discussion will be weighted on the formation of the Malaysian state as a product of the country's development under the capitalist world economy, with particular attention given to the highly patronizing political culture it inherited through colonialism. This paternalistic authority, embedded in the character of the state in its relationship with the people, has allowed the ruling elites to utilize economic nationalism as a means to justify its disproportionate political power over citizens. It has also enabled the state to exercise strict supervisory role over the country's major cultural and political institutions with the aim of subverting any internal political challenges from the citizenry and civil society organizations.

Finally, in chapter 8 "Communications Globalization and Prospects for Political Change in Malaysia, 1990-2011," the book will examine the impact of the new wave in global communications technology and rapid informational exchanges on the social-political landscape in Malaysia. This chapter will analyze whether greater and more intense communications between citizens and civil society groups could narrow the ethnic and religious divides that had historically prevented the mobilization of an effective alliance of movements against the state, and pave the way instead for the emergence of a progressive and multiethnic struggle for a multicultural democracy. The chapter closes with summarized findings of the research through the construction of a theoretical model.

For readers' convenience, the historical phases of British colonization of Malaysia with its different names for the country during the colonial period are highlighted according to chronological order in table 1.1 on the previous page. Occasional reference to this table is necessary to avoid confusion with the usage of various names for Malaysia during the different phases of its history.

Notes

1. C. Wright Mills, *Sociological Imagination* (New York: Oxford University Press, 2000), 143-65.

2. Nicos Poulantzas, *State, Power, Socialism*, Translated by Peter Camiller (London: Verso, 2001), 36-40.

3. Ronald Chilcote, *Theories of Comparative Political Economy: New Paradigms* (Boulder, Co: Westview Press), 175-79

4. Jorge Larrain, *Theories of Development* (Cambridge: Polity Press, 1989), 62-68.

5. Bertrand Badie and Pierre Birnbaum, *Sociology of the State* (Chicago: University of Chicago Press, 1983), 97.

6. Ali Kazancigil, *State in Global Perspective* (Paris: Gower-UNESCO, 1986), 134.

7. Seymour Martin Lipset and Jason M. Lakin, *Democratic Century* (Norman, OK: University of Oklahoma Press, 2004), 173-74.

8. Immanuel Wallerstein, *Geopolitics and Geoculture* (New York: Cambridge University Press, 1991), 7.

9. Edward Said, *Culture and Orientalism* (New York: First: Vintage Books, 1994), 162-67.

10. Martha Caso, *Invisible and Voiceless* (Bloomington, IN: Universe, 2011), 44-45.

11. Ali Behdad, *Belated Travelers: Orientalism in the Age of Colonial Dissolution (Post-Contemporary Interventions)* (Durham, NC: Duke University Press, 1999), 13-15.

12. Joe Feagin, *White Racial Frame: Centuries of Racial Framing and Counter Framing* (New York: Routledge, 2010), 38-39.

13. Miguel Darcy De Oliveira, "Deepening Democracy in Latin America," in *Global Civil Society 2007/8: Communicative Power and Democracy,* ed. Martin Albrow, Helmut Anheier, Marlies Glasius, Monroe Price, Mary Kaldor (London: Sage, 2008), 120-21

14. Ernest Gellner, "Civil Society in Historical Context," *International Social Science Journal* 43, no. 3 (August 1991): 495-500.

15. Benedict Anderson, *Imagined Communities: Reflections on the Origins and Spread of Nationalism* (London: Verso, 1983), 15-16.

16. Walker Connor, *Ethnonationalism: The Quest for Understanding (*Princeton, NJ: Princeton University Press, 1994), 150-59.

17. Bob Jessop, *Capitalist State*: *Marxist Theories and Methods* (New York: New York University Press, 1982), 250-51.

18. Rosa Luxemburg, *National Question* (New York: Monthly Press Review, 1983), 141.

19. Joseph Whitmeyer, "Elites and Popular Nationalism," *British Journal of Sociology* 53, no. 3 (September 2002): 333-36.

20. Karl Hack, "Theories and Approaches to British Decolonization in Southeast Asia," in *Transformation of Southeast Asia: International Perspectives on Decolonization,* ed. Marc Frey, Ronald W. Pruessen, and Tai Yong Tan (New York: M.E. Sharpe, 2004), 106-7.

21. The National Alliance changed its name to the National Front in 1974.

22. Samir Amin, "Crisis, Nationalism, and Socialism," in *Dynamics of Global Crisis*, ed. Samir Amin, Giovanni Arrighi, Andre Gunder Frank, and Immanuel Wallerstein (New York: Monthly Review Press, 1982), 167-72.

23. Ronald Grigor Suny, "Don't Paint Nationalism Red! National Revolution and Socialist Anti-Imperialism," in *Decolonization: Perspectives from Now and Then*, ed. Prasenit Duara (New York: Routledge, 2004), 176-178.

24. Muthiah Alagappa, "The Bases of Legitimacy," in *Political Legitimacy in Southeast Asia*, ed. Muthiah Alagappa (Stanford, CA: Stanford University Press, 1995), 31-33.

25. Robert Scalapino, "National Political Institutions and Leadership in Asia," *Washington Quarterly* 15, no. 4 (Winter 1992): 152-56.

26. Joseph Wong, "The Adaptive Developmental State in Asia," *Journal of Southeast Asian Studies* 4, no. 3 (September 2004): 351-52.

27. Ankie Hoogvelt, *Globalisation and the Postcolonial World: The New Political Economy of Development* (Baltimore: John Hopkins University Press, 2001), 48-51.

28. Jerry Kloby, *Inequality, Power, and Development: Issues in Political Sociology* (New York: Humanity Books, 2004), 134-35.

29. Jurgen Habermas, *Legitimation Crisis*, (Boston: Beacon Press, 1975), 4-8.

30. Walt Whitman Rostow, *Stages of Economic Growth* (Cambridge, UK: Cambridge University Press, 1970), 36-40.

31. Ronald Inglehart, *Modernization and Postmodernization: Cultural, Economic, and Political Change in 43 Societies* (Princeton, NJ: Princeton University Press, 1997), 226-30.

32. David McClelland, "Business-Drive and National Achievement," in *Social Change*, ed. Amitai Etzioni and Eva Etzioni (New York: Basic Books, 1964), 99-112.

33. Thomas Shannon, *Introduction to the World-System Perspective* (Boulder, CO: Westview Press, 1996), 116.

34. Raymond Duvall and John Freeman, "The State and Dependent Capitalism," in *World Systems Structure*, ed. W. Ladd Hollist and James Rosenau (W. Beverly Hills, CA: Sage, 1981), 223-42.

35. Samir Amin, *Unequal Development* (New York: Monthly Press Review, 1976), 150-55.

36. William Easterly, *The White Man's Burden: Why the West's Efforts to Aid the Rest Have Done So Much Ill and So Little Good* (New York: Penguin Books, 2006), 44-50.

37. Jeremy Seabrook, *Victims of Development: Resistance and Alternatives* (London: Verso, 1993), 20-22; Frank, Andre Gunder, *Crisis in the Third World* (New York: Holmes and Meier, 1981), 96-111; Magdoff, Harry "Third World Debt: Past and Present," *Monthly Review* 37, no. 9 (July 1996): 8-9.

38. Francis Fukuyama, "Democracy's Future: The Primacy of Culture," *Journal of Democracy* 6, no. 1 (January 1995): 3-9.

39. Ronald Inglehart and Christian Welzel, *Modernization, Cultural Change, and Democracy* (New York: Cambridge University Press, 2005), 44-47.

40. Christopher Chase-Dunn, "The World System since 1950: What Has Really Changed?" in *Labor in the Capitalist World Economy*, ed. Charles Bergquist (Beverly Hills, CA: Sage, 1984), 75-77.

41. Alvin Y. So and Stephen K. Chui, "Modern East Asia in World–Systems Analysis," in *World Systems Reader: New Perspectives on Gender, Urbanism, Cultures, Indigenous Peoples and Ecology*, ed. Thomas D. Hall (Lanham, MD: Rowman & Littlefield, 2000), 281-82.

42. Immanuel Wallerstein, *Capitalist World Economy* (Cambridge, UK: Cambridge University Press, 1997), 80-81.

43. World Bank, *World Development Report 1993* (New York: Oxford University Press, 1994), 1. First tier country is Japan. The second tier countries, often referred to as the Asian miracle economies, are sometimes been dubbed the "Asian Tigers." These are South Korea, Taiwan, and Hong Kong. Malaysia, along with Indonesia and Thailand, belongs to the third tier known as the Asia's newly industrializing economies (NIEs).

44. Kwang-Yeong Shin, "The Political Economy of Economic Growth in East Asia: South Korea and Taiwan," in *Four Asian Tigers: Economic Development and the Global Political Economy*, ed. Eun Mee Kim (San Diego: Academic Press, 1998), 22. Also read similar explanation in Bernard, M. and J. Ravenhill, "Beyond Product Cycles and Flying Geese: Regionalization, Hierarchy, and the Industrialization of East Asia." *World Politics* 47, no. 2 (January 1995): 175-77.

45. Ichiro Numazaki, "The Export-oriented Industrialization of Pacific Rim Countries and Their Presence in the Global Market," in *The Four Asian Tigers: Economic Development and the Global Political Economy*, ed. Eun Mee Kim (San Diego: Academic Press, 1998), 66-69.

46. Immanuel Wallerstein, *World System Analysis: An Introduction* (Durham NC: Duke University Press, 2004), 25-29.

47. Kenneth Bollen, "World-System Position, Dependency, and Democracy: The Cross-National Evidence" in *American Sociological Review* 48, no.4 (August 1983): 470-71.

48. Deitrich Rueschemeyer, Evelyn Stephens, and John Stephens, *Capitalist Development and Democracy* (Cambridge, England: Polity Press, 1992), 72-73.

49. Jeff Haynes, *Democracy and Political Changes in the Third World* (New York: Routledge, 2006), 5-7.

50. William Robinson, *Promoting Polyarchy; Globalization, US Intervention, and Hegemony* (Cambridge University Press, 1996), 1-13.

51. Democracy promotion by western states, especially the US, is often contradictory and limited to supporting procedural rather than substantive forms of democracy. Read Armine Ishkanian, "Democracy Promotion and Civil Society," in *Global Civil Society 2007/8: Communicative Power and Democracy,* ed. Martin Albrow, Helmut Anheier, Marlies Glasius, Monroe Price, Mary Kaldor (London: Sage, 2008), 77-78.

52. Fareed Zakaria, *Future of Freedom: Illiberal Democracy at Home and Abroad* (New York: W.W. Norton, 2007), 17-19.

53. Zakaria, *Future*, 89-95.

54. Mary Kaldor and Denise Kostovicova, "Global Civil Society and Illiberal Regimes," in *Global Civil Society 2007/8: Communicative Power and Democracy,* ed. Martin Albrow, Helmut Anheier, Marlies Glasius, Monroe Price, Mary Kaldor (London: Sage, 2008), 152.

55. Peter Garrett, "Meanings of Globalization: East and West," in *Handbook of Language and Globalization,* ed. Nikolas Coupland (Singapore: Wiley-Blackwell, 2010), 448-52.

56. Jackie Smith, *Social Movements for Global Democracy* (Baltimore: Johns Hopkins Press, 2008), 103-4.

57. Jack Donnelly, "Human Rights, Globalizing Flows, and State Power," in *Globalization and Human Rights,* ed. Alison Brysk (Los Angeles: University of California Press, 2002), 226-42.

58. Smith, *Social Movements*, 47-48.

59. Susan Strange, "The Declining Authority of States," in *Globalization Reader*, ed. Frank Lechner and John Boli (Malden, MA: Blackwell Publishing, 2007), 219-225; The removal of President Suharto from state power had been initiated by a conglomeration of civil society movements in that country, who mobilized their activism through e-mail and internet dissemination of information. This "second Indonesian revolution" led to, among other things, Indonesia becoming the third largest democracy in the world and the eventual independence of East Timor from nearly 15 years of Indonesian rule.

60. *The Star*, "Talco Spearheads Effort to Make Malaysia Facebook Capital of the World," *Star Online* 2011, www.thestar.com.my/metro/story.asp?file=/2011/2/20/central (accessed June 2, 2011).

61. Mary Douglas, "Traditional Culture: Let's Hear No More about It," in *Culture and Public Action*, ed. Vijayendra Rao and Michael Walton (Stanford, CA; Stanford University Press, 2004), 107-8.

Chapter 2
Transplanting the Old World: British Colonial State in Malaya, 1824-1942

The "discoveries" of kingdoms and civilizations outside of Europe by Spanish and Portuguese *conquistadores* in the sixteenth century opened up a new chapter in world economic history. Access to navigable sea routes helped expand European mercantile trade into the Americas, Africa, and Asia, making the transportation of goods and commodities between markets and production sources across continents much faster and with relative ease.

By the 1800s, the British in particular were able to exploit their technological achievements to institute a series of capitalist expeditions into Africa and Asia. Soon, the Britain and other European powers were engaged in bitter rivalries for territories and resources around the world. In the Malay Archipelago, British and Dutch seafaring expeditions penetrated deeply into the various Malay maritime kingdoms for the control of the lucrative East-West sea trades. Each sought to affirm their absolute imperial influence in the region.

Malacca and Johor-Riau Sultanates, 1400-1700

The rise of Islam as a global commercial force between the fifth and sixteenth centuries was a major historical event that created long-lasting impacts on the social and political development of the Malay world. The growth of the Arab-Chinese sea trade spanning and extending through the waters of Southeast Asia represented the oceanic version of the *silk route*.

The heavy commerce coming into the Malay Archipelago from all over the world would soon give rise to the prosperity of the Malay Malacca kingdom, which became one of the busiest *entreports* (trading ports) in the world. By the mid-fifteenth century, Malacca had flourished into a strong maritime empire encompassing much of Sumatra and the Malay Peninsula. The sultanate's economic influence was virtually felt along all the major sea lanes between the Indian Ocean and the South China Sea.

Conversion of Malays to Islam, almost *en masse,* had been one of the most important contributive factors to attracting large volumes of commercial traffic to and from the various caliphates throughout the Islamic world.[1] During the reigns of its various sultans, Malacca boasted of an efficient administrative system, helped by a strong navy that delivered almost unfailing service and protection for international ships and traders, especially against regional piracy.[2]

Malacca's economic vibrancy was captured by historian Fernand Braudel in his discussion of world-economies between the fifteenth and eighteenth centuries, mentioning that Malacca was the gravity that pulled the various world-economies together. He remarked that Malacca was "where everything and anything could be found, and whose network of commercial traffic was comparable to that of the Mediterranean and Atlantic coasts of Europe."[3] The flow of commodities and goods into Malacca around the year 1500 is shown in figure 2.1.

Following the Arab-Muslim trading period was another major global-historical event. This came in the form of the expansion of the mercantile economy beyond the European continent. As early as the late fifteenth century, several European traders had arrived in Malacca and soon found out it to be "the city that was made for merchandise."[4] Prized for its location and strategic control of the profitable spice trade, Malacca soon became the constant target of the powerful Portuguese *conquistadores*. Having been driven away by the Malacca navy in their earlier attempt, the Portuguese under Alfonso d' Albuquerque consolidated its armada to finally occupy the city-port in 1511. Under Portuguese rule however, Malacca was no longer the glowing cosmopolitan haven that thrived under the sultans. Having endured Arab occupation for centuries, the Iberians had developed extreme hatred for Muslims. Their fanatical mission and cruel disposition toward non-Christians chased out many local as well as foreign traders to other ports in the region, including Brunei and Johor-Riau.[5]

By the end of the seventeenth century however, the Dutch had emerged as a new dominant commercial power in Europe. They were especially reputed for their successful cargo-carrying role in the emerging capitalist economy. In their quest to assume greater control and monopoly of the spice trade in the eastern islands of Southeast Asia, the Dutch established the *Dutch United East India Company* (VOC). Supported by well-organized networks of capital and managed through a business philosophy divorced from religious convictions that had so spirited the Portuguese earlier, the VOC was to become the first successful transnational company operating at the global level.[6]

In 1641, the VOC managed to wrest control of Malacca from the Portuguese, finally ending the latter's political economic dominance in the region. Although the conquest of Malacca has often been told in history books as a "Dutch victory," the invasion could not have been possible without their alliance with the Johor-Riau sultanate, which actually provided the bulk of military operations. The gallantry of Bugis warriors from Sulawesi (Celebes), who took up arms on behalf of the Johor-Riau sultanate, had been particularly critical.

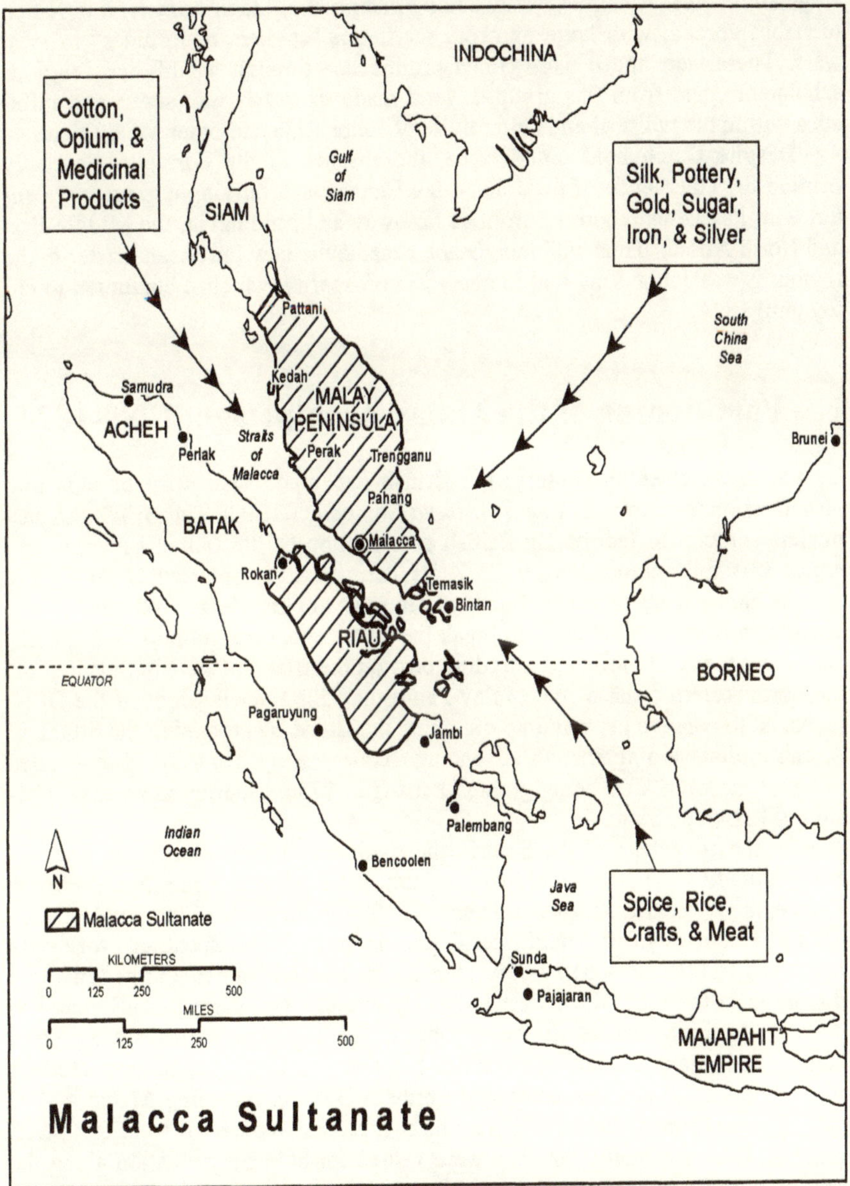

Figure 2.1: Map of the Malacca Sultanate 1500. The city-port of Malacca served as the oceanic version of the Eurasian inter-continental *silk route*.

The Bugis were especially renowned for their superb navigational knowledge and mercenary skills. Many among them had left their homeland in search of riches abroad, with large numbers serving as "soldiers of fortunes" in local wars. There were those who gained prominence through wealth and religious scholarship, and from this group, several made their way into status and influence within the political and cultural life of Johor-Riau and other Malay states.[7]

Despite Dutch hold on Malacca, the absence of the Portuguese actually marked the emergence of the Johor-Riau Empire as a thriving commercial center, with its clientele coming from as far away as Scandinavia, the Middle-East and North Africa.[8] Thus while the Dutch became the new European master in the region, it was Johor-Riau that increased in prosperity, which it continued to enjoy until 1824.

Partitioning of the Malay Archipelago, 1789-1824

By the mid-eighteenth century, the British had made successful inroads into Asia through their own *British East India Company* (BEIC). The BEIC was particularly crucial in facilitating British colonization of the Indian subcontinent, which was fully completed by 1757. By then, hostility between Great Britain and the Netherlands over the control of sea routes in the Malay Archipelago had become intense. In an attempt to break the Dutch economic monopoly in Southeast Asia, the BEIC founded a trading post on the island of Penang, located off the northwestern coast of the Malay Peninsula.[9] Sir Francis Light of the BEIC managed to connive his way into obtaining the island by promising the Sultan of Kedah military aid against an advancing Siamese army. However, Light failed to honor his word after being granted Penang in 1786, ushering in an easy invasion of Kedah by Siam.[10]

To the advantage of the British, the rivalry with the Netherlands was virtually halted by the Napoleonic war in Europe. Faced with a common enemy in France, the two parties signed a détente in 1824 in the form of the Anglo-Dutch Treaty. This agreement would later divide the huge Malay-speaking world into the Dutch and British spheres of influence. The Dutch obtained a large territorial dominion in the vast Dutch East Indies (Indonesia) spreading from Sumatra in the west to the Moluccas (Spice Islands) in the east. The British on the other hand, would gain a relatively smaller but more strategic set of protectorates throughout the Malay Peninsula and northern Borneo, including Malacca. The size of these British possessions may be miniature compared to what the Dutch received from the treaty, but they were valued for both their location along the east-west trade as well as for their abundance in sought-after crafts and raw minerals.[11]

While the Anglo-Dutch treaty provided its signatories relative peace with each other in the coming decades, it effectively severed the social, cultural, and economic relationships linking the various Malay kingdoms.[12] The Malay maritime network was gradually absorbed into the larger and more predominant European capitalist trading system, with the Johor-Riau Sultanate experiencing the biggest loss. Despite having contributed to the invasion of Malacca, Johor lost its southern Riau-Lingga Islands when they were annexed by the same side they had helped in the war against the Portuguese—the Dutch. The eventual dismemberment of this proud empire would rapidly kill off its bustling trade between the Straits of Malacca and the South China Sea, thereby marking the end of any vestige of Malay economic ascendancy in the region.

The British Straits Settlements, 1824-1942

With Malacca declining in its *entrepot* role, Dutch Batavia (Jakarta) on the island of Java emerged as Southeast Asia's new mercantile port. Although Penang did expand substantially in its commercial role, its location was too removed from the hub of regional maritime activity. This made it quite difficult for the British to divert much of the eastern trade away from the Dutch. Furthermore, the BEIC was obliged to comply with a policy of non-involvement in the Malay states, and therefore had been restrained from negotiating further treaties.

However, this policy sentiment was not shared by many within the BEIC. One of its officers, Stamford Raffles, aggressively proposed for deeper British involvement in the political affairs of the Malay state as a way to expand British commercial interests in the region. His immediate goal was to obtain the once-flourishing island of Temasek (Singapore) from the Johor sultanate, which could be utilized both as a geo-strategic economic center along the east-west trade corridor as well as a convenient entry point into the potentially lucrative areas of the Malay Peninsula. Despite the uncertainty of British government support, Raffles went ahead to exploit a succession crisis within the Johor-Riau royal house to enable the installation of Raja Hussein as puppet ruler of Temasek. After buying off Hussein in 1819, Raffles managed to completely take over the whole island, and placed it under BEIC control.[13]

By virtue of the 1824 Anglo-Dutch treaty, the British were able to secure its possessions of Penang, Malacca, and Singapore under the Straits Settlements government of India. Using Singapore as its administrative center, the British introduced a Charter of Justice in 1826 that legally bound all three ports through the standard enforcement of an English legal system. By the time the capitalist economy had firmly set into place, a Supreme Court system was established in 1868 to streamline the adjudication of an ever increasing number of civil and commercial proceedings.

True to Raffles' intentions, the Straits Settlements colonies would provide the BEIC with its launching pad into the Malay states, thereby linking the Malay hinterland with the outside world through a new network of mercantile trade. Nevertheless, despite this, British political involvement into the complex world of traditional Malay politics was to remain considerably limited. The *laissez-*

faire approach of the British government held back any serious effort on the part of BEIC to assume deeper political involvement in the various Malay states. This did not mean however, that there had been no unilateral attempts to expand British interests into the area. In 1831, the BEIC tried to push its land and judicial systems beyond the Straits Settlements into the strictly matrilineal Malay communities in Naning (northwest of Malacca). This was met with violent resistance by the Malays. A year-long conflict nearly squeezed the British dry of their finances and served as a vigilant reminder of the hazards associated with meddling into the affairs of Malay societies.[14]

The British Residential System, 1874-1895

Gradually, financial strains caused by a depletion of funds in 1874 saw the formal dissolution of the BEIC. The administration of the Straits Settlements was then passed on to the British colonial office in London. For centuries, tin had traditionally been mined by Malays for the production of crafts sold in the Asian and the Middle-Eastern luxury goods markets. By the nineteenth century, the utility of tin plates for industrial manufacturing in Europe spurred monumental demands for the commodity in western commodity markets. This subsequently urged the British to fortify their hold on tin production in the Malay states through the Straits Settlements.[15]

The coveted demand for tin had already attracted the first batches of Chinese migrants into Selangor and Perak. These foreign miners were organized by Chinese syndicates, or *kongsi*, which were in constant hostility with each other over resources and influence. Often, each *kongsi* was also aligned with a particular Malay provincial chieftain or warlord, who usually owned the mines. This meant that physical contestations of power between Malay warlords would also involve armed skirmishes between Chinese rival gangs. Such chaotic political conditions worried the British, whose commercial activity in the Malay states had already become a main source of imperial revenue for the Crown. However, British colonial authority was confined solely to the Straits Settlements at this time, and its policy of non-intervention overseas meant that there was little they could do to address the de-stabilizing political conditions in the Malay states.

However this changed in 1873. The opening of the Suez Canal enabled greater access for Europeans to their colonies in Africa and Asia. In London, the Liberal Party was replaced by the Conservatives, who advocated for more aggressive imperial campaigns abroad. Thus when a succession crisis in the state of Perak swayed one of its pretenders, Raja Abdullah, to seek British aid in his battle for the royal throne, the British government took the opportunity to reverse its isolationist policy in the Malay states. The governor of the British Straits Settlements in Singapore, Andrew Clarke, was dispatched to expeditiously draft the Treaty of Pangkor, which stipulated the conditions of their "assistance." These included British right to trade protection in the state and the prohibition of all other European powers from dealing directly with the sultan.[16] The signing of the treaty in 1874 saw Abdullah mount the Perak throne with the help of the British, who in return received the territory of Dindings near the mouth of the Perak River.

The treaty also enabled the British to establish their first *residential system* in the Malay states. Under this system, an appointment of a British Resident was mandated upon the sultan. The Resident's "advice" had to be sought by the sultan on all matters of state administration except those pertaining to Malay religion (Islam) and customary laws. The role of the Resident in effect, was beyond a mere advisor. His office represented British economic interests and political power in Perak. The advantages derived from the system's indirect rule soon paved the way for similar treaties and pacts with the other Malay states on the Peninsula. As in Perak, internal crises in the states of Selangor, Negeri Sembilan, and Pahang were exploited by the British as "just cause" for establishing in each of them, separate residential systems.[17]

Deeper involvement in the affairs of the Malay states was not without costs however. In 1875, Perak's first Resident J.W. Birch was assassinated by a disgruntled nobleman. Sporadic but fierce wars against British troops also took place throughout the Malay states from the mid-1800s to the early 1900s. Despite the use of modern weaponry, the British proved no match for the highly-skilled Malays, especially in the art of hand-to-hand combat. In the Negeri Sembilan War for example, British deaths exceeded that of Malays, but the latter suffered more casualties from British reinforcements of additional troops and weaponry. British retaliation was ruthless. Villages were burnt while suspected rebels were mercilessly hanged, shot, or exiled. The British wanted it known that these punishments served as reminders of the consequences of challenging their authority.[18]

Although the number of British officials was relatively small, the success of the residential system rested primarily on the Resident's direct ties with the sultans, whose responsibility under the system was to carry out all tax collections. This relationship effectively enabled the British to cover administrative expenses, extend investments opportunities, and procure direct management of lands and other sources of revenues in the respective Malay states.[19] Gradually, the residential system allowed the British to station its armed forces under the guise of "protecting" the respective Malay sultans. It is for this reason that the Malay states during this period were also known as the *Protected Malay States*.

It is an escapable fact that the British had enabled the sultan and his close aristocratic circle to secure the benefits of an emerging capitalist economy through fixed portions of taxes extracted from his subjects.[20] Aside from receiving formal British protection, the Malay sultan also personally gained from the residential system in terms of official power over his subjects. Most notably was the way British indirect rule had reinforced and institutionalized within a modern state structure, the sultan's traditional authority that had previously been subjected to numerous internal challenges. Pre-Islamic Malay cultural beliefs had always perpetuated the notion that the ruler stood at the apex of human society as a representative of God on earth. The relationship between ruler and subject was emphasized in the historical *Malay Annals* as one that "has been granted by God to Malay subjects that they shall never be disloyal or treacherous to their rulers, even if their rulers behaved evilly or inflicted injustice upon them."[21] Such sanctified position had accorded the ruler with the loyalty, devotion, and reverence from his subjects, and formed an unquestionable reality of Malay feudal life. An important aspect of this covenant is the concept of *daulat*, which is the unleashing of punishment by mythical forces against those who committed royal treason or *derhaka*.[22] For Malays, such beliefs have been deeply transfixed within their culture. Despite the embrace of Islam, paramount allegiance to the sultan has been an undisputed tradition imposed upon Malays at every level of social life.

However, this did not mean that Malays had no potential inclination for rebellion. Historian James Scott documented the prevalent occurrences of peasant resistance against authority in Malaysia in what he termed as "weapons of the weak."[23] These forms of resistance, which included non-participation in economic exchanges, the boycotting of goods delivered from authorities, willful and massive non-compliance with laws, demonstrations, and sit-ins could be traced to age-old Malay cultural resistance practices. Donald Nonini, in his study of the Malay peasantry, asserted that despite its rank-ordered structure, pre-capitalist Malay peasant society was communally cohesive and egalitarian, and that the ruler at times faced difficulties in exerting taxes.[24]

During the arrival of the British, the control of local trade and the distribution of wealth in many parts of the Malay states had been firmly held among the Malay chieftains or *orang kaya,* thereby slowly weakening the absolute reign of the individual sultan.[25] In many ways, the residential system virtually returned *de facto* Malay authority to the sultan by providing him formal recognition, prestige, and backing of the British military. By this, the British also gained circumlocutory control over the Malay masses and preserved the top-down structure of Malay feudal society. Historian Simon Smith affirmed this when he noted that "the reciprocity of the relationship between Britain and the Malay Rulers can be drawn into the wider debate on the extent to which such indigenous monarchs can be seen as collaborative elites upholding British interests."[26]

The residential system also laid the foundation of modern political structures in the Malay states to facilitate the further expansion of the capitalist economy. In 1877, the first State Council was introduced in Perak. The Council was, in effect, a rubber-stamping body comprised mainly of British notary appointees and corporate leaders, selected members of the Malay aristocracy, and a few Chinese merchants. An important function of the Council was to obtain the cooperation of leading members of the state and businesses as well as representatives of local communities in the passing of English laws relating to land leases and labor taxes, in order to expedite the extraction and production of much-needed raw material in the Malay states. Presided by a figurehead sultan, the power of the Council rested virtually on the British Resident. With the operational functioning of these councils throughout all the Malay states, any trace of traditional Malay governance firmly gave way to western bureaucratic administrative structures, whose power radiated from the all-powerful Resident.

Significantly, the ratification of commercial-centered regulations catered specifically to the needs of the growing tin mining industry. By 1878, export duties on tin accounted for 70 percent of Perak's revenues.[27] Although the British declared that all lands were vested in the jurisdiction of the sultan, the political separation between the colonial executive and the Malay ruler enabled the management of lands, especially those with known tin deposits, to actually reside with the respective Resident. Here, transactions of lands were strictly dealt with under uniformed English laws. In the decade between 1879 and 1889, general land regulations based on standardized leaseholds were introduced in Perak, Selangor, and Negeri Sembilan, to ensure the expediency of tin extraction and transportation to the Straits Settlement ports.[28]

The commoditization of lands also provided the impetus for greater agro-plantation activity in pepper, gambier, tobacco, sugar, tea, coffee, and later, rubber and palm oil. What followed was a proliferation of bountiful land concessions to Europeans, many of whom were friends and close associates of the Resident.[29] In 1888, the largest concessionaire in the state of Selangor, Hill and Rathbone, managed to obtain 999 year-leases for lands that totaled more than 10,000 acres for tobacco, coffee, and pepper.[30]

The introduction of proprietary rights to lands also entailed new tax laws pertaining to leases and ownership of lands. Although not yet widespread, major strips of land were now transformed into private property with prescribed rights and revenue obligations to the owner. For the first time in their history, Malays in rural areas were required to pay quit rent in return for leases on their own lands. Naturally, the Malay peasantry resented this since it imposed upon them additional financial burden. Consequently, these new laws also precipitated the sale and losses of Malay lands to newly-arrived migrant Chinese and Indian moneylenders.[31] As a result, many rural Malays were left destitute as they became unable to pay rent or buy back lands that had been placed as collateral under the new money-centered economy.

The rapidly growing capitalist economy also necessitated the regulation of labor to streamline wages and revenue collection. Prior to British residential rule, Chinese *towkays* (headmen or labor advancers) had been responsible for the recruitment of Chinese migrant workers into the Malay states under an indentured system known as the *truck* system.[32] Under this system, these headmen, with the help of secret society syndicates, would provide their workers with board, transportation, and expensive supplies through loans that often doubled the market interest rates. Such a mechanism aided in keeping the workers indebted to their recruiters.

The British were initially reluctant to interfere with the increasingly problematic system of Chinese labor management for fear that any action threatening Chinese business interests might lead to disinvestments by the more prosperous entrepreneurs. Nevertheless, a more efficient and organized labor-remuneration system to meet the demands of newly emerging industries was critically needed.

Hence, a *Protector of Chinese Labor* position was established in 1887 tasked with the supervision of the smooth transfer of large numbers of imported Chinese migrant workers into the Malay states from Singapore.[33] The position also doubled as a state portfolio that oversaw the registration of civic organizations aimed at monitoring Chinese secret societies and their activities. Later in 1895, a Labour Code was introduced, allowing for a clearer measurement of worker productivity through a new wage structure, and enabling revenues from labor taxes to be promptly collected for the state.

Another important impact of the British residential system on the economy of the Malay states was the increased use of monetary capital, manifested in both long-term fixed assets investments and short-term circulatory financing of daily operations. One of the earliest forms of investment funds was *revenue farming*, first introduced by the Dutch in Java as a means of tax collection from foreign merchants.[34] In the Malay states, this system was then emulated and adapted by the ruler of Johor, who in turn introduced it to ethnic Chinese businessmen in the Straits Settlements. This was particularly beneficial for the British since the Straits Settlement government had earlier been unable to enforce taxation among the mainly Chinese settlers under their jurisdiction. It was revenue farming that eventually allowed private Chinese individuals to purchase from the government, commissioned rights to collect taxes for a specified period on highly demanded items and activities among the Chinese community such as liquor, opium, and gambling.

Funds collected from these activities allowed early Chinese capitalists in the Straits Settlements to later dominate the tin industry and diversify their investments into production technology, retail, and banking. From 1870 to the late 1890s, these funds brought over steam-powered pumps that helped Chinese miners to efficiently extract tin deposits from sources located away from water. The smooth flow of both creativity and capital within the Chinese mining sector was the primary reason for initial British encouragement of Chinese entrepreneurial involvement in the modern tin industry.

British Colonial Involvements in Northern Borneo (Sarawak and Sabah)

The Anglo-Dutch Treaty of 1824 did not specifically mention the status of Borneo, although the Dutch had officially secured the southern and eastern portions of the Malay Archipelago. To stake their colonial presence throughout the region, the Dutch proceeded to enter into various treaties and agreements with the numerous sultanates, including those located along Borneo's southern coasts. However, the treacherous mountainous terrain dividing the island's northern and southern regions may have severely restricted any Dutch penetration into the north.

By the sixteenth century, Brunei had emerged as a prosperous and well-organized Malay-Islamic sultanate, ruling almost all of northern Borneo and attracting traders and merchants from as far as western Asia and China.[35] In the early nineteenth century, an English adventurer, James Brooke, became embroiled in Brunei's domestic conflicts between the sultan and his various chieftains. Expecting bountiful rewards, Brooke helped the royal court suppress the rebellions through the use of a relatively large private army that he had assembled from among the local people. For his effort, Brooke was able to obtain much more from the sultan than mere gifts. He virtually extorted the concessions of enormous tracts of lands along the northwestern coasts of Borneo, constituting almost two-thirds of the Brunei sultanate.[36]

As governor of his new territory, now named Sarawak, Brooke formally commenced his century-old *White Rajah* family dynasty in 1841. Through creative bargaining, Brooke also managed to command the authority of various ethnic Malay and the indigenous Dayak-Iban leaderships around the state. He cleverly expropriated native lands for the purpose of development by breaking up long-standing social-political alliances between Malays and Ibans, who had kept tight controls over the state's fertile areas and strategic outposts. Along the coastal areas, such campaigns became quite violent. In the pretext of combating piracy, many villages were indiscriminately attacked. In one incident, about 800 Malays and coastal Ibans were ruthlessly killed by attacks from British-backed state gun-ships.[37]

Rebellions were severely dealt with. In the guise of abolishing headhunting, the Brooke government would also raid Iban villages and burn their crops, forcing them to assume horticultural modes of production as a means to sustain their communities.[38] Through oppressive policies, the Brooke dynasty successively expanded its territorial dominion and ruled Sarawak as a private fiefdom in the ensuing decades. It was not long before Sarawak would eventually overpower Brunei, and in 1888, the sultanate was accorded formal "protectorate" status.[39]

In the northeastern end of Borneo, in the state known today as Sabah, large tracts of lands had been divided between the political authorities of the Muslim Sulu Sultanate of the southern Philippines and the Sultan of Brunei. In 1881, a group of British entrepreneurs from the British North Borneo Chartered Company (BNBCC) gained access into the interior and began operating land concessions for various commercial activities. Many were leased to private European planters, who opened up new economic settlements along the coastal areas of the state. Faced with chronic labor shortages, the BNBCC also brought in contract labor from China as well as encouraged transmigration of Malays from other parts of the Archipelago for work in these numerous agricultural estates.[40]

Unlike in the Malay States, the British colonial office was not involved in the administrations of Sarawak and Sabah. This was primarily due to the anticipated high costs of formally colonizing these states.[41] Since major resources found in northern Borneo were not as highly demanded in the world markets, it became more economical and less burdensome on the British national treasury to minimally maintain its colonial presence through the respective private entities; the Brooke family in Sarawak and the BNBCC in Sabah. Whatever the economic gains in northern Borneo, they would have still ended up one way or another into the British national economy through taxes levied on trade. At the same time, any loss incurred by these "private colonists" would not have likely placed the British government in serious economic difficulty.

In many instances however, the colonial office in London did not hesitate to provide grants and charters to both the Brooke dynasty and the BNBCC in order to help them bolster their respective state machineries with much needed weaponry. The British royal navy, for example, was often dispensed to assist the Brookes in suppressing piracy in Sarawak waters. The British government also often helped Sarawak in its border disputes with Brunei.[42] In 1912, the British entered into an official treaty with the Dutch to delineate the respective boundaries of Sarawak, Sabah, and Dutch Borneo (part of the Dutch East Indies). This ensured the Brooke government and the BNBCC from future encroachments by other European powers.[43]

One of the major successes of Sarawak's modern administration was attributed to the imposition of civil order emphasizing tribal allegiance to a central authority.[44] Similar to the Malay states, indigenous ruling hierarchies were coopted into the state's colonial machinery in order to indirectly impose political authority over the local people. Here, the Brooke dynasty would provide protection for the various local chiefs, who were expected to retain formal command over their subjects through the customary power they wielded in their respective territories. Notwithstanding that, the influence of indigenous chiefs was constrained by their being barred in obtaining new lands.

In 1867 a Supreme Council (later renamed the *Council Negeri*) was established comprising mainly of European officials, selected Malay and Iban leaders, and prominent local Chinese figures. A Chief Secretary's post was also introduced to foster close working relations and coordination between the state bureaucracy and the Council, which despite its consultative appearance, had some legislative powers in the enactments of codes applicable throughout the state. Real executive powers however, were in the hands of the Chief Secretary and the numerous British Residents, who headed each of Sarawak's territorial *Divisions* and who had his own council of local chiefs.

The complexities of an emerging capitalist economy also required the presence of British colonial personnel in Sarawak to adjudicate both civil and criminal cases pertaining to any matter outside tribal and customary life. For this purpose, the Brooke dynasty was able to recruit qualified administrators into the various state agencies for the handling of revenue collection, enforcing of criminal laws, and facilitating of commercial activities. It was the supremacy of the English legal system in Sarawak that allowed commercial transactions relating to land to be uniformly carried out away from the involvement of indigenous communities.[45] By the end of the nineteenth century, Sarawak recorded a trade worth $13.5 million in local currency.[46] Tobacco, coffee, sago, pepper, gambier, and later rubber, became main export crops, with the last two commodities generating the bulk of state revenues. Later in the twentieth century, with the decline in rubber prices, Sarawak's economy was sustained by the discovery of oil in Miri.

In contrast, the territorial administration of Sabah (formerly called British North Borneo) carried out by the BNBCC had been far less efficient. Lack of a strong bureaucracy and poor knowledge of local cultures proved to be astronomical handicaps for the colonial authorities.[47] In order to administer its geographically rugged regions and culturally diverse peoples, Sabah was divided into various *Residencies,* each with its own official Charter Resident. The BNBCC was neither as dynamic nor competent as the Brooke government in addressing state administrative matters and problems. The company remained primarily as a giant corporation aimed at raking out profits from the various plantations and land development projects it leased. At the top of its political hierarchy was the Governor, who was effectively responsible to the charter's shareholders and Board of Directors in London, and who often had little experience in governing a state.

Unlike the Malay States and Sarawak, the BNBCC's Advisory Council was also virtually an all-European affair, consisting primarily of businessmen and entrepreneurs associated with the charter. Due to its purely economic approach to administration, the BNBCC exerted coercive measures to extract unreasonably high taxes from the indigenous populations.[48] Since there had hardly been any initiative to acquire better relations with the various native peoples in the state, there was widespread resentment and defiance among the local population against state authority.[49] Coupled with mismanagement and inefficiency on the part of the BNBCC, it was not long before the state began to experience its many episodes of near bankruptcies even in the early years of colonial governance. Later however, the lucrative timber industry began to contribute to massive increases in state revenues, with high volumes in exports pushing the eastern coastal city of Sandakan to become one of the most important logging ports in the world—a status it enjoyed well into the twentieth century.[50]

The Federated Malay States (FMS), 1896-1948

As world market demands for tin and other industrial raw materials expanded beyond the nineteenth century, competition for colonial possessions began to heighten amongst Europe's leading industrial countries. The British government saw an impending need to secure their growing investments and capitalist interests in the Malay states against any political or economic trespass. The formation of a centralized colonial state in the form of the Federated Malay States (FMS) was a rationalization of this concern.

The residential system had its limitations. Since production of tin operations had to transverse borders of each of the separate Malay states, the desire for streamlined regulations dealing with land, labor, taxation, and communications among British capitalists became more urgent. As a result, a rather expeditious treaty was signed in 1895 between the British government and each of the four Malay rulers of Selangor, Perak, Negeri Sembilan, and Pahang that merged the four states into a federated colonial protectorate. In 1896, the Federated Malay States (FMS) came into being.

The FMS marked a formal and definitive colonial structure aimed at establishing a more comprehensive and unified polity in the Malay Peninsula. A federal civil service and a new system of courts, filled by Europeans, were created to effectively dispense the enforcement of English laws throughout the federation. Consequently, all civil and commercial transactions in the FMS were incorporated into a standardized federal system with the passing of the 1937 Civil Law Ordinance.[51] One of the more important introductions of western laws was the Torrens land appropriation system in 1897 that dictated the procedures for all official land title registrations. The Torrens system required that land proprietorship can only be recognized through tenure registration in the state's land office, and since only official land purchases or transactions could be placed under the registry, this system effectively transferred all formal land matters in the Malay states into the authority of the colonial state.

The Federation Treaty was said to be both ambiguous and confusing in its articulation. None of the Malay rulers had been adequately advised on the implications of greater integration of their states into a centralized structure.[52] The "British Protectorate" status of the federation meant that the British were now officially responsible for the federation's overall security while a centralized administrative system implied that the Malay states under the federation were now subjected to greater British colonial control. Under the new structure, there also appeared to be virtually no sharing of power between the states and the federal government. It would soon become apparent that policies and regulations formulated at the federal level would oblige their administrative operation and implementation at the state level as well.

The creation of the Federal Council in 1909 extended the colonial state's political jurisdiction over a wider range of financial and legislative matters affecting the FMS. Headed by the Governor of the Straits Settlements seated in Singapore (who also functioned as the High Commissioner of the Federated Malay States), the Council comprised the Resident-General, the four state sultans, and several European and Chinese trade representatives, whose interests in both Malaya and Singapore in many ways coincided with that of the colonial state. In this respect, the Federal Council was highly useful to Singapore and its merchant community, which viewed any inching toward closer political unification between the island and the FMS as potentially profitable. Besides financially boosting the city-port with additional revenues, tighter political links between the Malay states and Singapore would facilitate investment ventures for Singapore-based capitalists in the burgeoning economy of the FMS.

Prior to the formation of the FMS, each of the Malay sultans manifested his ceremonial sovereignty through his position as head of the state council, which at the very least endowed him with symbolic prestige and recognition as head of the state. Now, the sultans' subordinated presence as mere members of the Federal Council emblematically characterized the submission of their sovereignty to the Governor, who now headed the Council. As historian N.J. Ryan noted "In this Federal Council the sultans were no longer the rulers of their own states but advisers to others who were ruling their states for them."[53]

In 1911, the Malay rulers' position in relation to the federal colonial government further eroded with the creation of a federal secretariat, whose Chief Secretary assumed greater and more extensive powers than the now-dissolved Federal Resident-General. As chief executive officer of the secretariat, the Chief Secretary was able to effectively cement the FMS under as tight a control as a centralized administrative body could possibly function under a federated system. This was done clearly to bolster British colonial administrative authority in the FMS, so that its export-led economic development could be better facilitated and coordinated across the various Malay states under uniformed jurisdiction. To emphasize the power of the new branch of government, a federal capital was established in the mining town of Kuala Lumpur, where all federal departments and bureaucracies were eventually situated.

Another important feature of this federated structure was the federal appointment of British *District Officers*, whose tasks included the enforcement of law and tax collection at the lowest level of colonial administration—the local districts. As grassroots intermediaries, these officers were fluent in Malay and worked closely with the traditional Malay *penghulu*, who was chief of a parish called *Mukim*. These *penghulus* became salaried state personnel and were commissioned to ensure British policies were observed among the Malay rural population.[54] The close cultural linkages between *penghulus* and their local communities, each averaging a population of 2000, completed the effective incorporation of Malay rural communities into the colonial state system.[55]

The Unfederated Malay States (UFMS)

The success of a thriving FMS economy convinced the British of the potential benefits of bringing the other Malay states outside of the newly-created federation under its orbital influence. These states included the southern autonomous state of Johor and the four northern states of Perlis, Kedah, Kelantan, and Terengganu, which had remained under the suzerainty of the Siamese king.

The British had recognized the importance of maintaining friendly relations with the Siamese, especially when the latter served as a buffer between British Burma and French Indochina. Nonetheless, the vulnerability of the four northern states' borders to external penetration posed a major concern for the FMS colonial government. Several British merchants had already complained about the lack of protection for their investments in these areas, cautioning that the Germans and Americans had already attempted to broker commercial agreements with local rulers of areas close to the Malay Peninsula.[56]

Subsequently, a 1909 Anglo-Siam treaty was forced on the Siamese primarily to concede their four southern Malay states of Kedah, Perlis, Kelantan, and Trengganu to Britain.[57] Together with the independent Johor sultanate, these newly-released states were collectively referred to as the Unfederated Malay States (UFMS). Each state was designated British protectorate status, formalized by its acceptance of a British Resident Advisor. In return, Siam was promised assistance from Britain should the French decided to interfere with its eastern provinces. Under the agreement, Siam would also get to keep the rest of its southern Malay provinces of Pattani, Narathiwat, Yala, Satun, and Songkhla.

Functioning largely as territorial cushions against imminent external threats to the FMS, the UFMS were neither totally independent nor were they a centralized unit under British colonial rule. There had been no genuine interest in directly incorporating the UFMS into a political union with the more prosperous FMS. One reason had been that the northern UFMS states lacked any valued commodity usable for exports. Furthermore, the states' harsh geographical landscape and sparse populations also made it undesirable in terms of both investments and prospective human settlements for Europeans.

However, the lone southern UFMS state of Johor was different. Despite the presence of a British-endorsed state council, the state had greater autonomy than any of the other Malay states. The sultanate also possessed a well-organized modern bureaucracy that successfully managed a fast emerging agro-based mercantile economy. Importantly, Johor's location between Singapore and the rest of the Malay Peninsula made it highly strategic in terms of transportation, labor, and market flows. It became particularly critical for the British to eventually close in on Johor under its imperial influence, especially since Singapore's own security was largely dependent on the political economic stability of the state. It had not been uncommon for the British to utilize Johor's armed personnel for the enforcement of law and order on the island.

Hence, Johor's relative autonomy had become a thorny issue for the British. The state's glorious past under the Johor-Riau Empire and its reputation as a highly-regarded independent kingdom impelled Sultan Abu Bakar (1833-1895) to regard himself as standing above the other Malay rulers. Sensing that the pervasiveness of British policies throughout the Malay states would eventually extend into Johor, Abu Bakar sought to protect the state's sovereignty by promulgating a constitution that clearly defined the equal relations between the ruler and the Johor state council. Among other things, the constitution emphasized the sultan's institutional status as being separate from the council, which exempted him from any of its meetings and which subjected him to a kind of implicit transgression if he were in any way to involve himself in any of the council's proceedings.[58] This sort of action by the Sultan had sowed seeds of uneasiness in his relationship with the British, who became increasingly anxious at the uncertainty or even possibility of their long-term influence in the state. Thus the British sought an opening for which greater involvement in the state could be justified, which finally came in the form of growing state debt accumulated under the new ruler, Sultan Ibrahim.[59]

Figure 2.2: Map of British Malaya Incorporating the FMS and UFMS 1935

Unable to secure any financial support from London to relieve the growing budget deficit crisis, the sultan agreed in 1914 to accept a British Adviser accountable to the High Commissioner in Singapore. He also agreed to opening up the state's government machinery to European administrators as a way to "resolve" his state's financial problems.

The official acknowledgement of Johor's protectorate status under Britain signaled the complete absorption of both the FMS and the UFMS under an unofficially acclaimed *British Malaya* (please refer to map on figure 2.2 on the previous page). This was the beginning of a glorious period for the British in Malaya. Having secured one of the most highly-prized imperial possessions in the world, they were unrivalled in terms of colonial power and prestige.

Arguments for Greater Centralization of the Federated Malay States

By 1913, Britain, along with other western industrial countries, accounted for 15 percent of the world's population. This core region however, produced 80 percent of the world's manufactured goods and provided for 85 percent of the world's total investment funds.[60] The rapid pace of development in the FMS was very much dictated and fuelled by western market demands for raw material to be used in industrial end-product manufacturing. The unrivalled tranquility and fast-growing capitalist economy characterizing the years preceding the Second World War gave the British a sense of invincibility with regards to their position as colonial rulers in Malaysia and Singapore.

As capitalist development in Malaya became more intense, there emerged arguments for greater centralization of Malaya through direct colonial governance. This meant further increasing the powers of the federal government at the expense of each of the FMS states and its respective Malay rulers. Several of the European and ethnic Chinese capitalists, especially in Singapore, had expressed their frustrations at the colonial state's lack of coordination and pace in keeping up with the expanding trans-Malayan commercial networks, particularly in the transporting of resources and in the legislation of standardized transactions between the various states.[61] In a rapidly growing economy, the expediency of economic processes and laws across the Malay states became crucial for aiding the growths and prosperity of emerging colonial enterprises.

There was also the perception that the individual states had too much power, especially over land matters. Land had become an invaluable asset in the capitalist economy, and as trade and commerce intensified, there seemed to be sluggishness on the part of the state in dealing with the acquisitions and allocations of lands. It was thought that the most feasible solution to this problem lay in the consolidation of both the administrative and legislative bodies of each state through greater centralization of the FMS.

However, the major barrier to such a proposition was the status and position of the Malay rulers. These rulers' sovereign existence had been crucial in sustaining colonial rule in the Malay states, which also made any move toward greater unification of the FMS extremely difficult. By the 1930s, many of the sultans in the FMS had already expressed their displeasure in the way their political authority had greatly dissipated under the new federal system. Many, in fact, began to raise suggestions for greater decentralization of colonial state power as a way to regain some of their influence in the political decisions affecting their respective states. In 1932, the Sultan of Perak openly complained to Britain's King George V that the state councils of the FMS did not emit the scope of power it was understood to possess, not even when compared to those found in the UFMS.[62]

Naturally, the Colonial Office in London was not comforted by any move to further the power and role of the state council, and with it, the status of the sultan. Doing so was considered to be holding back the advances made at federalizing Malaya, thereby potentially disrupting the political rationalization process of the rapidly growing capitalist system. As the capitalist class became more prominent and influential in the economic life of both the FMS and Singapore, the colonial state became increasingly generous in executing laws and policies that advanced their economic interests in the colonies. Any erosion of confidence among entrepreneurs and investors with regards to the capacity of the federal government to foster and encourage investments was taken to be particularly detrimental to the general health of the capitalist economy in Malaya and to wider British imperial interests in the region.[63]

However, there were also many among colonial state officials and those within London's colonial office who were cautious about moving too rapidly toward a more cohesive state structure. Given the political and cultural complexities of the Malay states, a political looseness of the FMS had been essential in sustaining colonial rule. A decentralized system in other words, had been the embodiment of successful British colonialism in Malaya, especially so considering that it was through the sultans' feudal authority that the British had acquired and maintained the legitimacy to rule over the Malay states. Thus many thought it unwise to further dislodge the FMS sultans of their sovereignty and power since a weak Malay ruler may entail forceful rebellions by the masses, leading to potentially implosive situations that severely jeopardized long-term British colonial presence in the Malay states.

Furthermore, there had been increasing concerns regarding a central government's lack of preparedness in dealing with increasingly huge expenditures and large scale administration of all the Malay states. On this issue, some British officers, including the new High Commissioner Cecil Clementi, even proposed a disbanding of the Federation for the restructuring of both the FMS and UFMS under a looser confederation.[64] Many within the colonial establishment also shared the view that the present system or even that of a more decentralized structure could potentially appeal to the UFMS, enticing them into a larger coalition with the FMS.[65]

In the end, it was decided that the preservation of the colonial system through indirect rule was as equally a significant priority as the consideration given to rising capitalist class needs and interests. To resolve the issue and appease advocates on both sides, the British devised several modifications to the existing political structures. In displaying its commitment to safeguard the sovereignty of Malay rulers—a perception crucial to stabilizing the colonial state—each FMS state legislative body was expanded between the early to mid-1930s. Seats in the state council were added, with each state taking responsibility in matters of local health and public works.[66]

To further appease the sultans, the Federal Council accommodated thirteen Officials and eleven Unofficials, allocating extra seats for members of the Malay nobility. Under a new arrangement, the sultans' prestige was somewhat "restored" when they no longer became associates of the Federal Council. Instead, the respective state Residents would serve as official representatives of each of the Malay States in the Council, who must now seek prior "consultation" with his ruler before Council meetings.[67] By implementing these structural changes, the British managed to impress upon the Malay rulers that their position and power had been reinstated. In reality however, there proved to be neither an elevation nor reposition of the Malay rulers' status in their "advisory" role to the Residents. This was because in the actual decision-making process, these so-called consultative relationships had always taken on a procedural rather than participatory character.[68]

Furthermore, even with the increased Malay membership in the Federal Council, the real power still rested with the Federal Secretary and the High Commissioner. In any case, the Unofficial posts set aside for Asian representatives in the Council were also virtually semi-ceremonial positions. It was the Federal Secretariat, who performed the definitive role in policymaking despite the seemingly greater inclusion of colonial subjects through the Federal Council.[69]

In other words, the expansion of civilian participation in policy formulation and the conferring of perceived powers to the states in political decision-making were merely cosmetic than perfunctory. As long as the colonial state and its officials at the federal level were able to cater to the needs of the growing imperial economy through *coordinative* control of the FMS's finances and revenues, any perceived devolution of power to the individual states or Malay rulers would pose no major misgiving for the British. Real unification, it was thought, would inevitably surface from the benefits of a strengthened Malayan economy.[70]

The Colonial State and Capitalist Development in British Malaya

Sustaining the growth of Malaya's export-driven economy was the colonial state's most important goal. In this regard, accommodating the economic pursuits of the emerging European capitalist class in the FMS became a policy imperative. Through its federal administrative machinery, the colonial state was able to service such needs. For example, when further investments in tin production required expensive capital acquisitions, especially in the all-encompassing and technologically-advanced mechanized dredges, the colonial government responded by generously providing affordable leases of these huge machines to credible British investors.[71]

The colonial state also often helped with the management and appropriation of lands for the benefit of the capitalist class. The 1897 Land Enactment for example, which introduced the Torrens system, enabled large numbers of European capitalists with easy access to the most suitable lands for agribusiness, mining, and planting. Exploiting the masses of ill-informed Malay peasants, the British were able to persuade these farmers and landholders to part with their properties and thus make avail through the registration process, huge tracts of valuable areas for development by European entrepreneurs.[72]

However, the repercussions of Malays losing all of their lands to powerful corporations became equally detrimental to British political interests in the FMS, particularly with respect to the legitimacy of British rule through the sultans. Therefore, a 1913 Malay Reservations Act was eventually passed to identify several *Malay ancestral lands* that were to be set aside and prohibited from any type of large-scale agribusiness development.[73] Instrumental to sustaining British colonial rule in Malaya, this legislation was meant to preserve some aspects of Malay cultural rights relating to land and agriculture. The only exemption here was when minerals were found in these lands, in which case European capitalists should be permitted to enter and carry out their mining operations.[74]

These were prosperous times for the British colonialists, especially the wealthy business class. Financial backing, especially for new capital and technology, could be readily procured from the various agency houses in Singapore. Massive funds from these highly-accredited establishments, which came mainly from reinvested profits of local Chinese businesses and Indian moneylenders, formed large portions of loans supplied to individual Europeans.[75] Larger conglomerates and merchant houses from Singapore such as the Straits Trading Company, Guthrie, and Boustead also functioned as stock-broking houses that managed the marketing of tin and other commodities as well as the buying over of several Chinese-owned mines for long-term capital accumulation. Capital imports through these companies reached $14.6 million (Malayan currency) by the early years of the twentieth century, facilitating an increase in overall domestic industrial activity.[76]

Due to high manufacturing demands in the west, industrial consumption of tin tripled between 1870 and 1900. In the next thirty years, it doubled from previous levels, with the United States taking up the lion's share of the market.[77] In time, large-scale tin extraction and production methods would favor investments from joint-stock European companies, which had greater organizational and investment capacity compared to the smaller Chinese firms. More importantly, the colonial state's patronage of European industrialists through its influential networking with London financiers also greatly contributed to the success of these tin magnates, enabling an almost complete *Europeanization* of Malaya's tin industry by the time the Second World War arrived. By the 1930s, European mining corporations that were equipped with technologically-sophisticated expropriation methods contributed to nearly two-thirds of the total world tin production.[78]

The tin industry also almost single-handedly triggered all other infrastructure development throughout British Malaya. British colonial state presence in both the FMS and the UFMS ensured that the numerous development projects undertaken across the states were conducted with precise legal and structural-administrative synchronization. A well-organized public utilities sector provided the building of road networks over vast acres of lands that connected mining areas with processing centers. Thus movements of workers and commodities were also made more viable, facilitating the transformation of mining settlements into towns along the western coast of the peninsula. In 1901, the Federated Malay States Railways (FMSR), the precursor to the existing *Malayan Railways*, became fully operational. Like highways, railway lines in both the FMS and the UFMS were built less for social exchanges than for the efficient carrying of industrial goods, produce, labor, and capital. Within a few years, the provision of electricity, telegraph, and telephone services would accompany the rapid development in both land and rail communications.[79]

Aside from tin production, another major industry that became a mainstay of the FMS economy by the turn of the twentieth century was rubber. The first successful experimental planting of the rubber tree took place in 1878 in northern Perak.[80] Subsequently, various land regulations catering to agribusiness and tin extraction would also serve to encourage and promote rubber cultivation. The western land tenure system that gradually replaced customary Malay land laws unquestionably helped in transforming vast areas of virgin jungles into European rubber plantations. The rapid growth of the automobile industry in the United States and Europe in particular, further created a rubber boom in Malaya, increasing by five-fold the total land acreage allocated for rubber plantations between the years 1905 to 1908. Between 1909 and 1913, these numbers rose by more than 100 percent, and by 1916 rubber would surpass tin as Malaya's primary export revenue.[81] Malaya was now the world's largest exporter of rubber.

As with the tin industry, the FMS colonial state drew up various policies that were disproportionately advantageous to individual European rubber planters. Assistance was generously given in the form of capital acquisition and subsidies, which greatly factored in the growth of the whole British rubber industry in Malaya. Well-financed companies such as Guthrie and Harrison & Crosfield began to receive additional incentives to purchase Malay lands and old Chinese tapioca plantations for the planting of rubber trees. These would be in the form of generous tax cuts and other benefits pertaining to investments and loans.

Another famous corporate assistance program handed out by the colonial state for the benefit of large plantation owners and rubber companies was the *Stevenson Scheme*. World supplies reached a glut following the First World

War, which affected the demand for British rubber and subsequently, its price. The Scheme, initiated by Sir James Stevenson of the British Rubber Growers' Association, requested for the British government to limit across-the-board production of rubber in the colony in order to stabilize rubber prices. This effort materialized into the Export of Rubber (Restriction) Enactment in 1922.[82]

The FMS government, whose legislative council was dominated by state officials and leaders of the various large businesses tied in one way or another to rubber industry, swiftly ratified the enactment. The quota placed on rubber production greatly aided large-scale European plantation companies in Malaya, who had sufficient capital to vary the costs of meeting production ceilings. By the mid-1920s, return of profit registered by British rubber producing companies in Malaya, which controlled nearly 70 percent of total world production, reached £47.22 million on capital investments worth £35 million.[83]

The Scheme was repealed in 1928 after market prices for rubber flattened out. However, the global economic depression of the 1930s brought about another drastic fall in rubber prices. This, once again, placed big rubber conglomerates in dire straits with many European companies faltering on their production costs. To alleviate the spiraling effects of falling rubber prices on these companies, an International Rubber Regulation Agreement was initiated by the Malayan colonial state. It brought to the table in 1934, various signatories from major rubber producers in the region.[84] Stipulations from this agreement included a production quota system of a fixed number of production volume per signatory country, thereby safeguarding the production to price ratio for each of those countries. This agreement soon introduced an oligopoly of world rubber producers, which included the Netherlands and France, who were able to maintain profits from rubber production despite falling prices.[85]

These protective measures gave European rubber conglomerates in Malaya the security of stable rubber prices in the face of global competition and market fragilities. They also served to stave off competition from native smallholders during periods of price fluctuations. During the recession, large European rubber companies defaulting on their costs faced stiff contests from individual Malay and Chinese smallholders who were still able to produce and sell their products for marginal profits. However, regulations forcing all producers to restrict rubber production placed greater difficulties on smallholders, who often apportioned a larger percentage of their capital in rubber and thus were unable to cushion drastic and artificial price falls. Larger companies inevitably benefited from production restrictions since they had access to easier credits and other forms of state subsidies and thus were better able to absorb proportionate production cuts. These larger companies were also able to switch to or supplement their incomes by growing palm oil, a new plantation crop emerging mostly in Selangor and Johor.[86] In other words, the more powerful companies were able to dictate the terms of production to their advantage, which greatly affected the smallholders' share of output. Smallholders on the other hand, lacked any source of funds to help branch out to alternative cash crops or influence market prices.

It would appear that prior discussions surrounding the decision to constrain the volume of rubber production should have included the prior consultations of *all* rubber growers. However, no smallholder representative was included in committees that dealt with the Stevenson Scheme or the International Rubber Agreement. Instead they composed entirely of European entrepreneurs.[87] Before the Stevenson Scheme was implemented, smallholders accounted for a substantial average of 217,000 tons of rubber production compared to the larger estates' average of 260,000 tons. At the end of the 1930s, native smallholders' rubber production thinned to about 113,000 tons, while that of large estates went practically unchanged, as shown by their 246,000 ton production figures for the same period.[88]

Instrumental services provided by the colonial state for European capitalists had been evident since the late 1800s through state-backed and industry-related organizations such as the United Planters Association and Perak Chamber of Mines. These commercial organizations comprised of members who come from a pool of wealthy merchants and agricultural growers, as well as those involved with the management of large plantation and manufacturing companies. Many of these individuals were often linked to the state through a revolving door network of state officials and capitalists, who sat on the various state councils and other important state apparatuses.[89]

In contrast, colonial state relations with Malay peasants were a little more neglectful. For example, rice production from the predominantly Malay states within the UFMS accounted for nearly 80 percent of all supplies in British Malaya by the 1920s.[90] However, since rice was never a European staple diet even in Malaya, its significance in both consumption and sales had not been given due priority within colonial policy. In Kedah, known as "the rice bowl of Malaya," the absence of investments and aid left the sultan himself to initiate projects in the state's rice-growing areas.[91] The colonial state did help build a small irrigation scheme in Krian (northern Perak) in 1906, but the effort proved too burdensome for the peasants as increased taxation from the project overrode any benefit generated from production.[92]

A severe rice shortage from 1920 to 1924 was reflected by low rice production averaging out to only 224,000 metric tons per year, constituting only about 38 percent of total average consumption.[93] Such low outputs caused severe hardships to peasants both in terms of economic livelihood as well as communal subsistence. It was not until depleting rice supplies affected other aspects of economic life in the FMS, especially in the urban areas, that the authorities realized the considerable importance of addressing problems associated with traditional agricultural production. This is particularly so when extreme poverty and hunger have historically shown to be a dangerous recipe for revolution in many places around the world. In 1932, the Drainage and Irrigation Department was established, which provided some form of limited aid to a few rice farmers in the FMS. However, there still persisted a general lack of interest on the part of the colonial state to adequately support Malay agricultural life, which continued to beset rice farming as a relatively backward and uninspiring economic activity.[94]

Summary

British supremacy in the Malay States, which came by way of their initial presence in the Straits Settlement colonies, was a culmination of world systemic factors involving a series of European mercantile incursions into the Malay Archipelago. Through the use of their formidable naval and commercial fleets, the British would go on to victor over the Dutch and establish long-term colonial presence through their geo-strategic possessions in the Malay Peninsula and northern Borneo. Their new dominions in this region would soon be linked to production centers and consumer markets in Europe and the rest of the world through the rapidly expanding networks of the capitalist world economy.

As the Straits Settlements' economy developed into a more complete system, the British considered it necessary to secure their commercial interests in the Malay Peninsula by attempting to control the sources of raw material extraction and production located further inland. The dismantling of the BEIC eventually paved the way for deeper British political involvement in the Malay states.

Through the residential system, the British were able to pressure the various Malay rulers into accepting their imperial presence. In order to indirectly subjugate the Malay masses, the British also conferred recognition and military support to the various sultans, legitimizing both the British colonial authority and the Malay sultan as modern-day despots. Culturally imprisoned by a rejuvenated feudal structure, Malays would eventually find themselves to be the most disempowered group under the emerging capitalist economy. Loyalty to tradition and subservience to political authority would steadfastly remain as primary characteristics of Malay culture that persisted well into the twentieth century.

The residential system was also critical in rationalizing capitalist economic production, particularly in terms of facilitating and promoting intensive capital investments in land, labor, and technology through a host of English administrative laws dealing with wages, taxation, and private commercial rights. With the British *Resident* holding the ultimate decision-making power, the residential system also provided the precursory foundation for a more defined colonial structure throughout the FMS during the early twentieth century.

Soon, the Malay states became critical in providing Britain with precious raw materials for industrial production in Europe, thereby consolidating the power and affluence of the British capitalist class in Malaya. The formalization of the colonial state through the FMS further served the needs of this class by expanding investments and production opportunities as well as consumption markets. The establishment of the various state councils as well as the Federal Council was among the accompanying features of this administrative modernization, which usefully provided business leaders and state officials with consultative forums on various colonial administrative policies and strategies. In spite of its representative structure, the seemingly modern institutions were in effect, autocratic and discriminatory. This became particularly apparent when the various legislative bodies that came with the development of the colonial state effectively confined public policy participation in the FMS to the wealthy European business class.

During the early twentieth century, there emerged serious contemplative discussions among state officials and mercantile leaders regarding the balance needed between direct governance of the FMS through greater centralization, and maintaining the dispersion of the FMS states' powers through the federated structure. At the heart of the discussions was not whether the status of the Malay rulers' could be enhanced or that the political involvement of colonial subjects could be encouraged. Instead, they pertained to types of colonial structure that best rationalized Malaya's capitalist production.

In the end, the argument went in favor of maintaining some degree of "decentralization" through the federal political system. It was agreed that continued control of the Malay states behind the façade of peaceful cooperation with the Malay rulers was indispensable for British colonial rule in Malaya. This was mainly because British colonial legitimacy had been strongly embedded in the protection and maintenance of Malay rulers' sovereignty, especially their traditional authority over the Malay people. Here, it may have seemed that for the state, the immediate benefits that come with deeper unification of the FMS for capitalists, such as greater market accessibility and trade logistics, were not as critically important as preserving and promoting the health and longevity of the British colonial-capitalist system through the present arrangement.

However, it appeared that the federated structure had already been generous in advancing the needs of the British capitalist class. This was especially so when tremendous political powers were concentrated in the offices of the Malayan High Commissioner, British Chief Secretary, and the various state residents, who had the ultimate casting votes in councils and performed decisive roles in policies catering to the interests of the capitalist class. Unofficial memberships in these councils as well as other important state-endorsed economic associations too were also either appointed from a pool of compliant state dignitaries or from a circle of privileged local individuals, whose interests lay not in the struggle to widen democratic participation in the FMS but rather in the political economic opportunities that the state was able to extend to them.

Unlike in the Malay States, British colonization of northern Borneo was for the most part through large private realtors. The Brooke family in Sarawak and the BNBCC in Sabah took hold of all matters relating to their respective state's politics and economy, with the occasional backing of the British government when the need arose. The reluctance on the part of the British colonial office to take direct political charge of these states was mainly explained by the region's lack of economic value when compared to the Malay states. These private entities nevertheless served to secure the larger British imperial presence in Southeast Asia through the supplement and support of their trade and commerce with Malaya and Singapore.

Notes

1. Muhammad Yusoff Hashim, *Malay Sultanate of Malacca: A Study of Various Aspects of Malacca in the Fifteenth and Sixteenth Centuries in Malaysian History* (Kuala Lumpur: University of Malaya Press, 1992), 281-83.

2. R. McRoberts, "A Study of Growth: An Economic History of Melaka 1400-1510," *Journal of Malaysian Branch of the Royal Asiatic Society* 64, no. 2 (December 1991): 47-49.

3. Fernand Braudel, *Perspectives of the World* Vol. 3 *Civilization and Capitalism 15th -18th Century* (New York: Harper & Row, 1984), 484.

4. Quoted in Carl Trocki, *Opium and Empire: Chinese Society in Colonial Singapore, 1800-1910* (Ithaca, NY: Cornell University Press, 1990), 24.

5. Sarnia Hayes Hoyt, *Old Malacca* (Singapore: Oxford University Press, 1993), 31-32.

6. For an extensive history of the VOC, read Els M. Jacobs, *Merchant in Asia: The Trade of the Dutch East India Company during the Eighteenth Century* (Amsterdam: CNWS, 2006).

7. Gene Ammarrel, "Bugis Migration and Modes of Adaptation to Local Cultures," *Ethnology* 41, no.1 (Winter 2001): 55-57.

8. Barbara Watson Andaya and Leonard Andaya, *A History of Malaysia* (New York: St. Martin's Press, 2001), 82.

9. Andaya and Andaya, *History*, 111.

10. N. J. Ryan, *History of Malaysia and Singapore* (Kuala Lumpur: Oxford University Press, 1976), 94.

11. This treaty would provide the blueprint for the modern boundaries of Malaysia, Indonesia, and Singapore. See Andaya and Andaya, *History*, 125.

12. Andaya and Andaya, *History*, 127.

13. Anthony Wild, *East India Company: Trade and Conquest from 1600* (London: Harper-Collins, 2000), 86-91.

14. Andaya and Andaya, *History*, 126-7.

15. Andaya and Andaya, *History*, 136.

16. Nicholas Tarling, *Imperialism in Southeast Asia* (London: Routledge, 1999), 47-50.

17. Andaca and Andaya, *History*, 169-75.

18. Amin and Caldwell, *Malaya: The Making of a Neo-Colony* (Nottingham, England: Russell Press, 1977), 64-66.

19. Anthony Webster, *Gentlemen Capitalists: British Imperialism in Southeast Asia 1770-1890* (New York: St. Martin's Press, 1998), 167-200.

20. For extensive reading on how the Malay sultan and other members of the dominant class gained the spoils of British colonial rule, read Shaharil Talib, *After its Own Image, The Terengganu Experience 1881-1941* (Kuala Lumpur: Oxford University Press, 1984).

21. C. C. Brown, *Malay Annals* (Kuala Lumpur: Oxford University Press, 1976), 27.

22. The concepts of *daulat* and *derhaka* remain today as an essential and non-detachable component in the relationship between Malays and their rulers. For further

reading on the subject, read P.E. De Jong, "The Character of the Malay Annals," in *Malayan and Indonesian Studies,* ed. John Bastin and R. Roolvink (London: Oxford University Press, 1964), 235-41.

23. James. C. Scott, *Weapons of the Weak: Every Day Forms of Peasant Resistance* (New Haven: Yale University Press, 1985), 298.

24. Donald Nonini, *British Colonial Rule and the Resistance of the Malay Peasantry, 1900-1957* (New Haven, CT: Yale University Press, 1992), 23-30.

25. Jeyamalar Kathirithamby-Wells, "Political Authority and the Orang Kaya in the Western Archipelago circa 1500-1800," *Journal of Southeast Asian History* 17, no. 2 (September 1986): 256-58.

26. Simon Smith, *British Relations with the Malay Rulers from Decentralization to Malay Independence* (Kuala Lumpur: Oxford University Press, 1995), 7.

27. John H. Drabble, *Economic History of Malaysia, c.1800-1990: The Transition to Modern Economic Growth* (New York: St. Martin's Press, 2000), 63.

28. Donald Nonini, *British Colonial Rule and the Resistance of the Malay Peasantry, 1900-1957* (New Haven, CT: Yale University Press, 1992), 52.

29. J.C. Jackson, *Planters and Speculators: Chinese and European Enterprise in Malaya: 1786-1921* (Kuala Lumpur: University of Malaya Press, 1968), 252-53.

30. Philip Loh, *Malay States 1877-1895: Political Change and Social Policy* (Kuala Lumpur: Oxford University Press, 1969), 119-20.

31. Paul Kratoska, *Chettiar and the Yeoman: British Cultural Categories and Rural Indebtedness in Malaya* (Singapore: Institute of Southeast Asian Studies, 1975), 9-11.

32. Yen Ching Hwang, *Social History of Chinese in Singapore and Malaya 1800-1911* (Singapore: Oxford University Press, 1987), 110-12.

33. Yen, *Social History*, 118-20.

34. John Butcher, Howard Dick, and Nathan Dick, eds., *Rise and Fall of Revenue Farming Elites and the Emergence of the Modern State in Malaya* (New York: St. Martin's Press, 1993), 35-40.

35. Graham E. Saunders, *History of Brunei* (New York: Routledge, 2002), 70.

36. Saunders, *History of Brunei*, 74.

37. Andaya and Andaya, *History*, 126.

38. For extensive accounts of histories and experiences of rebellion suppressions during the colonial era, read Reed Wadley, "Punitive Expeditions and Divine Revenge: Oral and Colonial Histories of Rebellion and Pacification in Western Borneo, 1886-1902," *Ethnohistory* 51, no.3 (Summer 2004): 609-36.

39. Nicholas Tarling, "Brooke Rule in Sarawak and Its Principles," *Journal of the Malaysian Branch of the Royal Asiatic Society* 65, no.1 (1992): 14-19.

40. Ryan, *History,* 175-80.

41. John Darwin and Frederick Madden, *The Dependent Empire: 1900-1948, Colonies, Protectorates, and the Mandate* (London: Greenwood Press, 1991), 400-402.

42. L. R. Wright, *Origins of British Borneo* (Hong Kong: Hong Kong University Press, 1970), 146-48.

43. Andaya and Andaya, *History,* 187. The borders drawn from this agreement have remained between Indonesian Kalimantan and Malaysia's Sarawak and Sabah states.

44. Andaya and Andaya, *History,* 189.

45. P.M. Kedit. *Modernization among the Iban of Sarawak* (Kuala Lumpur: Dewan Bahasa Pustaka, 1980), 58-62.

46. Ryan, History, 184.

47. Andaya and Andaya, *History*, 195-96.

48. Amity Doolittle, *Property & Politics in Sabah, Malaysia: Native Struggles over Land Rights* (Seattle: University of Washington Press, 2005), 29-35.

49. K.G. Tregonning, *History of Modern Sabah (North Borneo 1881-1963)* (Kuala Lumpur: University of Malaya Press, 1965), 52-54. One of the more famous Malay dissenters in Sabah during the nineteenth century was Datu Mat Salleh, who led a rebellion against the BNBCC. Read more about the warrior in *Datu Paduka Mat Salleh (Hero of Sabah)1894-1900* (Kota Kinabalu: Borneo Books).

50. Andaya and Andaya, *History*, 223.

51. For detailed history of the introduction of English laws in Malaysia, read Sharifah Suhanah Syed Ahmad, *Malaysian Legal System* (Kuala Lumpur: Malayan Law Journal, 2007), Chapter 1.

52. Rupert Emerson, *Malaysia: A Study in Indirect and Direct Rule* (Kuala Lumpur: Oxford University Press, 1974), 53.

53. Ryan, *History*, 175.

54. Shamsul Amri Baharuddin, *From British to Bumiputera Rule: Local Politics and Rural Development in Peninsular Malaysia* (Singapore: Institute of Southeast Asian Studies, 2004), 16-17.

55. Wu Yin Hua, *Class and Communalism in Malaysia: Politics in a Dependent Capitalist State* (London: ZED, 1982), 30.

56. Andaya and Andaya, *History*, 196.

57. Wan Kamaruddin Che Man, *Muslim Separatism: The Moros in Southern Philippines and Malays of Southern Thailand* (Singapore: Oxford University Press, 1990), 10-15.

58. James de Veere Allen, A.J. Stockwell, and L. R. Wright, eds., *Collection of Treaties and Other Documents Affecting the States of Malaysia 1761-1963* (London: Oceana Publications, 1981), 80-82.

59. Andaya and Andaya, *History*, 203.

60. Ankie Hoogvelt, *Globalisation and the Postcolonial World: The New Political Economy of Development* (Baltimore: John Hopkins University Press, 2001), 18.

61. Smith, *British Relations*, 150-55.

62. Margaret Shennan, *Out in the Midday Sun: The British in Malaya 1880-1960* (London: John Murray, 2000), 141.

63. Andaya and Andaya, *History*, 248.

64. J. Sidhu, "Decentralization of the Federated Malay States 1930-34," *Peninjau Sejarah* 1, no. 66 (1966): 21-23.

65. Smith, *British Relations*, 160-61.

66. Andaya and Andaya, History, 250.

67. Ryan, *History*, 213-14.

68. Ryan, *History*, 166-70.

69. Smith, *British Relations*, 30.

70. Smith, *British Relations*, 250-51.

71. Andaya and Andaya, *History*, 210.

72. K.S. Jomo, "Plantation Capital and Indian Labour in Colonial Malaya," in *Indian Communities in Southeast Asia*, ed. K.S. Sandhu and A. Mani (Singapore: ISEAS, 1993), 293-94.

73. This enactment prohibited the sale of certain Malay lands to non-Malays. See Andaya and Andaya, *History*, 220.

74. Loh, *Malay States*, 124-27.

75. Loh, *Malay States*, 142.

76. Lim Chong Yah, *Economic Development of Modern Malaya* (Kuala Lumpur: Oxford University Press, 1967), 3-5.

77. Abdullah Azmi Abdul Khalid, *Trade of Malaya with Special Reference to the Federated Malay States* (Sydney: University of Sydney, 1981), 325-27.

78. Kok Peng Khor, *Malaysian Economy: Structures and Dependence* (Kuala Lumpur: Marican Press, 1983), 54-57.

79. Amarjit Kaur, *Bridge and Barrier: Transport and Communication in Colonial Malaya, 1870-1957* (Kuala Lumpur: Oxford University Press, 1985), 137-35.

80. The first seedlings were brought in to Malaya from Brazil by Henry Wickham, and planted in Taiping, in the state of Perak. See Voon Phin Keong, *Western Rubber Planting Enterprise in Southeast Asia 1876-1921* (Kuala Lumpur: University of Malaya Press, 1976), 1-10.

81. Andaya and Andaya, *History*, 214.

82. Voon, *Western Rubber*, 82.

83. Voon, *Western Rubber*, 164-65.

84. Drabble, *An Economic History*, 130-31.

85. European countries such as Netherlands and France were considered "rubber growing" powers by virtue of their colonies in Southeast Asia—Dutch East Indies and Vietnam respectively—which produced and exported huge volumes of the commodity.

86. Andaya and Andaya, *History*, 219.

87. Andaya and Andaya, *History*, 220-21.

88. Lim, *Economic Development*, 144.

89. Jomo, "Plantation Capital," 293.

90. R. D. Hill, *Rice in Malaya: A Study in Historical Geography* (Kuala Lumpur: Oxford University Press, 1977), 197.

91. Andaya and Andaya, *History*, 217.

92. T.G. Lim, *Peasants and their Agricultural Economy in Colonial Malaya 1874-1941* (Kuala Lumpur: Oxford University Press, 1977), 180-82.

93. Drabble, *Economic History*, 134.

94. Lim, *Peasants*, 184.

Chapter 3
The Making of an Unequal Multiethnic Society, 1850-1957

Market prices for tin and rubber reached an all time high from the late 1800s to the 1920s. Increased industrial manufacturing activities in Europe and North America had stimulated unprecedented demands for the processing of tin plates and rubber sheets, attracting greater investments in tin and rubber production throughout the world. Importantly, a scarcity of cheap labor in these industries would entail large migrations of workers from southern China and India for work in the tin mines, rubber plantations, and newly-opened urban areas throughout Malaya and Singapore.

The settling of these migrants in proximity to their places of work would mark the beginning of a new multicultural existence in British Malaya. With Malays residing in rural areas and working in traditional subsistence agriculture, the assignment of Chinese and Indian workers into the respective tin processing and rubber growing regions would create a demographically distinct and socially unequal Malayan landscape, defined uniquely along ethnic-occupational lines.

The Function of Migrant Labor in Malaya

European investments in the tin and rubber industries were said to be hampered by the lack of cheap workers suitable for work in the tropical climate of Malaya. The relatively small and unskilled Malay agricultural labor, whose traditional occupation was primarily in subsistence production, was said to be unprepared for a task that was heavily specialized and a reward system that was based on daily wages.[1] The importation of foreign workers into Malaya was both an economic and political imperative. A major feature of British colonial policy had been to encourage the appropriation of specific ethnic workers for specialized manual-type occupations. For the colonial state, a reliance on a particular ethnic group in all aspects of the economy could result in the indispensability and eventual empowerment of that group within the capitalist system. Furthermore, grievances regarding work conditions and wages might go beyond mere occupational issues and spill over into the realm of political contestation. It is for this reason that in a multiethnic society like Malaya, a racialized division of labor was encouraged to preclude any potentiality of a unified challenge against the colonial establishment. This was what the then Governor of the Straits Settlements, Sir Frederick Weld, implicitly meant when he stated that "it is advisable that, in a country like this, the preponderance of any one Eastern nationality should not be exceeded."[2]

An accompanying outcome of this ethnicized labor structure was the formation of a multiethnic but highly-stratified society, marked by distinct ethno-occupational living spaces and functional labor positions in the economy. The following sections will briefly examine the social history of each of the major Asian ethnic groups within the emerging ethnic-labor hierarchy; the Chinese, the Indians, and Malays and Bumiputeras.[3] Highlighted in the following discussions are the specific labor functions of each of these major ethnic groups within the modern capitalist economy.

The Ethnic Chinese

As mentioned briefly in chapter 2, the hiring of Chinese workers into the Malay states and Singapore was encouraged by the British to meet the demand for cheap labor within the lucrative tin mining sector. Many of these earlier migrants worked at the mercy of their wealthier Chinese recruiters while receiving little in terms of welfare and protection from the colonial state. Thus, not all of the Chinese who came to the Malay states arrived as workers in the tin industry. There were others who came to profit off the ever-expanding business opportunities located especially in the urban areas.

The earliest historical records of Chinese settlers in the Malay Peninsula can be traced to the days of the old Malacca sultanate of the fifteenth century. As the Straits Settlements came into being, expansions in agribusiness and commerce encouraged many from this affluent merchant community to move to the port-cities of Penang and Singapore.[4] Having maintained their unique cultural traditions for centuries, the Straits-born *Peranakan* or *Baba* Chinese, as they are popularly known, stand out from other Chinese groups by their assimilated Malay character, which includes their inability to speak a Chinese dialect fluently. These *Peranakans* also became naturalized British subjects under Straits Settlement laws, which accorded them privileged access to English schools and government jobs. As the capitalist economy developed, their commercial enterprises and skills grew along with it, with many finding employment in various professional fields in the urban areas.

Embracing the spirit of the colonial Empire, the *Peranakan* took in as much as possible the lifestyle of the colonial masters.[5] Through the Straits Chinese British Association, *Peranakan* businessmen made it clear that their political and entrepreneurial interests conflated with that of the British, with whom they identified closely even during the Anglo-Chinese wars of the 1850s. Prominent historian C.M. Turnbull remarked that the Straits-born *Peranakan* Chinese "leagued themselves with the ruling elite against the rank and file of their own countrymen."[6]

The early European-owned agricultural export industries in the Straits Settlements did not initially yield the adequate revenues for profits. The Chinese merchants, on the other hand, proved more successful. It was the *Peranakan* entrepreneur, who diligently undertook investments in the tapioca, pepper, and gambier-growing industries and generated prosperous returns on their export ventures into Europe. In 1890, three Malaccan Chinese, Tan Jiak Kim, Tan Jeong Saik, and Lee Cheng Lam, together with a handful of European capitalists, founded the first Chinese shipping conglomerate in Singapore—the Straits Steamship Company.[7]

The growth of the Malayan economy further attracted both sojourners as well as entrepreneurs from southern China seeking jobs and other business-related opportunities during the later part of the nineteenth century. The "tin rush" in Malaya especially brought in a huge influx of Chinese low-wage workers into the FMS. Many were grouped into secret society triads such as the *Hai San* and *Ghee Hin* for purposes of both protection and organization.[8] Leaders from such triads were also able to rise to prominence through partnerships with various Malay chieftains, who held the concessions and rights to mine. Several among the China-born migrants were also able to successfully chance upon various commercial pursuits that grew out of a rapidly developing capitalist economy. Amassing huge fortunes from investments and production opportunities, many became be part of the emerging local bourgeoisie in Malaya.

Unlike the *Peranakans* however, this class of China-born merchants would always distance itself from the British colonial administration. Through its own business association, the Chinese Chamber of Commerce, these elites preferred instead to direct their efforts to philanthropy work within the local communities. Although near-limitless opportunities in the Malay states and Singapore had made it possible for this group to experience intra-generational mobility, many remained fixed on plans to eventually return to the motherland. There had been little or no sentiment for their "land of bread and honey" that was Malaya.

By the turn of the twentieth century, ethnic Chinese businesses from both the *Peranakan* and China-born groups had dominated the banking, light industrial, and retail sectors of Malaya's economy. Among the notable Chinese merchants who built their commercial forte around these sectors included Tan Kah Kee, Tan Beng Swee, and Tan Kim Ching. This trio also successfully expanded their Singapore-based commodity trading and rice-milling businesses to other parts of Southeast Asia.[9] As the later migrant Chinese population outnumbered the *Peranakan* Chinese, the commercial domains of the latter would also be increasingly subsumed by that of the former.

Subsequently, the rapid tempo of capitalist development in Malaya became most evident in the fast growing urban areas of the FMS. The pull of the urban economy led to multiple arrivals of Chinese workers from the mining areas, many of whom had been freed from their initial contracts and were now in search of commercial opportunities in newly-opened towns.[10] The expanding consumer markets and increased job availability in these towns maintained this pattern of human movements well into the twentieth century, establishing the urban demography of the FMS to be largely associated with Chinese residents.

Wherever the Chinese established themselves, their economic networking followed. In serving the economic needs of a bourgeoning population, Chinese-owned banks and loan companies were always looking for new clientele from among those yearning to start their own businesses. The expansion of credit markets brought on by the arrival of new consumers was therefore highly encouraging for Chinese commerce. For the Chinese businessman, his ethnicity and clan membership availed him to relatively easy borrowings that no other ethnic group had privy to, giving him a niche in the retail and small commercial sectors of the emerging urban capitalist economy.

As the businesses of the newer China-born groups flourished, much of their earnings were channeled toward China through active bodies as The Chinese Chamber of Commerce and the Nanyang Chinese Relief Association. Financial contributions, donations, and investments from Singapore and Malaya would be funneled to a wide system of mainland Chinese interests ranging from assisting the growth of Chinese industries to the provision of funds for the war against Japan. As exclaimed by prominent China-born businessman and community leader Tan Kah Kee: "Malayan wealth must be drawn off for China."[11]

During the Japanese occupation of Malaya from 1942 to 1945, the Japanese colonial state recognized the crucial role of ethnic Chinese capitalists in the Malayan economy. In need of contributory investments for the war, the Japanese were careful not to disrupt the flow of local Chinese commerce in Malaya, allowing many prominent leaders from the various Chinese guilds to escape imprisonment or torture. Many were instead assigned important roles in the Japanese colonial administration through the Overseas Chinese Association (OCA), which among other things helped disbursed a mandatory $50 million military contribution to help the Japanese in their war campaigns.[12]

Under the Brooke dynasty in Sarawak, Chinese migration into the state was also directed at filling in the labor needs of the various mining, plantation, and agribusiness fields. Within a short time, the Chinese began to dominate the commercial as well as natural produce distribution networks throughout the state. Many had arrived to ply their trade in the city's local economy as well as in gold mining.[13] In Sabah, the Chinese were specifically channeled by the BNBCC into areas that were leased for economic development, namely for mining and agro-commercial ventures. Chinese labor was also bound for the Brunei border to work in the pepper and gambier plantations as well as in the newly-discovered timber-felling regions. Like in the FMS and Sarawak, the Chinese in Sabah also participated actively in the emerging urban economy and soon populated the new towns along the coasts.[14]

As an immigrant community, the Chinese were driven by political and economic hardships to take on whatever that was available in the market. This eventually led them to numerous job and business opportunities that came as a result of the rapidly growing capitalist economy. An important variable of success for the Chinese migrant community was attributed to the well-organized labor distribution networks within each family or clan-based organization. The structure of rights and obligations tied together family members, clansmen, and business associates into an efficient commercial system that was highly adaptable to the capitalist economy and facilitative of attaining success.[15] The willingness of many Chinese migrants to work for low returns also further pushed many from this group into newly available and relatively independent occupations such as petty trade, service provisions, and retail. With the family as its organizational unit, many Chinese businesses would develop into identifiably private and small enterprises that were passed down from one generation to another.

By the second decade of the twentieth century however, the mechanization of European tin production had caused an eventual surplus in cheap Chinese labor. Gradually, many unemployed men found their way into various crime syndicates and secret society memberships associated with the proliferation of vice and other socially disruptive activities.[16] Troubled by what they saw as these groups' scant regard for the law and increasingly defiant attitude toward authority, the British made sure the importation of Chinese workers into Malaya and Singapore came to an almost abrupt stop by the end of the 1920s.

The Ethnic Indians

By the late nineteenth century, rubber had already become a major export commodity for the FMS. Accompanying the growth of this industry was the demand for cheap labor, stimulated by the opening up of numerous European-owned plantations throughout the colony. British experience in Sri Lanka (Ceylon) and southern India convinced the FMS colonial state of the suitability of Indian workers for the tropical climate of the Malay States. The Governor of the Straits Settlements, Sir Frederick Weld was particularly enthusiastic about the introduction of low-wage southern Indian labor, seeing that the British-protected Malay states had a population of only about one million with vast areas of untapped resources yet to be exploited.[17] More than anything else, India was a British colony, making the recruitment task especially convenient. In 1907, a Tamil Immigration Fund was set up to subsidize this process.[18]

The hiring of Indian labor was initially undertaken by several private organizations through the *kangani*, which was an indentured system involving the selection of workers by a pool of commissioned village heads throughout southern India.[19] During the rubber boom in 1899 alone, more than 15,000 of these *kangani* laborers came to the FMS to work in various types of employment related to the rubber industry.[20] Conforming to British colonial ethnic-labor policy, an important stipulation in the employment of these laborers was its prohibitive use in the mining sectors.

Among the Indian migrant workers, a majority belonged to the Hindu-Dravidian cultural groups comprising the Tamil, Telegu, and Malayalee. One of the more apparent characteristics of these south Indian laborers had been their enormous poverty. Coming from the most disenfranchised class of Indians, these workers mostly ended up doing the least attractive menial jobs within the plantation and urban construction sectors. Interestingly however, Tamils from Sri Lanka came from relatively much higher socio-economic status and were specifically brought by the British to assist them in Malaya's colonial administrative services. It was similarly the case for many Sri Lankan Sinhalese, who were predominantly Buddhists and who fared much better than most other south Asian groups. They were for the most part, educated and skilled, which enabled them to fill in the various clerical jobs in the public services, while others opened up their own individual businesses in the urban areas.[21]

Relatively fewer Indians came from other parts of India. Among this minority, participation in the colonial economy was mainly in the mercantile and small commercial sectors. The Gujeratis as well as Bengalis were visibly the most highly-organized in their retail enterprises and the most ostentatious in terms of lifestyles. The Sikhs of Punjab, on the other hand, were mainly recruited into the police and constabulary forces of the British colonial army, with many among the better-educated able to transition into a range of higher-paid occupations.[22] There were also Muslim and Christian groups from the Coromandel coasts of southwestern India, who although sharing a similar language, lived quite separately from the majority Hindus due to their distinct cultural and occupational backgrounds.

The spectrum of class and ethnicity among Indians also intersect with the stark contrasts brought forth by the differences in social caste backgrounds. Members from the lower castes who occupied the lowest rungs of Hindu traditional society were often confined to the most physical but lowest paid jobs in both rural and urban areas of Malaya. The upper castes on the other hand, although sometimes possessing relatively little in terms of wealth, commanded a more esteemed position in traditional Indian society. It is not unusual that the prospects for upward mobility often correlated proportionately with caste.

The most influential among the ethnic Indians also often engaged in the money lending or *chettiar* businesses in the urban centers throughout Malaya and Singapore.[23] The lives of these upper caste Indians yielded little or no social contact with their lower caste counterparts other than perhaps in the course of work. In fact, many from this class made extra effort to disassociate themselves from the poorer Indian laborers. As mentioned by historian Sinnapiah Arasaratnam, "These (upper castes) people would use the word 'coolie' on (majority Tamils) in the same derogatory sense as the Europeans in Malaya."[24]

However, economic opportunities in the urban areas in Malaya did gradually provide for a number of Indians from various backgrounds with opportunities of entering the wage or salaried workforce. English education, in particular, made it possible for many ethnic Indians to penetrate significant social barriers in Hindu society. With such qualification, many were able to enter various occupations outside manual labor. Upper-class Indians, of course, were able to achieve much more, with many seeing their children through tertiary education to become lawyers, doctors, and other form of professional work.[25]

The majority of Indians during the colonial period however, would remain perpetually trapped within the impoverished existence of the rural estates and plantations, where disease and alcoholism plagued much of their communal life. Plantation work was in effect a form of captive labor tied to the exploitative conditions of colonial capitalist production as well as to a social system that defined the laborers' powerlessness and low status in society. For many ethnic Indians who were un-schooled or came from the lower rungs of the traditional social caste system, there was a tendency to become easily subservient to any type of authority, making them readily available for the most demanding and undesirable types of manual work.[26] Most noticeably, the inherently rigid caste system, which had allowed the British the power to suppress and control Indian workers in the various labor-based industries, remained widely practice well into twentieth century Malaya.

Faced with severely limited life chances, a substantial portion of ethnic Indians would remain confined to a social world associated with low-wage occupations throughout much of the country's modern history. As the stratified ethno-economic structure began to socially reproduce itself, social relationships between the majority of Indians and other ethnic groups in Malaya became considerably unequal and distanced.

Malays and their Agrarian Function

The official recognition given to Malays as the indigenous people of Malaya had been crucial for British colonial rule in both the FMS and UFMS. The preservation of Malay culture, especially their attachment to their lands, served the British with two important goals. First, it conferred sovereignty of the Malay sultan over the Malay people, which gave the British the legitimacy to provide "protection" for the sultan and his state. In such a relationship, the colonial state was then able to "indirectly" access these lands to determine their various allotments for development by European capitalists.

Second, the preservation of specific Malay lands purely for "cultural" use would confine Malay peasants to remain on their small plots as self-subsistence farmers or agricultural tenants. Land laws in the form of the Malay Land Reservation Enactment of 1913 and the Rice Lands Enactment 1917, as discussed previously, gave special rights to Malays with respect to the utilization of their lands for personal farming. Caveats were often inserted however, to stipulate that lands originally appropriated for rice production had to be cultivated only for rice and nothing else.[27] Penalties for transgression of these laws included confiscation of crops or heavy fines.

These policies produced two significant consequences for Malays under the emerging capitalist economy. One, it opened up lands outside Malay reservations to large British and Chinese agro-business ventures. Second, these enactments effectively discouraged many Malay farmers from any economic shift away from subsistence agriculture. Although some managed to grow rubber to supplement their small-hold incomes, most rural Malays were practically left out of any meaningful participation within the capitalist economy. This made sense from the colonial viewpoint. Any wealth accumulation or upward social mobility that comes with greater economic opportunities could have posed considerable political economic threats to the Malay ruler. British colonial policy was very much premised on upholding the sultan's supreme status over his subjects. Thus any potential political empowerment of Malays outside of the royal house would also likely jeopardize the colonial structure, and along with it, British interests throughout the Malay states.

Furthermore, the entrenchment of Malays in agrarian life was also meant to restrict substantial educational opportunities for the group. Educational empowerment of Malay always carried the potential risks for Malay political challenge against the authority of both the sultan and the British.[28] Importantly, any extensive social-economic opening through education would also furnish Malays with modern skills and knowledge that could eventually lead to demands for a greater share of rewards from Malaya's growing capitalist economy.[29] In other words, this would defeat the very rationale of a colonial rule that was heavily premised on the continued suppression of the masses.

By the turn of the century, the Chinese had already formed the largest non-Malay ethnic group in both the FMS and Singapore. The free labor character of Chinese workers advantaged them with access to various employment markets in the new economy. In terms of both social power and mere numbers, the emerging Chinese-educated professional classes far overwhelmed the Malay nobility class, upon whom the British depended for their continued colonial rule in Malaya. The British began to realize the impending danger associated with the educational and economic prominence of the ethnic Chinese, which could very well imperil the dominant position of the Malays and thereby destabilize the dynamics of indirect colonial rule in the FMS.

Hence the British saw the need to improve educational services for the Malay elite class by providing exclusive English education for selected Malay youths of various aristocratic backgrounds. This plan materialized in 1907 in an Eton-style residential school located in the royal town of Kuala Kangsar, Perak. Formally named *The Malay College*, the school was designed mainly to prepare "Malay males of good birth" for positions in the various state civil services. From this, a special Malay Administrative Service was also later established as a federal support branch to the European-dominated Malayan Civil Service .[30]

Unsurprisingly, calls by various Malay village chiefs to establish similar schools in their respective localities were rejected by the British.[31] This resulted in the majority of school-going Malay children confined to village-level education, especially in the communal religious *madrasah*.[32] As was the situation then, extreme resource inadequacy and ill-equipped infrastructure had placed these Malay schools worlds apart from those in urban educational settings, where the quality of teaching and skills preparation had been much superior and more relevant for modern occupations.

In this respect, the willingness on the part of the colonial state to provide quality educational services for elite Malays and its simultaneous reluctance to similarly extend such educational opportunities to a larger section of the community remained a firmly entrenched colonial policy function. If any improvement in the area of education was to be initiated for the masses of Malays, it would serve solely to make them "better farmers." In 1920, the Director of Education of the FMS commented that "the aim of the Government is not to turn out a few well-educated youths… rather it is to improve the bulk of the people, and to make the son of the fisherman or peasant a more intelligent fisherman or peasant than his father had been…"[33]

An effort to improve the *instructional* quality in Malay schools finally came with the founding of the Sultan Idris Training College in Tanjung Malim, Perak in 1922. Considered one of the more progressive moves by the colonial authority to provide some limited educational development for the relatively few Malay schoolteachers, the training college however failed to upgrade the quality of Malay education in general since infrastructural spending for schools remained a non-priority. Aside from later producing a handful of outstanding Malay teacher-cum-literary figures, the college also did little to directly or indirectly increase the overall life-chances of the average Malay beyond the agricultural sector. That an "improved" vernacular education was hardly a gateway for successive generations of Malays taking up salaried or even waged positions in the modern economy was evident by the end of the1930s when more than 90 percent of working Malays in the FMS remained as rural cultivators, rubber smallholders, and fishermen.[34]

The long-term consequences of these colonial policies on the economic prospects of ordinary Malays within the capitalist economy were particularly harmful. While few members of the Malay aristocratic families in the FMS did eventually secure comparatively higher rewards through their privileged positions in the civil services, the majority Malays was constricted to a rural life that was increasingly disconnected from the economic growth occurring in their own backyard.[35] The seclusion of rural life only further reinforced the closed-mindedness of Malay parents, who for a long time were not able to comprehend the social importance of modern education for their children.

The plight of Malays as an economically marginalized and highly impoverished community would remain well into the years after independence. The lack of educational and employment opportunities effectively disadvantaged them in their socio-economic standing with other ethnic groups, which would culminate into serious ethnic tensions in the years after Malayan independence. More importantly, the general disenfranchisement of Malays, coupled with their undying loyalty to the Malay ruler for leadership and direction, would eventually place them in a state of unrivalled political apathy.

Multi-Tiered Ethnic-Occupational Structure in Malaya

As the development of the capitalist economy intensified in Malaya, an ethnically-tiered social structure would inevitably emerge. At the top was a relatively small group of large-scale entrepreneurs dealing in the production of commodity resources as well as in the imports and exports of both manufactured and agricultural goods. This group consisted mainly of European capitalists, whose close association with the colonial state was mirrored in the latter's servicing of their economic interests.

The social world of these Europeans revolved in one way or another around the advantages obtained from Malaya's new-found wealth. Many would congregate and recluse in their lavish homes and luxuriant racquet clubs located in the most placid parts of the city, where the barring of non-Europeans from residences and memberships reflected the exclusivity of Caucasians in terms of both status and privileges.[36] Even those outside of the elite class would also distance themselves from the local population as a way to assert their identity of being part of the dominant group in colonial society.

Below this group lies another elite circle of entrepreneurs, who despite their material wealth but due to their ethnicity, was never really included in the social world of European elites. The successful Chinese capitalist community held ownership of numerous large companies dealing with a wide array of distributive, retailing, and wholesaling of consumer items and services.[37] This group was also responsible for the newly-emerging financial networks that circulated throughout the colonial economy, and whose esteemed positions in the local business guilds also made them eligible candidates for appointments to the various state councils seats.[38]

Among those also included in the lower ranks of the local bourgeoisie in colonial Malaya were several members of the Malay nobility. For this group, their distinguished traditional status had provided them avenues for higher education and relatively decent standing in the various state civil services. The experience gained from assisting the British to indirectly administer the Malay states also exposed these elite Malays to critical aspects of politics and modern state governance, which many will use to their advantage in later years to come.

Also, there was a small but rising English-educated middle-class comprising mostly of ethnic Chinese and Indians, who began to function as new social units in the urban capitalist economy. Although still distanced by culture and ethnicity, many were brought together through professional encounters or residential proximity. Many were employed either in administrative positions of the manufacturing and service sectors, or in civil service jobs located in cities and towns. Newer generations of these families would also attend the few good schools located in the cities as well as participate in important social events that opened them up to leadership positions within their own commnities.[39]

Meanwhile, the lower occupational tiers within the capitalist economy belonged to the lower-waged urban service workers and the manual laborers of the mining, plantation, and agricultural sectors. In the towns, distinct and segregated ethnic enclaves housed many of Malaya's poorer urban population. In terms of employment, the Chinese would partake in low-paying trades and services while the Indians were mainly hires in public and urban construction works. There was also an increasing number of Malay families in the major towns, who had either migrated from the countryside to ply their petty trades in the city or were part of outlying village communities that had been gradually absorbed into the various municipalities.

In the rural setting, inter-ethnic interactions were extremely rare due to the enormity of distances between hamlets, mines, and plantations. As the capitalist economy developed, large numbers of Chinese took on numerous economic functions as middlemen in small parishes or as private commercial farmers in the countryside.[40] While many from this group could hardly sustain a basic standard of living, they nevertheless fared much better than a majority of Tamil Indians, who were subjected to indenture-type work in the various rubber estates.[41] Grueling working conditions and continuing poverty marked the daily lives of both these groups, while the relatively closed nature of their communities kept them far apart from each other as well as from their upper class brethrens in the cities.

Finally, the most economically marginalized group was the rural Malays and other various but smaller Bumiputera groups in Malaya. Confined to the declining world of self-subsistence agriculture and rural craftsmanship, these native groups under the old economy were once successful traders throughout the Malay states.[42] As the capitalist economy encroached upon the Malay world, traditional Malay commercial activities became increasingly displaced by new networks of organized and profit-oriented Chinese and Indian businesses. This inevitably resulted in this community's detachment from the mainstream capitalist economy, where most would remain well into Malaya's independence.

Hence, residence was, for the most part, well-integrated into each ethnic group's specialized occupational functions. This meant that social distances were greatest between the lower-tiers of each ethnic community who lacked any substantial mobility or experiential exposure to the worlds outside their neighborhoods. Any interaction taking place between each ethnic group or between different social classes within each group rarely moved beyond the few impersonal exchanges of business transactions.

Ethnic-Occupation Formation in Northern Borneo

The capitalist economy had developed at a more sluggish pace in northern Borneo as compared to the FMS, but an ethnic-labor structure nevertheless emerged between Europeans, Chinese and indigenous groups. The Brooke government had politically categorized the peoples of Sarawak into three basic groups; Malays (including other Muslim indigenous groups), indigenous non-Muslims (majority from the Iban or Land Dayak group), and Chinese.[43] Crucial for the consolidation of Brooke's authority across the state had been this process of "racial-formation" along well-defined geographical areas that soon reflected each ethnic group's distinct economic activities.[44]

Immediately after suppressing the Brunei rebellion, the first Brooke *Rajah* in Sarawak, James, pardoned the various chiefs involved in the uprising and included them into the few selected ceremonial state positions.[45] Among the visible features of early capitalist development in Sarawak was the use of the English legal system to allocate lands for agro-business, mining and later, logging. Soon after resettling Malay communities away from Iban areas, specific vacant and arable lands left from these displacements were earmarked for various crop plantations. Imported low-waged Chinese labor would later be used to work these lands. Meanwhile, in towns and cities, the few Europeans there would be engaged either in government work or some aspects of high-level business management, while the bulk of lower-level urban economy was run by the various ethnic Chinese trades and services.

Similarly in Sabah, there had been a few selected members of the various indigenous nobility groups who were included in the lower ranks of the state bureaucracy, while the top and middle managements were filled mostly by British officers of the BNBCC. Outside of this elite group, the majority of the native populations remained heavily confined to subsistence agriculture, fisheries, and jungle produce collection.[46] The largely Muslim Bajau and Sulu groups for example, lived mainly along the eastern coasts of the state while the predominantly non-Muslim groups such as the Kadazan and Murut settled in the interior as farmers and horticulturalists dependent on the planting of rice and sago.[47] Like elsewhere in colonial Malaysia, imported Chinese labor was also used to work on newly-opened European commercial plantations and also in the low-wage employment sectors of the few urban areas around the state.

The absence of any political cohesion among the various indigenous peoples, attributed largely to these regions' distinct cultures and massive size, was advantageous to the colonial states in both Sabah and Sarawak. It enabled both the BNBCC and the Brooke administration to authoritatively control their territories, which compelled the various local groups in the respective states to acknowledge their political presence as colonial masters.

Emerging Ethnic Inequalities in Colonial Malaysia, 1930-1957

One of the most salient outcomes of an ethnically-tiered labor structure was the inevitable wealth and income inequities between the different peoples of Malaya. By 1941, the major migrant groups had numerically overwhelmed the indigenous Malays. Malaya's ethnic balance stood at approximately 2.4 million Chinese, 2.2 million Malays, 750,000 Indians, and 30,250 Europeans. About 80,000 more came from other groups that included non-Malay Bumiputeras, Eurasians, and Ceylonese.[48] By 1947, 60.8 percent of the non-indigenous population in Malaya and Singapore had been born within the country. A pattern of more permanent and diverse Chinese settlements also began to appear with the growing migration of women, thus narrowing their ratio to Chinese men from 513:1000 in 1931 to 837:1000 in 1947.[49]

The accompanying social inequalities brought forth by capitalist development in Malaya were captured through various economic indicators for the years leading up to independence from Britain in 1957. The most notable was the disproportionate wealth distribution between Europeans and the three main Asian ethnic groups. Using commercial land capital as measurement, Europeans owned 665 estates covering a size of 821,049 acres, followed by the Chinese with 299 estates and an area totaling 92,389. Indians, although relatively poor as a group, owned 119 estates with an area of 26,927 acres compared to Malays, who owned just 23 estates totaling less than 5,000 acres.[50] Although such statistics may not represent the accuracy of real-life living standards of the average person in each ethnic group, they nevertheless reflected the general comparative wealth level between each major group through average asset holdings.

The disparity in average incomes between Malays, Chinese, and Indians also illustrated the social-economic differences between each of these groups, particularly in terms of their class positions relative to the others along the stratification structure. By 1947, the Malays, primarily concentrated in low-return agricultural occupations, averaged an income per capita of $258 (Malayan dollars). The Indians, who had a considerable share of its members engaged in wage and salary jobs in estates and government services, did better with an average income per capita of $560. The Chinese, greater in population and more evenly distributed throughout the private and government sectors, acquired a heftier portion of revenues with an average income per capita of $656.[51]

This ethnic inequality structure would continue into the later decades after the Second World War, perpetuated primarily through sectoral-occupational differences between groups. By the 1950s, the ethnic Chinese had increasingly dominated nearly all local economic activities from small scale agribusiness to retail and trade. They also constituted the largest percentage among all Asian groups in the managerial, professional, and entrepreneurial job categories. Indians, for the most part, were still generally situated within the clerical and plantation sectors, while its urban elite class would gain a foothold over some aspects of traditional textile retail and lending services. Malays on the other hand, would remain prevalent within the agricultural sector, with a small portion occupying the lowest ranks of the armed forces and state bureaucracy.[52]

The uneven nature of capitalist development occurring across urban centers, rural areas, and agro-estates in Malaya also carried massive discrepancies in the provision of clean water, sanitation services, and accessible medical facilities. The correlations in postwar Malaya between provision of social services and ethnicity can be captured in the differences in ethnic infant mortality between the major groups. In 1947, the Malay infant death ratio was highest with 259 deaths per 1000 live births. This was followed by Indians with 199 deaths, and the Chinese with 141 deaths. Overall ratios declined ten years later in 1957, but for Malays and Indians, the numbers were still relatively high at 191 and 151 deaths per 1000 live births respectively.[53] These relatively high rates among Malay and Indian infants were symptomatic of the deprivation in healthcare and basic modern amenities that go along with the lack of economic and infrastructural development in regions associated with lower income farming and plantation work.

In Sabah and Sarawak, labor-ethnicization patterns produced by colonial capitalist development had also resulted in visible differences in the rates of social-economic progress between the various ethnic groups. Remuneration received from the traditional economy of Bumiputera and Malay groups, premised mainly on fishing, subsistence farming, and tropical produce collection was enormously less compared to the relatively few but rapidly transformative agribusiness and plantation-centered capitalist economy. Increasingly detached from mainstream economic activity, these rural-based ethnic groups were considerably divested of any opportunity for social growth and left far behind in the total development of the region.[54]

The case in Sabah was comparatively worse than in Sarawak. Bajaus and other indigenous Muslim groups who resided along the isolated coastlines of the state were virtually cut off from any modern development taking place in the s ate. Similarly for the Muruts, who mostly inhabit the inhospitable mountainous terrain of the interior, it would be about a decade or so later before they received any substantial form of modern healthcare that other ethnic groups may have already acquired in limited forms.[55]

In contrast, the urban Chinese, who became active participants in the local economy, were more likely to have taken advantage of better job and educational opportunities in towns and earned disproportionately higher average incomes than the various indigenous groups. This was similarly true for the few urban-dwelling indigenous families, who usually come from higher traditional circles within their respective groups. Several Kadazan Christians for instance, were able to fare much better than their compatriots in the outlying regions in terms of jobs and upward social mobility. Their association to the British, either through affinity in faith or as comprador elites, further made entry into a number of salaried state administrative positions more possible.[56]

In Sarawak, the ethnic composition of local Asian groups in 1961 showed Bumiputera Ibans as the largest group, constituting 31 percent of Sarawak's total population of 744,529. The Chinese constituted close to 30 percent, the Malays 18 percent, while other indigenous ethnics, including the Bidayuh and Melanau, making up the rest of Sarawak's major populations. Yet, the general breakdown of occupations in 1960 showed that most of the higher-income industry-related jobs were concentrated mainly among the ethnic Chinese, who dominated the commercial and manufacturing sectors with a total of 26,404 workers, followed by Malays with only 8,167 workers.[57]

Income inequality between ethnic groups in Sarawak was also implicitly reflected by the disproportionate ethnic group percentages in the higher-paying professional and technical services category. These included teaching, nursing, and lower level engineering jobs as well as occupations relating to the public services. By 1960, the Chinese had eclipsed other groups in this field with 3,194 workers, accounting for more than 50 percent of all workers in these relatively higher-end occupations. Malays constituted only around 15 percent of lower-paying service workers in the state, while all other Bumiputera groups, including the more populous Iban and Bidayuh, combined for 28 percent of this workforce, which were mainly located in the lower-end portion of this occupational category.[58] Similar to the situation in Malaya, the majority of Bumiputeras and Malays in northern Borneo remained heavily involved in low-intensity agriculture or seasonal horticultural practices with unstable and relatively meager earnings.

The wide disparity in job and wage distribution between the various ethnic groups in colonial Malaya as well as in Sabah and Sarawak was to generally persist in the decades to come. Such inequality would be reproduced by the "free market" nature of capitalist development in colonial Malaysia, one that the colonial authorities perceived as an accompanying feature of a rationalized social-economic arrangement.

Urbanization and Uneven Regional Development

Social disparities in Malaya and northern Borneo were also exacerbated by the nature of capitalist development that polarized the various ethnically-segregated residential and working spaces into unequal ethnic regions. Since colonial policy had prioritized specific development objectives based on revenue potentials, the impact of returns on economic investments in Malaya and northern Borneo on region and ethnicity was therefore seriously unbalanced. Triggered by heavy inputs in mining and rubber located mostly in the FMS states, spillover of development from these industries for example, took on a regional bias. As economic historian W.G. Huff put it, "The result was to shift the whole western coast of the Malayan economy onto a higher development plane."[59]

This meant that even within the FMS, expansions in the tin-mining and rubber-growing sectors made Selangor and Perak the wealthier and more developed states. It was in these two states too that social and economic infrastructure development, especially in the form of support services and supply networks for these industries, had been most rapid and concentrated.[60] Paved highways and rail lines serving to accommodate the tin and rubber industries, for example, were mostly built along the Selangor-Perak corridor, with Singapore, Kuala

Lumpur, Ipoh, and Penang serving as main artery points of all land communications.

In many ways, capitalist development in colonial Malaysia was also primarily an urban-centered process. The disproportionate flows of early public sector investments linked to the tin industry contributed to the influx of Chinese miners, laborers, and businesses gravitating toward urban areas. Here, the readily available networks of roads, telegraph services, and numerous public amenities significantly enhanced the mobility of Chinese populations in search for greater employment opportunities in the towns dotting along these major communication hubs. In time, cultural connections with other clan groups in the cities made urban life significantly comfortable for the Chinese, in terms of both social and economic capital provisions.[61]

Between the years 1947-1957, the drift into cities and towns grew at an average of 5.84 percent per annum. By 1957, there had been 36 urban centers with a population of 10,000, totaling nearly 26.6 percent of Malaya's population.[62] Although the Chinese still constituted the majority of urban populations, a demography that still prevails into the present time, migration rates for Malays also increased during this period at an average of 7.1 percent as compared to Chinese at 5.9 percent, and Indians, 4.6 percent.[63] Movements of Malays to urban centers were most widespread among the younger age groups, who were most affected by declining incomes from agriculture, and who hoped to seek better employment opportunities in towns.

The higher level of development taking place in the mainly European and Chinese-populated urban areas of Malaya also further widened the town-country social-economic gap. One of the major causes of this difference was the steady rise in consumerism within urban areas. As a vital catalyst to capitalist markets expansions, the urban consumer economy was now taking on a life of its own, fuelling multiple growths in economic activities as more and more people moved in to become part of an escalating system of demands and supplies of manufactured items and modern services. The rapidly vibrant consumer-production-sale cycles inherent in the urban economy was also accompanied by the provision of modern amenities that enhanced the quality of life for a substantial portion of urban residents.

On the other hand, the peripheral areas of the Malayan countryside experienced disproportionately slower rates of development since investments and exchanges coming from the cities were limited and rare. Businesses and commerce seldom gained a foothold outside the main towns due to the comparatively impoverished environment of the rural regions, which made it unlikely that rural populations were able to purchase profitable and sufficient volumes of consumer goods and services.[64] Furthermore, rice and small-hold agricultural produce were also items that rarely headed toward overseas markets during the pre-independence period as such there was no immediate incentive for high-level capitalist investments in the rural economy. Deplete of infrastructural development, the rural setting provided a stark contrast to the thriving and prosperous atmosphere of modern cities.

Unlike Selangor and Perak however, the other FMS states, Negeri Sembilan and Pahang, did not progress as rapidly. This was mainly due to these states' political economic uncertainties in investments associated with lack of marketable resources and geographical barriers that made transportation building less attractive. The inclusion of Negeri Sembilan into the FMS actually began with its role as a buffer region for the Straits Settlement of Malacca. In so far as minerals and strategic ports were concerned, this state was not able to offer the British much in the form of profitable investments. Pahang, the largest state in FMS and untapped in potential resources, was almost entirely covered by virgin jungle and in most part cut off by the Titiwangsa mountain range. Until the 1920s, the main mode of transportation in the state was the river system. By the time of its early phase of capitalist development, Pahang had already been too far behind the more advanced states along the western coast.[65]

Overall, there had also been a significant lack of development in the UFMS states of Perlis, Kedah, Kelantan, and Terengganu. Despite the establishment of a relatively modern bureaucracy, these states' traditional social-political systems reflected a predominantly semi-tributary system. Here, unlike in the FMS, local chieftains and regional lords still retained relative power in controlling the various trades in their respective regions. Furthermore, civil strife and political tensions arising from internal Malay rivalries and anti-British sentiments persisted well into the early part of the twentieth century, thwarting any incentive for deeper British political involvement in these states.

This meant that in the UFMS, any pull factor among British investors in setting up permanent settlements or among migrant workers searching for economic opportunities was essentially few and far between. Despite this, the small number of British and other European entrepreneurs that were in these states still acquired a hefty share of returns from whatever limited capitalist economic activity there was. This was also true of the sultan, who as a comprador class, enjoyed some of the revenues collected from various land concessions in timber and rubber.[66] With the exception of Johor, the confinement of relatively few processing plants to specific localities in the UFMS contributed to the relatively inconsistent and slower urbanization patterns when compared to the FMS.

Similarly, infrastructural framework and modern services in Sarawak also could not expand as efficiently or as rapidly as in the FMS in view of the absence of treasured commodities for exports and manufacturing markets. Furthermore, any economic activity relating to capitalist production in the state was also less sophisticated, and as such, the need for workers was also not as intense. As a result, new towns were slower to develop and major highways and roads had been virtually non-existent save for the few kilometers that linked particular economic areas within or between the larger towns. Major cities such as Kuching, Miri, and Sibu grew largely out of Chinese-centered trade or specific activity such as commodity processing or gold mining.[67]

In Sabah, capitalist development was even more sluggish than in Sarawak. There had been only scant attempts under colonial rule to construct railways and highways across a wide, rugged, and sparsely populated geographical landscape in a state that had not been known for high development potentials.[68] The few urban areas that seemed to thrive along the coasts of the South China Sea and Sulu Sea such as Jesselton (Kota Kinabalu) and Sandakan sprouted mainly around specific economic activities, namely timber processing and agricultural trades with the interior.

The comprehensive impact of these overall differences in regional economic development in colonial Malaysia was two-fold. While capitalist production under colonial rule may be considered exploitative to the numerous ethnic groups caught within its web of unequal ethnic-labor divisional and distributive systems, capitalism's potential in preparing life chances for workers can neither be ignored nor underestimated. With capitalist development came greater access to health and occupational opportunities that are considered useful platforms for generational social-economic mobility. In an emerging capitalist economy, residents in regions where such prospects are available tend to have greater life improvements compared to those areas where such opportunities were either deficient or absent. Importantly, with urbanization and economic growth also came opportunities for education and greater social interactions, which often provided for structural integrative processes crucial for popular political empowerment.

"Natural" Explanation for Social-Economic Hierarchy

Subsequently, the uneven regional development in Malaya and northern Borneo would considerably reproduce inequalities in income, wealth, and education levels between the various ethnic groups throughout these regions. That the British neither attempted to address or resolve these widening disparities was attributed largely to their stoic belief that social class differences were a "rational" and inevitable outcome of capitalist market competition. The basis of such a worldview was the belief that there were inherent biological differences between the major races in the world that predisposed each racial group to categorical variations in aptitude and skills development capacity. In this, the generally lower status of Asians relative to whites in the colonial social-economic hierarchy was often attributed to their "natural" physical, mental, and cultural inferiority to that of Europeans. These explanations were supported by now-defunct "sciences" such as *craniometry* and *eugenics*, whose research methodologies were often flawed and heavily biased toward the racist narratives and deep prejudices of the late nineteenth century western world.[69]

Hence, colonialism became a convenient instrument that sought to illustrate what these sciences claimed were immutable differences between Europeans and non-Europeans. Through colonial achievements, the British would also able to prove themselves as the most civilized, formidable, and virtuous people in the world. The justification for colonialism was further reinforced by the perception that because non-Europeans severely lacked similar qualities and attributes, there was an arduous obligation on the part of the British to spread their civilizational goodwill and technical expertise to these "lesser" traditions by way of colonial rule.[70]

At the same time, the rationalization of production systems was also contingent upon the exploitation of local labor, which resulted in the disenfranchisement of indigenous people through limitations of their access to educational, political, and economic resources. Hence, there existed a contradiction between suppressing colonial subjects on one hand, and the moral obligation to bestow European munificence on the other. Thus, reconciling this contradiction often required the British in Malaya to regularly assert the argument that keeping Malays in the agricultural sector was central to their cultural existence given the natural limitations of their occupational potentials.[71] Common colonial rhetoric often argued that Malays were innately suitable to a simple agrarian life and that moving them outside the world of subsistence farming would not only disrupt their customary life but it would also expose them to a complex world, of which they could never master.[72] This was clearly captured in the FMS Director of Agriculture's statement that: "Our trusteeship for the Malay people demands that we administer the country on lines with their welfare and happiness…than by causing them to forsake the life of their fathers for the glamour of new ways…world conditions beyond their orbit."[73]

Hence, colonial policies intended to keep Malays within the agrarian sector were premised mainly upon racist and unflattering depictions of the group as culturally backwards, socially inept, and beset by various forms of indolence.[74] Evidence of condescending accounts of Malays can be found in the numerous colonial-era ethnographic studies, novels, and travel writings.[75] Here, Malay social temperaments were often viewed in terms of child-like characteristics, which prevented them from fully grasping the demands of the new economy or appreciating the responsibilities of a modern lifestyle. In Malaya, such racist worldviews came from colonial administrators themselves, who assumed "expertise" in the scholarship of Malay culture and history. Frederick Weld, Governor of Singapore and Straits Settlements from 1880-1887 asserted: "I doubt if Asiatics will ever learn to govern themselves; it is contrary to the genius of their race...their desire is a mild, just and firm despotism that we can give them."[76] Similarly, former Hugh Clifford asserted that the Malays' economic deficiency was naturally determined and that it has shaped the Malay personality into assuming the life of perpetual shiftlessness and economic inertia.[77]

Nevertheless, such literature also often contained persuasive allusions to colonialism as a valuable and enlightening system that allowed for adaptations and growths of naturally degenerative non-western societies through their exposure to various aspects of western civilization.[78] In Malaya, figures such as Frank Swettenham were indeed more hopeful about Malays. Swettenham showered adorations on the Malay nobility, particularly in their ability to emulate the refinements of British culture and ideas. In this, Swettenham believed the common Malay to be lacking in the productive qualities of the western man because he was inherently medieval in character. However, he believed there was possibility for Malays to progress to a higher developmental phase if western values and work ethics were imposed through colonial rule could be successfully cultivated and absorbed.[79]

Stereotypes of indigenous peoples with regards to their natural "athleticism" or warrior-like qualities had also often been emphasized and rationalized for their recruitment into the military. Early writers of the Malay world such as D.E. Worcester referred the "racial nature" of Malays throughout the Archipelago as inherently barbaric, cruel, and warrior-like, thus predisposing them to the demands of warfare.[80] In a much more gracious manner, Frank Swettenham also described the typical Malay for example, as "naturally well-built, courageous, sportsman-like, and respectful of constituted authority."[81] It was precisely for these reasons that Malays and other indigenous groups in northern Borneo were considered "suitable material" for uniformed duties.

Such narrow and racist portrayals often ignored the realities of colonial rule, where the overwhelming poverty of Malays had mainly been a consequence of economic marginalization and occupational specialization under capitalism, made worse by regular discriminatory policies disadvantaging Malays as a group. Self-fulfilling prophecies of Malay backwardness and incompetence never took into account, for instance, the few brilliant Malay doctors, lawyers, and civil servants, who professionally outshone their British counterparts, but had neither been acknowledged nor promoted to higher ranks due to their race. Instead, it was the white male professional, no matter how inefficient or mediocre, who was always advanced to higher positions and praised for their "achievements."[82]

Malays were not the only ones adjudged from a deeply prejudiced and uncomplimentary discourse. The basis for low-wage Indian manual work in the rubber estates was unwaveringly racist as well. British imperial exploitation of Indian traditional caste hierarchies, staunchly practiced in southern India, sustained the extreme poverty of the majority of poor Tamil Indians who came to Malaya. Ascribed into their lowly status within Indian society and acculturated into an oppressed group under the British, the Tamils were willing to accept any type of work and abide by any given order in the course of many social economic interactions.[83]

Socially outcast and economically disenfranchised, the majority of poor Tamils inescapably developed a worldview of passivity and subservience. This was exactly the main reason the British favored Tamil Indians for cheap labor work in the first place. However, colonial justification of confining Tamil Indians to low-wage labor was often based on the generalized view that their docility and inclination to please authority were natural ethnic characteristics, and therefore suitably dispensed for untrained menial jobs. On this, many among the Europeans and British agreed that Tamil Indians were on the whole a "poor specimen, both in physique and morale...cowardly, and lacking in vitality...his blind admiration for the white man as rather pathetic."[84]

British attitudes toward Chinese migrants were conspicuously racist as well. To the British, the Chinese were generally ill-disciplined, lacking integrity, and unrefined. It was not uncommon to view the Chinese as the antithesis to western cultural values. Despite their high work rates, the Chinese were considered inassimilable as settlers or migrants in places like Britain, Australia, South Africa, and the United States. More importantly, since Chinese laborers came without women, they were often depicted as lusty, "animal-like," or sexually menacing. In an effort to drive the Chinese out of the labor market, renowned Australian feminist Rose Summerfield once used the moral high grounds to instill fear and resentment of the Chinese by claiming that "white women could not even walk the streets of the city without suffering the jeering catcalls and lewd eyes of Chinese beasts."[85]

In Malaya, where there had been a relatively small European merchant and professional community and an absence of a large European labor force, Chinese migrant labor became critically essential. Nevertheless, there was also a generalized belief in a Chinese character associated with lawlessness, criminal activity, and a penchant for filthy habits. During the early colonial period, for example, many Chinese were involved in the trading and exchanging of opium. The opium-based economy was an indirect result of a racist colonial policy to acquire taxes through the sales of the commodity for the consumption of Chinese men. Thus opium addiction was effectively encouraged by state policies, which soon became a main problem plaguing the Chinese community in both Malaya and Singapore. The link between opium and crime surfaced when the monopoly of opium sales became increasingly associated with the secret societies. Triad wars over opium became increasingly rife in Chinese neighborhoods, made worse by the deliberate dumping of Chinese workers in highly-dense and overcrowded localities surrounding factories and waterfront warehouses. Living conditions in these urban ghettoes were extremely appalling and ripe for the spreading of all kinds of health and socially-related diseases.[86] Interestingly, social problems related to opium use such as prostitution, gambling, and murder as well as the unhygienic conditions the lower class Chinese lived under were often linked back to the perceived natural unruliness of the Chinese rather than the social-colonial circumstances that gave rise to them.

Nevertheless, there was a kind of concealed but contemptuous admiration by the British toward the emerging Chinese capitalists. However, since these capitalists would soon pose as competitors to Europeans, the aggressive and thrift-like business approach of these capitalists was often perceived to be enigmatic of all Chinese. Descriptions of the Chinese as unscrupulous businessmen were not unlike those stereotypically constructed of Jewish merchants in Europe during the middle-ages. Just as how Jews were encouraged to invest and contribute toward the development of European capitalism but kept separate and excluded from European Christian society, the rich Chinese too were often grudgingly accepted for their economic utility while alienated for their culture and disparaged for perceived untrustworthiness.

The emergence of the wealthy Chinese business class did however give this group a more complementary standing when compared to other Asians, especially Malays. William Pickering, the first Chinese Protector in Singapore, summed up his justification of the social hierarchy in Malaya when expressing the impossibility of the Chinese being managed or governed by Malays, likening it to "white settlers of America submitting to the rule of the Indian chiefs."[87] Scant mention however, was made by colonial scholars and historians to the modernization policies formulated by the relatively prosperous Johor Sultanate, where Chinese labor was not only humanely organized under its Malay political administration, but also where relations between the two groups were not as tensed as in the FMS.[88]

These well-established but stereotypical perceptions about particular ethnic and racial communities often resonate and filter down into the grassroots, where prejudice and contempt against the "other" are often reinforced by the wide social distances that exist at this level among ethnic groups. Similarly, stereotypes and prejudices engendered during British colonial rule would be passed on to later generations of Malaysians as the premise for identifying each ethnic group by their so-called "natural traits." The following statement by a British colonial officer summarizes the popular identity of each ethnic group as constructed through the colonial lens: "...the Malays are far more reasonable (than the Irish), but just as cunning and tell more lies, I am beginning to like the Chinese in a sort of way, they are as obstinate as pigs and are always in court with paltry cases; as the paltry cases the *Klings* (Indians) are the worst and they are all regular lawyers and never speak the truth by accident."[89]

Racist descriptions of Malays as lazy, Chinese as greedy, and Indians as compulsive liars flourished into mainstream ethnic views well into the decades of independent Malaysia. A pioneering survey conducted by social researcher Alvin Rabushka in 1967 revealed in many ways and in varying degrees that the segregated and endocentric lifestyles among Malays, Chinese and Indians had been elemental in the maintenance of generalized perceptions about outsider groups. However, his study also showed that degrees of stereotypes and intolerance with regards to external groups tend to lessen when interpersonal contacts and friendships were formally established.[90] This is an important revelation. It explains that there are possibilities for better and more constructive inter-ethnic relations when there is increased convergence in class and social interests between specific sectors of the population.

Hence, it can be acknowledged that in justifying the relative positions of the various ethnic groups within the colonial stratification system, British rule became primarily responsible for initializing the various racist stereotypes of each ethnic groups in Malaysia.[91] At the same time, colonial rule also created a social system devoid of any meaningful inter-ethnic interactions or civic associations, which could have possibly reduced ethnic prejudices. Instead, the prolonged effects of unequal and distanced ethnic relations during colonialism would later materialize into inevitable ethnic tensions as nationalism and ethnic identity increasingly became central issues of debate in the formative years of Malayan independence. This will be highlighted in the following chapter.

Summary

The allocation of labor functions along ethnic lines had been a major rationalization process of capitalist production in colonial Malaysia. This ethnic-labor structure was essentially characterized by the demographic segregation of ethnic groups in the form of predominantly Chinese urban centers, Indian-dominated plantations, and Malay farming areas in the countryside. More significantly, the ethnic-labor formation process effectively delineated the social separation between Europeans as managers of the economy and Asians as workers, laborers, and farmers, thereby successfully maintaining the social-occupational distances between the colonial elite and their subjects.

This labor ethnicization policy had also given rise to the conflation between ethnic identity and occupation, through which an ethnic group's average wealth levels, educational rates, and social prestige relative to others were likely to be assessed and formally viewed. The absence and lack of integrated social space in colonial Malaysia further restricted any significant inter-ethnic exchanges that might otherwise have brought these groups socially and politically closer together. Instead, the specificity of occupational activity and the difficulty to move away from one's respective economic area resulted in a multicultural presence deeply entrenched in multiple dimensions of ethnic distances and prejudices. Segregated occupational and living areas as well as distinct and differentiated lifestyles and interests also meant that there had been little opportunity for significant social interactions between the different classes within each ethnic group.

As geographical specialization of economic activity invariably affected the rate of capitalist development in particular regions throughout Malaya and northern Borneo, urban areas that primarily grew out of manufacturing and mining, comprising mainly of ethnic Chinese and Indians, developed at faster and higher rates than regions where economic activities were associated with agriculture and fisheries. This was because the urban economy provided viability to modern social infrastructures as well as greater life chances, especially in the form of permeable entries into education and stable job opportunities. In contrast, the self-subsistent agricultural regions where Malays and indigenous groups constituted the majority population offered almost nothing in terms of social and economic capital since their occupational linkages with the wider capitalist economy were minimal at best.

Inarguably, the dynamics of multicultural relations in Malaysia, which became grounded on cultural differences, ethnic disparities, and spatial segregation, were acutely compounded by a racist colonial discourse aimed at justifying each Asian ethnic group's inferior social-economic position relative to Europeans. Consequentially, the unshakeable stereotypes that evolved from the rigid stratification structure would provide the major platforms through which each ethnic group would examine their cultural worth and identity as well as that of others within the rapidly emerging capitalist economy. Political economic uncertainties, exacerbated by ethnic suspicions arising out of the perceived motives of other groups under an increasingly vulnerable climate, would also form the basis upon which each ethnic group's political struggles and relationships with others were to be defined. This will be analyzed n the next chapter

Notes

1. M. R. Stenson, *Class, Race and Colonialism in West Malaysia: The Indian Case* (St. Lucia: University of Queensland Press, 1980), 14-16.

2. J. N. Parmer, *Colonial Labour Policy and Administration: A History of Labor in the Rubber Plantation Industry in Malaya c. 1910-1941* (Locust Valley, NY: J.J. Augustin, 1960), 19.

3. *Bumiputera* is a term given to indigenous groups in Malaysia, in which Malays constitute the majority. It is derived from Sanskrit meaning "children of the soil." Today, it is mostly used in reference to the indigenous peoples of Sabah and Sarawak.

4. Yen Ching-Hwang, "Overseas Chinese Nationalism in Singapore and Malaya 1877-1912," *Modern Asian Studies* 16, no. 3 (1982): 112-13.

5. Yen, "Overseas," 117-18.

6. C.M. Turnbull, *Short History of Malaysia, Singapore, and Brunei* (Winchester, MA: Allen and Unwin, 1989), 55.

7. Turnbull, *Short History*, 100-5.

8. Barbara Watson Andaya and Leonard Andaya, *History of Malaysia* (New York: St. Martin's Press, 2001), 136-38.

9. Turnbull, *Malaysia and Singapore*, 196.

10. Lim Chong Yah, *Southeast Asia: The Long Road Ahead* (Singapore: World Scientific Publications, 2009), 127-28. The indentured system under the truck or credit-ticket system was abolished in 1914 by the British to break the monopoly of Chinese labor supply and importation by wealthy Chinese businessmen. This move indirectly gave greater freedom and mobility for Chinese laborers.

11. Christopher Bayly and Tim Harper, *Forgotten Wars: Freedom and Revolution in Southeast Asia* (Cambridge MA: Harvard University Press, 2007), 120-21.

12. Cheah Book Kheng, *Red Star over Malaya: Resistance and Social Conflict During and After the Japanese Occupation of Malaya, 1941-1946* (Singapore: NUS Press, 2003), 45-47.

13. N. J. Ryan, *History of Malaysia and Singapore* (Kuala Lumpur: Oxford University Press, 1976), 120-21.

14. Danny Tze Ken Wong, *Historical Sabah: Community and Society* (Kota Kinabalu: Natural History Publications, 2004). Read chapters 1 to 3 on the origins and early life of Sabah's coastal towns that included Chinese migration into these urban areas and their participation in the economy.

15. Lee Sheng Yi, *Monetary and Banking System of Malaysia and Singapore* (Singapore: Singapore University Press, 1990), 250-51.

16. For further reading on the sociological factors and aspects of secret society formation in Malaya and Singapore, read Mak Lau Fong, *Sociology of Secret Societies: A Study of Chinese Secret Societies in Singapore and Peninsular Malaysia* (Kuala Lumpur: Oxford University Press, 1981).

17. Parmer, *Colonial Labour*, 19.

18. Saw Swee Hock, *Population of Malaysia and Singapore* (Singapore: Institute of Southeast Asian Studies, 2007), 36.

19. T.N. Harper, *End of Empire and the Making of Malaya* (Cambridge, UK: Cambridge University Press, 1999), 24-25.

20. K.S. Jomo, "Plantation Capital and Indian Labour in Colonial Malaya," in *Indian Communities in Southeast Asia*, ed. K.S. Sandhu and A. Mani (Singapore: ISEAS, 2006), 295.

21. R. Rajakrishnan, "Social Change and Group Identity among Sri Lankan Tamils," in *Indian Communities in Southeast Asia*, ed. K.S. Sandhu and A. Mani (Singapore: ISEAS, 2006), 541-43.

22. Kernail Singh Sandhu, "Sikhs in Malaysia: A Society in Transition," in *Indian Communities in Southeast Asia*, ed. K.S. Sandhu and A. Mani (Singapore: ISEAS, 2006), 560-67.

23. Kernail Singh Sandhu, *Indians in Malaya: Some Aspects of their Immigration and Settlement (1786–1957)* (Cambridge: University Press, 1969), 139.

24. Sinnapiah Arasaratnam, *Indians in Malaysia and Singapore* (Kuala Lumpur: Oxford University Press, 1980), 88.

25. Arasaratnam, *Indians in Malaysia*, 90-95.

26. Chandra Muzaffar, "Political Marginalization in Malaysia," in *Indian Communities in Southeast Asia*, ed. K.S. Sandhu and A. Mani (Singapore: ISEAS, 2006), 230-36.

27. T. G. Lim, *Peasants and their Agricultural Economy in Colonial Malaya 1874-1941* (Kuala Lumpur: Oxford University Press, 1977), 112-19.

28. William Roff, *Origins of Malay Nationalism* (Kuala Lumpur: Oxford University Press, 1995), 25.

29. Philip Loh, *Malay States 1877-1895 Political Change and Social Policy (*Kuala Lumpur: Oxford University Press, 1969), 154.

30. Read Rex Stevenson, *Cultivators and Administrators: British Policy toward Malays 1875-1906* (Oxford, UK: Oxford University Press, 1975) for further informational detail on British policy toward Malays during the early phase of British colonial rule in the FMS.

31. Requests by groups of Malays at the beginning of the twentieth century throughout the Malay states for English medium schools in their communities were turned down by the colonial education authorities. See Mustapha Hussain, Mustapha, Insun Mustapha, and K.S. Jomo, *Malay Nationalism before UMNO: The Memoirs of Mustapha Hussain (*Kuala Lumpur: Utusan Press, 2005), 97 and also Andaya and Andaya, *History*, 234.

32. A *Madrasah* is a religious school, specifically catering to the learning of rudimentary school subjects and basic scriptures of holy Islamic texts.

33. Quoted in Government of Federated Malay States, *Annual Report on the Federated Malay States 1920* (Kuala Lumpur: Government Printers, 1920), 20.

34. Roff, *Origins*, 123.

35. Roff, *Origins*, 110-13; Also read Syed Hussein Alatas, "Collective Representations and Economic Development," in *Modernization and Social Change: Studies in Modernization, Religion, Social Changes and Development in South-East Asia*. (Sydney: Angus and Robertson, 1972), 53-64.

36. For further insight to exclusive European life in colonial Malaya, read D. J. M. Tate, *Lake Club 1890-1990: In Pursuit of Excellence* (Kuala Lumpur: Oxford University Press, 1990).

37. Henry W. C. Yeung, "The Internationalization of Ethnic Chinese Business Firms from Southeast Asia: Strategies, Processes and Competitive Advantage," *International Journal of Urban and Regional Research* 23, no. 1 (March 1999): 110-20.

38. Yeung, "Internationalization," 122-26.

39. Chan Kok Eng and Tey Nai Peng, "Demographic Processes and Changes," in *Chinese in Malaysia,* ed. K.H. Lee and C.B. Tan (Kuala Lumpur: Oxford University Press, 2000), 72-75; Arasaratnam, *Indians,* 85-90.

40. Yen Ching-Hwang, *Chinese in Southeast Asia and Beyond: Socieconomic Dimensions and Beyond* (Singapore: World Scientific Publishing, 2008), 11-28.

41. P. Ramasamy, "Social Economic Transformation of Indian Plantation Workers," in *Indian Communities in Southeast Asia*, ed. K.S. Sandhu and A. Mani (Singapore: ISEAS, 2006), 320-25.

42. John H. Drabble, *Economic History of Malaysia, c.1800-1990: The Transition to Modern Economic Growth* (New York: St. Martin's Press, 2000), 45-47.

43. Stanley S. Bedlington, *Malaysia and Singapore: The Building of New States* (Ithaca, New York: Cornell University Press, 1978), 44.

44. John Henry Walker, *Power and Prowess: The Origins of Brooke Kinship* (Honolulu: University of Hawaii Press, 2002), 24-30.

45. Amarjit Kaur, *Economic Change in East Malaysia: Sabah and Sarawak since 1850* (London: Macmillan, 1998), 20-25.

46. Graham E. Saunders, *History of Brunei* (New York: Routledge, 2002), 60-65.

47. Sago is a type of starch extracted from certain types of palm indigenous to Southeast Asia. It is a staple food for many lowland indigenous peoples in the eastern portion of the Malay Archipelago. A form of flour can also be derived from sago, and is often commercially produced in the shape of pearls, which are offered as the main ingredient in the preparation of puddings. Large amounts of sago have been produced for exports to Europe and North America since colonial times.

48. Harper, *End of Empire,* 35.

49. Data and statistics for Malayan population between the years 1940-47, taken from M.V. Del Tufo, *Malaya: Report on the 1947 Census of Population*, (Singapore: Government Press, 1949), 58.

50. Drabble, *Economic History*, 161.

51. T.H. Silcock, "Approximate Racial Division of National Income," in *Political Economy of Independent Malaya*, ed. T.H Silcock and and E.K. Fisk (Berkeley: University of California Press, 1963), 276-80.

52. Data taken from Government of Malaya, *Census of Malaya 1957* (Kuala Lumpur: Government Printers, 1959), 10.

53. J.A. Palmore, Ramesh Chander, and Dorothy Fernandez, "The Demographic Situation in Malaysia," in *Population and Development in Southeast Asia,* ed. J.F. Kantner and L. McCaffrey (Lexington, MA: Lexington Books, 1975), 60-62.

54. For further reading on Sabah and Sarawak under colonialism, read Amarjit Kaur, *Economic Change in East Malaysia: Sabah and Sarawak since 1850* (London: Macmillan, 1998).

55. For in-depth history of the Muruts in Sabah read George Cathcart Woolley, *Timogun Muruts of Sabah* (Kota Kinabalu: Kota Kinabalu Natural History Publications, 2004).

56. Stanley S. Bedlington, *Malaysia and Singapore: The Building of New States* (Ithaca, NY: Cornell University Press, 1978), 136.

57. Michael B. Leigh, *Rising Moon: Political Change in Sarawak* (Sydney: Sydney University Press, 1974), 5-6.

58. Roy Bruton, *Farewell to Democracy* (Devon, UK: Merlin Books, 1993), 62-70.

59. W. G. Huff, *Economic Growth of Singapore: Trade and Development in the Twentieth Century* (Cambridge, UK: Cambridge University Press, 1997), 68.

60. Lee Boon Thong, "A Historical Analysis of Formative Settlement Patterning: A Background to the Klang Valley Dominance," *Malayan Journal of Tropical Geography* 25, no.2 (December 1994): 112-24.

61. Hans-Dieter Evers, "On the Evolution of Urban Society in Malaysia," in *Melaka: The Transformation of Malay Capital, c.1400-1980,* ed. Kernail S. Sandhu and Paul Wheatly (Kuala Lumpur: Oxford University Press, 1983), 333-36.

62. E. K. Fisk and H. Osman-Rani, eds., *Political Economy of Malaysia* (Kuala Lumpur: Oxford University Press, 1982), 85-86.

63. Fisk and Osman-Rani, *Political,* 105-106.

64. Fisk and Osman-Rani, *Political,* 77-80.

65. Andaya and Andaya, *History,* 181-82.

66. Shaharil Talib, *After Its own Image: The Terengganu Experience 1881-1941* (Kuala Lumpur: Oxford University Press, 1984), 221-22.

67. Bob Reece, *White Rajahs of Sarawak, a Borneo Dynasty* (Singapore: Archipelago Press, 2004), 25-27.

68. Kaur, *Economic Change,* 86-88.

69. Stephen Jay Gould, *Mismeasure of Man* (New York: Norton), 92-97.

70. Colonial discourse assumed non-Europeans to be naturally inferior to Europeans in many aspects. Hence, colonialism was often considered to be the platform or preparatory step toward civilizing backward peoples through cultivation of European enlightenment thinking. In this, colonialism was seen as a moral but difficult obligation on the part of Europeans, given the inability of non-Europeans to fully grasp and adapt to modernization. Such a view was acknowledged by many in the west to be scientific and true, and was thus used by many literary figures in their works. One particularly influential poem written by Rudyard Kipling to encourage American expansionism in the Philippines captured this sentiment by referring to colonial conquest and rule as "The White Man's Burden." For further reading on colonialism and racism, read, Edward Said, *Culture and Imperialism* (New York: First Vintage Books, 1994) and A.P. Thornton, *Imperial Idea and its Enemies* (London: MacMillan, 1985).

71. Milton J. Esman, *Ethnic Conflict* (Cambridge, UK: Polity Press, 1994), 22.

72. Charles Hirschman, "The Making of Race in Colonial Malaya: Political Economy and Racial Discourse," *Sociological Forum* 1, no.2 (Spring 1986): 331-50.

73. Quote taken from Christine B. N. Chin, *In Service and Servitude* (New York: Columbia University Press, 1998), 40. This statement was originally part of a working paper submitted as Working Council report to the Malayan *Federal Council Proceedings* in 1933 by A.R. Haynes, titled "Memorandum on the Extension of Rice Cultivation in the Federated Malay States: Need for a Definite Policy." Please read Chin, *Service,* 35-45, for further reading on British colonial policy and limitations of Malay educational and occupational opportunities.

74. Syed Hussein Alatas, *Myth of the Lazy Natives* (New York: Frank Cass, 1977), 110-15.

75. Daniel Goh, "Imperialism and Medieval Natives: The Malay Image in Anglo-American Travelogues and Colonialism in Malaya and the Philippines," *International Journal of Cultural Studies* 10, no. 3 (September 2007): 324-25.

76. Quoted in Emily Sadka, *Protected Malay States, 1874-1895* (Kuala Lumpur: University of Malaya Press, 1968), 17.

77. Hugh Clifford, *Stories by Hugh Clifford,* introduced by William R. Roff (Kuala Lumpur: Oxford University Press, 1967), 190.

78. Hugh Clifford, "Life in the Malay Peninsula: As it Was and Is," in *Honourable Intentions: Talks on the British Empire in Southeast Asia, Delivered at the Royal Colonial Institute 1874-1928,* ed. Paul Kratoska (Singapore: ISEAS, 1983), 228-29.

79. Frank Swettenham, *Nocturne and Other Malayan Stories and Sketches,* introduced by William R. Roff (Kuala Lumpur: Oxford University Press, 1993), 1-5.

80. D.E. Worcester, *Philippines, Past and Present* (New York: Macmillan, 1930), 75.

81. Swettenham, "Stories and Sketches," 16.

82. For further reading on European life in colonial Malaya, read John Butcher, *British in Malaya 1880-1941: The Social History of a European Community in Colonial Southeast Asia* (Kuala Lumpur: OUP, 1979).

83. Sandhu, *Indians in Malaya*, 57-58.

84. Quoted in M.R. Stenson, *Class*, 37.

85. Sascha Auerbach, *Race, Law, and the Chinese Puzzle in Imperial Britain* (New York: Palgrave Macmillan, 2009), 24.

86. Brenda Yeoh, *Contesting Space in Singapore: Power Relations and the Urban Built Environment* (Singapore: NUS Publishing, 2003), 38-39.

87. Rupert Emerson, *Malaysia: A Study in Indirect and Direct Rule* (Kuala Lumpur: Oxford University Press, 1974), 503.

88. Andaya and Andaya, *History*, 202-203. For more information on history of race relations in Johor, read Kenelm Burridge, "Racial Relations in Johore," *The Australian Journal of Politics and History* 2, no. 2 (May 1957): 155-60.

89. Quote taken from Margaret Shennan, *Out in the Midday Sun: The British in Malaya 1880-1960* (London: John Murray, 2000), 32.

90. Alvin Rabushka, *Race and Politics in Urban Malaya* (Washington DC: Hoover Press, 1973), 66-68.

91. Andaya and Andaya, *History*, 180.

Chapter 4
Fragmented Identities and the Rise of Pro-Western Elites, 1918-1963

Sustained colonial oppression in many areas of the global periphery would eventually invigorate and direct nationalist ambitions among colonial subjects toward the political liberation of their homelands. This culminated in a worldwide decolonization process after the end of the Second World War. The struggle for independence for colonized peoples was also based on the fundamental need to realize their long-held aspirations for civil liberty, justice, and rights that had been deprived under colonial rule. Importantly, the very denial of such rights had primarily been based on the so-called inferiority of their race or culture. For many among the colonized, the racist dimension of colonialism would elicit a collective sense of awareness that colonial occupation stood in the way of the future survival of their ethno-identity, culture, and religion. In these communities, this ethno-consciousness would eventually provide the spiritual motivation and drive for national independence. In multicultural colonial societies, such ethnonationalism would become the basis for each ethnic group's struggle for political empowerment in a post-colonial political arrangement.[1]

Divergent Ethnonationalisms

Since most European colonies in the developing world had essentially been shaped into multicultural structures, there came into existence in those societies a multiplicity of ethnic identities, each with its own ethnonational sentiments and goals embodied within the group's ethnonationalism. The unequal nature of ethnic relations made it unlikely that there could emerge an effective and unified multiethnic force within the struggle for national independence.

This was the case in Malaya. The wide social disparities between ethnic groups that developed under colonial-capitalist development, together with the accompanying racist approaches used to explain each group's so-called "natural" location within the colonial social hierarchy, resulted in ethnic relations in Malaya becoming inevitably distanced. These various social detachments were also aggravated by the absence of any structural integrative process during British colonial rule that could have fostered a visibly cohesive Malayan identity, often considered important in stimulating a collective struggle against the colonial state for national self-governance.

Furthermore, the formation of an ethnic group's ethnonationalism also often intersects with other important class and status-related interests, complicating the pursuit of national liberation as a collective struggle. Instead, distinct social-cultural experiences of each major ethnic group under a highly stratified colonial social structure had shaped within each of these groups, a unique but divergent set of political goals and objectives. This would later provide conditions ripe for ethnic conflicts. This chapter begins with the colonial experiences of each of the three major groups in Malaya—the Chinese, Indians, and Malays.

Origins and Nature of Chinese Ethnonationalism in Malaya

Coming from diverse geographic and sub-cultural backgrounds, ethnic Chinese migrants in Malaya and Singapore were initially grouped according to their respective clan and dialectic memberships. Popularly referred to as the *Nanyang*, or "southern overseas Chinese," this group's initial political interests pertained mostly to issues and crises within the confines of the Chinese homeland.

China at the turn of the twentieth century was faced with turbulent internal rebellions and foreign military encroachments. Fearing China's possible disintegration, a new Confucianist movement sought to revive China's glory by rejuvenating the Emperor's waning legitimacy, which they believed if strengthened, could serve to unify the Chinese against existing internal as well external sources of destabilization.[2] In their effort to bolster the movement, the neo-Confucianists solicited the financial support of the *Nanyang* Chinese, whose enduring patriotism as well as unfailing monetary remittances to the motherland had been well-known among the mainland Chinese. Many from this movement would eventually come to Malaya and Singapore to establish multiple news organs and political clubs aimed at instilling among the *Nanyang* their new Confucianist perspective in Chinese nationalism.[3]

True to Confucian philosophy, the reformists advocated for an open educational system, through which a pool of the brightest students in the country would be able to contribute their distinguished services to the emperor and China. This vision was fully supported by the *Nanyang* Chinese, who saw the idea of a similar merit-based Chinese education in Malaya and Singapore as an attractive vehicle for upward mobility for the majority of this community who anticipated a return to China. This led to the establishment of numerous Chinese schools throughout the major cities in Malaya and Singapore, whose China-centered curricula emphasized the unconditional reverence to the emperor. One of the major impacts of this somewhat streamlined Chinese education structure was the successful merging of the disparate Chinese provincial groups toward a more salient pan-Chinese ethnic identity in Malaya.[4]

Aimed at conserving Chinese culture through education, Chinese schools strictly maintained their emphasis on communal funding, or *minban xuexiao*.[5] A closed financing system from within members of the ethnic Chinese community was meant to ensure that Chinese education remained free of any external social and political influences, particularly westernization. It was for this reason that Chinese schools emerged as the force behind the successful proliferation of Chinese mainland ideologies in Malaya. Backed by the major business and commercial guilds, and working together with various Chinese cultural associations, these schools assumed a critical role in the preservation of Chinese culture for the subsequent generations of the *Nanyang* community in both Malaya and Singapore.[6]

The Confucian reformist agenda was not extensively supported in China however. On their heels was the nationalist movement led by Sun Yat Sen. Followers of his republican philosophy, also known as Chinese "revolutionaries," believed that so-called Confucianist reforms were merely superficial dogmas, and as such, were incapable of thrusting China into the league of powerful industrial nations. The revolutionaries in fact, placed the blame for China's ongoing political economic anomalies, ranging from its inability to halt foreign military incursions to its cultural obstruction of modernization efforts, squarely on the country's imperial institutions.[7]

Nevertheless, Sun's revolutionary approaches to systemic changes had initially seemed too alien and radical for the ordinary Chinese. The secular nationalism he was advocating for seemed far too removed from and incongruent with the traditional emphasis on filial piety, which had been the building block of centuries-old Chinese culture. Thus in order to project his republican ideals closer in affinity with Chinese traditional customs, Sun contrived a concept relating the state in terms of a larger family unit. The advantage and convenience of his *Sanmin Zhuyi* or *Three Principles of the People* lay in the gentle reorientation of loyalty owed to the emperor under the old system toward one devoted to the modern state and its political leadership.[8] By doing this, Sun managed to connect his authoritarian republican ideals to the traditional concepts of allegiance and respect for authority.

The ethnic Chinese community in Malaya and Singapore closely followed the debates as well as eventual confrontation between the Confucian reformists and revolutionaries on the mainland. Consequently, the triumphant 1911 revolution led by Sun's Kuomintang (KMT) party decisively brought the republicans to power in China. Once in power, one of Sun's first efforts to unite the country was through the use of Mandarin as the country's *lingua franca*. Following suit, Chinese schools in Malaya and Singapore turned to utilizing Mandarin as the standard medium of instruction, while adopting Sun's revolutionary doctrine as the bases of Chinese educational vision.

The KMT government subsequently sent inspectors to Malaya and Singapore to ensure that ethnic Chinese students here followed the same nationalist curriculum as the one used in China. Aided financially by local businesses, KMT associations soon became widespread throughout the region, with numerous party branches mushrooming all over Malaya. By the eve of the Second World War, the party had generated memberships of over 30,000, making it the largest political organization in both Malaya and Singapore.[9]

The influence of the KMT on the politics of Malaya and Singapore soon became increasingly forceful. Before long, a majority of Chinese-educated leaders here had become resentful of British authority, which they saw as consistently regulating the social-economic life of the *Nanyang*. To the Chinese in Malaya, the British were also heavily involved in the political affairs of mainland China, and thus were also part of the larger western conspiracy seeking to undermine the sovereignty of the Chinese. Hostility toward the British was impassionedly inflamed in Chinese schools, where discussions of national-political developments in China, especially those relating to the presence of foreign colonial forces, would be regularly featured in the classrooms, turning many students into fervent anti-colonial militants.

Concerned, the British took to supervising Chinese education through a strict registration process. This policy was "sugar-coated" by promises of fund appropriations and grant endowments for the construction and maintenance of Chinese schools. Despite its benevolent appearance however, it became obvious to the Chinese community that this move had been nothing more than to filter students and staff for anti-systemic activity in schools. Such scrutiny placed on Chinese education inevitably ruffled the ethnic Chinese leadership, who became increasingly aggravated with the British. Any gesture extended to the community from thereon would always be taken with skepticism and suspicion.[10]

Before long, a new struggle for power emerged in China between the KMT and an increasingly popular Communist Party of China (CCP). This new development on the mainland was again closely followed by the Chinese in Malaya and Singapore, who began to draw their attention to the impeccable organization and outward determinism of the communists in combating foreign forces in China. By the eve of the Second World War, communist and other forms of left-wing ideologies had successfully penetrated into many Chinese-dominated institutions in Malaya, especially within the numerous Chinese high schools.[11] Eventually, the infiltration of communists into the various trades union, consisting mainly of the Chinese working classes, would move Chinese ethnonational activism in Malaya toward the direction of left-wing politics.

Class Dimensions of Chinese Ethnonationalism

Throughout British colonialism, the Malay-assimilated *Peranakan* Chinese, who had been part of the earliest Chinese mercantile communities in Malacca, had gained a relatively advantageous position when compared to other local non-European groups. From their role as successful merchants in the old economy, many became prosperous entrepreneurs and urban professionals under the new capitalist economy. The success of this ethnic minority had largely been maintained by their close working relationships with the British and their status as Crown subjects under Straits Settlements law, which enabled their children open access to English schools.

The later wave of Chinese migrants came mostly between the late 1800s and early 1900s. In contrast to the *Peranakans*, this group generally worked in low-wage and manual-related occupations. As relative strangers to Malaya and Singapore, the China-born migrants interacted exclusively within their own clan groups, from whom they were also able to seek communal protection as well as obtain personal solace. When comparing to these newcomers, the relatively more wealthy and highly-westernized *Peranakan* considered their group to be superior to the newly-arrived Chinese. Many initially distanced themselves from the latter, of whom they referred to as *sinkek* (uncouth class).[12]

However, as the influx of newer Chinese outnumbered the *Peranakans*, the marked social divides between the two groups gradually faded. Many from the newer Chinese groups also began to attain high communal status and prestige through the enormous wealth they acquired in business and trade. Economic exchanges also often required deeper interactions between the *Peranakans* and the upper classes of the newer migrants. Eventually, many from the former group would blend into the larger Chinese-Malayan population through intermarriages, which occurred more frequently between the more educated and wealthier families. As a result, later generations of *Peranakans* began to voluntarily drift away from their *Malayanized* culture to take on the identity of the more powerful China-born Chinese.[13]

Throughout colonial rule in Malaya, leaders from the newer Chinese groups had also painstakingly steered their communities away from what they perceived as the "polluting" effects of multiculturalism. In fact, this had been one of the important premises upon which Chinese schools and associations were founded. Chinese-educated professionals and teachers took on the responsibility to ensure that the authenticity of Chinese culture would be preserved in Malaya both in practice and form. The more ethnocentric groups within this community would selectively hold the *Peranakan* as an example of Chinese cultural waywardness—an "unfortunate" by-product of both British colonialism and Malay cultural assimilation. Many would go as far as ridiculing and despising the *Peranakan* for not being "pure" Chinese.[14]

As the larger ethnic Chinese community became more entrenched in Malaya and Singapore, many among the newer generations became less attracted to any prospect of returning to the Chinese mainland. The wealthier classes especially, had established their fortunes and livelihood in their newly-adopted residence, and few would trade the pull of vast economic opportunities in Malaya for the chaotic conditions in China. Increasingly, many of those born in Malaya and Singapore began to consider no other place as their home than the local communities in which they were born, schooled, and worked.

Among the elite Chinese class, the resolve to remain as permanent residents in Malaya had become particularly urgent. Despite their ever-present allegiance to the original homeland, many among them yearned for a greater and more formal presence in their new land of opportunity. As a result, a large number of people within the ethnic Chinese community now began to seriously mull over their status as an important but excluded group in Malaya. There was increased confidence on their part to demand a greater role in the colony's political economic future. A main reason for this was attributed to the community's overall economic strength, which had now elevated them to a higher social standing to the native Malays or any other local group. Another factor had also been their population—the ethnic Chinese were slowly but surely surpassing other ethnic groups, including Malays, in both Malaya and Singapore.

The course of Chinese ethnonationalism at this juncture, as reflected in the concerns of their leadership, would gradually be geared toward greater political empowerment and participation in Malaya. A constant point of annoyance for them, however, had been the uncertainty of attaining full control of a land where the Malay sultans were still recognized as sovereign heads by the British colonial state. Chinese culture, especially as expressed in the principles of Confucian philosophy, did not provide any clear political guidelines for Chinese leadership in a foreign culture. There had been much difficulty among the Chinese leaders in Malaya to conceive their existence as an ethnic community under a larger and different national-cultural entity.[15] In places where the Chinese community lacked political organization or substantive numerical advantage, such as in the United States, the Dutch East Indies, or Thailand, the assimilative approach to permanent residence became the sole path toward co-existence. However, Malaya was different. The Chinese community here was the most politically organized and its economy the most prosperous. Thus, as historian Lucian Pye noted: "that any Chinese leader should be a subordinate to a foreigner is culturally unthinkable...any Chinese who acts as a leader must be an imposter if he is subservient to the Malay majority leadership."[16]

Subsequently, it was left to the various emerging ethnic Chinese leaders to deliberate the form, content, and trajectory of Chinese ethnonationalism in Malaya. By the dawn of the post-Second World War period when Malayan independence became a growing possibility, there emerged two major political variants within the Chinese-Malayan leadership. The mainly Chinese-educated group insisted that the ultimate appearance of an independent Malaya, inclusive of Singapore, must in some way reflect the political supremacy of the Chinese community, strengthened by close political affiliations with the Chinese mainland.[17] This heavily ethnocentric approach was especially attractive to other Chinese traditionalists who identified very closely with efforts to invigorate a more dominant Chinese presence in Malaya. Some among them had been known to be exceptionally scornful of British colonial authority and the Malay royal leadership for standing in the way of the community's full political autonomy. The more radical members of the Chinese-educated group would later become especially captivated by the Maoist doctrine of political change, especially in the use of violence, which they believed offered the most effective form of reaching real political transformation in Malaya.[18]

The second strain of Chinese ethnonationalism developed a little later than the first, and was associated mainly with groups that preferred a more moderate path toward greater Chinese political role in Malaya. Proponents of this view believed that the welfare of the ethnic Chinese in Malaya was inevitably dependent on their ability to successfully become full-fledged citizens in a multicultural Malaya.[19] In many ways, their concern was heavily focused on the economic prospects of citizenship under modern capitalist statehood. Theirs was the view that a peaceful and equal co-existence with Malays within a capitalist democratic system was particularly crucial in providing the political mechanisms available to protect their communal interests as well as advance their economic opportunities.[20] Furthermore, full citizenship privileges would also place the ethnic Chinese in a calculable and strategic position to obtain greater political concessions and resist long-term institutional assimilation.

This group of ethnic Chinese leaders comprised mainly of Malayan-born English-educated class as well as some Chinese-educated members of the middle-class. Although not all in this group came from privileged lineages, many have had or were part of families with extensive experience in local businesses and the colonial administrative services. There were also many who drew their ancestry through intermarriages with the *Peranakan*. Subsequent generations of this elite class continued to maintain the semblance of the British lifestyle; they spoke fluent English and were more likely to embrace the Christian faith. It also seemed to appear that as the ethnic Chinese became wealthier or more educated, they also were more likely to become more inclined in adopting a westernized political outlook. Having acquired reputable standing through professional and educational achievements, members from this group formed a collective imagination of a Malaya grounded on democratic ideals of equal citizenship across ethnic lines.[21] The eventual formation of the Malayan Chinese Association (MCA) was an outcome of this elite concern.[22]

In any event, overall subscription to any ethnonational goal was neither mutually exclusive in terms of political philosophy nor strictly aligned along educational background. There was however, the tacit acknowledgment among both ethnic Chinese leaderships that success in their organizational strategy rested largely on acquiring the support of the ethnic Chinese population.[23] This, however, was more difficult to achieve than anticipated, particularly for the westernized elites. There was a large presence within this ethnic community, who remained under perpetual economic servitude and without legal status in Malaya, and a considerable portion of whom were living in squalid conditions around the forest fringes or inside the many urban slums.[24] Many among them still had harbored hopes of returning to China with new-found wealth. Meanwhile, the more established but mainly non-English speaking urban classes found the ethnocentrisms of the Chinese-educated leadership more appealing. Caught within an uncertain and contentious atmosphere, this group found worldviews associated with cultural conservatism most identifiably sensible and comforting.

In many cases, the pursuit and value of political empowerment that preoccupied the attention of the elites was not equally shared or understood by many Chinese who were attempting to meagerly survive in a political climate that was becoming increasingly volatile. As the years toward independence neared, these two elite groups would be engaged in an intense and hostile battle to define and shape the path of Chinese-Malayan ethnonationalism in the way each saw as befitting the community's as well as their own group's future needs in Malaya.

Early Indian Activism in Malaya

The diversity of the ethnic Indian population in Malaya existed in a myriad of caste, class, and regional differences. This made the ethnic Indian social experience pretty much contingent upon the dynamics occurring between the person's membership within a particular regional or religious sub-group, his or her traditional social status, and his or her type of economic participation.[25]

Similar to the Chinese, the first generation ethnic Indians in Malaya had never developed any emotional imminence to their adopted homeland. As newly-arrived migrants, cultural and political ties were still very much bonded to India. The curricula of Indian vernacular schools located across Malaya for example, were more likely to orient students toward the history and events occurring in the Indian subcontinent than on the developments and histories of the Malay world. Furthermore, depending on which region the ethnic Indian came from, deeper allegiances were owed to the sub-culture of their ancestry.

However, unlike the Chinese, Indian political sentiments to the motherland were neither fully established nor as aggressive. This was largely attributed to the Indians smaller populations compared to the Chinese, their relative poverty, and lack of cogent experience, which as mentioned above, were still heavily divided along class, caste, and cultural lines. As such, there was never a period in which Indians desired for a takeover of the colonial government or visualized Malaya to be part of a larger Indian republic.

Due to the relatively low economic status of ethnic Indians, early Indian activism in Malaya also lacked the highly-charged ethnocentrism visibly manifested in Chinese ethnonationalism. Rather, it was mostly influenced by occupational experiences relating to labor exploitation at the hands of plantation and factory owners. Conditions of work were unbearable for many in the estates as was their inability to meet decent living standards through their measly wages. Although some form of minimum wage level was introduced by the colonial state's Labour Department, employers and owners rarely observed these requirements especially if they were more than likely to cut into their profit margins.[26] The effectual grounding of the majority of Indians to the oppressive semi-slavery conditions of plantation life in particular, virtually linked the ethnic Indian identity with extreme poverty and destitution.

Notwithstanding that, there were some efforts at addressing the plight of ethnic Indians, especially with the establishment of a Central Indian Association of Malaya (CIAM) in 1936. Affiliated with the Indian National Congress in India, leaders and members of this federal-based consortium included several influential people from the middle class, who were inspired by the Congress's social justice goals. The influence of the CIAM became particularly significant among ethnic Indian laborers in various local industries, where a series of successful strikes later occurred in the states of Selangor and Kedah after the war.[27] It was widely believed that these strikes were organized at the behest of communist-inspired unions, whose members managed to infiltrate the CIAM and other major workers' organizations.[28] Swift and harsh responses by the colonial state however, resulted in the disbandment of these movements and the setting up instead, of state-friendly workers' associations which monitored future labor activities in the plantations. With the elimination of the original unions by the late 1940s, civil protests involving Indian workers also gradually died out.

By the mid-1940s, many Indians in Malaya had begun to identify with the independence movement against Britain on the sub-continent. Anticipating the prospects of going back to India as free citizens, many across the diverse ethnic Indian sub-groups began to acquire an unprecedented pan-Indian national consciousness. The participation of hundreds of young men in the Indian National Army under the legendary Chandra Bose as well as the charitable contributions made by the wealthy classes in support of the Indian Independence League exemplified the devotion given by ethnic Indians from various backgrounds to the cause of Indian independence.[29] Expectedly, the support for Indian independence agitated the British in Malaya, who ordered the deportation of individuals caught in any form of anti-British activity. In any case, the eventual freedom won by India against the British in 1948 was recognized by ethnic Indians in Malaya as a proud accomplishment and the crowning glory of their contributions toward their motherland.[30]

Impact of Caste and Class on Indian Ethnonationalism

Due to persistent economic deprivation, continued illiteracy, and demographic confinement, social and political development for the majority of ethnic Indians in the rural areas had been highly elusive. There had been attempts by a few from the English-educated Indian groups before the Second World War to establish associational linkages with the Indian estate laborers toward some type of political grouping.[31] However, the dichotomous existence shaped by economic differences between the different classes was too precise; the social experiences of these lower income Indians in the rural areas were too far removed from the interests and daily lives of the upper classes.[32] It was not surprising that such attempts hardly materialized into any substantially unified political force.

Spurred on by the spirit of Indian nationalism against colonialism in India, a faint form of ethnic consciousness also began to emerge in Malaya, especially among the upper and middle classes. Coming mainly from an urban, English-educated background, many from this group were bonded by a shared lifestyle and the desire to further advance their political economic interests in their new land. By the early 1950s, there emerged across some of the major urban centers in Malaya, small cultural and recreational associations catering to specific religious, social, and economic needs of this community.[33] Although memberships in these organizations were expanded to include Indians from various subcultures, the helm of control and influence remained within the elite class, who consisted mainly of the higher caste Tamils and other smaller groups.

As an increasingly settled group, ethnic Indian elites realized that their political future in Malaya could be considerably bolstered by the leadership position in their ethnic community. They also felt obliged to ensure that their own direction was neither tied to involvements with Indian nationalism nor drawn to any form of anti-colonial activism in Malaya.[34] The experiences of earlier cohorts and union members immediately after the war had shown that any association with radical groups would likely be met with state scrutiny of movement or even deportation. Instead, a pro-establishment leaning would likely invite some respectable treatment from the colonial state, such as accessibility to and memberships in the various state councils and committees.

Conservatism soon became the philosophical foundation of the elite Indians I seeking to secure their political economic interests in a rapidly developing capitalist economy in Malaya. A major vehicle through which these interests were to be articulated was found in the Malayan Indian Congress (MIC). Initially established to help mobilize ethnic Indians in the cause of Indian independence, the MIC went through a brief period of experimentation with socialism before eventually transforming into a party that primarily served the political goals of the ethnic Indian elite.[35]

Like their ethnic Chinese counterparts, many Indian leaders envisioned a future Malaya that facilitated an expansion of their economic opportunities and the further boosting of their existing prestige to the highest levels of the social structure. Such a system cannot exist without the guarantees of equal political rights and civil liberties for all ethnic groups. Like the MCA, the MIC too hoped that their political legitimacy could be enhanced by their ability to represent their ethnic community in a multicultural political setting.

Finally, the Indian elite group realized that if Indians desired a more permanent status in Malaya, the failure to subscribe to a broader Malayan vision would place them at a comparative disadvantage with other ethnic groups. Thus there had to be more intense mobilization of ethnic Indians toward a pro-Malaya focus. The major obstacle for many however, came from their inability to fully discard any lingering attachments they may still have for the motherland. To overcome this, the Indian elite duly encouraged the enlistment of as many Indians to accept their destiny as Malayans while dismissing any expectation of holding dual Indian and Malayan citizenship as an unreasonable venture.[36]

Hence, the Indian elite was determined to persuade as many ethnic Indians in Malaya to subscribe to the idea of remaining as permanent residents despite the wide social distances and strong political barriers posed by class and caste differences within the ethnic population.

Origins of Malay Ethnonationalism

Discussions of Chinese and Indian ethnonationalisms are intricately related to discussions of Malay ethnonationalism, which in many ways emerged as a reaction against both the former. To the Malay rulers, the coming of the Chinese and Indians to the Malay states as transient laborers was seen as nothing more than as guests in their homes—that they were expected to leave. The unrelenting focus and respective allegiance of the majority of the Chinese and Indians toward China and India seemed to affirm that these groups had been mere voyagers who planned to head back to their lands of origin once they have amassed their riches and fortunes.

However, Malay rulers' apprehension of Chinese political economic power began with the startling realization of the enormous wealth imbalances between the two groups. Such concerns had initially been confined to internal discussions among various Malay sultans, and thus were hardly aired publicly. The rulers were further stunned with what they perceived as the Chinese leaders' voracity for greater political power despite their having been granted allocations of seats in the various state councils.

The Malay masses, meanwhile, were indifferent to the political developments outside of their community. Socially repressed by their sultans and economically neglected by the colonial state, the average Malay's scope of politics was confined to the daily well-being of his village and its shared issues. Strict abidance to a feudalistic culture precluded the common Malay from any ambition of greater political empowerment or participation; any such attempt would have been construed as challenging the authority of the Malay ruler. So dismal and unenergetic was the state of Malay politics by the start of the Second World War, it was not incorrect to mention that Malays may have been the least politically active among all major ethnic groups in southeast Asia.[37]

There had been however, small efforts by members of a relatively miniscule Malay literati movement in encouraging the growth of Malay ethnic consciousness in Malaya. The *Persatuan Guru-Guru Melayu Selangor* (Selangor Malay Teachers Union) established in 1921, and the Singapore Malay Union, established in 1924, were among the early self-help associations that pioneered discussions and debates on issues such as Malay unity and poverty.[38] Such dialogues were also prompted by awareness of rapid population growth of the Chinese community as well as public statements made by several of their leaders alluding to their demands for greater political power in Malaya. More seriously for this group of Malays had been the boldness on the part of some ethnic Chinese leaders to question the position of Malays as "rightful owners" of the Malay states, as exemplified by a Penang executive councilor's declaration: "Who says Malaya belonged to the Malays!"[39]

There also existed in the late 1920s, a rather limited Malay media catering to a mainly urban readership. In their circulation were newspapers and magazines such as *Warta Malaya*, *Majlis*, and *Majalah Guru*, which ran commentaries as well as public opinions relating primarily to the economic hardships faced by the Malay community.[40] However, due to constraints in both financial support and subscription, these media had relatively short-life spans. This was not at all surprising considering literacy in the Roman script as well as rates of educational proficiency among Malays had been relatively low during the interwar period.[41] Expectedly, the media failed to inspire any significant political discourse on Malay ethnonationalism or stimulate among the masses any form of greater and more widespread political activism.

Nevertheless, the ground-breaking role of the Malay media in initiating early discussions on Malay political economic issues did provide two important consequences. One, it gave rise to a number of prolific Malay writers, who were able to tread the experience of covering important political issues either by participating in these media discussions or by holding editorial positions in several of the newspapers. Even after many of the newspapers had closed down, a new wave of literary figures such as Ishak Haji Muhammad, Zainal Abidin Ahmad, and Ahmad Noor would continue to critically direct the conversation of Malay politics toward a higher and more emphatic level through their own novels and writings.[42]

By the Second World War, an increasing number of educated Malays would participate in greater and more intensive discussions on the state and future of Malay political affairs. The resulting discourse provided a deliberative framework revolving around three critical aspects of Malay cultural identity—the Malay language, Islam, and the Malay monarchy. The Malay language was considered a central feature of Malay identity that bound the various Malay states and their peoples into a common consciousness. The prestige of the Malay language as a historical language of international trade and diplomacy in the region also made it a basis for social organization among the Malay subgroups throughout the Archipelago. As such, there was emphasis given by many who participated in these discussions on the importance of formalizing the Malay language at the national level in order to enhance the status of Malays in Malaya.

Another important unifying force found in Malay culture was Islam. As the most followed religion throughout the Malay world, Islam served as the political premise on which Malay social life and identity had been profoundly expressed and manifested. Intertwined with the Malay cultural aspect of Islam was the institutional role of the Malay sultan or ruler, to whom Malays submit their unreserved reverence. In old Malay-Hindu culture, the ruler or *Raja* was always presumed to be "God's representative" in Malay society. As Malays became Muslims, the same mythology was transplanted into the sultan's role as "God's caliph or steward on earth."[43] As mentioned earlier, it was British colonial rule that would finally strengthen the sultan's supreme position in modern Malay society by additionally tasking it with the guardianship role of Islam.

The early ideological contestation in Malay identity politics would touch on issues of whether Islam or secularism should be prioritized, or whether a system based on Malay republican ideals or a monarchy should be given greater weight in outlining the content and direction of Malay political future. This was important for the few nationally-conscious Malays, who had become critically aware that the shape and character of Malay ethnonationalism had to be clearly articulated around rationally defined social-political criteria before Malays could ever embark on their struggle for greater sovereignty and freedom in their own land.

Emergence of Malay Progressive and Conservative Factions

The earliest known Malay reform movement consisted of scholars who came from the local *madrasah* school system and eventually found their way to the centers of higher learning in Cairo, Jerusalem, and Baghdad. While pursuing studies there, several became attracted to the wide array of discussions and debates surrounding Islam and modern society, especially with regards to Islam's relationship with capitalism.[44] Among the major outcomes of their experiences in the Middle-East was a new-found spirit in Malay ethnic consciousness, In 1923, a small circle of Malay students attending the renowned Al-Azhar University in Cairo, together with some students from the Dutch East Indies (Indonesia), formed an association known as the *Perhimpunan Indonesia Malaysia* (Indonesia Malaysia Convention).[45]

Upon their return, this group brought with them their newly-acquired approaches to and emphases on the teaching and practice of Islam, particularly in the obligatory struggle for a just and equal society. Several members from this group soon embarked on a social reform philosophy expressed mainly through their writings in novels and books as well as in the columns of the Malay and Indonesian press. Known as the *Kaum Muda* (young generation), this group's target audience was very much regional in scope. Their main message called for the "cleansing" of Malay-Islamic culture from the corruption and injustices of the existing feudal practices that had thus far been responsible for stifling the progress of the native peoples in both Malaya and the Dutch East Indies.[46] This group believed that only through the restoration of genuine Islamic principles, which prioritized the values of education, innovation, and social justice, would Malays be able to build strong social-political institutions in order to adapt and advance in the new economy.[47]

The message of the *Kaum Muda* was an interesting blend of progressive secularism and Islam that emphasized a moderate approach to life. They were also steadfast in their views that Islam was not incompatible with modernity, since the principles of individual hard work, scientific pursuit, equality of women, and democratic governance were very much implicated in the basic tenets of Islam.

Importantly, the *Kaum Muda* refuted the so-called infallibility of the Malay ruler, and criticized Malay reverence for the monarch as "un-Islamic." This group believed that as long as Malays continued to subscribe and enslave themselves to "pre-Islamic" rituals, there would be continuing difficulties for them in achieving competency and excellence in the modern world.

The primary target of contempt by the *Kaum Muda* had been the custodians of the traditional Malay establishment, referred to as *Kaum Tua* (traditionalists). This group of conservatives stood firmly behind the authority and prestige of the Malay royal court and claimed that devotion to the sultan and acknowledgement of his absolute powers were the foundations of Malay-Islamic cultural existence. As far as the *Kaum Tua* was concerned, cultural aspects of Malay social and political life, especially those pertaining to the Malay ruler, should not be subjected to debate or dispute since it could eventually lead to the eventual destabilization and disintegration of the larger Malay society.

Open expressions made by the *Kaum Muda* against the salient aspects of Malay traditional culture were naturally worrisome for the *Kaum Tua*. It was not long before the British too were taking notice of this group and its reformist discourse. To the colonial state, the group's critical views of the Malay monarchy were considered potentially "subversive." A mass following of the group could eventually threaten the absolute position of the Malay sultan, and with it, the legitimacy of British rule in Malaya. To avert such possibility, the colonial authorities fortified the sultan's authority as head of religion in his state through the introduction of a salaried bureaucracy for religious affairs.[48] The aim was to streamline conservative versions of Islam in the various Malay states that would serve to recognize and uphold the sultan's position as head of the Malay people and their religion. Such a move proved successful for the British; the sultan's authority and influence among Malays further deepened through the various state-appointed religious leaders. Faced with formidable social and political barriers in the form of an illiterate and tradition-bound Malay populace, the *Kaum Muda* was not able to extend its ideas and influence in Malaya beyond the circle of a few followers.[49]

In the early 1930s, another form of Malay political activism emerged. Popular left-wing ideology which had taken root in Indonesia began to spill into Malaya and Singapore. Many among the younger Malays were captivated by the prospects of an independent Malay nation premised on a socialist political system that delivered equal rights to its citizens. Relatively small in number, this group comprised mostly of Malay-educated intellectuals in the local Malay teaching colleges and schools, who had often been involved in regular political debates and exchanges within various Malay grassroots organs such as the *Suara Rakyat* (Voice of the People). Heavily influenced by the concept of a worker and peasant-based republican system, many of these left-leaning writers and activists began to mobilize themselves into a more prominent association in 1938 in the form of the *Kesatuan Melayu Muda* (KMM or Union of Young Malays). The KMM would go on to advocate for the creation of the *Melayu Raya*

(Greater Malaysia/Indonesia) that would bring Malaya and the Dutch East Indies under a large socialist union.[50]

Primarily driven by socialist ideals, members of this movement were highly critical of all existing Malay establishments, particularly the Malay bourgeoisie, for their close political relationships with the British.[51] As in the case of the *Kaum Muda*, the British quickly responded by enforcing tight monitoring of the KMM and their socialist-revolutionary political agenda. The British would later ban the organization just before start of the Second World War, with several of its members incarcerated without trial under the colonial Defense Regulations.[52]

During the Japanese occupation, the new occupiers would release the organization's members and channeled many of them into their own patron association called *Pembela Tanah Air* (PETA or Defenders of the Motherland). For purposes of propaganda, the Japanese maintained many of the KMM's goals within PETA, especially the proposal for a joint Malaya-Indonesia independence scheduled to take place in 1945. The Japanese however, had never been serious about granting any type of self-rule to either Malaya or Indonesia, and therefore hardly prepared any time-line or significant steps toward independence. When Japanese rule collapsed in 1945, some members of the former KMM took upon themselves to unilaterally declare Malaya's independence, which occurred about forty-eight hours after the official Japanese surrender.[53] The British nullified the pronouncement, and in their full return to Malaya, used their police force to round up and detain several important Malay left-wing activists and KMM members.

Although the KMM had pioneered an important contribution to the growth of modern Malay ethnonationalism, they were nevertheless confronted with the same political impediments that besieged the *Kaum Muda* earlier. Much of the KMM's political objectives were considered too complex and radical for the ordinary Malay, who remained unconvinced of the possibility of independence as well as highly resolute in abiding by his cultural expectations, especially those relating to his relationship with the sultan.[54] Most importantly, the KMM also had to contend with the extensive power of the British and their influence over the Malay comprador class, which unwaveringly protected the sultan, leaving the organization effectively isolated in its struggle.[55]

The further weakening of Malay left-wing and progressive factions in Malaya would open up for the Malay traditionalists, significant latitude to consolidate their leadership within the community. Soon, an emerging Malay conservative bourgeoisie began to appear in the form of an English-educated class, who had worked closely with the British from within the lower ranks of the Malayan colonial bureaucracy. Members of this upper circle came primarily from the various Malay aristocratic families and were likely to have been schooled and socialized within a common privileged royal environment.

As junior officers of the colonial administrative services, this group had been highly knowledgeable of state policy matters and had been in touch with the latest current events affecting Malaya. They were especially aware of the potential threats posed to Malays by the burgeoning Chinese population, whose massive economic power could easily overrun the Malays in their own *tanah air* (homeland).[56] Antagonized by the adamant requests from Chinese leaders for greater political involvement in Malaya, these Malay elites sought to counter what they viewed as the "rapacious demands" of the Chinese leadership through the continued protection of the Malay royal institution, which became the undisputed symbol of Malay "ownership" of Malaya.[57]

For the Malay elites, there had emerged an imperative for the rulers' official and ceremonial positions to be continually upheld even if it meant having to achieve it through sustained British presence in Malaya. Through British colonial rule at least, there was official recognition of the FMS, the UFMS, and Malaya (Anglicized version of *Tanah Melayu* or *Malay Land*) as the homelands of the Malays, especially in the documentations embedded in Britain's various treaties with the Malay rulers.[58] On these grounds, the Malay elites were reluctant to accept the uneasy multicultural existence that had accompanied Malaya's capitalist development, where the ethnic Chinese community proved to be far superior in terms of economic advancement and education. As trained lawyers and professionals, the Malay elites were well aware of the connotations that liberal citizenship may entail in jeopardizing what limited social privileges they enjoyed thus far as members of the Malay aristocracy and colonial establishment. This conservatism of the Malay elite was to become the essence of Malay ethnonationalism in the coming years.

Impact of Japanese Occupation on Malay and Chinese Ethnonationalisms

The Japanese imperial army landed in Malaya from the north in 1941 and swiftly defeated a rather highly-disorganized British defense force that awaited them in the south. Although the Japanese occupation of Malaya from 1942 to 1945 was relatively short, it was undoubtedly a watershed period in Malaya's political development.

Eluding any reference to its own colonial objectives, Japan presented its invasion of Southeast Asia as one which sought to liberate Asian homelands from European rule. Its *Greater Asia Co-Prosperity Sphere* policy was aimed at impressing upon peoples in this region the potential benefits of being under Japanese trusteeship, including economic cooperation and eventual self-rule.[59] In Malaya, the Japanese attempted to exploit Malay elite disillusionment with the British for failing to protect Malaya by encouraging their participation in the new colonial administration. While many of the Malay elites refused, others grudgingly relented.

At the same time, the Japanese military administration formed a state constabulary unit, the *kempeitei*, whose function was to ferociously weed out local resistance against its occupation. Specifically targeted were Malaya's ethnic Chinese, whose unrelenting allegiance to China made them a suspicious "fifth column" community. The fact that many Chinese had joined the communist-inspired armed resistance movement called the Malayan People's Anti-Japanese Army (MPAJA) only fuelled Japanese mistrust of this ethnic group. The scope of Japanese anti-Chinese campaign was extensive; between February and March 1942, about 5,000 Chinese were reported to have been systematically executed by the Japanese in Singapore alone, with thousands more killed in Malaya.[60] The consistency of this effort in the early years of the occupation made it seem to appear as a particular crusade in ethnic-cleansing.

Meanwhile, the Japanese maintained the same ethnicization of labor that the British had created. They filled the state's local policing units with considerable numbers of Malays and Indians, which was truly unfortunate. Although Malay personnel were rarely used in the arrest, detention, and execution of ethnic Chinese civilians, the mere presence of Malays in the Japanese Imperial army was sufficient for the Chinese to follow an oversimplified representation of a Malay-Japanese alliance against their community. This was despite the thousands of Malays who were also mistreated and sent to labor camps throughout Southeast Asia by the Japanese during the war, with others escaping or helping other resistance groups, including the British-trained Force 136 of the Malay Regiment.[61]

Heightened levels of hostility between Malays and Chinese during Japanese colonial rule would be seriously felt after the war. A somewhat reckless British policy during the interregnum period between the Japanese surrender and formal British resumption of colonial rule in 1946 would exacerbate and inflame the existing tensions between the two groups. An ad-hoc British Military Administration (BMA) temporarily undertook both the security and governing functions of Malaya and Singapore, and in the absence of a strong local armed police force, engaged the services of the MPAJA to assist with the maintenance of law and order.[62] This gesture was partly a payback to the MPAJA for their role in resisting the Japanese occupation. What unraveled thereafter was perhaps one of the darkest chapters of ethnic relations in Malaysia's history. The predominantly Chinese MPAJA took advantage of their newly-found power to conduct a campaign of vicious vendettas against anyone they suspected of collaborating with the Japanese during the war. In most of these cases, such acts of atrocity were inflicted against helpless Malay villagers.[63] Suspects who were tortured or killed were picked out primarily on suspicion, while verdicts of executions passed by the numerous "show trial courts" were decided on extremely feeble evidence.[64]

Retaliation by Malays, although not widespread, was equally harsh. Interpreting these events in terms of willful Chinese attacks on Malays, several formed their own armed groups and attacked suspected Chinese perpetrators. Incidentally, such incidents occurred mostly in areas of close economic competition, where latent tensions arising from social economic inequalities and pent-up antagonisms easily exploded into senseless reprisals. High-level conflicts also extended to areas where the Chinese outnumbered Malays, but were relatively few in Malay-majority states.[65] These physical clashes, would claim thousands of lives, prompting historian Cheah Boon Kheng to describe this period as "MPAJA's reign of terror."[66]

The political repercussions of Japan's relatively short occupation of Malaya had unmistakably changed the nature and course of the country's future politics. One of its major impacts was the re-invigoration of Malay political consciousness, which for the previous decades had been cautiously stifled under British colonial rule. For the Malays, the easy defeat of the British by the Japanese significantly altered their previously-held perception of British invincibility. It also became common knowledge to many Malays that a substantial number of British commercial expatriates, colonial officers, and their families had abandoned Malaya even before the Japanese arrived, thereby putting in question Britain's sincerity in protecting Malays and their land. These events compelled many English-educated Malays, especially the bourgeoisie class, to seriously rethink the role, position, and future of the Malaya without British patronage.

Similarly, the harsh treatments meted out against the Chinese by the Japanese helped to significantly mobilize various Chinese sub-ethnic groups and social classes into a more identifiable pan-Chinese ethnonational identity in Malaya. As the Chinese began to seriously ponder over their own future in Malaya, their own ethnic solidarity became a much-needed bulwark against the power of the British and Malays, both of whom they feared would permanently marginalize them in their newly-adopted land.

Decolonization and the Malayan Union, 1946-1948

The momentum of liberation struggles swinging in favor of anti-colonial forces would virtually open the floodgates for effective decolonization in many parts of the global periphery. After the Second World War, support for colonized peoples' rights to self-determination and independent statehood was strengthened by the missions and goals of the newly-formed United Nations.[67] Compelled to abide by world human rights principles embedded in the organization's various charters, Britain sought to display its progressivism by promising their colonies' eventual political independence.

However, the rise of socialist and revolutionary organizations throughout these colonies, especially in spearheading independence movements, gave colonial powers such as Britain much cause for worry. Several European powers such as France and Netherlands were particularly indisposed to the idea of national independence for their colonies, especially where left-wing forces were part of the liberation movement. These countries had anticipated huge economic losses if they granted total independence to their coveted imperial dominions in Asia and Africa. Their refusal to concede independence sparked full-scale liberation wars in places such as Algeria, Vietnam, and Indonesia.

The British on the other hand, were not entirely reluctant to allow political independence for their territories, especially when there could be high economic and military costs involved in maintaining these colonies and fighting liberation wars. Nevertheless, it would have also been against their economic interests to leave behind a politically unstable Malaya vulnerable to a communist or ultra-nationalist takeover. More significantly, Britain needed to retain and maximize its revenues from Malaya in order to rebuild its own economy and crumbling infrastructure left behind by the ravages of war. Its balance of payments had severely plummeted while Malaya's was increasing from the exports of much-needed raw materials to the west. By the late 1940s, Malaya's sale of rubber to the United States alone were valued at approximately US$405 million, compared with total exports from the United Kingdom to the same country, which were less than US$400 million. Malaya was indisputably the most vibrant economy in the Far East, and its per capita income in 1950 exceeded even Japan.[68]

As a critical component of its economic recovery plans, Britain needed its "bread and butter" to be politically settled before independence could be considered. If, as an inevitable reality, Britain were to grant independence to Malaya, it had to be accompanied by assurances that the new Malaya would continue to perform its role in the world economy as suppliers and markets for capitalist production. Therefore, it became critical for Britain that as they left Malaya, they would have eased in a new local leadership that was friendly and facilitative to their capitalist interests.

Hence, a stable Malaya became both a political and economic imperative. One of the potential sources of instability however, came from the imminent threat of ethnic violence. As noted earlier, divergent ethnonational goals, competing economic aspirations, and mutual ethnic suspicions between the various ethnic groups, especially Malays and Chinese, had culminated into serious ethnic unrests in the aftermath of the Second World War. This led the British to believe that unless a unified nation is forged, disruptions and threats to its economic interests in Malaya would continually resurface from a society divided along ethnic loyalties.[69]

One of the ways in which the British sought to alleviate and eventually resolve ethnic problems in Malaya was to gradually fuse the different ethnic groups into a common national identity. The Labour government in Britain, especially, was of the opinion that the ideal system for Malaya lay in a nationally-integrated capitalist democracy, driven by a centralized political structure that granted equal citizenship to all ethnic groups. The creation of the Malayan Union in January 1946 was the basis for this project.

There were two primary aspects of the Malayan Union that were considered fundamental departures from the old colonial structure. First, Malaya was to be initially ruled as a direct colony, incorporating the FMS, UFMS, and the Straits Settlements of Penang and Malacca under one government.[70] In this respect, the long-standing debate between advocates of centralization and decentralization of Malaya had eventually turned in favor of the former. Centralization through the Malayan Union was to cogently create a common political structure to ensure that future Malayans were united under a capitalist democratic banner and remained under British influence.

The Malayan Union also required that the individual Malay states in both the FMS and UFMS submit their sovereign status to an all-powerful central government, which was in turn, answerable to the Crown Office in London. This meant that the individual Malay states were no longer "autonomous" protectorates, but entities absorbed under a larger colonial structure. Despite the rulers' reluctance to accept their sudden relegation in rank, they were nevertheless coerced into signing the proposal, turning the relatively loose federation within the old British Malaya into a centralized Malayan Union.[71]

The centralized political system additionally posed some major points of concern for the Malay elites. A major component of the Malayan Union involved the granting of *jus soli* (by birth) citizenship and equal political rights to ethnic Chinese and Indians. This citizenship process meant that alongside Malays, all other ethnic individuals born in the country would also automatically qualify for Malayan citizenship. Even if a non-Malay person was born outside Malaya, he or she would still be eligible for citizenship if residence in Malaya or Singapore had been for 10 out of 15 years before 1942. Qualification was even extended to adults whose father qualified automatically for citizenship. Anyone else wishing to apply only had to fulfill the residency requirements of 5 out of 8 years of his or her life within Malaya.[72]

While the liberal approach to Malayan citizenship was perhaps heavily influenced by the political philosophy of the Labour government that took office in London immediately after the war, it was also thought to serve as a preparatory framework for a post colonial Malaya reflective of those found in many British Commonwealth countries such as Canada and India. Here, equal citizenship was seen as a way to cultivate a sense of *Malayanhood* among the different ethnic groups in Malaya, which the British hoped would provide long-term political remedy for ongoing ethnic hostilities in the country. The British had considered the non-Malays as essential in the development of the Malayan capitalist economy, and it was critical that they remained a permanent part of the new Malaya.

The conservative Malay elite were not at all amused, however. They saw this proposal as eroding any possibility of Malays to re-stake their claim of being "masters" of their own land. The English-educated Malay elite felt betrayed by the British and reviled them for insensitively reneging on past agreements and treaties that at the very least recognized the institutional sovereignty of the Malay sultans.[73] To them, an independent Malaya had always been viewed as a resumption of Malay political governance that historically began with the ancient Malay kingdoms, and interrupted only by periods of European and Japanese colonialisms. The constitutional structure of the Malayan Union which deemphasized the role and recognition of the Malay monarchy was not expressive of such a notion.

More importantly, the Malay elite also feared that the granting of full citizenship to massive numbers of non-Malays could inevitably compromise the protection of Malay special rights to land, the Islamic religion, and government employment, thereby condemning the largely impoverished Malays to similar plights of indigenous peoples in North America, Australia, and Palestine.[74] As far as their own class interests were concerned, the Malay elite also felt that the eventual disappearance of the Malay nation and culture in the new Malaya could very well jeopardize the very source of their political economic existence.

Exasperated, the Malay elite saw an urgent need to quickly dismantle the Malayan Union. Their observations of events transpiring in other British colonies seemed to illustrate that a persistent show of public action against the colonial state could be the most effective approach in rescinding the union. The problem however was in generating nation-wide support from a relatively apathetic and apolitical Malay population, who were further divided along provincial loyalties.

Nevertheless, the Malay elite did possess the charisma within its leadership to sufficiently appeal to the growing number of active Malay social movement through highly emotive ethnonational sentiments designed specifically to drum up support for the "Malay cause" against the Union. Within a short time, the conservative Malay bourgeoisie began organizing cross-country road trips into numerous grassroots communities located in small towns and rural vicinities to explain the poignancy of the Malayan Union plan, focusing on its impact on the future sovereignty and status of Malays in the country.[75] An important emphasis here had been on the inevitable relegation of Malays to mere citizens, where entitlements and privileges to their own lands would now have to be equally shared with ethnic Indians and Chinese.

Such rhetoric proved successful. For once in their modern history, large numbers of Malays from various backgrounds came together under the collective umbrella of the United Malay Nationalist Organisation (UMNO), formed in 1946 as a response to the Malayan Union. Aware that they would be subsumed by the economic powers of the Chinese, many Malays began to identify with UMNO's proclamation of "Malaya for the Malays."[76] Many saw it as a justified rallying call to reassert the dominant place of Malays in a Malaya they had always believed as rightfully theirs to rule. During these events, the small Malay urban middle class emerged as a politically conscious group. Those who were closely following the unfolding of events, including some on the left, suddenly found the conservative temperament of Malay ethnonationalism particularly soothing.

Within the space of several weeks, UMNO managed to convince the various groups under its consortium to boycott all events relating to the Union, particularly the various Advisory Councils that were set up by the British for purposes of discussing citizenship and other ethnic-related issues.[77] Although the show of force by UMNO across Malaya spanning the years from 1946 to 1948 was relatively peaceful, it did gain in momentum to become vociferously defiant. A contagion of Malay ire quickly spread across the Malay Peninsula, sending a stern message to those complicit with the Union proposal to beware of the consequences of their actions. The UMNO leadership even made it clear to the various sultans that each one of them would be disowned by the people should they maintain their conspiring role in the Union. The sultans' shunning of the inauguration ceremony of the Malayan Union's first governor, Sir Edward Gent, was at the insistence of UMNO.[78]

The irony in the whole Malayan Union episode was that the British had intended to push through their proposal by exploiting what they perceived as the lack of political will among Malays to challenge British authority. Instead, the plan backfired and inadvertently triggered off a new wave of Malay political activism that had apparently been missing for the past decades. For the first time, uncountable numbers of Malay women, the young, and the elderly fiercely participated in UMNO's street protests and marches.

Hence, it did not take the British long to realize the potential costs of a Malayan Union in the face of a highly unreceptive and increasingly aggressive Malay populace. There were increasing signs that some Malays might even deliberate toward militancy, which worried the British since such factions could also cozy up with left-wing groups and eventually ignite a series of mass-based civil disturbances. The postwar years had certainly become a volatile period for everyone, and touching the nerve of Malay sensitivities would have possibly invited ethnic unrests of unprecedented proportions.

In view of the potentially high political economic risks coming from a destabilized Malaya, the British decided that it was not worth further pursuing the full enforcement of the Union and its laws; the plan disintegrated after a mere two years of official existence. The British now had to work fast toward putting together a new political structure that could develop and sustain a capitalist democratic system in Malaya, one which served to accommodate British and western economic interests in the region.

The end of the Malayan Union coincided with the propulsion of the conservative Malay elite within UMNO into the forefront of Malayan politics. This "revolt" by the English-educated Malay elite against the colonial establishment occurred so swiftly that the ethnic Chinese and Indian elites hardly had time to fully absorb and disseminate to their respective communities the positive implications of the Malayan Union in terms of its constitutional privileges and liberal citizenship laws.[79] Malay rebellion against the full implementation of the plan had effectively aborted any such effort into permanent oblivion.

Reconfiguring British-Malay Elite Ties: The Federation of Malaya Agreement, 1948

The seemingly insuperable problem of nation-building in Malaya came in the way of constructing a unified nation-state from among a culturally diverse, ethnically divided, and socially unequal society. A unification process of such magnitude would have required decades of integrationist policy implementation, something which the British had deliberately side-stepped for reasons of obvious political expediency and economic profitability. The British realized, perhaps a little too late, that its colonial labor-ethnicization policy had culminated into a system that perpetuated rigid ethnic boundaries and competing ethnonational visions. In other words, the fragile ethnic co-existence emanating from its own "divide and rule" policy had come back to haunt them in the form of potential instability in Malaya.

Nevertheless, the end of the Malayan Union and the rise of the Malay elite meant that the British had no choice now but to engage UMNO in upcoming discussions to ensure that maintaining the capitalist system became a vital precondition to Malaya's eventual independence. This was especially so when increased communist activity loomed over the region.[80] Lessons from the Malayan Union evidenced the British that the most pragmatic form of post-independent governance in Malaya necessitated a reversion to some sort of federated administrative structure that assured the sovereignty of each of the Malay states and its ruler. Traditional loyalties had still been very much alive among Malays, and any move to lower the esteem or status of any of the Malay ruler would have entailed massive political problems for the British.

Furthermore, it became unmistakably apparent as to who now possessed the ultimate political power within the Malay community. The English-educated Malay elite of UMNO had already consolidated their demonstrative role as guardians of Malay ethnonational interests and hegemony in Malaya after their inspiring fight to abolish the Malayan Union. Thus it became inexorable for the British to reconfigure their old alliances with the Malay conservative elite in order to be on the "right side of history" and avert the rise of any popular Malay support for socialist or Islamist groups. Here, the British would take every precautionary measure to ensure that any future dialogue on independence excluded Malay socialists from the former KMM, who now have a platform in the newly-formed Malay Nationalist Party (MNP).[81]

That the British dealt only with the pro-capitalist Malay conservatives on every social-dimensional level became increasingly clear. For example in 1947, a group of Malay teachers from the *Maahad Illhya Assyarif* Islamic School in Perak proposed a progressive plan to aid poor Malay farmers through community-based credit and cooperative banking programs using Islamic financing practices.[82] The effort, embedded in the group's Center for Malay Economy in Malaya, needed British support. However, since the colonial state had always been wary of any initiatives run by socialist or Islamist organizations in Malaya, the request was conveniently ignored. In contrast, the British did not hesitate in helping launch a similar project in the form of the Rural Industrial Development Authority (RIDA) in 1950 that served the groundwork for future affirmative-action programs mostly benefiting the Malay bourgeoisie.[83]

Interestingly, any federated structure in Malaya would definitively exclude Singapore. A major reason is economics. For the British, the unification of Malaya and Singapore had to be carefully weighted. There was urgency in recouping as much revenues as possible from the remaining colonies toward Britain's reconstruction efforts at home. The British had acquired an external debt in excess of £3.4 million and were on the verge of national bankruptcy.[84] Malaya's exports of tin and rubber provided the British with a major source of its gold reserves while Singapore separately remained as one of the few places left in which Britain still maintained direct control of its international commerce. Losing both Malaya and Singapore in such expedient manner would have been detrimental to whatever was left of their imperial influence.

Britain was also becoming increasingly alarmed at the growing communist activism in Singapore. Here, the British felt certain that should they leave Singapore hastily, a communist takeover would all but undermine major British economic interests and operations in Southeast Asia. Thus by the time the British were convinced into gradually leaving India in 1946, the debate on the status of Singapore as part of an independent Malaya became more settled toward exclusion.[85] In 1948, the Federation of Malaya was formed incorporating all the FMS, UFMS, and former Straits Settlement states excluding Singapore.

The most important postcolonial objective, as far as the British were concerned, was for Malaya to perform well in the world economy under a government that remained stable and welcoming to western capital. For this to materialize, the valuable contributions of non-Malays toward Malaya's economic production and trade necessitated their permanent residency in Malaya. Citizenship for non-Malays, however, was still a potentially explosive issue, and the British were at a crossroads on this problem. As the Malayan Union events had illustrated, the proposal to confer equal status and voting privileges on large numbers of non-Malays had already evoked a hostile response from the Malay elites. On the other hand, the exclusion or even marginalization of a significant portion of the country's population and labor force would unavoidably threaten the full productive capacity of the country's capitalist economy.

The British solution to Malayan citizenship issues remained fixed on their desire to move toward some form of integral political system, in which those who considered themselves loyal to Malaya would be given automatic citizenship. Despite the annulment of the Malayan Union, the British still appeared to prefer the development of some type of transcendent Malayan nationality to represent the Malayan nation.[86] This was an important prerequisite for the British, who viewed an ethnically-diffused political system as the safest and most effective structural mechanism to de-emphasize ethnic and cultural allegiances, which they perceived as the primary source of ethnic problems in the country.

More importantly however, the British were also of the adamant opinion that an ethnically-integrated political system worked best if it were helmed by multiethnic elites affiliated with the leadership of issue-based political parties. They also envisioned the central feature of an elite-driven capitalist democracy in Malaya to be based on a leadership that was able to understand and identify with western standards of governance and values. This included the intrinsic support for a capitalist democratic political structure and the upholding of a "free market" approach to macro-economic transactions and trade. Such a comprehensive system would help advance the capitalist economy in an independent Malaya, protect capitalist class interests, both local and foreign, and serve to ensure the control of labor through the political marginalization of the peasantry and working class.

UMNO as Dominant Malayan Political Party

Although the Malay elite within UMNO had been aggressively at odds with the British over the Malayan Union proposal, they were nevertheless appeased by the institutional contents of the Federation of Malaya agreement that gave them greater and more extensive political hegemony of their country. As the British pressed ahead for an ethnically-integrated Malayan political system, the issue was now whether UMNO, whose political goals had been passionately grounded on the notion of a Malay-based Malaya, could be persuaded to agree to the fruition of a multiethnic political alternative.

UMNO president Onn Jaafar, the aristocrat who meteorically rose to heroic status for his role in opposing the Malayan Union, sensed that the British were serious in withholding independence as long as ethnic politics was the order of the day.[87] He was also sure that the British would back his candidacy for Malayan leadership if he undertook a position of greater flexibility on some of the issues relating to citizenship and political empowerment for ethnic Chinese and Indians. Thus in 1950, Onn surprisingly recommended for the party he had helped found to open its membership to non-Malays. To the majority Malays in UMNO, such suggestion signaled a sweeping departure from the very life-force that catalyzed the party's spirit for Malayan independence. To the staunchly conservative UMNO members especially, the party's very existence was entrenched in the safeguarding of Malay political rights in Malaya. Allowing competing ethnic interests to access UMNO would not only seem to compromise Malay political hegemony, but also defeat the very rationale of the party's thematic "Malaya for Malays" struggle. It is interesting to note that prior to this, only the leftists, who later formed the MNP, had dared suggest any transformation of the party into a multiethnic entity, resulting in the group's eventual alienation from Malay mainstream politics. Likewise, Onn's suggestion was immediately rejected, after which he left UMNO to form the multiethnic Independence of Malaya Party (IMP).

With Onn in the IMP, the British became increasingly worried. On one hand, UMNO possessed almost sole representation of the Malay electorate, but seemed deficient of a strong charismatic leader capable of simultaneously holding Malays together and pulling the party out of its ethnic focus. Onn seemed to possess the most suitable persona of the pro-capitalist and westernized Malay leader they had sought, but the IMP had only a few Malay followers. In any case, the British decided to throw their weight behind the IMP, since it was the only party they saw sufficiently capable of realizing their notion of a western-friendly and multiethnic Malaya.[88] With the recruitment of several more prominent non-Malay leaders into its fold, the IMP looked set to be groomed into its national leadership role.

The 1952 municipal elections became a crucial litmus test. UMNO was to run against the British-favored IMP along with a host of other ethnic-based parties, including the very wealthy Malayan Chinese Association (MCA). Facing a shortage of funds, the task to perform well in the campaigns was rather daunting for UMNO—until an unexpected event followed. The MCA, lacking penetrability into the electorate, sought UMNO's help. By the time of the elections, many Chinese in Malaya had not qualified for the residency requirements and became ineligible to vote. Many had also left Malaya or deported for communist-related activities.[89] A considerable portion of the remaining ethnic Chinese population was also quite hostile to the political philosophy of the MCA, especially its pro-capitalist and western orientation.

Hence, a remarkable sequence followed. The Chinese elites in the MCA had agreed to finance UMNO campaigns in return for being allowed to contest on UMNO's political tickets in predominantly Malay areas. Realizing the mutual political benefits to be gained from this relationship, both parties agreed to help each other out in preparing for the upcoming elections. And gain they did. This informal *quid pro quo* political agreement between UMNO and MCA produced a winning formula. Not short of money or logistical resources, the UMNO-MCA front won nine out of the twelve seats in the 1952 elections, making it the dominant political coalition ahead of independence.

In 1953, this coalition expanded under a new name—the National Alliance—to include another elite-led ethnic party, the Malayan Indian Congress (MIC). This inter-ethnic elitist political alliance, supposedly premised on each party's political representation of their respective ethnic group and interests, went on to win that year's elections by a much wider margin.[90] By the time of Malayan independence in 1957, the National Alliance would widen its membership to allow several more smaller parties into its coalition.

Ethnic Elite Collaboration

The lesson in political cooperation for Malaya's new elites was valuable. In a country that was now theirs to rule, it became difficult to ignore the incentives for such collaboration. It dawned on the Malay, Chinese, and Indian elites that political realities associated with capitalist development in Malaya, namely in the preservation of social and economic interests, obliged them to put aside some of the pervasive and contentious issues in inter-ethnic relations and instead, work together as a formidable ruling class.[91]

The common denominator that glued these Malayan elites together was unmistakably apparent; they were bonded by the influence of English education, which had been crucial in westernizing their social and political outlooks. These elites also enjoyed social privileges associated with their esteemed positions in their own communities, and were now looking ahead to entering the circle of power at the national level. While the Malay elite was focused on seeing its group take over the political functions left behind by the British in the new Malaya, non-Malay business elites began to see themselves in same light as the European capitalists who had influenced much of Malaya's corporate policies in the past. Importantly, a less noticeable characteristic shared by these elites was that although each group attempted to generate for their parties the political support and legitimacy from among the lower classes, these elites hardly had any significant social relationship or interests with these social-economic groups.

Subsequently, the further strengthening of the Alliance's collaboration would require outlining the fundamental principles defining the political relationship between UMNO, MCA, and MIC. This would involve discussions toward solving some of the sensitive issues relating to language, citizenship, and culture. Of prime importance to the Malay elite in UMNO was addressing the economic progress of Malays and the protection of their cultural rights if long-term Malay support for the party were to be sustained. The majority of Malays were illiterate and impoverished, and in such state of affairs, UMNO would inherit a support base that was too deficient in both income and education to be able to contribute to the party or gain from the growing capitalist economy. Implicitly, an educated and economically sustainable Malay citizenry would also guarantee UMNO with an effective barrier against non-Malay political challenges since it would be able to ward off possible conspiring efforts by non-Malays to potentially marginalize them in the future.

More than anything else, a totally disenfranchised Malay ethnic group would also indirectly lead to the insignificance of the Malay elite as a political power, and eventually serve as a recipe for Malay grassroots revolution. Such a scenario would be detrimental to the political interests of both UMNO and the other parties in the alliance since each was considerably dependent on the Malay electorate for its legitimacy. Hence, it became imperative that Malays "catch up" with the other ethnic groups, even if it meant attaining it through the use of reverse discriminatory policies. In this, UMNO insisted that the special position and rights of Malays as the indigenous people of Malaya required their preferential access to educational and commercial opportunities, which should be guaranteed and enshrined in the final draft of the Federal Constitution.[92]

The political calculations made by the MCA and MIC were premised on the *realpolitik* dictates of a system closest to a multiethnic coalition, through which major political compromises and concessions could be brokered between the Malay and non-Malay elites on constitutional issues of citizenship, cultural rights, and language. The non-Malay elites pledged to recognize the special position of the sultans and Malays as well as to the proclamation of Malay and Islam as the official language and religion of the new federation.[93] In return, the non-Malay elites were successful in their requests for the institutionalization of *jus soli* citizenship for all non-Malays who were eligible. This meant that the stipulations embedded in the Malayan Union proposal were practically revived. These citizenship proposals were now acceptable to the Malay elite in view of the fact that by 1955, the Malay population had superseded the Malayan-born Chinese, albeit marginally.

Gradually, the broader definition and context of Malaya as a national entity was reconstituted to include all other ethnic groups. It was eventually understood even by the Malay elite that the concept of Malaya embodying an exclusively Malay identity was no longer considered a realistic description of the multicultural society that Malaya had developed into. The notion of "Malayan" was then constructively transformed, through the Constitution, into a pluralist concept. Significantly, the assurance that Malays would assume ultimate political leadership in the country would be operationalized by UMNO's *primus inter pares* (first among equals) status within the ruling alliance. This would among other things, automatically secure a Malay Prime Minister so long as the National Alliance remained in office.[94]

The British were initially skeptical of this ethnic power-sharing structure, and had not been convinced of its viability and success in the coalescing of a united Malayan nation as long as ethnic-based interests remained the foundation of the political system. However, the Alliance moved ahead tenaciously from their newly-found electoral strength toward further affirmation of their leadership status in the new Malaya. The first nationwide elections in 1955 demonstrated the effectiveness of this ethnic power-sharing synergy, in which UMNO in particular, proved to be the masters of the political game. Having pioneered the Malay ethnonationalist struggle and taking advantage of its new role as "protector" of Malay rights, the party's elite was able to mobilize the Malay masses fully behind the Alliance. In this, UMNO was also able to convince Malay voters to decide on non-Malay politicians from the MCA or MIC even if they stood in contest over Malay opposition candidates from other parties. Consequently, the results of the 1955 elections were more than convincing. The opposition took a huge beating with the National Alliance winning all but one seat and taking up 87 percent of all popular votes.[95]

Desiring to leave Malaya with a sense of completion and relief, the British would become increasingly comforted by the success of this collaborative political arrangement. More importantly, the elitist and western orientation of the Alliance's leaderships would sustain the political economic linkages between Malaya and the capitalist world economy that was favorable to British production, investment, and market interests in the region. To help prepare the Malayan elite with experience in self-rule at the federal level, the British created a local Member system, in which several Officials and Unofficials of the Legislative Assembly were appointed to various ministerial portfolios.[96] When Malaya gained independence in 1957, these individuals served as the country's first cabinet of ministers.

There was now full realization within the leaderships of the MCA and MIC with regards to the criticality of the current ethnic-power sharing structure in sustaining their own ultimate political survival. Given the historical complexity of ethnic relations in the country, especially the highly unpredictable nature of Malay political behavior, these ethnic elites knew very well that the consolidation of the collaborative system was the lifeline to their own future growth and development in Malaya (later Malaysia). Thus any incongruity of political or economic views had to be resolved through mutual political bargaining and concessions. Due to their subordinate power however, it follows that the non-Malay elites should, at least superficially, appear to appease the concerns of the Malay community, who provided the crux of political support for the Alliance.

This power-sharing political arrangement, known as *consociationalism*, has been proposed, at least in theory, as a practical approach to resolving politically litigious conflicts between ethnic and cultural groups in many multiethnic societies.[97] It also contains some major flaws however. The elitist nature of Malaya's consociational structure for example, risked eclipsing the democratic essence of consensual power-sharing governance, rendering the system to be one in which prioritization of elite class-related interests would overshadow efforts in the pursuit of justice and equality for all citizens. Ethnic representation through elite-based political parties in this case, would not necessarily translate into the collective representation of each respective group. Rather, it would more likely serve to mask the convenient disbursement of political power exclusively among the country's various ethnic leaderships.

Nevertheless, the groundwork for Malayan consociationalism seemed ideal for the country's elites, and was soon set in motion. As the Malay elite in UMNO became increasingly confident of their pole position in the new Malaya, the non-Malay elite within the Alliance too would become increasingly pleased with the economic advantages derived from being part of this new ruling class. The identification of the Malay elite with the helm of national politics and the association of ethnic Chinese elite with the corporate leadership in the country was to become the foundational relationship between these two groups within the National Alliance. Soon, membership within this ruling inner circle would expand to include the elites from Sabah and Sarawak as Malaya merged with these two states into a larger federation.

The Federation of Malaysia, 1963

The People's Action Party (PAP) of Singapore under Lee Kuan Yew, which won the mandate to lead the island toward independence in 1959, had consistently pressed for the island's merger with Malaya. This was partly because Singapore had historically been dependent on its larger northern neighbor both economically and militarily. It was also part of Lee's view that a larger Malaya, inclusive of Singapore, would serve to consolidate his party's power in the island's increasingly unstable political climate.

However, neither the enthusiasm nor the urgency of the PAP was shared by the UMNO elites, who failed to see any political advantages in the incorporation of Singapore into the Federation. A major reason for this has been Singapore's citizenship laws, which under British colonial rule had allowed large numbers of ethnic Chinese into its electorate, a situation with which UMNO found extremely uneasy if Singapore were to be part of Malaya. In addition to this, UMNO leaders were also not too thrilled about taking on the burden of handling Singapore's increasingly turbulent unrests involving communist-inspired Chinese school students and trade union members that had placed the city in a state of constant alerts and curfews. This threat was further exacerbated by the breakaway of the PAP's leftist faction from the party to form a formidable opposition, the Socialist Front, whose coming to power was seen to threaten not only the capitalist economy of the island but also that of the whole region.

However, upon deeper reflection, UMNO was forced to rethink its reluctance on the possible merger. Tunku Abdul Rahman, the first Malayan Prime Minister, had remarked that if left unchecked, a communist Singapore would more than likely invite a greater Soviet or Chinese presence in the region and therefore pose a serious threat to the security of Malaya. To prevent Singapore from becoming Malaya's "Cuba," the Malayan leadership decided to indirectly involve UMNO in the political affairs of the island through some form of unity government with the PAP.[98]

At the same time, discussions were already underway for a merger between Malaya and the northern Borneo territories of Sabah, Sarawak, and the sultanate of Brunei. The threat of communist penetration into the region, it was thought, could be better contained if there was an effective countervailing force in the form of a reliably strong and pro-capitalist *Greater Malaya* or *Malaysia*, incorporating Malaya and northern Borneo. The British and Americans seemed to welcome this proposal with some historiographies even pointing out that the whole idea was mooted by the British, who were more than willing to relinquish their Borneo colonies in the interest of fortifying the security of the Southeast Asian region against nationalist and left-wing forces.[99]

While political events in Brunei had compelled the sultanate to opt out from the Malaysia plan, the United Nations proceeded in 1963 to hold plebiscites in Sarawak and Sabah in order to gauge public sentiments on joining Malaysia. In Singapore, a similar referendum was carried out. When the results showed favorably for a merger with Malaya, the Federation of Malaysia was subsequently established on September 16, 1963. The creation of Malaysia certainly provided a political lifeline for Singapore's PAP as Malaysia's police force went on to effectively suppress the city's riots and allowed Lee to jail his leftist opponents. Later however, irreconcilable differences between Malaya's UMNO and Singapore's PAP over issues of Malay special privileges, distribution of power, and electoral access resulted in the island being brusquely kicked out of the Federation in 1965.[100] The PAP, representing its electoral interests in predominantly Chinese constituencies in Singapore, demanded parity of political power with UMNO in the federation. This not only angered UMNO but also the MCA, who saw itself as the primary ethnic Chinese party in Malaysia. This expulsion of Singapore would mark the first and only time in modern world history where a relatively affluent province or state was officially ousted from a larger country due to political differences.

Emergence of Ruling Elite in Northern Borneo

By the end of the Second World War, massive financial problems and unending internal discords compelled both the Brooke dynasty and the BNBCC to respectively surrender their sovereignty in Sarawak and Sabah over to the British government. Both these states became Crown Colonies and remained so until their merger with Malaya and Singapore to form the Federation of Malaysia in 1963.

As part of the Malaysia plan, the National Alliance extended invitations to various ethnic-based political parties in Sabah and Sarawak to join its consociational power-sharing arrangement at the federal level under the National Alliance. In anticipation of the merger, these ethnic leaderships had formed their local parties in order to safeguard their own political interests. Many of these elites were part of the privileged circles of their own respective ethnic groups, who had either served under the colonial government or come from successful business families, as in the case of the ethnic Chinese. The realization among these ethnic elites of the benefits to be gained from being part of Malaysia became crucial in consenting to their states' inclusion into the larger federation.

In Sarawak, the two biggest parties in the early 1960s were the Sarawak National Party (SNAP) and the Sarawak United People's Party (SUPP). Although primarily catering to native Dayak and Iban elite interests, SNAP eventually opened its doors to other local ethnic groups, primarily Malays and Chinese. The SUPP was originally established in 1959 as a communist party, which in alliance with the Partai Rakyat Brunei (PRB) had demanded for the establishment of a socialist northern Borneo state. After the leftists were deported from Malaysia, the party began a moderation process, focusing mainly on the advancements of Chinese cultural and educational interests in the state. In Sabah, the United National Kadazan Organisation, representing the ethnic Kadazan-Dusun populations, and the left-of-center *Pertubuhan Pasokmomogun Bersatu* (United Pasokmomogun Organisation) maintained the largest followings.[101]

All these major political parties save the SUPP in Sarawak readily accepted the National Alliance invitation. The predominantly ethnic Chinese SUPP had been wary of Sarawak's admission into Malaysia, especially with respect to the potential impact of federal policies on Chinese education in the state.[102] Nevertheless, in the 1963 state elections, both the Sabah and Sarawak alliances of parties went on to win the mandate for negotiating the terms of entry into the Federation. These agreements resulted favorably for the elites on both sides of the South China Sea. Given the special circumstances surrounding their inclusion into Malaysia, Sabah and Sarawak have also enjoyed greater privileges and autonomy than the other states in Malaya, namely in the preservation of exclusive local land rights, extensive state legislative powers, and strict immigration control.[103] It may be surprising to many that until the time of writing, citizen travelers from west Malaysia still needed to produce their passports upon arrival in these two states.

Being part of the federation certainly accelerated the emergence and development of many more political parties in these two states. Although elites from Sabah and Sarawak have appeared guarded against possible manipulation by Malaysian federal leaders, it has also become obvious that the profitable links between the two factions have caused their relationships to become more than cordial over the years. Furthermore, persistent internal party clashes, in-group rivalries, and competing personal interests have regularly impeded any unification or consolidation of these parties into a formidable political force, one that could seriously challenge the Malayan elite. Historian Michael Leigh noted this when commenting on the political culture of Sarawak: "this political division within racial communities provided a ready basis for compromise, forcing factions to seek allies outside their community in the quest for political power."[104] This was especially so when those who displayed readiness for cooperation with the federal government were often treated more propitiously.

Furthermore, any hint of dissent was not tolerated by the National Alliance government. In 1966, Sarawak Chief Minister Stephen Ningkan of SNAP was forcefully replaced by another Iban politician, Tawi Sli, who appeared to have been more amenable to policy suggestions from Kuala Lumpur.[105] In 1967, Sabah Chief Minister Mohammed Fuad Stephens, having displayed a semblance of brevity in calling for more state rights, was quietly pressured out of office. He was replaced by the philanthropic and charismatic pro-federalist Datu Mustapha Harun of the United Sabah National Organisation.[106]

Decades of unquestioned submission to the Brooke dynasty and the BNBCC have imbibed a tradition of deference within many Bumiputera elites in Sarawak and Sabah to external authority, particularly when it involved sustaining or acquiring local political advantages. Today, the benefits of the relationships between the Malayan leadership and that of these two states have been mutually gratifying. While many of the allying elites in Sarawak and Sabah have succumbed willfully to the directives of the Federal government, they too, in return, have reaped immense power, wealth, and privileges from being part of a larger ruling class in Malaysia.

Summary

The fragmented political identities of the Malayan people, compartmentalized into various competing and conflicting ethnonational goals, had made it quite difficult for a popular Pan-Malayan national consciousness to surface. Each of these ethnonational ambitions tended to emphasize the politically divergent and incommensurable aspects of their political goals from that of other groups, which would later cause efforts toward a functioning post-independent multicultural democracy rather problematic.

While the highly-distanced relationship between each of the ethnic groups suited the British well during colonial rule, it certainly impeded their plan for the development of an integrated society crucial for a stable post-colonial Malaya. Thus the Malayan Union presented a hastened attempt by the British to preserve their interests through a centralized political system, but which overlooked the existing complexities of conflicting ethnonational aspirations that defined the nature of ethnic relations in Malaya. For any type of integrationist project to successfully materialize into institutional permanence, the omnipresent ethnic and class hostilities among and between the different participating groups must first be effectively addressed and alleviated. Such a process, of course, would have required a systematic and consistent approach to civic association building, the successful outcome of which could not possibly have taken place within one generation. In this respect, the rushed implementation of the Malayan Union reflected on the part of the British, either their failure to understand the political dynamics of ethnic relations in Malaya or their advertent neglect to foster any inter-ethnic goodwill during colonial rule.

The Malayan Union's citizenship proposal was cleverly exploited by the Malay elite in UMNO as a means to mobilize mass Malay support behind the organization. Driven by the fear of being displaced from their land by ethnic Chinese and Indians, Malays soon subscribed to the ethnonationalism as propagated by UMNO to reach an unprecedented level of public activism. The success in getting the Malayan Union repealed indeed signaled the coming of age of the Malay elite class, who also realized that they had much to lose if Malay political hegemony dissipated under the weight of an unequal multiethnic social structure. For UMNO, the most profitable result of this struggle was its transition from an almost ad-hoc social movement to the most formidable political organization in Malaya. In the end, UMNO's emergence as a dominant political force turned out to be beneficial for the British as well, thus affirming that collaborative political ties with the Malay elite had always been the most effective recipe for stabilizing British influence in Malaya. As the period toward independence neared, the British needed to ascertain that only "acceptable" candidates had access to the country's leadership. In this, the legitimacy and leading role of UMNO among Malays in the future of Malaya would eventually receive full support from the British, who were more than comforted by its pro-western stand.

In preparing for Malaya's independence, the British advocated for the formation of a capitalist democratic state in Malaya, in which every Malayan, including ethnic Chinese and Indians, could participate in self-governance. This was critical if the capitalist system was to flourish in Malaya, especially in the context of cold war politics that essentially dictated the contents and character of western foreign policies after 1945. The eventual formation of the National Alliance comprising Malaya's various multiethnic elites in this case, was to be a blessing for to the British. The conflation of political economic interests between the elites of Malaya's major ethnic groups was crucial in bringing them together as political allies. The English-educated class of each ethnic group stood to be the most advantaged in terms of power and resources, and also the most exposed to the demands and expectations of a modern capitalist statehood.

This awareness enabled this class to foresee their role in the future of Malaya much clearer than those from the lower classes. It also allowed each of these elite groups to set their respective ethnonational goals along a discourse that served to advance their own class-related interests within the community. In short, members of Malaya's multiethnic elite possessed the capability to effectively utilize their status as well as common political economic interests as a means towards their political ends in ways the lower classes were not able to.

Hence, the consociational strategy taken by the ruling coalition to advance the political economic interests of its elites also heralded the introduction of a formal but non-substantive capitalist democracy in Malaya that was to be highly accommodative of western and capitalist interests. The elite focus of this interethnic political arrangement, furthermore, served to strengthen as well as legitimize exclusive representation of each ethnic group's interests solely through the power and authority of their leaderships. In this respect, the new Malaya appeared to be not much dissimilar from the old Malaya—political control of the masses remained the primary framework for effective capitalist state governance. Meanwhile, the same cold war politics that helped usher in the pro-western multiethnic elites to power in Malaya had also provoked left-wing movements into aggressively pushing for the establishment of a socialist state. Their historical accounts will be discussed in the following chapter.

Notes

1. The term ethnonational is used to specifically imply ethnic, and not national, ambitions and goals, since it refers to the summed derivation of each ethnic group's unique social and political experiences.

2. Yen Ching-Hwang, "Overseas Chinese Nationalism in Singapore and Malaya 1877-1912," *Modern Asian Studies* 16, no. 3 (1982): 399-400.

3. Cheah Boon Kheng. *Red Star over Malaya: Resistance and Social Conflict During and After the Japanese Occupation of Malaya, 1941-1946* (Singapore: NUS Press, 2003), 8.

4. Victor Purcell, *Chinese in Southeast Asia* (London: Oxford University Press, 1965), 147.

5. Tan Liok Ee "Baggage from the Past, Eyes on the Future: Chinese Education in Malaysia Today," in *Ethnic Chinese in Singapore and Malaysia: A Dialogue between Tradition and Modernity,* ed. Leo Suryadinata (Singapore: Time Academic Press, 2002), 156-58.

6. Carl Trocki, *Opium and Empire: Chinese Society in Colonial Singapore, 1800-1910* (Ithaca, NY: Cornell University Press, 1990), 10-12.

7. Marie-Claire Bergere, *Sun Yat-Sen,* translated by Janet Lloyd (Stanford CA: Stanford University Press, 1998), 141-45.

8. David Strand, "Community, Society, and History in Sun Yat Sen's Sanmin Zhuyi," in *Culture and State in Chinese History,* ed. Theodore Huters, R.B. Wong, and Pauline Yu (Stanford CA: Stanford University Press, 2002), 332-36.

9. T.N. Harper, *End of Empire and the Making of Malaya* (Cambridge, UK: Cambridge University Press, 1999), 33-34.

10. Barbara Watson Andaya and Leonard Andaya, *History of Malaysia* (New York: St. Martin's Press. 2001), 226-28.

11. C.F. Yong, "Origins and Development of the Malayan Communist Movement, 1919-1930," *Modern Asian Studies* 25, no. 4 (October 1991): 627-60.

12. Tan Chee Beng, *Chinese Overseas: Comparative Cultural Issues* (Hong Kong: Hong Kong University Press, 2004), 95-96.

13. Tan, *Chinese*, 94.

14. Yen, "Overseas," 401-2.

15. For extensive information on ethnic Chinese concepts of nation and community in colonial Malaya, read Tan Eng Teik, *Rhetoric of Bangsa and Minzu: Community and Nation in Tension, the Malay Peninsula, 1900-1955* (Sydney: Monash Asia Institute, 1988).

16. Lucian C. Pye and Mary W. Pye, *Asian Power and Politics: The Cultural Dimensions of Authority* (Cambridge, MA: Harvard University Press, 1985), 251.

17. Yen Ching-Hwang, "Historical Background," in *Chinese in Malaysia,* ed. Lee Kam Hing and Tan Chee-Beng (Kuala Lumpur: Oxford University Press, 2002), 30-31.

18. Milton J. Esman, *Ethnic Politics* (Ithaca: Cornell University Press, 1994), 59.

19. Heng Pek Koon, "The Chinese Business Elite in Malaysia," in *Southeast Asian Capitalists*, ed. Ruth Thomas McVey (Ithaca, NY: Cornell Southeast Asia Program Publications, 1997), 128-29.

20. Andaya and Andaya, *History*, 206.

21. Esman, *Ethnic*, 60-61.

22. Sharon Carstens, *Histories, Cultures, Identities: Studies in Malaysian Chinese Worlds* (Singapore: Singapore University Press, 2006), 124.

23. A. Collins, "Securitization, Frankenstein's Monster, and Malaysian Education." in *Pacific Review* 18, no. 4 (December 2005): 568-70.

24. Kumar Ramakrishna, "Making Malaya Safe for Decolonization: The Rural Chinese Factor in the Counterinsurgency Campaign," in *Transformation of Southeast Asia: International Perspectives*, ed. Marc Frey, Ronald W. Pruessen, and Tai Yong Tan (New York: M.E. Sharpe, 2003), 166-67.

25. Sinnapiah Arasaratnam, "Malaysian Indians: The Formation of Incipient Society," in *Indian Communities in Southeast Asia*, ed. K. S. Sandhu and A. Mani (Singapore: Institute of Southeast Asian Studies, 2006), 184-86.

26. M.R. Stenson, *Class, Race and Colonialism in West Malaysia: The Indian Case* (St. Lucia: University of Queensland Press, 1980), 35-40.

27. Amarjit Kaur, *Wage Labour in Southeast Asia since 1840* (New York: Palgrave-Macmillan, 2004), 78-79.

28. Tai Yuen, *Labour Unrest in Colonial Malaya* (Penang, Malaysia: Universiti Sains Malaysia Publications, 1999), 37-40.

29. Arasaratnam "Malaysian Indians," 209.

30. A. Mani, "Indians in Singapore Society," in *Indian Communities in Southeast Asia*, ed. K.S. Sandhu and A. Mani (Singapore: ISEAS, 2006), 784.

31. Susan Oorjitham, "Urban Working-Class Indians in Malaysia," in *Indian Communities in Southeast Asia*, ed. K.S. Sandhu and A. Mani (Singapore: ISEAS, 2006), 505-507.

32. T. Marimuthu, "The Plantation School As an Agent of Social Reproduction," in *Indian Communities in Southeast Asia*, ed. K.S. Sandhu and A. Mani (Singapore: ISEAS, 2006), 470-75.

33. Shanthini Pillai, *Colonial Visions, Postcolonial Revisions: Images of the Indian Diaspora in Malaysia* (Newcastle, UK: Cambridge Scholars Publishing, 2007), 82-105.

34. Chandra Muzaffar, "Political Marginalization in Malaysia," in *Indian Communities in Southeast Asia*, ed. K.S. Sandhu and A. Mani (Singapore: ISEAS, 2006), 221-22.

35. Rajeswary Brown, "The Contemporary Indian Elites," in Indian Communities in Southeast Asia, ed. K.S. Sandhu and A. Mani (Singapore: ISEAS, 2006), 240-45.

36. Kernail Singh Sandhu, *Indians in Malaya: Some Aspects of their Immigration and Settlement (1786–1957)* (Cambridge, UK: University Press, 2010), 810.

37. D. G. E. Hall, *History of Southeast Asia* (London: Macmillan, 1964), 753.

38. Mohammad Azizudin Sani, "Freedom of Speech and Democracy in Malaysia," *Asian Journal of Political Science* 16, no.1 (April 2008): 87-90.

39. Quoted in Mustapha Hussain, Insun Mustapha, and K.S. Jomo, *Malay Nationalism before UMNO: The Memoirs of Mustapha Hussain* (Kuala Lumpur: Utusan Press, 2005), 136.

40. Mark Emmanuel, "Viewspapers: The Malay Press of the 1930s," *Journal of Southeast Asian Studies* 41, no.1 (February 2010): 5-6.

41. Original Malay script used Arabic alphabets but this was soon replaced by the Roman letters. The use of the latter allowed more expedient accommodation of modern terminologies and concepts. The majority of Malays however were not used to the Latin alphabet, since community schools continued with the Arabic script well into the period of independence.

42. Emmanuel, "Viewspapers," 8-10.

43. The *Sejarah Melayu*, an oral anthology of Malay feudal and pre-feudal histories as recounted by court authorities, noted the role of the Malay ruler as being absolute and divinely legitimized. For further reading on this subject, read C.C. Brown, *Malay Annals* (Kuala Lumpur: Oxford University Press, 1976).

44. Muhammad Reduan Othman, *Islam dan Masyarakat Melayu: Peranan dan Pengaruh Timur Tengah* (Kuala Lumpur: University of Malaya Press, 2005), 205-210.

45. William Roff, *Origins of Malay Nationalism* (Kuala Lumpur: Oxford University Press, 1995), 254-57.

46. Wendy Mukherjee, "Kaum Muda and Kaum Tua in West Java," in *Islam: Essays on Scripture, Thought, and Society: A Festschrift in Honour of Anthony H. Johns,* ed. Peter G. Riddell and Tony Street (London: BRILL, 1997), 310-315.

47. Taufik Abdullah, *Schools and Politics: The Kaum Muda Movement in West Sumatra 1927-1933* (Singapore: Equinox, 2009), 22-24.

48. Cheah, *Red Star*, 10.

49. K.G. Tregonning, *Papers on Malayan History* (Singapore: University of Malay Press, 1962), 165.

50. Cheah, *Red Star*, 44.

51. Andaya and Andaya, *History*, 249.

52. Hussain, Mustapha, and Jomo, *Malay Nationalism,* 140.

53. See Hussain, Mustapha, and Jomo, *Malay Nationalism*, 287-93. The Japanese surrender was proclaimed on August 15, 1945. Indonesian nationalists Sukarno and Hatta declared their country's independence on August 17 without including Malaya, prompting some members of the former KMM to declare Malaya's independence unilaterally.

54. Hussain, Mustapha, and Jomo, *Malay Nationalism*, 136-44.

55. Roff, *Origins,* 255.

56. Hall, *History*, 754.

57. Roff, *Origins*, 235-237.

58. Shamsul Amri Baharuddin, "Economic Dimension of Malay Nationalism," *Developing Economies* 35, no. 3 (September 1997): 244.

59. The *Greater East Asia Co-Prosperity Sphere* was in effect, a doctrine aimed at assimilating populations across all Japanese colonial territories in Asia through familiarity with Japanese history, culture, and language. It was also designed to keep Asia's peoples, markets, and resources under Japan's military control. For more information on this topic, especially with regards to perspectives of the war through Japanese lens, read John Dower, *War without Mercy: Race & Power in the Pacific War* (New York: Random House, 1986), 262-93.

60. Yoji Akashi, "Japanese Policy towards Malayan Chinese." In *Japan and Southeast Asia: From the Meiji Restoration to 1945*, ed. Wolf Mendl (London: Routledge, 2001), 284.

61. Abu Talib Ahmad, "The Malay Community and Memory of the Japanese Occupation," in *War and Memory in Malaysia and Singapore*, ed. Patricia Pui Huen Lim and Diana Wong, (Singapore: Institute of Southeast Asian Studies, 2000), 88-90.

62. Harper, *End of Empire*, 55-57.

63. Andaya and Andaya, *History*, 253.

64. Charles Cruickshank, *SOE in the Far East* (Oxford: Oxford University Press, 1983), 195-210.

65. A. J. Stockwell, *British Policy and Malay Politics during the Malayan Union Experiment 1945-1948* (Kuala Lumpur: Oxford University Press, 1979), 146-48. In predominantly Malay areas, there had been few occasions of hostility with the Chinese since the level of capitalist competition would also have been minimal.

66. Cheah, *Red Star*, 170-77.

67. Article 21 (3) of The Universal Declaration of Human Rights 1948 reads: "The will of the people shall be the basis of the authority of government; this will shall be expressed in periodic and genuine elections which shall be by universal and equal suffrage and shall be held by secret vote or by equivalent free voting procedures."

68. Drabble, *Economic History*, 13.

69. A. J. Stockwell, "British Imperial Policy and Decolonization in Malaya, 1942-52," in *Southeast Asia: Colonial History Volume 5*, ed. Paul Kratoska (London: Routledge, 2001), 211.

70. Ronald Hyam, *Britain's Declining Empire: The Road to Decolonisation 1918-1968* (Cambridge, UK: Cambridge University Press, 2006), 72-83. Although the economies of Malaya and Singapore were inextricably linked, the British decided to exclude Singapore from the Union. Singapore's role in the world economy had always been as an international *entreport*, attracting commerce and investments through free-trade. Malaya on the other hand, generated its earnings through duties on exports of raw material as well as on imports of manufactured goods. Furthermore, any type of unification between Malaya and Singapore would have added the predominantly Chinese population in Singapore to the already huge ethnic Chinese population in Malaya, thus numerically overwhelming the Malays.

71. Andaya and Andaya, *History*, 244. The sultans had conceded to the Malayan Union plan partly to make up for their role in consenting to Japanese rule. Sir Harold McMichael, the British special envoy, constantly reminded them of this as he engineered the procurement of their signatures.

72. Andaya and Andaya, *History*, 246-47.

73. Andaya and Andaya, *History*, 255.

74. Ariffin Omar, *Bangsa Melayu: Malay Concepts of Democracy and Community, 1945-50* (Kuala Lumpur: University of Malaya Press, 1993), 49.

75. Hashim Salleh, "Globalization and the Challenges to Malay Nationalism as the Essence of Malaysian Nationalism," in *Nationalism and Globalization: East and West*, ed. Leo Suryadinata (Singapore: ISEAS, 2000), 134-35.

76. Firdaus Abdulllah, *Radical Malay Politics: Its Origins and Early Development* (Petaling Jaya, Malaysia: Pelanduk, 1985), 57-59.

77. John Nagl, *Counterinsurgency Lessons from Malaya and Vietnam: Learning to Eat Soup with a Knife* (New York: Praeger. 2002), 62.

78. Cheah Boon Kheng, "Erosions of Ideological Hegemony and Royal Power and the Rise of Post-War Malay Nationalism," *Journal of South East Asian Studies* 19, no. 1 (March 1988), 25.

79. C. M. Turnbull, *Short History of Malaysia, Singapore, and Brunei* (Winchester, MA: Allen and Unwin, 1989), 242-243.

80. Timothy Lomperis, *From People's War to People's Rule: Insurgency, Intervention, and Lessons from Vietnam* (Chapel Hill, NC: UNC Press, 1996), 204.

81. Turnbull, *History*, 244.

82. Nabir Abdullah, *Maahad Ilhya Assyarif, Gunung Semanggol 1934–1959* (Bangi, Malaysia: National University of Malaysia, 1976), 124-29.

83. Shamsul, "Economic Dimension," 246-247.

84. Hua Wu Yin, *Class and Communalism in Malaysia: Politics in a Dependent Capitalist State* (London: ZED, 1982), 73.

85. Karl Hack, "Theories and Approaches to British Decolonization in Southeast Asia," in *Transformation of Southeast Asia: International Perspectives on Decolonization*, ed. Marc Frey, Ronald W. Pruessen, and Tai Yong Tan, (New York: M.E. Sharpe, 2004), 109-110.

86. Diane Mauzy, "From Malay Nationalism to Malaysian Nation?" in *After Independence: Making and Protecting the Nation in Postcolonial and Post-Communist States*, ed. Lowell Barrington (Ann Arbor, MI: University of Michigan Press, 2006), 51.

87. R. S. Milne, and Diane K. Mauzy, *Malaysian Politics under Mahathir* (London: Routledge, 1999), 125-128.

88. Cheah Boon Kheng, *Malaysia: The Making of a Nation* (Singapore: Institute of Southeast Asian Studies, 2002), 26.

89. C. F. Yong, "The Origins and Development of the Malayan Communist Movement, 1919-1930," *Modern Asian Studies* 25, no. 4 (October 1991): 641-45.

90. In-Won Hwang, *Personalized Politics: The Malaysian State under Mahathir* (Singapore; ISEA, 2003), 58.

91. K.S. Jomo, *Question of Class: Capital, the State, and Uneven Development in Malaya* (Singapore: University of Singapore Press, 1986), 247.

92. Shamsul, "Economic Dimensions," 243. Article 153 of the Federal Constitution reads: "It shall be the responsibility of the Yang di-Pertuan Agong (King) to safeguard the special position of the Malays and the legitimate interests of other communities in accordance with the provisions of this Article." The Second Clause adds: "the Yang di-Pertuan Agong shall safeguard the special position of the Malays by reserving positions of such proportion as he may deem reasonable in a) the public service b) educational facilities and c) business licenses."

93. Shamsul, "Economic Dimensions," 244.

94. Mauzy "From Malay," 53.

95. Cheah, *Malaysia*, 91.

96. Stockwell, "British Imperial," 214.

97. For more information on consociational theory, read Arendt Lijphart, *Thinking about Democracy: Power Sharing and Majority Rule in Theory and Practice* (New York: Routledge, 2008).

98. Milne and Mauzy, *Malaysian Politics*, 19.

99. Tan Tai Yong, *Creating Greater Malaysia: Decolonization and the Politics of Merger* (Singapore: ISEAS, 2008), 1-13.

100. Gordon P. Means, "Soft Authoritarianism in Malaysia and Singapore," *Journal of Democracy* 7, no. 4 (October 1996): 316.

101. James P. Ongkili, *Nation-Building in Malaysia, 1946-1974* (Singapore: Oxford University Press, 1985), 169.

102. Stanley S. Bedlington, *Malaysia and Singapore: The Building of New States* (Ithaca, NY: Cornell University Press, 1978), 96-99.

103. Andaya and Andaya, *History*, 272.

104. Michael B. Leigh, *Rising Moon: Political Change in Sarawak* (Sydney: Sydney University Press, 1974), 39.

105. R. S. Milne and K.J. Ratnam, *Malaysia: New States in a New Nation* (London: Frank Cass, 1974), 14-15.

106. Andaya and Andaya, *History*, 277-78.

Chapter 5
The Leftists in Malaya, 1945-1963

Where divergent ethnonational goals impeded the formation of a united nationalist agenda, the class-centered approach of socialism seemed to have provided a broader and more inclusive nationalist alternative for many independence movements in the world's periphery. In neighboring Dutch East Indies (Indonesia) for example, Soviet-styled leftists had assumed a significant role in that country's national independence that they were also able to inspire their counterparts across the Straits of Malacca on pursuing a similar objective in Malaya.

However, the largest and most influential communist organization in Malaya and Singapore, the Malayan Communist Party (MCP), had its origins rooted in the Chinese mainland. With their support base generally confined within the Chinese working class, the MCP took advantage of the declining postwar economy to embark on the struggle for Malayan national independence through the creation of a Malayan socialist state. For Britain, the control of an independent Malaya by an adversarial left-wing government, bent on nationalizing the economy, was an outcome they wanted to avoid. This chapter examines the extent to which the MCP could have successfully spearheaded an alternative nationalist front for Malayan independence. It will also look at the world systemic response by Britain and the western world in addressing the leftist challenge in the region, and its impact on the effectiveness of the movement.

The Malayan Communist Party (MCP)

The Malayan Communist Party (MCP) emerged as the earliest and most active left-wing political organization in pre-independence Malaya. Borne out of the General Labour Union in 1930, it served to replace its precursor, the Nanyang Communist Party.[1] Mass unemployment caused by the economic depression of the late 1920s had provided the MCP with support from a pool of discontented industrial workers in Singapore. By the early 1930s, unofficial membership in the MCP had reached nearly 15,000.[2] From the onset, the MCP had been declared illegal by the British colonial state. At the party's formal inauguration in

Singapore, the colonial police arrested many of its leaders and deported several of the foreign guests in attendance, including a man by the name of Ho Chi Minh.[3]

In 1936, the Chinese Communist Party (CCP) in China forged an alliance with the Kuomintang (KMT) in the form of the *National Salvation Movement*. Both parties had agreed to temporarily put aside their political differences in an effort to help liberate China from Japanese occupation. In Malaya, the MCP, together with the local KMT, emulated the mainland merger and established their own *United Front*. This alliance would be highly beneficial for the MCP as it allowed the party valuable access to KMT members in Malaya.

Support for the MCP, especially among the urban Chinese-educated classes would climax during a period known as the *Malayan Spring*. This was a brief phase of unprecedented political tolerance in Malaya, partly attributed to the relatively liberal policies of the Labour Party in Britain, which came to power in 1945. The MCP happened to be an important beneficiary of this policy. The social-progressive approach of the Labour government allowed for the operational presence of socialist movements in Malaya. This did not in any way imply however, any willingness on its part to endorse organizations that openly advocated for a Leninist or Moaist type totalitarianism.[4] This meant that the MCP and other leftist organizations were free to run their memberships so long as their political goals refrained from supporting a revolution in Malaya and were not in any way threatening British interests in the region. Another reason for the accommodation given to the MCP had been Britain's official acknowledgement of the party's insurgency efforts against the Japanese through its armed wing the MPAJA during the war. Some of the "rewards" given to the MCP came in the form of the legalization of the party as well as the appointment of several of its leading members to the Governor's Advisory Council in Singapore.

In spite of this however, there had always been an air of mutual caution in the relationship between the British military and the MCP. Aware of the party's strong affiliations with China and having witnessed the ruthlessness with which the MPAJA carried out its policing duties during the immediate postwar period, the British military had always taken a distrustful stand toward the party.[5] Likewise, the MCP was disdainful of the British, whose return to Malaya they viewed as an audacious attempt to reassert the Empire's declining glory. As a sign of its readiness for any imminent armed confrontation with the British, the MCP had assigned its secret arsenal of weapons in the care of former officers of the now disbanded MPAJA.[6]

Meanwhile, the MCP also made full use of its new-found prestige and the relative political freedom of the early postwar years to demand a series of institutional and political reforms. Embodied within the party's *Eight Principles,* these stipulations pertained primarily to freedoms of expression, the ability for workers to go on strike, and a minimum wage for industrial workers. More importantly, the MCP also insisted on the right of the Malayan people to vote in a national assembly for the eventual creation of an independent Malayan republic. As expected, the British were not willing to lend any serious consideration to these demands, especially the one related to a fully functioning electorate in Malaya, which could potentially allow the communists to come into power.[7]

In the same vein, the MCP had anticipated the disinclination on the part of the British to possibly accede its rule in Malaya to any left-wing party. At the same time, they also believed that any major military confrontation against the British was not forthcoming at that point in time, especially when the latter assumed superiority in terms of both personnel and weaponry.[8] Instead, the MCP decided on building up its existing support base from among the mainly urban ethnic Chinese working class, who not only looked to the MCP for labor-related reforms but also passionately lauded communism's highly-organized commitment to the liberation campaign in China.

Importantly, the social hardships emanating from a ruined post-war economy once again provided a conducive and favorable climate for workers' support for the MCP. The near-devastation of the Malayan capitalist economy had, among other things, encouraged numerous employers to carry out prolonged suppression of wages, which had caused immeasurable suffering among lower-income workers. Thus the MCP naturally attracted a large number of labor activists and civil groups for its relentless efforts in seeking employment-related remedies on behalf of workers. Soon, the effective reach of the MCP and those sympathetic to its cause would seep into the various leadership ranks of major civil society groups and labor unions in both Malaya and Singapore.

The MCP and Labor Unions

Through the help of many of its members in the various workers' unions, the MCP became the driving force behind the conglomeration of the General Labour Unions in both Singapore and Malaya into a larger and more consolidated Pan-Malayan Federation of Trade Unions (PMFTU) in 1946. Within a short time, the PMFTU had controlled 241 out of 277 registered unions with members comprising 70 percent of the labor force in Malaya and Singapore.[9]

The strength and vigor of the PMFTU spurred on hundreds of workers to declare a series of nationwide strikes throughout Malaya. A substantial number of factories, shipyards, and even public transportation networks were systematically paralyzed in the first few months after the call for strike. In February, 1947, alone, 171,000 man-days were lost in Singapore, while in Malaya it was 96,000.[10] A number of these strikes occurred without any serious violence, with some even yielding impressive outcomes. In the cases of the Malayan Collieries and Singapore Traction Company disputes for example, workers managed to obtain increases in wages as well as improved working conditions.[11] However, there were also incidents in which aggressive street demonstrations culminated into bloody clashes with police, leaving scores of people dead.

The violent nature of some of these confrontations sufficiently distressed the British into seriously reassessing their relationship with the MCP. Furthermore, the party had also boldly supported Mao Zedong's *new democracy* agenda, which among other things called for the transition of colonies in the global periphery into independent communist states.[12] In many of its speeches and meetings, the MCP overtly applauded socialist uprisings in Indonesia, the Philippines, and Vietnam, and called for spiritual and political camaraderie among various left-wing groups throughout the region.[13] Against the backdrop of cold war politics, Britain saw the drastic need to block any possible communist accession to power in Malaya.

The MCP and Ethnic Chinese Support

The MCP plan for an independent *Malayan People's Democratic Republic* had always included Singapore. The city-port was the industrial heart of the Malayan capitalist economy, making it the bastion of labor activism in Southeast Asia. The island's self-contained geographical layout and significant Chinese working class presence, in particular, had been crucial in the successful mobilization of various forms of labor unions that housed all types of workers, ranging from teachers to cabaret dancers.[14] These socio-economic factors provided the MCP with what it believed to be a strong source of support for a possible revolution in Malaya, starting from a heavily-Chinese populated Singapore.

It is for this reason also, that from the beginning, the approach of the MCP, both in vision and membership, took on a China-focused orientation. In fact, the initial struggles of the MCP had been primarily concentrated in the extension of Chinese Communist Party interests into Malaya. The party's Central Executive Committee also comprised mostly of ethnic Chinese members, some coming directly from the mainland. This partially explained the party's use of Mandarin in the majority of its communications and informational exchanges.

Maintaining the party's large ethnic Chinese following also had to do with sustaining its huge sources of funding coming mainly from the various Chinese business associations such as the Chinese Chamber of Commerce. It is not surprising also that in so doing, the MCP needed to present itself as advancing the political cause of the *Nanyang* Chinese, whose goals were very much embedded in the notion of a "Malaya for the Chinese."[15] As such, it was not uncommon for the MCP to have also made explicit references to the creation of a Malayan socialist republic, hinging considerably on the vanguard of a strong Chinese working class and the removal of the Malay feudal elite.[16]

The almost non-detachable relationship between the MCP and local Chinese cultural organizations would soon form a blurry line between the party's identity as a communist organization and its vehicular utility in the pursuit of Chinese ethnonational ambitions in Malaya. This apparently upset the international communist body, Third International Comintern, which had prescribed a purely class-based approach to communism's struggle across the globe.[17]

The All-Malaya Council for Joint Action (AMCJA)

The MCP's heavily Chinese following truly discredited its appearance as a multiethnic representation. The MCP soon realized the imperative of expanding its support base beyond the ethnic Chinese business and cultural associations as well as various trades union in order to commence upon a more effective and broader campaign for the national liberation of Malaya. To achieve this, the party began cooperating with several other left-leaning organizations in both Singapore and Malaya, and bringing them together under the umbrella of the All-Malaya Council for Joint Action or AMCJA.[18]

Formed in 1946 as a conglomeration of mainly non-Malay civil society groups, the AMCJA was highly supportive of the Malayan Union and its equal citizenship laws. Among the more prominent political organizations in this coalition was the Malayan Democratic Union (MDU). Established in 1946, the MDU comprised of several English-educated non-Malays that included distinguished Singapore-based socialists such as Gerald De Cruz, Philip Hoalim, John Eber, and Lim Hong Bee.[19] Seriously concerned with the militant UMNO-inspired Malay protests against the Malayan Union proposal, the MDU feared that a Malay-centered independent Malaya would spell the end of non-Malay ethnic and cultural interests in the country.

Egged on by MCP agents within AMCJA, the MDU, together with other constituent bodies within the coalition such as the Associated Chinese Chamber of Commerce, the Straits Chinese British Association, the Malayan Indian Congress (MIC), and the Pan-Malayan Federation of Trade Unions (PMFTU), initially called for a united and independent socialist Malaya incorporating Singapore. The coalition's proposed constitutional structure emphasized the provision of a Malayan nationality with equal citizenship and rights for all individuals living in Malaya and Singapore, which of course, appealed to the many non-Malay communities in both these places. By 1947, the AMCJA membership was said to have grown into the tens of thousands.[20]

Malay Leftists and PUTERA

Shortly after the end of the Second World War in 1945, prominent Malay socialists Dr. Burhanuddin Al-Hilmy, Ahmad Boestamam, and Ishak Haji Muhammad founded the Malay Nationalist Party (MNP). Soon, other Malay leftists initially allied to UMNO also became disapproving of the party's increasingly conservative outlook and followed suit into either joining the MNP or focusing on their own workers' organizations.[21] The MNP had initially subscribed to AMCJA membership in 1946 but left soon after, fearing that its lack of legitimacy and support among Malays would further isolate its struggle for a Malay socialist state. This was especially crucial after UMNO had publicly labeled the party as "Malay traitors."[22]

In the aftermath of the Malayan Union protests, the MNP became highly critical of the way the British began to engage only the Malay bourgeoisie in their discussions regarding the proposal of a Federation of Malaya. The party's request for a share in Malaya's new leadership had been palpably disregarded by both the British and UMNO. The MNP subsequently created its own *Pusat Tenaga Raayat* (Peoples' Labor Center) or PUTERA. This conglomeration comprised of left-leaning Malay-Muslim organizations such as the *Angkatan Pemuda Insaf* (Liberated Youth Corps), the Peasants Union, the Islamic *Hizbul Muslimin*, and the women's arm of the MNP, *Angkatan Wanita Sedar* (Women's Awareness Corp).

Like the KMM, the MNP leadership had been greatly mentored by Soviet-schooled Indonesian communists such as Mokhtaruddin Lasso, Alimin, and Tan Malaka.[23] The legacy of the KMM within this party can also be traced through its ultimate goal of forming a political union between Malaya, Indonesia, and Singapore in the shape of a Malay socialist state or *Indonesia Raya*. In major ways, the MNP's socialist platform and staunch support for a Soviet model socialist system focusing on economic justice and worker equality paralleled its understanding of the political realities surrounding a multicultural Malaya. Thus it was not surprising that the MNP became the first leading Malay organization to openly state that an independent Malaya must embrace the rights of ethnic Chinese and Indians as full Malayan citizens.[24] This outward support for ethnic equality in Malaya and Singapore opened up the possibility for closer relations between PUTERA and the AMCJA.

AMCJA-PUTERA Leftist Coalition

The MCP's wish for a larger coalition of socialist organizations in Malaya and Singapore was soon granted in March 1947 when the MNP led-PUTERA joined forces with AMCJA to provide Malaya its first ever broad-based political alliance.[25] The coming together of the two socialist blocs into a coalition mirrored their immediate need in attempting to prevent the creation of a capitalist Federation of Malaya, which was being brokered between the British and UMNO following the abrogation of the Malayan Union.

With a membership of more than 150,000, the AMCJA-PUTERA was a heavily diverse assortment of communists, socialists, Chinese merchants, trade unionists, Malay nationalists, and even Islamic scholars. Despite this, the AMCJA-PUTERA worked remarkably swift to draft an alternative constitution for Malaya called the *People's Constitution*. The main principles of the proposed constitution included the following articles.[26]

1. A United Malaya, inclusive of Singapore;

2. A fully elected central legislature for the whole of Malaya;
3. Equal political rights for all who regarded Malaya as their real home and as the object of their loyalty;
4. Malay rulers to assume the position of fully sovereign and constitutional rulers, accepting advice not from British advisers but from the people through democratic institutions;
5. Matters of Muslim religion and Malay custom to be under the sole control of Malays;
6. Special attention to be paid to the advancement of indigenous Malays;
7. Malay as official language of the country;
8. Foreign affairs and defense of the country should be the joint responsibility of the Government of Malaya and His Majesty's Government (Britain);
9. The term *Melayu* or Malay should be the title of any citizenship or national status in Malaya; and
10. The national flag of the country should incorporate the red and white of the Indonesian national flag.

This alternative constitution was a result of diligent discussions between the leaderships of the various factions of the AMCJA-PUTERA.[27] With expeditious crafting of its contents, the proposal reflected the contributions and compromises made by each group with regards to their major concerns in the political structure of an independent Malaya. This included the highly controversial issue of Malayan citizenship. The AMCJA was adamant in including the provision for all Malayan citizens, equal rights to political, economic, educational and cultural opportunities, irrespective of race, ethnicity, or gender. To accommodate the goals of worker-centered socialist groups, the coalition's constitution also made sure there was prioritization in employer protection of all workers through safe and fair working conditions, a minimum wage, and a national social security system. The proposal also championed the right to strike for workers if stipulated work conditions are not met to standards.[28]

While the AMCJA initially concentrated mainly on the urban non-Malay working class as its support base, it broadened its outlook and recommendations to include the dormant Malay peasantry, whose future support and contributive role in a socialist state was considered by PUTERA to be extremely vital. Articles 4, 5, and 6 of the People's Constitution, which served to secure the status of Malays as the indigenous groups, were drafted with this in mind. Despite the mention of special allowances for special Malay development (Article 6), there was however, nothing in the constitution that pointed to any special citizenship rights allocated specifically for Malays, as advocated by UMNO.

Article 9 was an interesting point. The concept of *Malay* under the People's Constitution was somewhat de-constructed to include other ethnic groups in Malaya.[29] The MNP in particular, had been uncomfortable with the British concept of *Malayan*, which did not clearly address whether Malaya was a single nation-state or a multiethnic country. Instead, the MNP insisted on the comprehensive categorization of *Malay* (as the people of Malaya) to be inclusive of all ethnic groups who officially affirmed nativity to Malaya and considered Malaya as their country of citizenship. The implication here is that although the various ethnic groups will have the freedom to practice their respective religions, language, and cultural heritage, they would all nevertheless be officially referred to as Malays. This newly-constructed identity would be enhanced by the recognition of the Malay language as the official language of Malaya, as emphasized in Article 7, and its eventual fluency by all of Malaya's citizens.[30] This nationalization process would have been comparable to the Americanization process in the United States, where despite the multiethnic composition of America created by the country's immigrant heritage, literacy and fluency in the English language would gradually provide the determining aspects of American citizenship and identity.

Despite the seemingly progressive nature of this proposal, the British rejected the AMCJA-PUTERA constitution and along with it, any possible discussion with the coalition. The reasoning given was that the British had never been interested in negotiating with groups they had sought to exclude in the first place, namely the various MCP-led trade unions and the Malay leftists.[31] Alienating left-wing groups was a central priority for the British, who were resolute in preparing Malaya as a capitalist democracy. Intent in perpetually keeping Malaya under its influence, the British were not about to allow any alternative system to jeopardize this long-term objective, especially one that would ultimately "convert" the Malay masses into obedient socialists.

In response to the snubbing by the British, the AMCJA-PUTERA decided to initiate a *hartal* (stoppage of economic activity for a specified period) on October 20, 1947.[32] This event, which has rarely been discussed in local mainstream texts, became a showpiece of highly-coordinated strikes by a consortium of bodies, many of whose members had never physically met in any common forum. It was however, visible to many who witnessed the *hartal*, be it in the deserted streets of Kuala Lumpur or the silent docks of Singapore, that the mass compliance with the stoppage of work was highly successful. Supported by strong networks of trade union and urban service worker groups, Chinese factory workers, Indian coffee shop owners, and Malay trishaw pullers who heeded the call for the single-day strike, the *hartal* cost the economy an estimated £4 million loss.[33]

Quick End to the AMCJA-PUTERA Coalition

The British were undaunted by the test of challenge from the MCP-inspired AMCJA-PUTERA, and carried on with the Federation of Malaya declaration in 1948.[34] The emergence of a relatively strong leftist alliance in Malaya however, compelled the British to become more determined in their cooperation with the conservative UMNO. This was especially so when close working relations between the two served to prevent any possible alliance between the Malay masses and the Malay leftists. In this respect, the British hoped that the restoration of Malay monarchies' prestige and their sovereignty under the federation agreement would entail the elevation of the Malay bourgeoisie over other social forces in Malayan politics.

Aiding the British in their plan to structure in a capitalist democracy in Malaya was the Malayan economy, whose rejuvenated growth in the late 1940s had been induced by increased global demands for raw material exports, especially rubber. By the time the AMCJA-PUTERA attempted to push ahead for the next major political action, opportunities emerging from a growing Malayan economy had already began to pull apart the political alignments between the major factions within the coalition. The massive defection of the financially strong Chinese mercantile community, namely the Associated Chinese Chambers of Commerce, was to mark the beginning of the end of the short political marriage between AMCJA and PUTERA. For this group of commercial-minded financiers, there seemed to be better gains made not only from the recovering economy but also from cooperation with the British, who began baiting their leaders with leadership positions in the new Malaya.[35]

The loss of Tan Cheng Lock, a prominent member of the English-educated *Peranakan* elite, was a particularly big blow for the coalition. Tan had been attacked from nearly every side of the political spectrum. The British had been especially disappointed with him for captaining the AMCJA-PUTERA and practically working shoulder to shoulder with leftist groups. The Malay-speaking *Peranakan* Chinese was also ostracized by many within the Chinese-educated community for obliging the Malay leftists in the articulation of Malay nationality provisions under the People's Constitution. To save his political future in an independent Malaya, he speedily opted out of the AMCJA-PUTERA, leading an exodus of other English-educated Chinese out of the coalition. Together with other prominent Chinese elite, he later co-founded the Malayan Chinese Association (MCA) in 1949.

In a move to save the AMCJA-PUTERA, a second *hartal* was called. However, by then, the coalition was already on its way to permanent collapse. Despite its brief success as well as potential for greater accomplishment, the AMCJA-PUTERA coalition never regained its influence. In retrospect, the relatively quick end to this fragile entity was hardly surprising. One major reason for this is found in the inherent philosophical inconsistencies and implicit ethnonational concerns among the coalition's members. For example, it seemed to appear that the ultimate goal of the MNP for an independent Malaya had been strictly tied to its political union with a socialist Indonesia in the form of a Malay-dominated socialist republic. Emulating the governing structure of a Russian-dominated Soviet Union, the political framework of the *Indonesia Raya* was to produce two beneficial consequences for the Malay socialists. One was that the proposed political union would demographically enlarge and strengthen the Malay population in Malaya, as part of the dominant group in a politically unified Malay-Indonesian state. This would make Malay-speaking groups the overwhelming ethnic group in the new political entity, thus providing Malay socialist leaders with the bulwark it needed against any type of external pressure threatening their political economic interests in either Malaya or Indonesia. Second, the combined sizeable population of these two countries, along with their valuable natural resources and vast territory, would potentially transform the proposed *Indonesia Raya* into an emerging Malay superpower capable of acting on equal terms with the United States, Soviet Union, India, and China. As MNP's president Dr. Burhanuddin Al-Hilmy declared, "there is no room in this world of the atomic age for small isolated countries.... the free Malaya of the future should become part of Indonesia."[36]

Similarly, ethnic Chinese members within this coalition were not able to move away from their own exuberant ethnocentrisms.[37] The Chinese-dominated Chambers of Commerce and the MCP, despite struggling on opposite ideological platforms, converged on similar sentiments for a Chinese-dominated Malaya. The subtle chauvinisms emanating from this group can often be reflected in condescending statements made by those within the higher circles of the AMCJA. In one of his speeches, AMCJA chairman Tan Cheng Lock implied that the enhancement of Malay social progress could be attained through their coexistence with the Chinese under one nation since "inferior races are raised by living in political union with races intellectually superior."[38]

There had also been obvious instances of superseding class interests displayed by the AMCJA leadership in the articulation of its political vision. For example, despite its left-wing appearance, the MDU basically represented the interests of a Singapore-based English-educated non-Malay professional elite.[39] The party's brand of socialism was different from that of the MCP or MNP, and those who really understood its *Fabianist* approach to social reform were often part of a small urban intellectual circle.[40] The MDU identified the road to socialism to be a gradual, evolutionary process that required a series of social restructuring led by the urban intelligentsia. In this respect, the MDU's socialist vision seemed contradictory and confusing to its coalition audience, most of whom prioritized an immediate British withdrawal from Malaya and Singapore. Thus it was hard to follow, for example, that while the party propagated for a socialist self-governing Malaya, it also advocated for Malaya to remain part of Britain for as long as possible in order to benefit from the country's membership in the British Commonwealth.[41]

Finally, in the absence of extensive informational channels and a more generous time frame, discussions regarding the larger structural goals of the AMCJA-PUTERA coalition inevitably excluded the large mass of people, whose interests and welfare were supposedly at the center of the coalition's political efforts. It became clear that for the most part, the leaderships of the various component organizations seemed considerably detached from that of the lower and working classes. Much of the parties' actions were also decided at the upper echelons of the various organizations, without any real or effective participation from or representation of groups at the grassroots level. The major personalities behind this coalition also belonged to an idealistic group of men and women, whose political ambitions and daily lives were effectively out of touch with the social economic realities faced by the illiterate and impoverished masses living in the rural areas, urban slums, and plantations. For the Malay peasantry in particular, memories of MPAJA vigilante justice were still hauntingly fresh that many would have had serious misgivings about any alliances with Chinese leftists. Similarly, the focus of the ethnic Chinese and Indian working classes remained entrenched in either their daily economic survival or in their hopeful return to their respective motherlands. Many were too ill-informed or simply unexposed to the constitutional and political implications relating to an independent Malaya.

Hence, while the AMCJA-PUTERA had been more effective in generating support for the *hartal* among particular trade unions and working class groups, it had yet to stamp its mark or even meaningfully impress the rest of the population with its socialist goals and aspirations. To be fair, had the coalition been given more time to achieve this, the ratification of the federation agreement could have perhaps been postponed by a rejuvenation of their collaborative efforts to include more effective and pervasive actions against the colonial state.

In any case, despite the break-up of the AMCJA-PUTERA, the coalition should be remembered for its pioneer work in Malayan inter-ethnic political cooperation. The People's Constitution had been the first piece of nation-wide legal proclamation drafted by a diverse group of Malayans. For its Chinese and Indian leaderships, this experience lent political self-reflection regarding their status in Malaya, which truly provided them with a sense of genuine attachment to being Malayan. Such inter-ethnic cooperation had been truly exemplary and even inspired a future project in multicultural cooperation—the UMNO-MCA political alliance, which came later, was in effect, modeled after this coalition.

Declining Union Activism, 1948-1950

To maintain the federation as a capitalist system, the British made sure there was total suppression of left-wing activism in Malaya. In 1948, the British colonial administration reacted to the numerous civil unrests by strictly enforcing the prewar Societies and Trade Union Ordinances. These laws enabled the state to oversee the sources of organizational funding of various civil associations and unions as well as filter these groups' memberships for potentially "subversive" elements. This was exceptionally harmful for the various labor organizations that had previously cherished their autonomous status.

The Registrar of Societies as well as the Registrar of Trades Union was also empowered to decide on the legality of particular associations based on these criteria. Such power allowed them the ability to declare an association illegal if its organizational goals and pursuits were seen to be detrimental to state capitalist interests. This was the case in 1948, when the Registrar of Trade Union in Singapore refused to renew the PMFTU's registration on account of "irregularities" in membership fees and union leadership eligibility.[42] The PMFTU's deregistration was particularly harsh for the MCP, which lost its main supply of funding and source of membership recruitment.

Union activism in Malaya and Singapore further waned by new policies implemented by the colonial state aimed at effectively preventing public action by workers. This included the state's "shoot to kill" police laws where enforcement officers were given wide prerogative powers to use their ammunition on suspected "perpetrators of public peace."[43] Such severe steps taken by the colonial state were sufficiently effective in containing any likelihood among unionists, especially the less passionate ones, in participating in worker-related demonstrations or strikes.

Another important factor in helping workers steer away from any form of activism was Malaya's growing economy. The postwar economic chaos that had earlier brought on harsh living conditions in both Singapore and Malaya began to significantly subside. Along with it fell the general outward discontentment among the majority of workers who were now focusing instead on their immediate wage increases and wider economic opportunities. This augured negatively for left-wing trade unionism, which had been fervently active before the war and reached its peak during the early years of the post-war period.[44] By the end of 1949, there had been a drastic membership drop in Malaya—from 70,037 members in January to 42,288 in December of that year.[45]

The newly-structured workers' unions were radically different from the ones that existed just after the war's end. They were more accommodating and pliant in their approach, especially since leadership had to be screened and endorsed by the colonial state. Many among them preferred the advantages of working with employers in solving work-related issues, placing the future of union activities to be carefully monitored under some form of state-employer patronage. This eventually constrained union members' ability to politically wrestle for better employment benefits. For the MCP, losing the support of these unions meant that the party also lost its political grip on the working class in Malaya.

MCP and the Malayan Insurrection, 1948-1955

Unable to effectively carry out its planned urban revolutionary approach, the MCP armed itself and retreated to the hinterlands of Malaya. After attending a communist youth conference held in Calcutta, India in 1948, the MCP decided the time was ripe for a more aggressive struggle for Malaya's liberation. This was especially so when the consensual mood at the meeting pointed toward the timely and necessary use of violence in the overthrow of colonial forces throughout the periphery.[46] The new secretary-general of the MCP, Chin Peng, agreed that the party had no other realistic choice than to adopt strategies for an armed take-over of Malaya.

Utilizing a Maoist-style battle strategy, the MCP aimed for the targeted destructions of various economic infrastructures, especially those that provided vital lifelines for capitalist production in Malaya. To replenish its dwindled support based, the MCP reached out to the predominantly impoverished Chinese population living in the outskirts of rural settlements. Through these mostly illegal settlers, the MCP hoped to carry out the groundwork for the supplies of food, arms, and information to its new military wing, the Malayan National Liberation Army (MNLA).[47]

Many of these undocumented Chinese settlers had either been landless or recently retrenched from work, and driven by economic hardship and displacement to illegally reside on tracts of lands primarily appropriated for large-scale agribusiness activity. Constant disputes over land use often erupted between these squatters and European plantation owners, who often called in the police to physically remove scores of families from their homes. These settlers' experiences and hardships were fully exploited by the MCP, whose cadres regularly came to inspire and incite the settlers in using aggressive means to resist forcible evictions, including taking up firearms. This, several of them did. When a string of attacks on European managers and plantation owners resulted in several of them killed, the British colonial authorities immediately imposed a state of emergency throughout Malaya and Singapore in June 1948.[48]

Under the new Malayan Emergency Regulations, the police were conferred wide discretionary powers to detain and arrest any suspected individual without a warrant. Law enforcement officers were also allowed to intrude upon private premises if they believed the occupants were tied to any form of insurgent activity. To deter communist sympathizers from accessing caches of weapons and ammunitions, the Regulations also stipulated that the unlawful possession of firearms would automatically mandate the death penalty. All left-wing groups and activities were also outlawed.

The consequent battles between the colonial state and the MCP were ruthless on both sides. The offensive launches by the MCP against were often in the form of terrorist-style strikes that often resulted in losses of civilian lives. In turn, the colonial state, with fresh reinforcements of British troops from all over the empire, indiscriminately burned down significant numbers of primarily Chinese villages and squatter areas in order to purge the MCP of its grassroots support. In one infamous incident near Batang Kali in west-central Malaya, a group of Scots Guardsmen massacred 24 suspected MCP sympathizers, who actually turned out to be ordinary day laborers.[49]

Committed to cutting off the civilian population from the MCP, undercover police officers began penetrating into the party's supply network, known as the *Min Yuen*.[50] The success of these secret operations on each side greatly depended on the detection of underground information relayed through networks of secret messengers or "running dogs."[51] The discovery of adversaries and betrayers among members was equally harsh on both sides. The colonial state often detained, interrogated, or even executed individuals who provided resources to the enemy. The MCP too, behaved just as brutally against those they assumed to be state informants or moles. In the larger scenario, the major strategy taken by both sides of the conflict seemed to be pivoted on the implantation of fear among the population in order to prevent them from cooperating with the enemy.

Gradually, the MCP began to experience a sizeable growth in party membership among Malays too. With the disbanding of the AMCJA-PUTERA coalition and the banning of left-wing Malay organizations, the more radical Malay leftists chose to join their few counterparts already in the MCP. The most prominent figure was party committee chairman Musa Ahmad, who was formerly from the MNP. Others included Abdullah C.D, Rashid Maidin, Ibrahim Mohammed, and top woman member, Shamsiah Fakeh. Malay peasant sympathy for the MCP was considerably significant in the predominantly Malay states of the former UFMS, where the all-Malay Tenth Regiment of the MCP managed to generate a notable following.[52]

A high point in the insurgency for the MCP came in 1951 when their agents assassinated the British High Commissioner of Malaya, Sir Henry Gurney.[53] Although the murder of the highest ranking officer of the colonial state provided the MCP with a moral victory, the people of Malaya on the other hand, were shocked by the incident. More than anything else, they were awakened to their own vulnerability amidst the widespread violence. Condemning the MCP for its attacks on civilians, the Malayan public began to throw their full support behind the campaign against the communists.[54]

The tide of war began to turn against the MCP, soon after. The links between the rural Chinese settlers and the MNLA were also being effectively severed. Much of this success was attributed to the deployment of a similar counter-insurgency tactic used by the British during the Boer War in South Africa. During that war, the British forced hundreds of Boer civilians into camps in order to break the support lines between the Boer population and their fighters. In Malaya, the introduction of the Briggs Plan in 1950 resembled this strategy. Here, massive numbers of ethnic Chinese, nearly 400,000 in total, were resettled away from MCP underground lines and into newly-formed and heavily-guarded "Chinese New Villages."[55] The plan eventually starved the MCP of its vital supply and information sources.

Gradually, the Briggs Plan expanded to include programs designed for improving the quality of life for many of these new villagers. It included relatively generous provisions of running water and electricity as well as basic education and health services. The British especially looked to the Chinese elite within the MCA for financial assistance as well as basic social support services for these villagers.[56] The idea of course, was to wean the villagers' allegiance away from the MCP, specifically by reorienting their focus toward a more sustainable future in a capitalist Malaya. In time, many were able to gain Malayan citizenship and take advantage of new economic opportunities that in the previous decades were virtually inaccessible to this community. This did not mean that the hardships of these new villagers were easily lifted as many remained poor throughout the generations. However, this new approach in counter-insurgency was sufficiently effective in weakening the MCP, and it did provide a much better option for the conflict weary communities. As rationalized by Sir Gerald Templer, the commander of Malaya's Armed Forces and Malaya's new High Commissioner: "the answer (to the Communist problem) lies not in pouring more troops, but in the hearts and mind of the people."[57]

Regional-Global Effort against Communism: The Fall of the MCP, 1955-1960

The United States had warned the world that the spread of communism resembled a "domino effect." The viral nature of communist ideological infiltration, according to the Americans, could only be contained and eliminated through the use of aggressive strategies, including the pouring of money and arms to support capitalist regimes in areas of conflict throughout the world. Particularly concerned with communist insurrections in Southeast Asia, the United States called for coordinated diplomatic and military efforts to protect the region against communist forces, culminating in the establishment of the Southeast Asia Treaty Organization (SEATO) in 1954.[58]

The SEATO agreement was also intended to bring back and consolidate western influence in Southeast Asia. Appearing initially to be the NATO (North Atlantic Treaty Organization) equivalent in this region, SEATO however lacked much of the intensity of the former in terms of both policy prioritization and military cooperation. If anything, SEATO seemed to be a preparatory framework for deeper US military intervention in Indochina.

Although Britain and the United States were partners in efforts to insulate the world economy from global communist advancements, both of these countries were also discreetly competing for long-term geopolitical influence in Southeast Asia, always considered one of the most vitally important economic regions in the world. The British were however, at a comparative disadvantage to the Americans in terms of both their financial capacity and military prowess. They had been particularly frustrated with the drawbacks of losing their political influence in Thailand, long served as a buffer state in Southeast Asia, and which had now become a tight regional partner of the United States. In view of this, the British were determined not to lose their remaining influence in Malaya and Singapore to any other power.[59]

That the SEATO membership also included Australia and New Zealand was a big help to the British. As members of the British Commonwealth, these two countries understood the significance of Britain's task in protecting its remaining imperial interests in Malaya and Singapore. The participation and support of both Australia and New Zealand in Malaya not only helped affirm British Commonwealth presence in the few remaining British outposts in the region, but it also helped toward maintaining a communist-free Asia-Pacific region critical to the national security of both these countries. In the following years, Britain's burden in fighting the communist insurgency in Malaya would be eased by these countries' commitment in providing their share of military personnel and resources.[60]

By the mid-1950s it became increasingly apparent that the MCP was losing the war in Malaya. Lacking public support and reeling from the success of the Briggs plan, the party's armed units were increasingly pushed northwards toward the Malayan-Thai border. This was a highly advantageous development for the emerging leaders of Malaya, who needed a decisive conclusion to the communist insurgency in order to expedite Malaya's declaration of independence. Hence, the leaders of the National Alliance, together with several others from Singapore, decided to offer political amnesty to the MCP in order to quickly put an end to the insurrection. An important condition for the MCP was for its members to surrender their weapons and renounce their struggle for a communist Malaya. It was also evident to both the Malayan leaders and the MCP that once Malaya attained its independence there would be no further grounds for the MCP to wage its "war of liberation." If anything, continued communist insurrection from thereon would be conveniently portrayed by the new Malayan state as a terrorist campaign against the people of Malaya.

The two parties finally met for further negotiations in the border town of Baling in December 1955. Although the MCP made it known that it had hoped to be part of the new Malaya, the party nevertheless refused to succumb to the major terms of agreement as determined by the Malayan elite.[61] Instead, the MCP offered its own counter-proposals, which included its right to exist as a political party in Malaya. This was however, a stipulation the British and Malayan leaders were obstinately against and had been unwilling to consider. The terms of these negotiations posed serious disadvantages for the MCP, who by now had seriously lacked the resources as well as any popular support it needed to back up its demands. The Malayan elites, on the other hand, were enjoying its burgeoning legitimacy derived from the recent 1955 elections. They carried into the meeting all the confidence in the world to duly reject any of the MCP proposals and forced the party to withdraw from the talks empty-handed.[62]

The turning point of the communist insurgency came in the last big battle near Teluk Intan, on Malaya's western coast in 1958. The insurgents were soundly beaten by Malayan troops, sending what was left of the remaining MNLA units into hiding in southern Thailand. In 1960, the Emergency was officially declared over. Throughout the course of the insurrection, a total of nearly 7,000 insurgents were killed and another 4,000 captured or surrendered. Also, nearly 1,500 Malayan troops, 500 Commonwealth personnel, and around 2,500 civilians perished in the twelve-year war.[63]

Leftist Rebellion in Brunei and Sarawak, 1962

Throughout the 1950s, communist presence in Indonesia was strengthened by the country's strong alliance with the Soviet Union. Its president, Achmad Sukarno, also embarked on a close working relation with the *Partai Komunis Indonesia* (PKI or Communist Party of Indonesia). Playing off one political faction against another within his administration had been part of Sukarno's infamous divisive strategy aimed at securing his ruling power against internal political challenge. By the early 1960s, the cozy relationship he had established with the Soviets was abandoned for closer relations with China.[64] In view of these developments, Britain undertook a giant effort at the height of regional cold war politics to contain any further strengthening of communist forces into its area of interests by encouraging the formation of a greater Malaya, or Malaysia.

The creation of Malaysia subsequently sparked diplomatic protests from neighboring Philippines and Indonesia. A major point of contention against the federation had been that both countries disapproved the inclusion of the northern Borneo territories of Sabah, Sarawak, and Brunei, into the federation. The Philippines claimed that Sabah historically belonged to the Sultanate of Sulu, and as such, should be lawfully governed under the Philippine Republic. Indonesia's Sukarno added, quite rightly in some respects, that the formation of Malaysia was a neo-colonial attempt by the British and the United States to reassert western hegemonic influence in Southeast Asia. Thus influenced by his PKI advisers, Sukarno declared the federation illegal and that it contravened the spirit of non-alignment in the region. While the Philippines broke off diplomatic relations with Malaysia, the Indonesians waged a more aggressive campaign of *Konfrontasi* (Confrontation), calling for the "crushing" of the new federation at any cost and through any means.[65]

In the midst of this controversy was the oil-rich sultanate of Brunei, which had pretty much been a docile British protectorate since 1888. By the late 1950s however, the PKI had managed to push its influence into northern Borneo to eventually support the 1962 Brunei rebellion against the pro-British Sultan, Sir Omar Ali Saifuddin. Initially, Brunei was invited to join Malaysia, to which the sultan gave his full blessings. However, the socialist *Partai Rakyat Brunei* (Brunei Peoples' Party or PRB), who had won all 16 elected seats of the 22-seat Brunei Legislative Council, opposed the move.[66] Instead, the PRB called for the return of Sarawak and Sabah to Brunei through the formation of a socialist Northern Borneo Federation.

Advised by the British and Malayan leaders, the Sultan promptly rejected the PRB proposal and postponed the opening of the 1962 Legislative Council.[67] The suspension of the semi-electoral body was met by attacks on police stations, the palace, and public buildings, as well as by the occupation of several towns and villages by the PRB's North Kalimantan Army.[68] However, quick and decisive action by the British to use its armed Sarawak Rangers successfully suppressed the insurgency, followed by an official proclamation from the Sultan of Brunei that the PRB had been banned and that its members' actions were considered treasonous. In a staunchly Malay kingdom such as Brunei, this effectively translated into a public command for Bruneians to sever any remaining support for the rebellion. Some key leaders of the PRB such as A.M. Azhari, and Yasin Affendy fled into exile in Indonesia, where many still remained.[69] With Borneo's valuable oilfields deemed too vulnerable to both internal and external threats, the British thereon decided against Brunei joining Malaysia. Suppression of the Brunei rebellion also spelled the end of any democratic process in that country, which remains today as one of the few absolute monarchies in the world.

In 1965, an alleged communist coup attempt in Indonesia initiated by the PKI was foiled by the pro-western faction of the armed forces under General Suharto, with considerable support from the United States.[70] By 1966, the confrontation with Indonesia was declared over and diplomatic relations were normalized between the two countries. The exchange of ambassadors was also resumed between Malaysia and a fully US-supported Philippines, leaving the region relatively free from any serious communist threats.

Summary

This chapter examined whether ethnic and cultural divisions prevalent in colonial Malayan society could have been bridged by class-based ideologies such as socialism or communism. It posed the issue of whether a class struggle agenda could have successfully mobilized an ethnically-divided society into a unified grassroots-based anti-colonial movement in Malaya.

The findings of this chapter seem to point to several major issues during the postwar period that worked against the realization of such a goal. One, it became apparent that the heavily-Chinese MCP and the Malay leftists of the MNP were still very much tied to their own subtle but obdurate forms of ethnonationalisms. Even if the AMCJA-PUTERA coalition survived for a few more years, the MCP's China-oriented agenda and the MNP's *Indonesia Raya* objective would have further polarized the coalition's organizational aspirations into two divergent directions. Second, the discussions and decisions occurring within the coalition assumed a common set of problems and realities faced by the masses. The urban experiences of the Chinese working class for example, were very distinct from the rural hardships faced by the Malay peasants. Any reconciliation of these realities toward a cogent national goal would have required massive and highly-coordinated contribution from all sides of the coalition, which would have been difficult if each of the two main parties remained committed to its own ultimate but distinctive goals.

Furthermore, it would have been an uphill task to persuade Malay peasants to fully embrace a socialist revolution that effectively threatened the sovereignty of their traditional rulers, especially if it had any thread of association with the highly-despised MPAJA. It would also have been difficult to imagine Chinese-educated workers furnishing their support for a socialist Malaya that perceivably worked toward de-emphasizing Chinese ethnic identity. Even more telling was the distinctive class-related worldviews of each leadership faction, which did not fully take into account the interests of the grassroots it needed to mobilize in order to initiate a leftist revolution in Malaya and Singapore. Without earnest and genuine political convergence of the various ethnic and class distinctions toward a common vision, the leftist struggle in Malaya remained merely ideological in nature.

Importantly, the MCP's initial goal of bringing the various left-wing groups into the AMCJA-PUTERA coalition was related to the immediate efforts in blockading the Federation of Malaya agreement. When the federation came into being, there seemed to be no other consensual issue that could link the coalition together. As the deteriorating conditions of the postwar period gradually gave way to a rapidly improving economy, worker activism in Malaya seemed to also dissipate. The effective decline in left-wing as well as trade union memberships was further hastened by the colonial state's harsh emergency laws that aimed at violently suppressing anti-systemic activity among various civil society organizations.

Finally, through the use of superior military and logistical resources, the United States and other western countries made sure that money and human power were always available to help pre-empt or eliminate leftist challenges against capitalist states throughout the world. With the gradual demise of socialist activism in Malaysia, the question lingers as to what other alternative integrative ideologies could foster a common and popular national consciousness in Malaysia. Without any, the notion of a mass-based united democratic front in an ethnically-divided Malaysia has continued to be problematic.

Notes

1. Barbara Watson Andaya and Leonard Andaya, *History of Malaysia* (New York: St. Martin's Press. 2001), 251.

2. John Nagl, *Counterinsurgency Lessons from Malaya and Vietnam: Learning to Eat Soup with a Knife* (New York: Praeger. 2002), 60.

3. C.C. Chin and Karl Hack, *Dialogues with Chin Peng: New Light on the Malayan Communist Party* (Singapore: NUS Press, 2005), 61-63.

4. For further information, read Andrew Defty, *Britain, America and Anti-Communist Propaganda, 1945-1958: The Information Research Department* (London: Routledge, 2004), 1-25.

5. Since the MPAJA (Malayan People's Anti-Japanese Army) had been the armed wing of the Malayan Communist Party, many of its members were also MCP members.

6. Cheah Boon Kheng, *Red Star over Malaya: Resistance and Social Conflict During and After the Japanese Occupation of Malaya, 1941-1946* (Singapore: NUS Press, 2003), 257-58.

7. Cheah, *Red Star*, 233-34.

8. Chin and Hack, *Dialogues*, 265.

9. Meredith Leigh Weiss, *Protests and Possibilities: Civil Society and Coalitions for Political Change in Malaysia* (Stanford, CA; Stanford University Press, 2006), 66.

10. Man-days are calculated by taking the quantity of work divided by unit-size, and multiplied by the man-hours required to do one unit.

11. M. R. Stenson, *Industrial Conflict in Malaya* (London: Oxford University Press, 1970), 197-98.

12. Christopher Bayly and Tim Harper, *Forgotten Wars: Freedom and Revolution in Southeast Asia* (Cambridge MA: Harvard University Press, 2007), 427.

13. Bayly and Harper, *Forgotten*, 117-19.

14. C. M. Turnbull, *Short History of Malaysia, Singapore, and Brunei* (Winchester, MA: Allen and Unwin, 1989), 224.

15. Bayly and Harper, *Forgotten*, 121.

16. Karl Hack, *Defence and Decolonisation in Southeast Asia: Britain, Malaya and Singapore, 1941-1968* (London, Routledge, 2001), 115.

17. T. N. Harper, *End of Empire and the Making of Malaya* (Cambridge, UK: Cambridge University Press, 1999), 89.

18. Vidhu Verma, *Malaysia: The State and Civil Society in Transition* (Boulder, CO: Lynne Rienner, 2002), 60-61.

19. Yeo Kim Wah, *Political Development in Singapore 1945-1955* (Singapore: Singapore University Press, 1973), 88-90.

20. The total number is unclear, and claims of hundreds of thousands may in itself be an overestimate. For more information read Weiss, *Protests*, 72.

21. Ahmad Boestamam, *Merintis Jalan ke Punchak* (Kuala Lumpur: Kejora, 1972), 87.

22. James P. Ongkili, *Nation-Building in Malaysia, 1946-1974* (Singapore: Oxford University Press, 1985), 63-64.

23. Yeo, *Political*, 20-21.

24. Mustapha Hussain, Insun Mustapha, and K.S. Jomo, *Malay Nationalism before UMNO: The Memoirs of Mustapha Hussain* (Kuala Lumpur: Utusan Press, 2005), 342.

25. Cheah Boon Kheng, *Red Star over Malaya: Resistance and Social Conflict During and After the Japanese Occupation of Malaya, 1941-1946* (Singapore: NUS Press, 2003), 300.

26. Information taken from Hussain, Mustapha, and Jomo, *Malay*, 342-43

27. Hussain, Mustapha, and Jomo, *Malay*, 345-47.

28. Ongkili, *Nation Building*, 55-60.

29. Ariffin Omar, *Bangsa Melayu: Malay Concepts of Democracy and Community, 1945-50* (Kuala Lumpur: University of Malaya Press, 1993), 212-15.

30. Hussain, Mustapha, and Jomo, *Malay*, 346.

31. Stenson, *Industrial*, 177.

32. Hussain, Mustapha, and Jomo, *Malay*, 347.

33. Bayly and Harper, *Forgotten*, 369.

34. Ongkili, *Nation-Building*, 73.

35. Harper, *End of Empire*, 90-93.

36. Quoted in Muhammad Ikmal Said, "Ethnic Perspectives of the Left," in *Fragmented Vision*, ed. Joel S. Kahn and Francis Loh (Honolulu: University of Hawaii Press, 1992), 264.

37. Weiss, *Protests*, 73.

38. Tan Cheng Lock, "One Country, One People, One Government" (speech delivered at the *Presidential Address at Meeting of General Committee of the MCA*, Penang, October 30, 1949), 9

39. Harper, *End of Empire*, 85.

40. Many socialists and socialist movements have criticized the Fabianist brand of socialism, which came to be popular within the various British labor movements. Some critics even pointed out that Fabianist socialism functioned as masqueraded capitalism. According to Leon Trostky, the Fabianist aim had initially been to rescue England and capitalism from the working class by propagating a social solidarity struggle headed by the bourgeoisie rather than a genuine class struggle against the capitalist elite. For further reading on this subject, read Leon Trotsky, *Writings on Britain* (London: New Park, 1974), 48-50.

41. Bayly and Harper, *Forgotten*, 200.

42. Ian Morrison, "The Communist Uprising in Malaya," in *Southeast Asia, A Colonial History: Peaceful Transitions to Independence*, ed. Paul Kratoska (London: Routledge, 2004), 183-84.

43. Stenson, *Industrial*, 179-80.

44. Stenson, *Industrial*, 199-200.

45. Michael Morgan, "The Rise and Fall of Trade Unionism, 1945-1950," in *Malaya: The Making of a Neo-Colony*, ed. Mohamed Amin and Malcolm Caldwell (Nottingham, UK: Russell Press, 1977), 191-92.

46. Anthony Short, *Communist Insurrection in Malaya 1948-1960* (London: Oxford University Press, 1976), 43-45.

47. Nagl, *Counterinsurgency*, 63-64. The MNLA was in effect, a rejuvenation of the old MPAJA.

48. Mohammed Amin and Malcom Caldwell, *Malaya: The Making of a Neo-Colony* (Nottingham, England: Russell Press, 1977), 216. Major changes in political office were also made by the colonial state to strengthen its resolve on the communist problem in Malaya. The Governor of Malaya, Sir Edward Gent was quietly removed from office and replaced by Henry Gurney, the former Chief Secretary of British Palestine.

49. Bayly and Harper, *Forgotten*, 449-50.

50. Leon Comber, *Malaya's Secret Police, 1945-60: The Role of the Special Branch in the Malayan Emergency* (Singapore: ISEAS, 2008), 79.

51. For an excellent source on the war of attrition between the MNLA and the Malayan state, read Noel Barber, *The War of the Running Dogs* (London: Cassells, 2007).

52. Short, *Communist*, 209.

53. Hack, *Defence*, 123-124. Sir Henry Gurney's civilian entourage was ambushed while it was traveling toward Fraser's Hills, a popular mountain retreat for Europeans. He was killed while attempting to protect his wife from the ensuing crossfire. After this incident, it became a practice for military convoy to accompany state dignitaries on their travels.

54. Ongkili, *Nation Building*, 79.

55. Nagl, *Counterinsurgency*, 72-74.

56. Nagl, *Counterinsurgency*, 75.

57. Quoted in Richard Clutterbuck, *Conflict and Violence in Singapore and Malaysia 1945-1983* (Boulder, CO: Westview Press, 1985), 3.

58. Hack, *Defence*, 243-245. The founding SEATO members were the United States, the United Kingdom, France, Australia, New Zealand, the Philippines, Thailand and Pakistan.

59. Hack, *Defence*, 95-100.

60. Jeff Grey, *Military History of Australia* (Cambridge, UK: Cambridge University Press, 2008), 208-209.

61. Comber, *Malaya's* 284-86.

62. Nicholas Tarling, *Cambridge History of Southeast Asia: From World War Two to the Present* (Cambridge, UK: Cambridge University Press, 1999), 50.

63. Comber, *Malaya's*, 6-7.

64. For more information on the relationship between the PKI and Sukarno in the formative years of Indonesia's "guided democracy," read Rex Mortimer, *Indonesian Communism under Sukarno: Ideology and Politics 1959-1965* (Jakarta: Equinox Publishing).

65. *Konfrontasi* is a Malay-Indonesian word for confrontation. Declared by Sukarno, this policy involved significant but limited extents of armed combats and battles between the two countries. For more information on the *Konfrontasi,* read Will Fowler, *Britain's Secret War: The Indonesian Confrontation 1962-66* (New York: Osprey Publishing, 2006) and Greg Poulgrain, *The Genesis of Konfrontasi: Malaysia, Brunei, and Indonesia 1945-1965* (London: Crawford House, 1998).

66. Harun Abdul Majid, *Rebellion in Brunei: The 1962 Revolt, Imperialism, Confrontation, and Oil* (New York: Palgrave Macmillan, 2007), 46-55. The initial Federation of Malaysia proposal was for the inclusion of Brunei as part of Malaysia.

67. David Easter, "Keep the Indonesian Pot Boiling: Western Covert Intervention in Indonesia, October 1965-March 1966," *Cold War History* 5, no. 1 (February 2005): 22-44.

68. Harun, *Rebellion*, 105-106.

69. David Easter, *Britain and the Confrontation with Indonesia 1960-66* (New York: St. Martin's Press), 50-53.

70. Easter, *Britain*, 64-66.

Chapter 6
Dependent Development and State-Capital Alliance, 1957-2011

Malaysia's ethnic power-sharing system has provided an economic environment accommodative to foreign capitalists, allaying anxieties on the part of western powers with regards to any potential disruptions to their capitalist production processes as well as markets security in the region. An expanding industrial economy has also furnished Malaysia's ruling elites within the National Alliance (National Front after 1974) with the wealth creation opportunities and long-term political monopoly they needed to stay in power. However, the road to full industrialization for any developing country requires generous incentives from capitalists for massive investments in technology, labor, and product development. For this purpose, the Malaysian state has assumed extensive control over the country's economy in order to procure these investments as well as ensure that the flows and distributions of resources would benefit the state, its ruling elites, and major investors.

Import-Substitution Development, 1957-1970

Throughout the 1950s and 1960s, Malaya's natural resources were its only lifeline to the world economy. Rubber re-emerged briefly as a sought-after commodity during the Korean War, but in time, American stockpiling practices and the introduction of synthetically manufactured rubber kept the price of natural rubber consistently low in the international market. The Malayan ruling elites were very much aware that their political survival pivoted on a buoyant economy. By the 1960s, it became apparent that the increasing destabilization of world commodity prices, coupled with the inability of developing countries to influence production and exports of raw materials, would force the Malaysian state to consider alternative paths to economic growth. Following the footsteps of other developing countries with light industrial infrastructure, the state chose the route of economic self-sufficiency through import-substitution as a way to overcome the burden of paying for expensive industrial imports.

Still very much an agrarian economy, Malaya's approach to import-substitution development could only be stimulated by a constant supply of capital investments from outside the country. Hence, at the strong recommendation of the World Bank, the Pioneer Industries Ordinance 1958 was passed by the Malayan parliament to help the country draw much-needed investments for these industries. The heart of the ordinance aimed at allowing for provisions of generous tax benefits and subsidization of infrastructure development in the form of transportation networks and industrial estates for foreign corporations in their quest to start up local infant industries in Malaya. It was hoped that these corporations would help out their local "pioneer" counterparts, or in some cases, local subsidiaries, with higher-end market and technical support.[1]

In 1960, the Malayan Industrial Development Finance Limited was established as a serious step toward providing incentives for foreign corporations to directly invest in the various import-substitution industries, namely automobile assembly, electronics, and textiles.[2] The goal was for these pioneer companies to eventually encourage greater domestic, namely Malay, capital participation and investments through joint ventures between local and foreign companies. It was in these industries too that the private sector was to generate low-skilled labor employment among the local population.

Effective protection rates for many of these companies increased from 15 percent in 1962 to 45 percent in 1966, imparting enormous profit-taking advantages to primarily foreign-owned interests.[3] Although the import-substitution approach was meant to open up greater local commercial and industrial activity in Malaya, it virtually gave foreign companies extensive control over the economy through full ownership of their local subsidiaries. Foreign corporation ownership grew from 38.5 percent of all large business concerns in 1959 to 54.7 percent in 1971. Activities arising from import-substitution industries contributed to more than half of industrial growth in Malaysia over the same period.[4]

At the onset of independence in the mid-1950s, the ethnic Chinese business community had traditionally run Malaya's local commerce, which grew out from a commodity circulation structure controlled by a few large European oligopolistic firms. Chinese capital within the local commercial networks was mainly connected to the production and distribution of goods as well as services in transportation, retail, construction, and real-estate.[5] Capital directly linked to the international commodity circuits was primarily invested in production chains along the export and import sectors in medium or light industrial manufacturing and raw commodity processing such as tin-smelting, timber-related production, and export food processing.[6]

A majority of these ethnic Chinese businesses was organized along kinship monopolies, making them virtually impenetrable commercial fortresses. As a consolidated merchant community, Chinese capitalists were thus able to exploit significant opportunities provided by the import-substitution economy. Chinese finance and light manufacturing investments, for instance, received impressive boosts from import-substitution industrial activities since these sectors functioned as supplementary capital for many small-scale industrial joint ventures with foreign firms. Local Chinese commerce was also able to grow through their material and services supply networks for the overall expanding urban-based economy. This was especially true in areas of construction, retail, and wholesaling.[7]

In contrast, Malay economic participation in the 1960s continued to perform miserably. Malay and Bumiputera businesses could not move beyond the traditional cottage industries and small sub-contracting works. Import-substitution industrial activities tended to benefit only a handful of Malay entrepreneurs with likely political links to the inner circles of UMNO. For lack of capital and experience, many of these Malay businessmen also often established joint partnerships with the more established Chinese entrepreneurs in setting up various pioneer status companies.[8]

The timing and volume of foreign direct investments (FDI) throughout the 1960s became critical in determining the pattern and rate of Malaysia's national economic growth, which was slowly becoming industry-based. The country's gross domestic product (GDP) grew an average of 4.7 percent from 1961 to 1965 and about 5 percent during the period 1966 to 1970.[9] While it was true that foreign corporations profited the most from Malaysia's economic growth, local Chinese capital also gained relatively huge returns from its own investments during this period, especially since its supplementary role in the economy had not been in any direct competition with foreign capital.[10]

There had been much concern among many Malays regarding the vast amounts of ethnic Chinese wealth flowing within Malaysia's economic growth during this period. Interestingly, there seemed to have been scarcely any mention of the huge profit margins acquired by foreign companies and their expatriates, who raked in the largest share of corporate earnings and held the highest volumes of assets under the state's import-substitution policy of the 1960s.

Continuing Ethnic Inequality in Malaysia, 1957-1970

The early years of independence saw a deepening inequality between non-Malays and Malays. In 1957, the mean monthly income for Malays was US$140, while the median was US$112. Although these figures climbed by 23 percent (US$172) and 9 percent (US$122) respectively in 1970, Chinese mean and median household incomes increased at much higher rates. They were, respectively, by 26 percent to US$381, and 20 percent reaching US$269 for the same year. Despite their general poverty, the ethnic Indian group's mean and medium incomes too were also slightly higher than Malays in 1970, standing at US$260 and US$191 respectively.[11]

In terms of the country's sector-based employment, a 1968 data revealed that 65.8 percent of Malays still participated in low-wage agricultural and plantation work, compared to 31 percent Chinese and 51.8 percent Indians. The ethnic Chinese also still dominated the more lucrative commercial, manufacturing, mining, and services sectors. Nearly 64 percent of all Chinese employment was in these sectors, while only 37.8 percent of all Indian workers and 30.2 percent of all Malay workers were involved in the same occupational sectors.[12]

Although several rural development programs had been implemented in the first decade after independence, the tight linkages between the urban economy and import-substitution led growth disproportionately favored higher investments in urban public infrastructure. In fact, half of all public expenditure developments under the First and Second Malaya Plans (1955-65) and First Malaysia Plan (1966-1970) were channeled toward urban-based projects.[13] The overall spread of private investments too, leaned toward urban communications, transportation, and other services sectors.

A result of these unbalanced investments and unequal state spending leaning toward urban development, significant spillover effects began to greatly benefit the mainly urban Chinese and Indian populations and their businesses. To some extent, it also provided better opportunities for the few Malays there, whose income levels rose relative to that of their compatriots living in the countryside. Greater emphases on urban services also affected the distribution of social services provision across the urban-rural divide. For Malays, its impact was reflected in overall poorer health among rural residents. Although health care delivery had become more widespread throughout the country by 1970, the farming and plantation communities still lagged behind cities and towns in terms of quality improvements. A major consequence of this was that infant mortality rates in 1970 were still higher for most Malays and Indians compared to the Chinese, despite improved rates for all groups since 1957.[14]

More significantly, the urban-rural social-economic comparison can also be highlighted in the differences in general poverty rates across ethnic groups during that period. Between Malays and Chinese, the incidence of poverty was much higher for Malays, at 65 percent in 1970 compared to the Chinese, which stood at 26 percent. In Sabah and Sarawak, the 1976 data showed poverty rates for Bumiputera groups in Sabah and Sarawak to be higher at 67.1 percent and 68 percent respectively, when compared to the Chinese in both these states, which were 22.2 percent and 29.6 percent respectively.[15]

The continuing poverty rates for Malay-Bumiputera groups throughout the 1950s to the mid-1960s began to worry some of the politicians in UMNO, whose political legitimacy had primarily been derived from its role in advancing Malay social-economic interests. Fearing that increased Malay economic backwardness would sway the party's constituents toward the opposition, UMNO, through the state, institutionally addressed the problem in a nationwide dialogue held in conjunction with the Malay Economic Congress in 1965. Following this, the state established the *Majlis Amanah Rakyat* (Indigenous People's Trust Council) or MARA.[16] As a public trust agency, MARA would hold equity shares acquired by the state on behalf of only Malays and other Bumiputera groups, aimed at stimulating and increasing Malay-Bumiputera share of national asset holdings in the national economy. In order to service Malay capital investments, a state-backed financial institution, the Bank Bumiputera Berhad, was also founded. The idea was for the creation of a pool of small but organizationally-equipped Malay grassroots enterprises, strong enough to eventually compete in Malaysia's small-scale retail markets. The ultimate goal was for this group of Malays to eventually work their way up to the top of the commercial ladder, and thus create more jobs and opportunities for other Malay-Bumiputera businesses.

By the mid-1960s however, the majority of Malays had become increasingly disillusioned with UMNO's assurances of higher living standards since it became glaringly obvious that Malays on the whole, had remained fixed at the bottom of the economic ladder. At the same time, the more prosperous ethnic Chinese community began to express their bottled dissatisfaction over state preferential treatment for Malays, which they felt were being taken at their economic expense. Ethnic tensions at this time were also aggravated by disagreements over the primacy of the Malay language as the medium of communication in Malaysian schools.

Consociationalism in the Balance: The Battle over Language and Education

In preparing for Malaya's independence, the British colonial state had suggested for a streamlined national education system that not only would help achieve a more efficient management of educational resources throughout the country but also stimulate a collective Malayan identity through a comprehensive assimilative process. For this purpose, the Barnes Committee in 1950 recommended that all government schools use Malay and English as their media of instruction while allowing other major vernacular languages as supplementary subjects for any student wishing to formally learn his or her own ethnic language.[17]

The MCA, in attempting to capture its elusive legitimacy with the larger Chinese population, formed its own Fen Wu committee in 1951 to counter the Barnes proposal for a nationalized educational curriculum. The committee rejected any move that would result in any inconsequentiality of Chinese education, and reiterated the pledge to maintain the autonomy of Chinese schools within the national education system. Advocates of the Barnes findings pointed out that the Fen Wu approach would render useless the role of education as an integrative social process. UMNO, however, in supporting its alliance partner's effort to generate greater Chinese support, expressed its preference for the MCA proposal. The enactment of the Education Ordinance 1952 virtually ascertained the autonomy of Chinese schools from national (English and Malay) public schools.[18]

However, in 1956, another nationwide study culminating in the Razak Report reasserted the position that national schools should ultimately serve a structural assimilative function to help unify Malaya's various ethnic groups toward a national identity.[19] Seven years would pass before this report materialized into the National Language Act 1963, which mandated the prioritization of national unification efforts in education through the expansive utility of the Malay language. Amended in 1967, the Act also authorized for the eventual development of the Malay language as the primary language in all public secondary schools. The Act also declared that although all elementary schools, regardless of medium of instruction, were to be fully assisted by the state, only Malay and English schools had funding access at the secondary level. Students from Chinese and Tamil-instructed schools who wished to attend these secondary schools would have to learn Malay and English for one year in order to be absorbed into the national educational mainstream.[20] The state's goal here was to subsequently lessen the educational significance of the Mandarin and Tamil languages under a Malay-based national curriculum.

Chinese cultural associations in Malaysia, who often performed the custodial role of ethnic Chinese culture, have always rejected any integrationist approach through education, and have been the least inhibitive in opposing any measure they saw as threatening the autonomy of Chinese educational interests. A coalition of Chinese associations spearheaded by the *Dong Jiao Zong* (National Chinese Schools Association) declared that the 1967 Act limits the rights of Chinese schools to operate independently of state control.[21] In emblematic defiance, this group advocated for a separate Chinese education system, in which Mandarin would be used as a medium of instruction in all Chinese schools from the elementary stage right up to the national tertiary level. The proposal included the construction of *Merdeka University,* aimed at catering exclusively for Chinese school students.

Meanwhile, Malay conservative groups dismissed such recommendations as presumptuous, reinforcing their argument that the National Language Act had not actually gone far enough in stressing Malay as an official national language. As it was, they argued, Malaysia was the only country in the world outside of China and Taiwan, where Mandarin had been extensively used as a teaching language in both state and privately-run schools. Conferring greater freedom to existing vernacular schools, they claimed, would cause the country's already segregated education system into becoming more deeply entrenched along ethnic-cultural lines.[22]

Persistent efforts by Chinese cultural associations to preserve and advance Chinese language and education had been part of a larger struggle by the leaders of the Chinese-educated community against what they saw as resoluteness on the part of the state to sustain Malay hegemony. Such sentiments were heightened during Singapore's short membership in Malaysia, when the island's People's Action Party (PAP), in its attempt to expand its support from among the country's ethnic Chinese, had openly called for the removal of Malay protective status and special rights in the country. After Singapore's expulsion from the federation, this unrelenting effort was taken up by the predominantly Chinese Democratic Action Party (DAP), a Malaysian splinter of the PAP. The complementary relationship between ethnic Chinese cultural activism and political support for the DAP would from thereon reflect the Chinese community's overall struggle against what they felt was state-endorsement of their second-class status in the country.

The years leading up to the 1969 elections were increasingly tensed. Many Malays were becoming extremely unhappy with the Alliance, especially the rising middle class, who saw the fruits of economic growth being limited to only a privileged few.[23] Many Malays in the urban areas had become increasingly exasperated at the relatively scarce economic opportunities available to them in the cities. They also believed that the *laissez faire* nature of the economy mostly advantaged the ethnic Chinese, whose power and monopoly in the markets enabled their enterprises to institute discriminatory measures against prospective Malay hires and businesses.[24] On the other hand, there seemed to be widespread anguish among the majority of non-Malays that the state's preferences for Malay workers in some sectors of the economy impeded the functioning of a merit-based economy. They believed that the market's most talented and qualified should be selected for key business and government positions. Such arguments were often used to justify the reluctance of ethnic Chinese enterprises to either recruit Malay employees into their organizations or allow Malay businesses admission into Chinese-controlled commercial networks.[25]

It was not surprising then that against the backdrop of persisting inequalities and highly passionate issues of economy, education, and language, the 1969 parliamentary elections became one of the most heated in Malaysia's history. The outcomes of these elections were to test the resolve and credibility of the National Alliance in defending and sustaining the country's consociational system. Instead, the results of the 1969 elections were extremely disappointing for the ruling elites. Despite holding on to overall victory, the Alliance's winning margin was heavily reduced with the MCA experiencing catastrophic losses in all of its constituencies, indicating almost overwhelming Chinese support for the DAP and Labour Party. UMNO too, collected its fewest Malay votes since independence, with most of them transferring to the opposition Pan-Islamic Party (PAS), which recorded its highest ever voting count.[26] Thus, if anything, these elections also indicated general Malay dissatisfaction with UMNO, especially over the party's failure to enhance the community's socio-economic status.

The elections would also ultimately be remembered for the tragic events that followed. The decision by the Chinese-dominated DAP and Labour Party to hold a celebratory parade in the streets of Kuala Lumpur proved disastrous. Documentation regarding the actual events that day remained hazy but most eyewitness accounts pointed to a heavily boisterous and incendiary procession passing through various Malay enclaves, where racist exchanges and taunting on both sides may have triggered physical encounters between the groups, and which soon spread out onto the outlying neighborhoods. Hostilities worsened with news of the killing of a Malay family by Chinese youths as they exited from a cinema in a Chinese neighborhood. From here, counter-attacks against Chinese individuals and businesses would eventually escalate into unprecedented ethnic violence throughout the capital city. The ensuing days of rioting left hundreds, mostly Chinese, dead and badly injured.[27]

As tragic as it was, the May 13, 1969, incident became a significant lesson of history in the way that it marked the inevitable consequence of the failure to address the social reproduction of ethnic disparities and distances emanating from the labor ethnicization structure. Considered to be the worst ethnic riots since the country's independence, the May 13 disaster also entailed a new era in Malaysian politics that considerably renewed the legitimacy and power of the country's ethnic Malay leadership in UMNO.

Ensuring UMNO Hegemony: The New Economic Policy (NEP)

A state of emergency was declared following the riots, with the Malaysian parliament subsequently suspended from 1969 to 1971. The federation was governed through a National Operations Council (NOC), dominated by members of UMNO, the ruling alliance, and senior security personnel. The Malaysian state's utmost priority was to assure investors and bankers that it was able to restore the country's political stability. Another urgent matter that needed serious attention for UMNO was the retrieval of Malay confidence in the party, particularly by proving that it was still relevant and devoted to the safeguarding of their special rights and privileges. Prime Minister Tunku Abdul Rahman, portrayed as being too liberal and accommodating toward other ethnic interests, was made a partial scapegoat for his poor handling of the unrest and was eventually forced to resign from public office. Waiting in the leadership wings was a newer group of UMNO elite, who were not the least apologetic in taking a less ambassadorial stance toward reasserting Malay and UMNO political hegemony in the country.

To reinstate order, UMNO's "new guards" publicly vowed to prevent the replication of the 1969 riots but also openly emphasized the significance of economic parity between ethnic groups as a precondition for national unity and ethnic harmony in Malaysia. The state also alleged that the historical and deliberate exclusion of Malays within the private economic sector had been one of the major contributing factors to the ongoing economic inequality between Malays and Chinese. According to the NOC, while the non-Malays complained of state assistance to Malays, especially in the public sector, "no mention was ever made...of the almost closed-door attitude to the Malays by the non-Malays in large sections of the private sector in this country."[28]

More specifically, the state implied that Malay social economic welfare had first to be seriously addressed if capitalist development and national economic growth were to be effective and successful. Since occupational discrimination was understood to be one of the major contributing factors to sustaining Malay-Bumiputera disadvantages, the state sought to introduce corrective economic measures aimed at enhancing the life-chances of Malays and Bumiputeras through greater private sector participation and wider educational opportunities. These proposals culminated in the launching of the New Economic Policy (NEP) in 1970. As a general vision, the NEP aimed at attaining poverty alleviation and national unity through the reduction of social-economic inequities between Malay-Bumiputeras and non-Bumiputeras by 1990.[29] The policy's specific implementation was focused on repairing the disproportionate ethnic-occupational structure left behind by British colonialism through state-led redistribution of job opportunities and economic resources along more balanced ethnic-income ratios.

In its implementation, the NEP was inarguably pro-Malay-Bumiputera. The rationale for this, according to the state, lies in the notion that since Malays and Bumiputeras had been the most economically-deprived groups under colonial rule, it was only justified that they be given disproportionately greater help in accessing the country's revenue-generating sectors after independence.[30] However, while there was emphasis on recruiting more Malays and Bumiputera groups in corporate and private sector employment, there was little mention of balancing the public services with greater admittance of non-Malays. The state was unabashedly silent on this matter, alluding to the implicit acknowledgement that UMNO was still the *de facto* leader within the Alliance, and that Malays should unquestionably be given the predominant role in governance.

To ensure the success of the NEP, strict compliance with the policy was expected of all corporate and commercial sector institutions in the country, regardless of whether they were locally or foreign-owned. In order to raise the average wealth levels of Malays and Bumiputeras, the NEP's underlined objectives involved various programs in assisting greater Malay and Bumiputera equity ownership. In 1970, Malay capital constituted only 2.5 percent of total corporate holdings, compared to the Chinese at 22.5 percent and foreigners at 60.7 percent, signifying little change from the pre-independence period.[31] Under the NEP, the target was for the accumulation of 30 percent Malay-Bumiputera share of the country's corporate assets by the year 1990. To achieve this goal, the state sought to increase expenditure and investments allocations in NEP-marked projects as well as in state-owned banks and trust companies, where Malay-Bumiputera management in these organizations would also be expanded.[32]

Despite criticisms regarding the discriminatory nature of the policy, the NEP proved to be one of the most successful affirmative action programs in the world. It became the show-case of successful state social-economic planning, not measurably found anywhere else outside Malaysia. This is especially so when the overall impact of this policy was the reduction of both rural and urban poverty by more than 30 percent.[33] By 1990, it had successfully elevated the average Malay income closer to non-Malays, whereby the ratio of mean income differentials between Chinese and Malays narrowed from 2.23 in 1970 to about 1.9 in 1989. The ratio between Malays and Indians also improved from 1.70 to

1.29 for the same period.[34] In Malaysia's eastern states, income difference ratio of Bumiputeras to ethnic Chinese in Sabah further decreased from 3.46 in 1976 to 2.50 in 1989, while in Sarawak it lowered from 3.40 to 1.88 for the same years.[35]

For UMNO, the relative success of the NEP boosted its image among Malays and Bumiputeras. The party would take credence for its ability in elevating the quality of life of the average Malay, who as recently as the early years of independence, had languished in the darkness of illiteracy and immersed in the backwaters of economic underdevelopment. For this, Malays began to see themselves as increasingly indebted to and dependent on the state, particularly UMNO, for their social-economic livelihood and political future.

At the same time however, the ruling elites in UMNO had to also reconcile the party's contradictory obligations to uphold its consociational relationship with non-Malay parties within the alliance on the one hand, and execute its preferential policies for Malays and Bumiputeras on the other. The state does this by constantly reminding all Malaysians that the existing consociational arrangement had been borne out of a "social contract" between the various ethnic groups, in which Malays had relented to full citizenship of non-Malays purely on the condition that the latter would recognize the special rights of Malays and Bumiputeras as indigenous groups. Policies such as the NEP were seen to qualify as part of these special rights. Thus it was to be understood that the dominant position of Malays as well as the NEP should not be subjected to dispute or questioning by any Malaysian citizen. Any disruption of the present system, the state often explains, would entail the return of ethnic instabilities similar to the ones that led to the 1969 riots.

To legitimize its arguments, the state often refers to Article 153 of the 1957 Federal Constitution, which refers to special considerations for Malays and Bumiputeras with regards to scholarships, public service, and trade permits.[36] After 1970, the state would gradually translate these special provisions as "special rights," which were to be explicitly applied to a range of social-economic benefits encompassing housing discounts, employment preferences, and asset creation. This interpretation of the constitution has become a point of debate among Malaysians today especially since the spirit behind the Article may not have implied for these special rights or privileges to go beyond land allocation and government employment. Nevertheless, it has already been ingrained in the Malay mindset that the prioritized provision of social and economic resources has become their exclusive rights of citizenship.

UMNO also had other intentions behind the NEP. One was to use the policy to enlarge the Malay-Bumiputera middle-class, whose economic stability would help provide strong political and financial support for the party.[37] Operationalizing this task rested on extending generous educational opportunities for Malays and Bumiputeras through special quotas in local college admissions and scholarships to universities abroad. Without doubt, the educational component of the NEP became one of the most successful aspects of the policy. The early 1970s saw numerous state technical and science-themed boarding schools rapidly established across the country catering to tens of thousands of mainly Malay and Bumiputera children from relatively humble social backgrounds.[38]

Since their inceptions, these "residential" institutions have been supported and maintained mostly by funds from the federal government through its ministry of education. They also often attracted the best of resources, and as such, offered their students with the highly enriching educational experiences not found in most other public schools in the country. Throughout the 1980s and 1990s, thousands of these students, together with other high-performing Malay-Bumiputera students from around the country, were able to further their tertiary studies in various science and technical fields in the United Kingdom and the United States through exclusive state scholarships that covered both their tuition and living expenses. Others preferring to stay home were also provided special places in the various local universities. In time however, the number of domestic universities and colleges were increased to promote greater student enrollment within the country while the smaller number of state scholarships for overseas studies have expanded to include non-Malay-Bumiputera students as well.

It is indisputable that without full state sponsorship and special preferential treatments in education, it would have been unfeasible for many Malays and other historically-disadvantaged Bumiputera groups to undergo any inter-generational class mobility within a relatively short period of time. In this respect, building an economically stable and greatly indebted Malay-Bumiputera professional class has been a successful strategy on the part of the UMNO ruling elite to assure the party of its long-term support from an increasingly large and influential base. For a relatively long time, UMNO has held the Malay middle class hostage to its constant reminders that their economic future was contingent on their loyalty and contributions to the party.

Shifts in Regional Capital Flows

More importantly, the NEP as a comprehensive social engineering project could not have been made possible if not for a consistently strong national economy. Although much of Malaysia's wealth came from its increasing oil revenues, the country's growth was also helped by world systemic factors that favored a major change in development approach. This came in the form of regional capital flows that had extended from the northeastern Asia economies into the emerging production centers and consumer markets of Southeast Asia.

The regional industrialization process in East and Southeast Asia occurred in systematic-geographic stages. Injections of US funds into Japan after the Second World War helped accelerate that country's ascent toward an industrial powerhouse by the 1950s. By the beginning of the next decade, the first wave of regional capital flows began to transverse across eastern Asia. These were primarily in the form of investments from Japan and the United States gravitating toward the low value-added labor areas of South Korea, Taiwan, and Hong

Kong, primarily for the re-exports of electronic components and manufactured products to western markets.[39]

As a result, these countries became cheap industrial labor centers and markets for Japanese industrial products and services. Powered by an import-substitution strategy and substantial technology acquisition from parent, mainly American, companies, these northeast Asian countries were able to successfully latch on to the buyer-driven commodity chain for consumer production of apparel, toys, and footwear, mainly for foreign firms during the 1960s.[40] Soon, special accessibility to US markets was also extended to these countries' home products, fuelling the remarkable export-driven growths of "Asian miracle economies" in the coming decades.

Malaysia's location in this dynamically changing region would also provide it with opportunities for rapid industrial development. By the 1980s, high costs of capital and labor in the East Asian economies caused outflows of investments into the lower-cost Southeast Asia labor region, creating the second wave of downward capital flow. Having started out with an import-substitution economy, Malaysia's growth strategy increasingly focused toward the expansion of commodity-based and light industrial exports. The success of the NEP was highly contingent on sustained economic growth, which was only achievable through the continuous exports of manufactured products. The state was confident that Malaysia was able to expand its exporting capacities since its well-established infrastructure and generous oil revenues could be counted on to prepare the country for higher-level manufacturing activities. This will be discussed in the next section.

Export-Led Economic Growth, 1970-1990

The early implementation of the NEP was embedded in the Second to Fifth Malaysia Plans. Throughout the decades of the 1970s to 1990s, the policy's social programs were pretty much focused on continued rural development, commercialization of agriculture, and Bumiputera educational development. Its economic projects, on the other hand, were in the process of being intricately tied in one way or another to the fostering of greater Malay and Bumiputera participation in export-oriented industrial activities.[41]

For Malaysia's ethnic Chinese, the 1969 riots became a reminder of the manner in which Malay docility could easily transmute into uncontrollable rage when provoked into an ethnic crisis. The majority of ethnic Chinese was careful not to be publicly criticizing NEP for fear of riling up Malay ethnic sentiments, or worse, reprisals. Instead, Chinese-Malaysians, as main domestic savers, chose to vent their displeasure by allocating their monies in overseas markets and banks. From 1975 to 1985, there had been around RM12 billion in ethnic Chinese capital flight from Malaysia.[42]

In the absence of much-needed local capital, FDI again became the principal source of jump-starting the NEP programs. In the 1970s, the capital flow in the light industrial commodity chains of both producer and buyer-driven manufacturing rapidly moved from the second-tier developing countries of South Korea, Taiwan and Hong Kong toward third-tier countries of ASEAN (Association of Southeast Asian Nations). These shifts signaled the intense search for lucrative investments in low and semi-skilled labor, particularly for apparel production and electronic component assembly.[43]

This second wave Asian capital flow provided the Malaysian state with a well-timed opportunity to absorb incoming investments. To accommodate the development of these industries, the Free Trade Zones Act 1971, in particular, enabled the state to help establish numerous multi-million dollar export processing zones (EPZ) around the country.[44] Among the major transnational corporations that took advantage of these facilities were Motorola, Intel, Hitachi, Monsanto, Ericsson, and Nippon Steel Glass, with more companies following suit for investments in information technology, textiles, and higher-end electronics assembly.

By the mid-1970s, Malaysia had become a haven for low-costs electronic and computer production for western and Japanese firms. A majority of the workers hired in these EPZs had been young females from Malay peasant families. Despite being lowly-paid and non-unionized, these girls' employments were nevertheless seen as highly rewarding opportunities by poor rural families within the Malay community, who depend on their daughters' supplementary incomes to survive in a declining agricultural economy.

By the time elections resumed in 1974, UMNO had successfully consolidated its authority within the National Alliance (now renamed as the National Front) through overwhelming Malay support for the party. UMNO became largely responsible for the ruling coalition's 64 percent winning margin in that elections, which was the widest since the country's independence. Reigning supreme among its coalition partners allowed UMNO to unreservedly introduce new legislations aimed at advancing its NEP programs through various industrialization projects. The passing of the Industrial Coordination Act (ICA) in 1975, for instance, gave the state considerable supervisory powers over company-related investments in Malaysia through the Capital Issues Committee. This Committee became responsible for ensuring portioned allocations of at least 20 percent corporate shares going toward newly-emerging UMNO-controlled companies. The power to manage investments in Malaysia was further consolidated through conditions for licensing and permits, tied to the appropriation of specific percentages of capital stock ownership to Malaysian citizens.[45] Having acquired considerable influence in the country's capital accumulation process, the state was now able to work toward achieving NEP Malay corporate equity targets while providing ample room for other ethnic elite businesses to also benefit from the country's industrial growth.

Foreign investors were initially cautious about the ICA guidelines, especially its stipulations on Bumiputera equity requirements, but the potentials as well as incentives accompanying such investments were too attractive to ignore. Costs of production and infrastructure provisions were among the most competitive in the world, made even more appealing by the state's lowering of ceilings on stock allocation quotas.[46] Subsequently, the state even appeared to liberalize a majority of its previous restrictions on investments with the introduction of the Promotion of Investments Act in 1986. Among other things, the Act enabled foreign companies that exported at least half of their output to be given options in the form of generous tax holidays and benefits. Further exemptions from certain licensing were also made available to both foreign and Malaysia companies, made possible by wider discretionary powers conferred upon Trade Ministry officials.

From 1961 to 1990, Malaysia received nearly 30 percent of all investments coming into the ASEAN region, second only to Singapore. From 1981 to 1990, in particular, these investments tripled to more than US$12 billion.[47] Escalating production costs in Japan and East Asia were exploited by the state in the form of its "Look East" policy to attract more capital from this region into the country. Frustrated at the unwillingness of investors from the United States and western countries to share technological knowledge with their Malaysian subsidiaries, the government of Dr. Mahathir looked toward Japan for inspiration and economic goodwill. The Malaysian state was particularly impressed with the *Japan Incorporated* approach to development. In emulation, the state would officially design its own *Malaysia Incorporated* to emphasize the permeable roles between the state and the country's corporate sector in enhancing efficiency and productivity of the national economy. In line with this policy, generous incentives were given to Japanese and other northeast Asian companies in order to entice injections of funds from this region, which by the late 1980s, had become Malaysia's principal investors.[48]

In tandem with the "Look East" policy was the state's Industrial Master Plan in 1985. The main objective of this plan was to help bring the Malaysian economy closer toward industrialization by encouraging foreign corporate investments in heavy industrial projects through numerous tax incentives for joint partnerships with local corporations. It was hoped that such ventures with reputable foreign companies, especially Japanese, would materialize into high levels of technology transfers, badly needed to boost the export-building capabilities of local companies. The largest among these local corporations, the Heavy Industry Corporation of Malaysia (HICOM) was specifically set up as the country's first state-subsidized hi-tech engineering corporation, and was backed by state-imposed protective tariffs. Soon, a wide array of other heavy industrial production projects, including steel and cement, were undertaken through the procurement of large scale and mainly Japanese investments. By 1987, manufacturing had surpassed agriculture as the country's main economic sector, with a percentage GDP share growth from 9 percent in 1965 to 24 percent in 1990.[49]

Intensification of State-Capitalist Network in Malaysia

Even in the early years of the NEP's implementation, much of the large-scale local capital holdings in Malaysia still remained in the hands of the MCA-linked Chinese commercial networks. The MCA's main company, the Multi-Purpose Holdings Berhad, was for a long time, the largest in the country. As mentioned previously in the book, the economic prowess of the MCA had traditionally furnished the ruling National Front with their financing needs ever since Malaysia's independence.

Many within UMNO however, saw the over-reliance on the MCA as hampering the institutional autonomy of the party.[50] Hence, under Dr. Mahathir Mohamad (1981-2003), the UMNO leadership made sure that rapid industrial development of Malaysia coincided with the rise and ascendancy of a Malay capitalist elite closely linked to the party. An UMNO-affiliated entrepreneurial class was seen to be advantageous to the ruling elite since it would enable the party to run its own financing through the proxy ownerships of state-held assets. This way, UMNO would be able to safeguard its long-term economic interests and maintain its role as the primary political organization in the country. At the same time, it was hoped that a successful Malay capitalist class would also hasten the effort toward fulfilling the NEP's targeted Malay-Bumiputera corporate equity goals of at least 30 percent by 1990.[51]

The Mahathir administration's approach to creating a Malay capitalist class differed from earlier efforts to increase Malay-Bumiputera equity participation, which was based on an "upward" wealth creation process. The traditional approach involved state-assisted capital accumulation through quasi-public bodies formed under various legislative acts in the 1970s.[52] State enterprises, functioning either as trust agencies or investments vehicles for Bumiputera equity, were often connected to the state machinery through interlocking membership and management structures. State statutory companies, such as the Permodalan Nasional Berhad (PNB or National Equity Corporation) and Perbadanan Nasional Berhad (National Trade Corporation) were essentially state-run investment arms for Malay-Bumiputera public asset holdings. Malays and other Bumiputeras were thus encouraged to deposit their savings into PNB's major twin-subsidiary trust schemes, the Amanah Saham Nasional and Amanah Saham Bumiputera, in order to generate guaranteed returns in the form of huge annual dividends. By 1992, PNB had churned out around RM22.7 billion (US$7.5 billion) in corporate stock, making it the second largest stockholder in the Kuala Lumpur Stock Exchange.[53]

Since Malaysia was among the world's leading oil-exporter, revenues from Malaysia's exponentially growing oil and gas industry had become the main financial lifeline for the state to help maintain many of these companies. Accessibility to petroleum money through the state-run oil company Petronas had also earlier enabled these state corporations to purchase large colonial-era British conglomerates such as Guthrie, Harrison & Crosfield, London Tin, and Sime Darby, thereby completing the "nationalization" of resource-based industries in Malaysia.[54] The state also formed various economic development corporations and public enterprises in the late 1970s that dealt in a spectrum of economic activities, and whose subsidiaries proliferated and diversified into agricultural product marketing, land redevelopment, construction, light manufacturing, real estate, and even banking. Much of the holdings of these companies were held by the state, and whose profits were to be extensively redistributed toward Malay-Bumiputera equity in the form of exclusive commercial projects, savings, investments profits, and other forms of asset-building.

The profitability of these companies hinged mostly on the state's ability to maintain them financially, which in turn was heavily dependent on a continuously thriving economy. During economic downturns however, the price elasticity of raw materials placed many of these companies in numerous financial difficulties. Researchers Salih and Yusof reported that from a sample of 269 state agencies and non-profit bodies in the early 1980s, there had already been accumulated losses of RM137 million (US$42 million).[55] The state conveniently attributed these companies' poor performances to poor management and lack of incentives inherent within their functions as public bodies. Thus under the Mahathir administration, many of these state bodies were gradually privatized into a range of commercial and manufacturing companies. It was hoped that state alliances with industrial capital would be strengthened through stakes in these companies, and long-term direct state expenditures that had begun to strain the national budget due to declining world commodity prices could be reduced.[56]

Hence, privatization also served another important purpose. Under Mahathir, the state now claimed that a "trickle down" effect would be a more expeditious and secure method in attaining the targeted Malay equity objectives. Privatization was also to become a blanket policy to enable the buying of as many public bodies as possible, including service and utility providers, for companies under UMNO patronage. In other words, privatization was to allow the handing over of these enterprises, many with paid up capital, to UMNO-connected capitalists for immediate profit-taking and wealth creation. From 1983 to the early 1990s, various high performing public companies were corporatized through buy-outs, public listings, and equity sales. Among these included the National Electricity Board (renamed *Tenaga Nasional Berhad*), HICOM, Pernas Hotel Chains, Malaysian Shipping Lines, Peremba (a subsidiary of the Urban Development Authority), Malaysia Airlines, Malayan Railways, and Telecom Malaysia (renamed *Sistem Telekom Malaysia*).[57]

The close alliances between state and capital were further manifested in the revolving door structure between these companies and UMNO, where the latter would arrange for management and major shareholder positions in these companies to be rotated among its trusted nominees, many of whom were staunch party supporters.[58] By the late 1980s, it had become quite apparent that UMNO was using revenues generated from these conglomerates to build up both its political and financial empires. Among the emerging enterprises in the 1980s most strongly connected to the party were the Fleet Group, Renong Berhad, TRI (Tajudin Ramly Industries), and Land and General. By the 1990s, a number of prominent UMNO-linked Malay millionaires had emerged from these state-capital alliances. These included then Finance Minister Daim Zainuddin, Rashid Hussain, Halim Saad, Wan Azmi Hamzah, Tajudin Ramly, and Azman Hashim.

In time, a significant number of prominent ethnic Chinese capitalists connected to the MCA also began to exploit its close relationship with UMNO in order to take advantage of the abundant commercial opportunities made available by a prospering economy and the NEP. Many became willing participants in the new corporate economy to cash in on the profitable returns and other forms of privileges derived from the strengthening of their political and economic ties with UMNO. Many of these benefits came in the shape of preferred allocations of lucrative equity holdings in newly-acquired companies, state protection of specific businesses and market monopolies, and the security of electoral votes in predominantly Malay constituencies. In some cases, UMNO-linked businesses even hired and left the actual running of their companies to their ethnic Chinese partners or subsidiaries. Termed *Ali Baba* ventures, these arrangements effectively defeated the whole rationale of developing Malay expertise in commerce and business. In turn, many MCA-connected elites would also provide UMNO-endorsed Malay professionals with influential positions in their companies' Boards of Directors, while it was also not uncommon for several ethnic Chinese capitalists linked to the MCA to assist in the campaign financing of its individual UMNO patrons.[59] In many ways, the NEP had successfully consolidated the political relationship between the ruling elites in UMNO and the MCA through their common network of crony capitalists and commercial partnerships that they had established through the years.

To date, Malaysia has the largest number of billionaires in Southeast Asia. These distinguished tycoons have produced a combined personal net worth exceeding US$50 billion. The ten richest individuals in the country in 2011 are as listed in table 6.1 on the next page. As in years past, many from the traditional Chinese elite families such as Robert Kuok, Lee Kim Hua, and Lee Shin Seng continue to monopolize the highest wealth brackets. Their mercantile monopolies in agriculture-based production, retail, and banking have diversified into a host of large commercial holdings in real estate, gaming, media, and construction.[60] The *nouveaux riches* billionaires such as Ananda Krishnan, Vincent Tan, and Mokhtar Albukhari, on the other hand, have gained immense privileges in one way or another through their close associations with the various major political parties within the National Front. Among the country's millionaires have also included individuals with family connections to current and former political figures, members of the royal families, and former civil servants.

As part of Malaysia's capitalist class, these groups of wealthy entrepreneurs are allied to the state through mutually beneficial relationships based on generous monetary contributions and prioritization of projects, markets, and contracts. Helming the country's largest enterprises, these corporate executives form the exclusive circle of close confidants to the ruling elites within the local state-capitalist alliance, which has continued to immensely reap off Malaysia's industrial development.

Malaysia's Export Economy under Globalization, 1990-2011

Malaysia's manufacturing growth, like other Southeast Asian economies, had been heavily reliant on foreign direct investments (FDI).[61] The country's Gross Domestic Product (GDP), which expanded from a mere US$2.44 billion in 1960 to about US$237 billion in 2010, correlated proportionately with the rise in FDI. The country's GDP and total FDI for selected years 1960-2010 are as illustrated in table 6.2 on the next page.

Although FDI had been crucial in transforming Malaysia into a manufacturing economy, one of its major downsides has been the repatriation of much of the returns on capital to their parent companies located abroad. This is because a huge portion of these investments remain entrenched in the outsourcing of product assemblies and market expansion of retail and other types of services for major companies headquartered overseas. Thus, Malaysia's industrial growth has provided little in the way of product development or technological transfers that could fully benefit local industries. This meant that while increased foreign earnings from exports has helped stabilize Malaysia's balance of payments and economic growth, the huge outflows of profits tended to offset substantial growths in longer-term domestic investments in local technological development.[62]

Table 6.1: Top Ten Malaysian Billionaires, 2011

Billionaire		Major Commercial Areas	Net worth (US$)
1.	Robert Kuok	Real estate, palm oil, media	12.5 billion
2.	Ananda Krishnan	Telecommunication, broadcasting	9.5 billion
3.	(Mrs.) Lee Kim Hua	Casino, recreation, gaming	6.6 billion
4.	Lee Shin Seng	Palm oil, real estate.	5.0 billion
5.	Quek Leng Chan	Finance, investments, real estate	4.8 billion
6.	Teh Hong Piow	Finance, investments, insurance	4.7 billion
7.	Yeoh Tiong Lay	Real estate, power, communications	2.7 billion
8.	Mokhtar Albukhari	Construction, transport	2.5 billion
9.	Vincent Tan	Gaming, recreation, real estate	1.2 billion
10.	Tiong Hiew King	Media, finance	1.2 billion

Source: Data calculated from Forbes website at www.forbes.com/lists/2011/84/Malaysia-billionaires-11MDRG.html.

Having assumed a supplementary and subsidiary role in the larger capitalist world economy, Malaysia's industrial growth has practically remained attributable to its function as a haven for lower-cost technical labor and as a provider of new markets for consumption goods. The lack of technological expertise and product research capacity of many of its local companies has largely inhibited the country's ability to move beyond the present stage of industrialization. Subsequently, Malaysia's own state-linked corporations have also become highly vulnerable to the volatility of an increasingly globalized world economy. A main cause of this has been the prevalence of penetrative information technology within business operations, which has encouraged aggressive and unimpeded movements of financial transactions and capital flows from one market to another, and across national borders.

Hence, ever since capital markets began deregulating in the early 1990s, short-term speculation aimed at extracting quick profits has become increasingly feasible and more attainable, making this type of investment the single largest flow of international investments worldwide.[63] This free flowing capital, helped greatly by market deregulations, had also been responsible for the Asian financial crisis that reverberated throughout the region in 1997, which almost brought down the otherwise healthy economies of newly industrializing countries such as South Korea, Taiwan, Thailand, and Indonesia. When the government of Thailand, where the crisis began, reacted to its increasing debt by devaluating its currency, a contagion of investor panic suddenly swept throughout East Asia.[64] In Malaysia, speculators began selling off the Malaysian ringgit while longer term investors immediately pulled their funds altogether, nearly collapsing the market.

Table 6.2: Gross Domestic Product (GDP) and Foreign Direct Investments, (FDI) for Malaysia, 1960-2010.

Economic indicator	1960	1970	1990	2000	2008	2010
GDP (US$ billion)	2.44	4.28	44	93.8	222.2	237.8
Total population (million)	8.1	10.5	17.7	21.8	27.7	28.4
Total foreign direct investments (US$ billion)	N/A	0.094	2.33	0.554	7.38	9.1

Source: Information calculated from Department of Statistics Malaysia, *Yearbook of Statistics 2010* (Kuala Lumpur: Government Printers, 2011) and other earlier annual editions of the book.

As a result, UMNO-related companies, whose loans had been leveraged by the state and pumped into real estate, banking, and other massive construction projects, instantly generated huge debts. The state acted quickly by pegging the Malaysian ringgit to the US dollar to stop the currency from further sliding while also refusing aid from the International Monetary Fund, which typically requires the imposition of unpopular austerity measures. Instead, the Malaysian state established a National Economic Advisory Council (NEAC) led by Prime Minister Mahathir to draft out its own major corporate adjustment initiatives.

Closely monitored by the Bank Negara (Central Bank), the state carefully followed the NEAC guidelines, which among other things recommended for the setting up of two new institutions to run as the Council's operating agencies. One was Danaharta, which began acquiring and managing non-performing loans within the banking system, while the other was Danamodal, which worked on recapitalizing weak financial institutions. By the middle of 2001, Danamodal had successfully "rehabilitated" eight out of every ten major financial companies, while Danaharta managed to absorb nearly US$10 billion or 82 percent of total gross bad loans up to that period.[65]

The state would unilaterally decide for these publicly-run institutions to utilize billions of ringgits in order to save Malaysian companies and banks from folding over. Here, Malaysia's rich petroleum and gas reserves, as always, performed the role of the state's fiscal guarantor. Ready access to revenues from the state petroleum company Petronas has made possible the numerous bailing-outs of fledgling UMNO-linked corporations belonging to party cronies and families of the ruling elite whenever the occasion warranted it. Among the most controversial bailouts arising out of the 1997 financial crisis was that of shipping conglomerate Konsortium Perkapalan, a privatized company owned by Prime Minister Mahathir's son, Mirzan. A *Bloomberg Businessweek* report dated November 9, 1998, stated that strong objections by then Deputy Prime Minister Anwar Ibrahim against the use of Petronas to buy out the company sparked the souring of his relationship and eventual enmity with his superior Dr. Mahathir.[66]

In any case, bailing out state-linked companies has practically become a national ritual. Even after the dust of the financial crisis had settled, there has been a continuing series of rescues of such companies mainly from mismanagement and corruption. The failure of many of these companies to expand into more formidable entities is also indirectly related to their role as nothing more than subordinate partners of larger foreign corporations. The alliance between foreign and local capitalists, or political nominees who assume those positions, has been borne out of advancing the larger companies' interests in Malaysia. In many such relationships, foreign capitalists were not hesitant in dispensing kick-backs or bribes in order to stipulate one-sided terms against their local partners, who in turn, were more than eager to be complicit in placing their personal gains over the organizational interests of their companies.

The national automobile company Proton and its subsequent "rescue mission" is a good case in point. While the car was being produced under license from Mitsubishi Motors Corporation of Japan in the 1980s, constraints set by the parent company with regards to marketing strategies, supply network, royalty payments, and most importantly, technological transfer virtually impeded Proton's ability to compete in international markets. This partnership was, in effect, Mitsubishi's strategy of stamping its competition in the region against long-time rivals Toyota, Honda, Mazda, and Nissan, and therefore was used to acquire as much profits as possible from the sale of their automobile in Malaysia. By the time the company became Malaysian-owned, it had sorely lacked the technological capacity for exports, incurring massive losses and debts arising from excessive production costs and low overseas sales.[67] Meanwhile, Mitsubishi is still guaranteed of its profits from the various aspects of supplies, research, and royalties derived from whatever limited technological transfers to Proton under the licensing agreement.[68]

It was believed that about US$2 billion worth of taxpayers' money may have been pumped into the company to save it from total financial ruin.[69] The automobile company ended up being held by Khazanah Nasional, the state's newest and largest investment arm. Efforts to either sell off the national car or concede its major shareholding equity to a foreign auto company had often been opposed and branded by many in UMNO as "unpatriotic."[70] Despite the company's failure to perform in the export market, UMNO cronies nevertheless had secured their share of profits from the taxpayer bail-outs, which also saved them from accountability for losses. Many have also profited from their hold on the car's domestic distributorship through *Edaran Otomobil Nasional*, whose sales have been helped by high state tariffs on imported cars. In the meantime, the majority of Malaysians have been forced to buy this locally-made and substandard automobile as they have no other reasonably priced alternative within their purchasing options.

Many other high-profile UMNO-linked companies such as United Engineers Malaysia and DRB-HICOM had been specifically created to lead the country's heavy industrialization efforts. Instead, they ended up either being recipients of billions of ringgits in salvage money or reduced to procuring state contracts for outsourced infrastructural projects.[71] For example, Renong, a once-upon-a-time blue chip company connected to UMNO, had been awarded preferential allocation to build and operate national expressway projects. After the 1997 financial crisis, the company received nearly US$3 billion in tax write-offs and zero coupon bonds to pay off foreign creditors.[72] Despite given direct state assistance, none of these once-hopeful companies has even adequately survived in the domestic markets, let alone become world players.

Particularly distressing for Malaysians has been the increased use of public funds from sources outside of Petronas to buy out these companies' massive debts. For instance, UMNO proxy Rashid Hussain and his company Rashid Hussain Bank (RHB), Malaysia's second largest banking company in the 1990s, were faced with more than US$1 billion worth of financial obligations. The tabs for RHB were taken over by the Pahang State Economic Development Corporation, Danamodal Berhad, and the Employees Provident Fund, the country's top workers' pension house, which eventually took over the burden of owning this failing company.[73]

The nature and process of these controversial bail-outs have also often been non-transparent. In many cases, this has allowed their top executives evade public scrutiny and criticisms. After-the-fact revelations would eventually shed some light into the way many of these purchases had been conducted, and most often they would involve state investment companies such as Danaharta and Khazanah Nasional, or Petronas taking over hefty portions of shares from the various UMNO nominees at above market prices. This of course, was done solely for the purpose of cutting these shareholders' personal losses. By the time any information of such transactions became publicly available, their paper trails would disappear and securely concealed so that prosecuting bodies and courts would find it "difficult" to bring down charges on corrupt capitalists and officials. In some cases, the courts have also been known to simply rule in partiality to the state and its crony companies.[74]

The case of Port Klang Free Trade Zone (PKFZ) clearly exemplifies the cloud of secrecy under which state-capitalist collaborations operate, and behind the veneer of which, such companies were often afflicted with massive cost overruns. For PKFZ, these amounted to more than RM4.5 billion in taxpayer money. An international audit investigation ultimately led to several top personalities charged with criminal breach of trusts, including the former president of MCA Dr. Ling Liong Sik.[75] Notwithstanding this, many Malaysians have serious misgivings about Dr. Ling actually being handed down a guilty verdict. In 2007, the late Eric Chia, former president of national steel company Perwaja and close associate of the National Front ruling machinery, was acquitted of embezzlement charges in connection with billions of ringgits losses and the eventual bankruptcy of the corporation.[76]

Another striking feature of these state-linked companies has also been that many of them had been relatively successful public organizations before they were privatized by the state or left at the mercy of its crony capitalists. The case involving the national airlines Malaysian Airlines (MAS) exemplifies this. Its CEO Tajudin Ramly, an UMNO crony, managed to buy controlling shares in the corporation at what was likely to be sub-market prices. He was then able to enrich his family and other close business associates through irregular and undisclosed sub-contracting transactions. These contracting works proved inefficient, resulting in the airline being previously one of the most successful air carriers in the world to having suffered a loss of more than RM8 billion within a few years.[77]

A similar case involved one-time traditional powerhouse Sime Darby, whose major equity holder was PNB. In 2010, it was reported that the corporation had ran up a budget deficit amounting to nearly RM1 billion. The opposition Pan-Islamic Party (PAS) questioned as to how a corporation whose Board of Directors comprised of past prominent politicians and distinguished civil servants, and which had utilized huge amounts of public funds for investments and purchases, was not able to document its transactions using a proper auditing system.[78] In order to divert public pressure away from the board, whose members comprised of the country's elite class, Sime Darby sacked its Chief Executive Officer instead. To date however, nothing has been done in the way of explaining the staggering losses and the people directly responsible for them.

That Malaysians have been affected by the misappropriations of their moneys to bail out top corporations in trouble is not as directly impacting when compared to the lowering quality of life caused by unfair state corporate welfare practices. This was evident in the price spiking of electricity supply. Malaysia's under-used power grids in the 1990s had provided the country's ruling elites and their crony capitalists with immense profiteering potentials. After public funds had been used to expand its massive infrastructure, the national power company *Tenaga Nasional Berhad* (TNB), whose operations had already been subsidized by Petronas, was forced into rather dubious outsourcing contracts with five major independent power providers (IPP) for the right to supply Malaysia's electricity. According to a *Harakahdaily* report dated June 6, 2011, companies belonging to National-Front linked entrepreneurs Yeoh Tiong Lay, Ananda Krishnan, Mokhtar Albukhary, and Lim Goh Tong were among the largest beneficiaries.[79]

Despite Petronas's continuing subsidies to both TNB and the five IPPs, electricity tariffs have also been consistently passed on to consumers. In explaining the latest and highest price inflation occurred on June 1, 2011, the state revealed that "competitive market forces" had compelled the elimination of consumer subsidies in order to curb over-usage. What it failed to mention however was that the IPPs had been guaranteed at least 20 percent return on investments as stipulated by the agreement with TNB, regardless of the circumstances of usage.[80] The removal of consumer subsidies meant that tax payers have been burdened with additional high costs of living in order to ensure these companies' huge profits.

Through the years, Malaysians have not able to address their grievances beyond taking them to opposition parties, whose petitions for further inquiries often get submerged under the might of the ruling party and the state-controlled court systems. The general patterns of privatization, subsidization, losses, and bailouts of state-linked companies as well as traditional rent-seeking economic linkages between the state and its coalition of proxy capitalists have increasingly defined the structural character of Malaysian state-corporate alliances. This in part explains the consistent failures and short life-spans of many of these companies. Often, the personnel that man the top positions of these enterprises have been political appointees rather than experienced executives and professionals in their fields. Additionally, the modes of earnings for many of these state-linked companies have mostly come by way of speculative buy-outs, subcontracting works, or transitory assembly roles rather than full-scale production operations. If the state had hoped for these companies to lead the country into full industrialization, the mission has certainly sputtered. The continuing saga of scandals and backroom intrigues has further made attaining industrialization through civility in governance and economic competitiveness rather unrealistic and far-fetched.

More importantly, another major reason why Malaysian companies have experienced non-substantial industrial growth has also been owed to the country's marginal position within the world economy, and the resulting dependency of Malaysian corporations on the investments of and supply-oriented relationships with western and Japanese TNCs. Over-reliance on this external sources of capital have also effectively diminished Malaysian industrial prospects for research and technological development, which in turn has undermined and stood in the way of enhancing local productive and exporting capacities. This unswerving dependency also encourages local capitalists and comprador entrepreneurs to steer away from building up internal productive capabilities and instead go for quick profit-taking as economic *rentiers*, thereby reproducing the cycle of non-productivity of their companies. The continuing deficiency in overall competency has severely stunted the development of high-end and value-added manufacturing and services badly needed to see Malaysia through to a maturing level of industrial growth.

More problems will come for Malaysian companies when the Asean Free Trade Area becomes fully operational. Officially commenced in 2010, the phased implementation of regional free trade would require Malaysian companies to compete without tariff protection for a variety of products ranging from agricultural produce to finished consumer items. The inability to sustain their own markets at home would leave these companies at the peril of other more efficient competitors from abroad. Similarly, without a comparative regional advantage, these state-linked corporations would also be unable to exploit the removal of trade barriers in markets outside of Malaysia.

More worryingly, the Malaysian economy has witnessed the outflow of FDI to cheaper wage regions such as Indonesia, China, and Vietnam. In 2006 there was approximately US$6 billion outflow of capital from Malaysia, including those from its own state-linked companies. This was double the amount of about US$3 billion the previous year.[81] In fact, continued investments outflow of Malaysian companies, who now prefer to profit from overseas purchases and contracting, reached US$7.9 billion in 2010. There is much concern, of course, that such exodus of domestic sources of local jobs and skill development would make it difficult for the state to meet its objectives of transitioning Malaysia into a "high income" economy.[82] In order for this goal to even near realization, the Malaysian economy must register a consistent 7.5 percent annual growth rate.[83] Given the highly globalized economic atmosphere and declining investments, this would seem a formidable task. It would compound the already difficult effort to push the country onto a higher development stage, owing to its relatively marginal position in the capitalist world economy and the dependent as well as limited nature of industrial development. This increasingly bleak outlook would sooner or later affect the legitimacy of the state in achieving national economic development through industrialization.

The fact that the state could authoritatively decide on all of the country's economic policies, to the extent that these policies have allowed state alliances with capitalists to expand outside the interests of the national economy, also illustrates the incredible political power it has assumed since the 1969 elections. Through paramountcy in political power, the ruling elites in Malaysia have been able to use the various social and political institutions at their disposal to conceal or distract public attention away from the various resultant problems of Malaysia's capitalist development process, including widespread corruption and social economic inequalities. A more detailed discussion of this will be carried out in the next chapter.

Summary

Industrial development in Malaysia has provided its ruling elites with the control and access to the economic resources they badly needed to remain in power. This is especially the case with UMNO, whose continued reliance on Malay electoral support has compelled the party to take advantage of economic growth in order to further advance Malay-Bumiputera economic opportunities through various affirmative-action policies favoring these groups. The eventual insecurity of dependency on external sources of capital, both foreign and ethnic Chinese, would eventually materialize into the party's nurturing of its own capitalist class through the largest and most extensive of these policies, the NEP. It is through these party-connected entrepreneurs that UMNO has sought to strengthen its economic power base and extend its political longevity. Additionally, the close relationship among UMNO-affiliated Malay capitalists and their trusted ethnic Chinese and Indian partners linked to the National Front illustrates the larger elitist nature of the current consociational arrangement, which has enabled these elites to access and obtain numerous political economic advantages derived from Malaysia's industrial development.

The character of the country's industrial development however, has become increasingly unstable due to the globalizing nature of the capitalist world economy. The near collapse of the national economy under the weight of heavily globalized market transactions had caused much of Malaysia's state-linked companies to accumulate massive and recurring debts. Nevertheless, the intricate and interconnected character of state-capitalist alliances in Malaysia has made it possible for many of these companies to access and utilize public funds in order to bail out their troubled businesses. In many cases, much of the public money and assistance used to rescue many of these corporations from impending bankruptcy has also been exploited by the ruling elite and their crony entrepreneurs to profit off their corporate losses.

Malaysia's ruling and capitalist elites are not the only ones to have fortuned off the country's economic growth. Foreign capitalists have also siphoned off their share of spoils as well. Malaysia has been disadvantaged from the start by its economically dependent position in the capitalist world economy. Lacking technology and capital, the country has primarily survived on foreign direct investments as an important source of fuelling its industrial development. Accommodating the needs of foreign corporations has mainly come in the form of infrastructure provisions and generously flexible investments policies that often sidestepped or totally excluded essential research and technology transfers for local industrial development. At the same time, restrictions on export markets and production contents imposed upon local manufacturing partners have also constrained the expansion of home-grown and competent Malaysian enterprises, which would otherwise represent the country's indicative hallmark toward a fully industrialized economy. As a result, state-linked companies have not been able to develop localized skills and capabilities needed for high-end manufacturing and services provisions and have often resorted to chancing upon profits through the convenience of their *rentiership* positions.

Overall, the larger and more important consequence of Malaysia's dependent development has been its persistent social inequalities, which would continually threaten the stability of the current political arrangement. Malaysia's capitalist development in this respect remains non-extensive in reach, while corruption among its ruling and business elites, who seek to stay in positions of power through the control of the country's economy, has become more rampant and widespread.

Notes

1. K. S. Jomo, *Question of Class: Capital, the State, and Uneven Development in Malaya* (Singapore: University of Singapore Press, 1986), 220.
2. Chi Sek Choo, "Accelerated Industrialization and Employment Opportunities in Malaysia," *Geoforum* 13, no. 1 (January 1982):15-18.
3. Raja Mohar Raja Badiozaman, "Foreign Investment: The Malaysian Experience" (paper presented at the *Annual Lecture of the Malaysian Economic Association*, Kuala Lumpur, Malaysia, November 1976), 4.
4. Lutz Hoffman and Tew Nee Tan, "Patterns of Growth and Structural Change in West Malaysia's Manufacturing Industry," in *Readings on Malaysian Economic Development*, ed. David Lim, (Kuala Lumpur: Oxford University Press, 1975), 142-45.
5. Jomo, *Question*, 215.
6. John Drabble, *Economic History of Malaysia, c.1800-1990: The Transition to Modern Economic Growth* (New York: St. Martin's Press, 2000), 244-45.
7. Drabble, *Economic*, 243.
8. Harold Crouch, *Government and Society in Malaysia* (Sydney: Allen & Unwin, 1996), 20-21.
9. Drabble, *Economic*, 186.
10. Jomo, *Question*, 237.
11. Ishak Shari and Rugayah Mat Zin, "Patterns and Trends of Income Distribution in Malaysia, 1970-87," *Southeast Asian Review* 25, no. 4 (April 1990): 106.
12. M. Zainuddin Salleh and Zulkifly Osman, "The Economic Structure," in *Political Economy of Malaysia*, ed. Ernest Kelvin Fisk and H. Osman-Rani (Kuala Lumpur: Oxford University Press, 1982), 135-37.

13. Pang Eng Fong, "Race, Income Distributions, and Development in Malaysia and Singapore," in *The Chinese in Southeast Asia*, ed. in Linda Lim and L. A. Gossling (Singapore: Maruzen Press, 1983), 317.

14. Kamaruddin Sharif, "The Demographic Structure," in *The Political Economy of Malaysia*, ed. Ernest Kelvin Fisk and H. Osman-Rani (Kuala Lumpur: Oxford University Press, 1982), 71.

15. Drabble, *Economic*, 278.

16. Terence Edmund Gomez and K.S. Jomo, *Malaysia's Political Economy: Politics, Patronage, and Profits* (Cambridge, England: Cambridge University Press 1997), 21.

17. Cheah Boon Kheng, *Malaysia: The Making of a Nation* (Singapore: Institute of Southeast Asian Studies, 2002), 34.

18. Yen Ching-Hwang, *Chinese in Southeast Asia and Beyond: Socieconomic Dimensions and Beyond* (Singapore: World Scientific Publishing, 2008), 220-26.

19. Loo Seng Piew, "Schooling in Malaysia," in *Going to School in East Asia*, ed. Gerard Postiglione and Jason Tan (London: Greenwood Publishing, 2008), 212.

20. Diane Mauzy, "Language and Language Policy in Malaysia," in *Language Policy and National Unity*, ed. William R. Beer and James E. Jacob (Totowa, NJ: Rowman and Littlefield, 1985), 167-69.

21. Amy Freedman, *Political Participation and Ethnic Minorities: Chinese Overseas in Malaysia, Indonesia, and the United States* (New York: Routledge, 2000), 79.

22. Karl Von Vorys, *Democracy without Consensus* (Princeton, NJ: Princeton University Press, 1975), 270-75.

23. Zakaria Ahmad, "The Political Structure," in *Political Economy of Malaysia*, ed. Ernest Kelvin Fisk and H. Osman-Rani (Kuala Lumpur: Oxford University Press, 1982), 95.

24. John Funston, "Writings on May 13" (paper presented at Seminar Aliran Kini dalam Sains Kemasysrakatan dan Kemanusiaan, National University of Malaysia, Bangi, Malaysia, October, 1974), 23-24.

25. Von Vorys, *Democracy*, 280-85.

26. James P. Ongkili, *Nation-Building in Malaysia, 1946-1974* (Singapore: Oxford University Press, 1985), 203.

27. Von Vorys, *Democracy*, 334-37.

28. NOC, *May 13 Tragedy* (Kuala Lumpur: Government Printers, 1969), 22.

29. For more information on the NEP, read Zakaria Ahmad and Sharifah Alatas, "Malaysia: In an Uncertain Mode," in *Driven by Growth*, ed. Paul Morley (New York: M.E. Sharpe, 1999), 186-89.

30. Tham Seong Chee, "Ideology, Politics and Economic Modernization: The Case of the Malays in Malaysia," *Southeast Asian Journal of Social Science* 1, no. 1 (August 1973): 50.

31. Gomez and Jomo, *Malaysia*, 19.

32. Gomez and Jomo, *Malaysia*, 24.

33. Faridah Jamaluddin, "Malaysia's New Economic Policy: Has It Been a Success?" in *Boundaries of Clan and Color: Transnational Comparison of Inter-Group Disparity*, ed. William Darity Jr. and Ashwini Deshpande (New York: Routledge, 2003), 167.

34. Muniappan Perumal, "Economic Growth and Income Inequality in Malaysia 1957-1987," *Singapore Economic Review* 34, no. 2 (October 1989): 35-37.

35. Data calculated from Tables 2.17, 2.18, 5.29 and 5.30, Shireen Mardziah Hashim, *Income Inequality and Poverty in Malaysia* (Lanham, MD: Rowman and Littlefied, 1998).

36. Article 152 of the Federal Constitution upholds the Malay language as the official national language. Article 153 (2) compels the King to "...safeguard the special provision of the Malays and natives of any of the States of Sabah and Sarawak and to ensure the reservation for Malays and natives of any of the States of Sabah and Sarawak of such proportion as he may deem reasonable of positions in the public service (other than the public service of a State) and of scholarships, exhibitions and other similar educational or training privileges or special facilities given or accorded by the Federal Government, and when any permit or license for the operation of any trade or business is required by federal law, then, subject to the provisions of that law and this Article, of such permits and licenses."

37. Shamsul Amri Baharuddin, "The Economic Dimension of Malay Nationalism," *Developing Economies* 35, no. 3 (September 1997): 252-53.

38. Shireen Hashim, "The NEP and Changes in Poverty and Income Distribution," in *Sustaining Growth, Enhancing Distribution: The NEP and NDP Revisited*, ed. J. Yahaya, N.P. Tey and K.K. Yeoh (Kuala Lumpur: CEDER, 2003), 5-7.

39. Michael Borrus, "Left for Dead: Asian Production Networks and the Revival of US Electronics" (working paper No. 100 presented at Berkeley Roundtable on the International Economy, San Francisco, CA, September 1997), 134-36.

40. Gary Gereffi, "Commodity Chains and Regional Divisions of Labor in East Asia," in *The Four Asian Tigers: Economic Development and the Global Political Economy*, ed. Eun Mee Kim (San Diego, CA: Academic Press, 1998), 104-105.

41. Drabble, *Economic*, 197.

42. J. V. Jesudason, *Ethnicity and the Economy: The State, Chinese Business and Multinationals in Malaysia* (Singapore: Oxford University Press, 1989), 180-89.

43. Ichiro Numazaki, "The Export-oriented Industrialization of Pacific Rim Countries and their Presence in the Global Market," in *The Four Asian Tigers: Economic Development and the Global political Economy*, ed. Eun Mee Kim (San Diego: Academic Press, 1998), 70-73.

44. Mitchell Bernard and John Ravenhill, "Beyond Product Cycles and Flying Geese: Regionalization, Hierarchy, and the Industrialization of East Asia," *World Politics* 47, no.2 (January 1995): 171-75.

45. Nokuyuki Yasuda, "Malaysia's New Economic Policy and the Industrial Co-Ordination Act," *Developing Economics* 39, no. 4 (December 1991): 331-32.

46. Yasuda, Malaysia's, 346-47.

47. Drabble, *Economic*, 240-241.

48. Alasdair Bowie, *Crossing the National Divide: State, Society and the Politics of Economic Transformation in Malaysia* (New York: Columbia University Press, 1991), 115-17.

49. Rokiah Alavi, *Industrialisation in Malaysia: Import Substitution and Infant Industry Performance* (London: Routledge, 1996), 175-78.

50. Jomo, *Question*, 247.

51. Robert E. B. Lucas and Donald Verry, *Restructuring the Malaysian Economy* (New York: St. Martin's Press, 1999), 199-202.

52. Fujio Hara, "Malaysia's New Economic Policy and the Chinese Business Community," *The Developing Economies* 19, no. 4 (December 1991): 358-59.

53. Sally Cheong, *Bumiputera Controlled Companies in the KLSE* (Petaling Jaya: Corporate Research Services Sdn. Bhd, 1993), 165-67.

54. Keiko Saruwatari, "Malaysia's Localisation Policy and its Impact on British-owned Enterprises," *Developing Economies* 29, no. 4 (December 1991): 384.

55. Kamal Salih and Zainal Aznam Yusof, "Overview of the NEP and Framework for a Post-1990 National Economic Policy: Options," *Malaysian Economic Review* 24, no. 2 (March 1989): 22-25.

56. Rugayah Mohamed, "Public Enterprises." In *Privatising Malaysia: Rents, Rhetoric, Realities*, ed. K.S. Jomo (London: Westview, 1995), 77-78.

57. Drabble, *Economic*, 200-201

58. Bowie, *Crossing*, 182.

59. Heng Pek Koon, *Chinese Politics in Malaysia: A History of the Malaysian Chinese Association* (Singapore: University of Singapore Press, 1988), 132.

60. Heng Pek Koon, "The Chinese Business Elite in Malaysia," in *Southeast Asian Capitalists*, ed. Ruth Thomas McVey (Ithaca, NY: Cornell Southeast Asia Program Publications, 1997), 128-30.

61. Paul Krugman, *Return of Depression Economics* (New York: W.W. Norton & Company, 1999), 161-65.

62. K. S. Jomo, *Growth and Structural Change in the Malaysian Economy* (London: Macmillan Press, 1990), 130-31.

63. Jagdish Bhagwati, *Wind of the Hundred Days: How Washington Mismanaged Globalization* (Boston, MA: MIT Press, 2001), 4-6.

64. For full information on the 1997-98 Asian financial crisis, read Stephen Haggard, *Political Economy of Asian Financial Crisis* (Washington D.C.: Institute for International Economics, 2000).

65. Mustapa Mohamad, "The Case of Malaysia after the Financial Crisis and the Way Ahead" (paper presented at the Forum for Economic Transition and Change, Northern University of Malaysia, Sintok, Malaysia, October 2001), 6.

66. Bloomberg, "How a Blood Feud in Malaysia Spun out of Control," *Bloomberg Businessweek* 1998, www.businessweek.com/archives/1998/b3603140.arc.html (accessed July 15, 2009).

67. Jeff Tan, *Privatization in Malaysia: Regulation, Rent-seeking, and Policy Failure* (London: Routledge, 2008), 158-59.

68. K. S. Jomo, ed., *Japan and Malaysian Development: In the Shadow of the Rising Sun* (New York: Routledge, 2001), 270-72.

69. *Asia Sentinel*, "Bailout Alert in Malaysia," *Asia Sentinel*, www.asiasentinel.com/index.php?option_content&tas=viewed=510Itemid=32 (accessed June 12, 2009).

70. Anil Netto, "Bumpy Road for Proton," *Asia Times* 2005, www.atimes/atimes/SoutheastAsia/GG30Ac01.html (accessed March 20, 2008).

71. Tan, *Privatization*, 185.

72. K. S. Jomo, "Malaysia Props up Crony Capitalists," *Asian Wall Street Journal*, December 21, 1998, A6.

73. *New York Times*, "Malaysia Takes Control of No.2 Bank Company," *New York Times* 1998, www.nytimes.com/1998/12/01/business (accessed December 2, 2010).

74. Marhalim Abas, "Government Need Not Reveal Syabas Deal: Appeals Court," *Malay Mail* 2011, www.mmail.com.my/content/64939 (accessed April 2, 2011). In this case, the privatization of water supply in the state of Selangor had been awarded to an UMNO crony company called Syabas. A residents' group filed the action in court and won the right to view documentation regarding transactions relating to the purchase of company. The Appeals Courts however overruled the decision for reason that the group had no standing in the matter.

75. *My Sinchew*, "Ling Applies to Transfer Case to High Court," *My Sinchew.Com* 2010, www.mysinchew.com/node/44378 (accessed January 12, 2011).

76. Raphael Wong, "Eric Chia Acquitted of CBT," *Star Online* 2007, thestar.com.my/news/story.asp?file=2007/6/37/nation (accessed June 11, 2009).

77. Abas Marhalim, "MACC to Meet MAS to Discuss Tajudin Case," *Malay Mail* 2010, www.mmail.com.my/content/47639 (accessed September 12, 2010).

78. Shazwan Mustafa Kamal, "PAS Looks to Fill PKR's Shoes" *Malaysia Insider* 2010, www.themalaysianinsider.com/malaysia/article.html (accessed June 12, 2010).

79. *Harakahdaily*, "Najib Told to Answer Former TNB Boss." *Harakahdaily* 2011, harakah.net.my/index.php/berita-utama.html (accessed July 16 2011).

80. G. Vinod, "DAP Calls for New IPP-TNB Deal," *Free Malaysia Today* 2011, www.freemalaysiatoday.com/2011/05/31/dap-calls-for-new-tnb-ipp-deal (accessed June 31 2011).

81. UNCTAD, *World Investment Report 2007: Transnational Corporations, Extractive Industries, and Development* (Geneva: United Nations Publications, 2007), 41.

82. The year 2020 has been designated by the state as the year Malaysia would achieve industrialized status through a high income economy.

83. Caroline Hong, "Investments Outflows Spark Debate in Malaysia," *Straits Times* 2010, www.asianewsnet.net/home/news.php.html (accessed September 12, 2010).

Chapter 7
Sustaining Elite Dominance: Economic Nationalism and Institutional Control, 1980-2011

Amid persistent ethnic-class inequalities, widespread corruption, and an elusive industrialization goal, Malaysia's ruling elites have nevertheless maintained their political legitimacy and power under the consociational system. This has been achieved over the years through, among other things, the propagandizing of economic nationalism as a means to subdue Malaysians under a false sense of unity, and the excessive penetration of state executive powers over the country's major political institutions in order to pre-empt or stifle popular challenges against the ruling elites of the National Front.

However, as Malaysia's path to full industrialization is made more difficult by an obtrusively globalizing environment, the ruling elites' ability to protract their political absolutism through economic growth also becomes weaker. As a result, the state has resorted to a further "strangulation" of the country's already-asphyxiated democratic process, making it unmistakably clear that Malaysia's elite-driven capitalist democracy may push closer toward authoritarianism.

Persistent Ethnic-Class Inequalities

The dependent nature of capitalist development in a particular country often results in wide or continuing gaps between the privileged few and the rest of the population. In places where democratic institutions are weak, the capitalist system allows an extensive degree of worker abuse and exploitation by powerful class interests, often facilitated by the state's hesitance, and even unwillingness to prioritize freedom, social justice, and civil liberties on behalf of workers and citizens. In such systems, there is very little likelihood that national economic benefits could be equally or proportionately shared among the people. For those in the lower levels of the class hierarchy, avenues for upward mobility become virtually non-existent. The capitalist system's vulnerability to elite class manipulation often entails, as a corollary, the social reproduction of inequalities and the entrenchment of weaker social groups in perpetual poverty.

This is true of Malaysia. In spite of the successes attained in elevating the general socio-economic status of Malays and Bumiputeras as well as in the narrowing of Malay and non-Malay income gaps, the NEP has not significantly closed the widening class inequalities among Malays.[1] A main reason for this has been the class-biasness of the NEP's implementation. Although the primary aim of the policy has been to assist the poorer sections of the Malay community by opening up better access to educational and economic opportunities, the benefits derived from the policy's implementation however have been partially predisposed toward those with greater resources.

That every Malay and Bumiputera was eligible for NEP privileges meant, in most cases, those in the upper classes were often placed in a better position than their compatriots from the lower classes to fully exploit these advantages. A large part of this has to do with the fact that families from higher income and wealth levels usually were better informed about the implications of the NEP and thus were better prepared to position themselves and their families ahead of others in the pursuit of opportunities. Most Malay and Bumiputera children from relatively wealthy or middle class backgrounds were also more likely to inherit comparatively higher amounts of social, cultural, and economic capitals than those from more modest origins, thereby enhancing their competitiveness in areas of education, occupation, and wealth creation. The higher classes also often have greater proximity to people with authority, who may be able to help them enroll in prestigious schools or obtain immediate approvals for scholarship applications. This is affirmed by economic analyst, Ozay Mehmet, who said: "the method of awarding scholarships is heavily biased toward the richer Malay households. To a lesser extent, it also favors the richer Chinese and Indians."[2]

Here, class, more than ethnicity, seemed to present the decisive factor in the extension of one's life chances in Malaysia. It must be noted again that a substantial number of non-Malay businesses had been given privileged access to participation in state-related projects under the NEP. Additionally, many non-Malay urban residents also benefited from the spill-over of infrastructure investments that came along with national capitalist development under the various NEP industrialization programs. Since there was often no effective mechanism to reduce the effects of class-based partialities in policy implementations, the reproduction of various existing social inequalities often accompanied overall capitalist development in Malaysia.

In this respect, the NEP and other development policies have tended to heavily subsidize both the Malay and non-Malay upper classes, resulting in higher levels of advantages and benefits accruing within the upper echelons of Malaysian society. This problem became too prevalent by 2010 that the National Economic Advisory Council (NEAC) finally acknowledged in its inaugural report that despite the NEP, income growth since 1990 has been strong primarily at the top 20 percent of Malaysian income earners while the bottom 40 percent of households has experienced the slowest rise in average income.[3]

Intra-ethnic disparity for Malays as represented by the Gini coefficient index on income inequality remained about the same—from 0.46 in 1970 to about 0.47 in 2007. The situation was rather similar for non-Malays as well. Inequality in incomes stuck around the same figures for the year 2007 as they did in 1970 for both the ethnic Chinese and Indians, as represented by Gini coefficients of 0.43 and 0.41 respectively.[4] One may point out that Malaysia's Gini indexes seem to display more positive indicators than many other developing countries in the world. While this is true, one must also be aware that Malaysia is a relatively small country of 28 million people with a considerably more developed economy. The concern here is on the continuing nature of inequality rather than the quantitative aspect of the index itself.

More significantly however, despite the NEP's implementation, the incidence of poverty was also still highest among Malays. In 2007, it stood at 5.7 percent, followed by Indians at 2.5 percent and Chinese at 0.6 percent for the same year.[5] The ethnic Chinese, meanwhile, have generally maintained their economic supremacy despite special advantages given to Malays and Bumiputeras. This is hardly surprising since the rapidly expanding national economy had opened wide-ranging business opportunities in infrastructure construction, services provision, retail, and consumer commodity production. These have materialized into considerable recruitment and participation of a variety of workers at every level and section of a growing manufacturing economy, yielding expansions in the professional, managerial and retail employment sectors where non-Malays still dominated.

Thus average ethnic Chinese and Indian household incomes actually increased through the NEP years from 1971 to 1990 by 20 percent and 9 percent respectively. The ratio of mean income of ethnic Chinese relative to the national income was also highest among the major ethnic groups in 2007 at about 1.3, compared to Indians at 1.0, and Malays 0.8.[6] On top of that, the non-Malays' combined share of total equity also rose from 34 percent to 54.6 percent by the end of 1990. Malay-Bumiputera equity share meanwhile fell short of the 30 percent NEP target despite its rise from 2.3 percent in 1971 to 20.3 percent twenty years later.[7] Hence, the equity objective of the NEP remained unfulfilled by1990, the year of the policy's designated expiry. As discussed in the earlier chapter, this was hardly surprising since ethnic Chinese capitalists and foreign investors have been among the major beneficiaries of the various capital-related NEP investments in the country.

In light of these persistent social inequalities, the Malaysian ruling elite has reason to be anxious. Such indicators do not fare well among some segments of well-informed Malays, who have been historically critical of state policies affecting their group. Although the NEP has virtually locked Malays into an ideologically dependent relationship with UMNO, especially in cultivating the belief that the party's commitment and capacity to enhance Malay economic aspirations has no equal rival, the party's relationship with a growing Malay middle classes has remained vulnerable during periods of elections. There have been instances where the more educated urban Malay population would openly raise concerns regarding the inadequate progress made among the poorer Malays amidst overall national prosperity. The spread of such doubts cast on UMNO potentially places the party in poor public image among the rural population. For UMNO, there is persistent fear of the repeat of the political troubles caused by the loss of Malay support during the tumultuous 1969 elections that nearly cost the ruling elite its leadership hold on the country.

Hence, there is always guarded caution on the part of the ruling elite with regards to any uncomplimentary revelation of its social-economic policies. The legitimacy of UMNO might well be compromised if for any reason Malays and Bumiputeras became displeased with the way state policies have failed to perform to expectations, especially with regard to the distribution of economic benefits. Therefore, the party is obliged to consistently vocalize and display its perfunctory relevance in defending "Malay rights and interests" at all costs, especially during times when support from Malays seems to be low or at risk.

Sadly, such task has often come in the way of instigating contempt and hostility against non-Malays. This is achieved by inculcating the belief among Malays of an impending national political takeover by non-Malays if they were not united in throwing their support behind UMNO.[8] Such fear tactics show both the boldness and desperation on the part of UMNO to retain its influence among Malays at any price. Interestingly, non-Malay elites within the National Front have seldom countered the deliberate antagonisms posited by their colleagues in UMNO against their own ethnic groups. This is hardly surprising however, considering that these elites have derived their own political power from their close consociational relations with UMNO, and are therefore mindful of getting in the way of these divisive political strategies drummed up by the lead party.

The rationale behind these deliberate and sustained provocations against a discordant citizenry is commonly shared by ruling elites in other multicultural societies. The defining fear among these elites in such societies often pertains to the plausibility of popular and concerted citizen efforts for greater equality, freedom, and empowerment chipping away at the uncontested powers of the state. Since resolving problems of inequalities through resource redistribution often entails major economic concessions on the part of the elite, it has not been exceptional in countries where democratic institutions are fragile for the state to apply direct suppression of popular anti-systemic forces. In many of these countries, the state becomes extremely heedful of any organized effort on the part of civil society movements and opposition parties, whether through the electoral franchise or collective grassroots organizations, to influence and mobilize the masses toward political change. Similarly, in Malaysia, the state often seeks to maintain social-political distances between ethnic groups as a way to prevent serious challenges against the National Front and thereby safeguard its ruling elites' hold on power.

The following sections will critically analyze the various ideological and administrative measures that the ruling elites have taken to avert serious citizen challenges to their power and to ensure National Front victories at the electoral polls. These include the propagation of economic nationalism to consolidate the legitimacy of the state and the consociational structure as well as extending state executive control over the country's major social-political institutions in order to coagulate the ruling elites' vulnerable power and authority.

Elite-Driven Economic Nationalism

The shape and focus of Malaysian economic policy shifted onto a different gear in 1991 with the introduction of the National Development Policy (NDP) to replace the expired NEP.[9] In its essence, the NDP involved ideologically connecting the projected benefits of state-led industrial development with the larger aspiration of Malaysian citizens to equally participate in and benefit from an economically developed and prosperous society.[10] The economic dimension of nationalism was craftily embedded in the assumption that the viability as well as attainability of full industrialization in Malaysia is possible only through whole-hearted public support for state development policies. Here, the notion of economic growth was to become highly instrumental in binding Malaysians from all ethnic backgrounds toward the common goal of industrial development.

For the ruling elites, economic nationalism was to provide the legitimacy that often comes with rapid economic growth and higher quality of life for all Malaysians. As the NEP had successfully served to generate Malay economic ethnonationalism prior to 1990, the NDP was to be taken a step higher and function as an economic nationalist instrument for a wider spectrum of Malaysians. This is particularly so with regards to the ethnic Chinese, whose evasive support for the National Front remained a substantial impediment to the ruling alliance's complete monopoly of Malaysian politics. The effort to draw the interests of non-Malays toward the NDP was critical in view of the improbability of achieving a fully industrialized economy in Malaysia without the intense participation of local private capital and labor. In a way, the NDP appeared to reach out to non-Malays by attempting to shift its ideological platform beyond the ethnic confines of the NEP.

Hence, while not de-emphasizing the Malay-Bumiputera preferential goals, which still remained an observable aspect of the NDP, the state began outwardly highlighting the critical collaboration of all Malaysians toward accomplishing a united goal, one that was premised on the attainment of a fully developed and industrialized society benefiting all citizens. To formalize this effort, UMNO and the National Front proceeded to encapsulate the spirit of economic nationalism within its comprehensive *Wawasan 2020* (Vision 2020) project.

The larger theme of the *Wawasan 2020* centers on efforts toward a fully industrialized Malaysia by the year 2020. However, according to this ideology, the route to this goal lies not solely in high economic performance. There are philosophical paradigms that need to be addressed, developed and cultivated in order for Malaysians to overcome some of the major social, political, and economic challenges that accompany the transition toward a fully industrialized society. These challenges can be met through the following:

a): Establishing a united Malaysian nation made up of one *Bangsa Malaysia* (Malaysian Nationality).
b): Creating a psychologically liberated, secure, and developed Malaysian society.
c): Fostering and developing a mature democratic society.
d): Establishing a fully moral and ethical society.
e): Establishing a mature, liberal, and tolerant society.
f): Establishing a scientific and progressive society.
g): Establishing a fully caring society.
h): Ensuring an economically just society, in which there is a fair and equitable distribution of the wealth of the nation.
i): Establishing a prosperous society with an economy that is fully competitive, dynamic, robust, and resilient.

The *Wawasan 2020* still represents the quintessence of state-led industrial development in Malaysia. If any significant success was owed to the state with regards to attaining this economic nationalist vision, it would come from the almost crusading nature of its promotion. Throughout the 1990s and into the first decade of the new millennium, the state made sure that the spirit of *Wawasan 2020* was entrenched into every aspect of Malaysian life. Malaysians were constantly reminded of the *Wawasan 2020* goals reverberating through numerous government-endorsed patriotic songs, plays, documentaries, and media advertisements on state-run television, radio and other media outlets.[12]

Supplementing the effort to keep Malaysians focused on the *Wawasan 2020* goals has been its supplementary *Malaysia Boleh* (Malaysians can do it) campaign, served to drive the imagination and confidence of Malaysians toward world-class accomplishments in various fields.[13] Many of these achievements, such as in sports, were often highlighted to accredit the state for its support and endorsement of the various successful athletes and their programs. Other efforts, such as sending an "astronaut" into space, were specifically designed to generate awe among its citizens with regards to the state's role in motivating Malaysians to reach what the state considers, world level achievements. Many Malaysians have been critical of these efforts however, such as in the case of the astronaut. Here, the country has no operational space program, and had instead spent millions of dollars training a space "participant" through a joint Russian initiative. Such "feats" were nevertheless impressive enough for the majority of rural folks in the UMNO support base, who followed these events through the narrated lens of various state-owned media.[14]

At about the same time the *Wawasan 2020* campaign was launched, another state-centered doctrine was being heavily promulgated in the shape of the much-debated "Asian values" philosophy. Introduced by technocrats in Malaysia and Singapore, this ideology advanced the notion that industrialization in Asian societies can only be successfully attained through the subscription of Eastern and Confucianist approaches to development. These include strict abidance to civic discipline, collective and individual self-restraint, and citizen trust in state leadership.[15] With specific references to the successful industrialization of South Korea, Taiwan, and even Japan under the strict patronage of the state, advocates of this worldview pointed how these countries managed to uniquely attain rapid economic growth through the collective subscription of their unique cultural values of hard work, discipline, and loyalty. Conversely, they stressed, overemphases placed on western individualism and political freedom have proven counterproductive to the political and economic stability of many developing countries. There were, they argued, "irreconcilable" cultural differences pivoted in the distinctness between the collective goal orientation of eastern societies and the western world's prioritization of individual liberty and freedom, which often came at society's expense. Critics, however, have viewed the Asian values doctrine as nothing more than a substantiation of the state's patronizing role in the politics and economy of the country, and lcss to do with cultural-philosophical incompatibilities in governance and development.[16]

Nonetheless, the state has portrayed the *Wawasan 2020* as illustrative of the "Asian" approach to economic prosperity along a scripted and guided path to national development. Despite the banal nature of many of these propagandas, few would publicly scoff at their frivolity, especially when they occur alongside a vibrant national economy. In fact, public admiration and salutations given to UMNO and the National Front for charting the country toward economic growth have turned the ruling elites into the definitive and symbolic representation of *Malaysia Boleh*. This has served well for the state not only in terms of justifying the soundness of its policies but also in distracting citizens from the country's many real-life problems in the form of increased state authoritarianism, widespread corruption, and continuing social inequalities that have accompanied Malaysia's rapid economic development.

On the whole however, it became fortunate for UMNO and the National Front that the implementation of the NDP occurred during a period of unprecedented industrial growth. Confidence in the national economy that brought in fresh penetrations of investments from the late 1980s to the mid-1990s allowed Malaysia to perform at an impressive 8.4 percent average annual real GDP (Gross Domestic Product) growth rate, with average savings rate standing around 34 percent of Gross National Product. Driven by a meticulously crafted Industrial Master Plan, exports in manufactured products reached 80 percent of GDP, stimulating exceptional demands in capital and consumption goods.[17] As a middle-income country, Malaysia compared favorably to Ireland, Portugal, and Spain, and was placed ahead of many countries in Latin America and Eastern Europe in economic performance.

With the national economy prospering, there left little room for doubt among many Malaysians that state-led industrialization was successfully transforming their country toward higher-end development. Economic growth also triggered further confidence in the security of returns on investments, which brought in many bankers and corporate enterprises to Malaysia seeking to take advantage of what they saw as a highly conducive and stable environment for profit-making. Rapid growth during this period also certainly gave considerable legitimacy to the ruling National Front, especially from the middle class who were beginning to see the economic and social benefits flowing in their direction.[18] Any criticism of the NDP during this period of prosperity would be outwardly countered by the evidencing of a thriving economy and stable political climate that state-led industrialization provided.

Nevertheless, if economic nationalism was instrumental in mobilizing and legitimizing Malay-Bumiputera support for UMNO under the consociational system, it also threatened to be the source of the party's potential downfall. Expectations of economic development are often high, and for economic and industrial growth to contain any justifiable value, its dispensing of rewards must be carried out fairly and justly. In other words, as a legitimizing tool, economic nationalism requires the state to visibly and consistently realize the needs and hopes of Malaysians by the actual delivery of higher living standards and greater life opportunities for all of its citizens. Economic growth as a unifying national goal is rendered ineffective when a considerable number of the population hardly gained from national prosperity.

Hence, just as the *Wawasan 2020* economic nationalist rhetoric had been successful in unifying Malaysians behind the state's social economic policies during the rapid growth years of the 1990s, the same economic nationalism narrative became subjected to critical scrutiny when soaring living indexes, increased unemployment, and declining purchasing power were widely felt in times of economic downturns. This was the case in the aftermath of both the 1997 Asian financial meltdown and the 2008-09 global market crises when mounting public disillusionment and doubts regarding the state's timely attainment of *Wawasan 2020* began to surface. By 2010, reduced investments and a sluggish manufacturing sector caused by worldwide capital fallouts began to seriously affect Malaysia's export-led industrial development. Skepticism of state policies began to grow among substantial numbers of Malaysian and foreign analysts, who were now pessimistic about the state's ability to realize its ambition of Malaysia becoming a fully-industrialized and higher-income country by 2020.[19]

Meanwhile tensions grew as ethnic Chinese and Indians began to attribute the drastic decline in economic growth to the state's pandering of Malay capitalist interests. Malays, in turn, were aggrieved with the way these groups hinted for the removal of some of the Malay-Bumiputera requirements as a means to halt investor outflows and alleviate the ailing economy. Economic hardships and increased competition over perceivably scarce resources in Malaysia have often been historically associated with the invigoration of ethnic tensions, as had occurred in the late 1940s, late 1960s, and in the mid-1980s. Against the backdrop of increasingly hostile exchanges and mounting ethnic antagonisms over the country's educational and economic policies, new Prime Minister Najib Razak launched the *One Malaysia* campaign in April 2009 to resuscitate national unity and re-establish public confidence in the state, especially for the benefit of foreign investors.

The *One Malaysia* campaign would eventually serve as a thematic prelude to UMNO's newest showcase of economic nationalism—the New Economic Model (NEM). In mid-2009, the NEAC recruited a number of foreign experts to help draft the NEM. The first official report of the NEM openly addressed major structural weaknesses afflicting Malaysia's industrial development, but focusing mostly on bloated state budgets and over-subsidization of social services and essential goods. Also included in the various proposals were addressing the "brain drain" problem, the institution of more flexible regulations dealing with low-wage foreign workers, and the upgrading of the Malaysian Industrial Development Authority into a one-stop center for investments.[20]

The language used in the NEM seemed to prioritize a "free market" approach to economic development. It hinted the liberalization of many state protective policies aimed at delivering better and more conducive conditions for foreign investors, who welcomed any policy move away from state assistance or subsidies to specific groups. Also, private investors have not been too supportive of any type of extraneous requirement attached to stipulations on loans and investment policies; most have relented grudgingly in fulfilling state preferential quotas for Malays. In turn, there have been lingering concerns on the part of the state that foreign investments would flow toward other locations with fewer structural obstacles on business transactions. In a climate of globalized and open competition, the NEM seems to manifest the state's preparedness in trimming down its pro-Malay-Bumiputera policies, if anything else to encourage greater investments and higher growths in the country.[21]

Nevertheless, the Malaysian state has been confronted with major difficulty in attempting to balance its neo-liberal economic agenda on one hand, and its traditional appeasement of the Malay-Bumiputera electorate through various preferential economic policies on the other. A genuinely "Malaysian" approach to economic nationalism through the NEM has been seen to elicit positive responses from the non-Malay community, whose loss of faith in past reforms saw them, and even talented Malays, emigrate for better pastures abroad.[22] However, the cost of attempting to cut back on Malay-Bumiputera economic privileges could also prove potentially destabilizing for the state. This is especially so in view of the virulent attacks from Malay right-wing factions within and outside of UMNO against the party's leadership since the introduction of the NEM. Expectedly, the underlying objective of the NEM has evoked strident responses from those who had already posited misgivings about the policy. A new wave of ultra-conservative Malay groups, who had formed an umbrella organization called the Malay Consultative Council, asserted that the NEM looked to seriously compromise Malay-Bumiputera special interests purely for the pursuit of national economic growth.

The largest among these groups, Perkasa, has proclaimed in its inauguration, that its mission would unconditionally focus on pressuring the state for continued protection of Malay "special rights" through the upholding of Malay political hegemony or *ketuanan Melayu.*[23] Additionally it has urged the state not to blindly succumb to the immediate demands of economic growth, which it believed would only be highly advantageous to the ethnic Chinese and Indian communities. Perkasa has especially been notorious for its political demagoguery, often attacking non-Malays for what it sees as their proclivity to undermine Malay political power in Malaysia. Interestingly, Perkasa has neither been reprimanded for its criticisms against the NEM nor for its racist overtones. On this, some observers are even convinced that the organization is endorsed by former Prime Minister Dr. Mahathir, and serves as a vehicle for right-wing factions within UMNO to eventually take over the party from the more accommodating elites in power.[24]

In any case, the Malaysian ruling elites have walked a fine line with its *One Malaysia* and NEM policies. On the one hand, UMNO and the state are forced to contemplate liberalizing the economy in order to solicit much-needed investments for industrial development through the *Wawasan 2020* objectives. On the other hand however, UMNO has not been able to "open up" the economy without potentially troubling the Malays, who have formed the customary political base for both the party and the National Front.

That the sudden emergence of reactionary Malay groups has successfully unsettled the state into withholding the NEM's full implementation could be seen in the way many officials have retracted or denied earlier statements regarding the possible phasing out of state preferential treatment for Malays.[25] Some have relented to the voice of Malay ethnocentrism in order to be on the right side of the political spectrum in the event that conservative and right-wing factions managed to assume considerable influence within the party. Others in UMNO have become significantly concerned over the possible sway of Malay political support for right-wing political forces. In *The Star* newspaper report dated July 6, 2010, the country's Deputy Prime Minister Muhyiddin Yasin was quoted as saying that Malays could neither economically survive nor politically endure the onslaught of "external forces" threatening to displace them from their leadership position without the strict patronage of UMNO.[26] Such statements coming from a high-profiled politician in UMNO reflected the philosophical quandary within which the party has found itself. There has been increasing difficulty in reconciling the paradox of economic nationalism that advocates for the unity of all Malaysians through the *Wawasan 2020* goals on one hand, while sustaining the party's historical relevance through the *ketuanan Melayu* agenda on the other. There will be greater problems down the road in terms of long-term political economic instability if UMNO continues to side-step the more genuine problems besetting the Malays or allows the country's multiethnic relations to further deteriorate.

It also must not be lost that the aim and rationale of state policies are grounded on the pursuit and preservation of elite class interests. Economic nationalism as a legitimization strategy is often only supplementary to the larger and more effective approach used by the ruling elites in many developing countries to systematically sustain their political dominance and authority through direct political control. Ever since Malaysia's independence, the National Front has shown that it would not hesitate in suppressing basic civil liberties and freedom in the face of impending threats against ruling class interests. This is often made possible by the ubiquitous presence of the state in almost every social and political institution in the country, which enables the state to manipulatively manage the country's democratic process to the advantage of the ruling elites, thereby rendering ineffective Malaysia's check and balance governing system.

State Institutional Controls

Continuous and overwhelming support of the Malay electorate for UMNO has indirectly preserved the historical durability of Malaysia's elite-driven consociational system. The state's political power and hegemony over other social forces in Malaysia has been further strengthened by its manipulation of the country's democratic process. Since the 1980s, Malaysia's industrialization path has been dotted by tremendous executive control over the country's major democratic institutions, particularly the legislature and judiciary. The exploitation of the country's monarchy as well as the media has also provided the state with a cultural framework within which it is able to define for Malaysians, expectations of citizen loyalty to the state and its authority. Finally, the state's continued use of colonial-era "emergency" regulations has considerably curtailed civil activism within the parameters of what the state delineates as "lawful."

Control of Electoral Process

An independent legislature often represents the most cherished institution in a country's democratic system. In genuine democracies, the executive branch seldom interferes with the running of the parliament or legislative assemblies, since doing so would contravene the basic tenet of representative government. However, many states do frequently manipulate their electoral processes by directly or indirectly regulating legislative actions, expanding the number of appointed assembly seats, or influencing electoral outcomes favorable to the regime and its ruling elite.

As a federation, Malaysia practices a three-tiered government structure located at the federal, state, and local levels. In a single representative-constituency system similar to Britain's, the triumphant political party in national elections forms the majority in parliament. This normally ensures the passing of legislations favorable to the party. The majority party would also establish the government of the day and appoints its head as the Prime Minister, who in turn, selects members of his cabinet of ministers.[27]

The federal parliament in Malaysia comprises two chambers: the *Dewan Negara* (House of appointed Senators) and the *Dewan Rakyat* (House of elected representatives). In each state within the federation, the state assembly consists only of one house of elected state representatives. This assembly is controlled by the party with the most votes from the previous elections, who would also form the state government and appoint the state's chief minister. For the entire history of independent Malaysia, the UMNO-led National Front has assumed control of the *Dewan Rakyat* mainly through Malay electoral support. Helped by a relatively prosperous economy, the ruling coalition (National Alliance before 1974) has triumphed in every election from 1959 to 2008 (See table 7.1 below).

The control of the country's electoral process and constituency structure has also enabled the National Front almost certain victory for a majority of its candidates in both parliamentary and state-level elections. This has, in most cases, given the ruling coalition a constant majority in the country's legislative assemblies, thereby conferring upon the National Front indomitable political powers at both federal and state levels. Throughout Malaysia's history, voting down of federal enactments or policy proposals in both the *Dewan Rakyat* and *Dewan Negara* has rarely, if not ever, occurred. In this respect, the Malaysian prime minister, usually appointed from the presidency of UMNO, has acquired almost unrivaled power in both administrative and legislative capacities.

Table 7.1: Federal Election Results Malaysia, 1959-2008

Election year	**National Alliance (National Front from 1974)**		**Political Opposition**		
	Percent of total seats Won	Percent of total votes	Percent of total seats won	Percent of total votes	Total seats contested
1959	75	N/A	25	N/A	104
1964	81	N/A	19	N/A	104
1969	66	49.3	34	50.7	144
1974	87	60.7	13	39.3	154
1978	84	57.2	16	42.8	154
1982	85	60.5	15	39.5	154
1986	83	55.8	17	41.5	177
1990	70	53.4	30	46.6	180
1995	84	65.2	16	34.8	192
1999	76	56.5	24	46.5	193
2004	90	63.9	10	36.1	219
2008	63	52.2	37	47.8	223

Source: Election Commission of Malaysia, "Federal Election Results," *Suruhanjaya Pilihanraya* 2011, semak.spr.gov.my/module/5_KerusiDR.php (accessed January 5, 2009); Zakaria Ahmad, "The 1999 General Elections: A Preliminary Review" (paper presented at Trends in Malaysia Seminar, Singapore, December 1999), 8.

As mentioned earlier in the chapter, acquiring and sustaining Malay-Bumiputera support for the ruling front is pivoted on the state's assurances, whether through demagoguery or fear tactics, that only UMNO could permanently safeguard their political economic interests. The ethnic Chinese and Indian elites within the National Front have also learned well to consent to the accommodations of Malays and Bumiputeras since electoral victories for UMNO also benefit the non-Malay elites in the National Front's component parties. Over time, these elites have become all too cognizant of the organizational as well as personal privileges derived from the consociational ruling structure and the centrality of Malay political support to their own parties. This is particularly so when many of them have also campaigned and stood for political office in predominantly Malay areas.

Similarly, a strong showing by the National Front in the east Malaysian states of Sarawak and Sabah also often translates in the securing of the respective Bumiputera and ethnic Chinese elites' political economic interests in these states. Sarawak's Parti Pesaka Bumiputera Bersatu, together with Sabah's Parti Bersatu Sabah (PBS) and United Pasokmomogun Kadazandusun Organization, have often vigorously propagated to their own electoral constituencies that the advantages derived from the NEP and the generous autonomy conferred upon these two states under the federation would have been unattainable without these parties' sustained participation within the consociational ruling structure. More importantly, these local elites have also been helpful in alleviating some of the general resentments and apprehensions among the Bumiputera groups in east Malaysia pertaining to potential encroachments of Malay political interests into Sabah and Sarawak.[28]

The task to acquire continuous Malay-Bumiputera votes in elections has also been made easier by the gerrymandering of electoral boundaries to maximize the number of predominantly Malay constituencies in the rural and smaller urban areas. State-initiated constitutional amendments have allowed more than 15 percent disparities in population figures between constituencies, resulting in much larger populations of mainly-non-Malay areas often located within single opposition-held constituencies. The resulting large numbers of predominantly Malay electoral areas have effectively aided the National Front in winning many of its parliamentary and state seats. Due to these boundary manipulations, the overwhelming victories of the ruling alliance in terms of seats do not actually reflect the often close contests in terms of voter percentages. In the 2008 federal elections for example, the National Front won only 52 percent of total votes, yet obtained 63 percent of total parliamentary seats (see table 7.1).[29]

In Malaysia, a single parliamentary constituency also extends over multiple state constituencies. This usually means that when a political party secures a parliamentary seat in the federal elections, it is very likely that it would also win those state constituencies geographically located under that area in separate state-level elections. The symmetry of voting patterns and the ensuing results between parliamentary and state seats simplify the coordination between state and federal governments on matters relating to land concessions, investments distributions, building projects, highway constructions, and voting registration. This way, areas supporting the National Front could be easily identified for purposes of funding and development. This assertion holds true considering that the National Front has always made it difficult for various financial assistances to find their way into the opposition-held states.[30] This is affirmed by an official statement made by deputy prime minister Muhyiddin Yasin of UMNO, who openly stressed that state-level development funds, given through the respective members of parliament, are meant only for National Front constituencies.[31]

Such a policy approach poignantly captures the relentless effort by UMNO and the National Front to weaken the political legitimacy of the current Pakatan Rakyat (Pakatan) opposition coalition. A long standing dispute arising from the federal treasury's withholding of award payments to the Pakatan-led state of Kelantan for oil exploration and drilling within its coastal areas illustrates this point.[32] The official justification for holding off these royalty payments has consistently pertained to "technical problems" in determining the maritime border between Kelantan and the exclusive economic zone (EEZ). The National Front government claims that since explorations and drillings occur within the EEZ, Kelantan could not be compensated for such payments. However, this has not been the experience of National Front-led states of Sabah, Sarawak, and Terengganu, which have been receiving their share of money from the outflow of oil well outside their territorial waters.[33]

Although a third tier of government exists at the local level, the Malaysian state had abolished all municipal elections by 1972 after they were suspended in 1965 during the confrontation with Indonesia. The federal government decided that autonomous local governments had been too prone to "administrative inefficiencies" that they would function more effectively if members of the various boards and councils were politically appointed instead.[34] Today, the daily operations of local governments are budgeted mostly from state governments, with federal supervision coming in from the Ministry of Housing and Local Governments.

It would be worth noting however, that urban areas are also heavily Chinese in population. Municipal boundaries are also more likely to territorially overlap with the larger districts that formed state assembly seats. Under the current structure, urban electoral areas are territorially separate from the surrounding rural constituencies, which are greater in number. Due to majority ethnic Chinese population, city districts are more likely to vote for the opposition in state and national elections. Thus doing away with the elections of municipal councilors at the local level prevents the performance of city and district government policies going against the interests of the ruling National Front coalition in those areas.

Another mechanism indispensible for state control of the electoral process in Malaysia has been the Elections Commission (EC).[35] The EC is primarily tasked with the management of electoral events and voter registration drives as well as the reconfiguration of electoral boundaries in accordance with population changes. It is here that the state is able to periodically carry out "boundary delimitation" efforts to ensure that any population growth can be adjusted to benefit UMNO and the National Front. The redrawing of electoral maps has also helped fragment communities that have traditionally been under or at risk of falling to opposition candidates.

In recent years, complaints and allegations by opposition candidates regarding voting fraud, bribery, and illegal voter registration have become increasingly rampant. As a neutral body, the EC is responsible for addressing any irregularity arising from voting and campaigning during elections. However, the EC has been known more for looking away and allowing National Front politicians and their supporters the ability to use the system to their advantage.[36]

Affirming this point was the case involving the Prime Minister Najib Razak, caught on camera bribing voters RM5 million worth of project money in the Sibu constituency 2010 by-election if they picked the National Front candidate. A *Malaysian Insider* newspaper article dated May 20, 2010, reported that the EC and other state agencies simply passed the buck with regards to the filing of complaints by opposition leaders, resulting in no action being taken against the premier.[37] That the EC refused to reprimand the Prime Minister was hardly surprising since the memberships of the EC comprise of former top civil servants, while its secretariat is staffed directly from the federal bureaucracy, which carefully vets all appointments and promotions in various state agencies.

Another area of contention with regards to the electoral process has been media coverage. During elections, airtime has been given almost solely to National Front candidates and their campaigns. Repeated proposals to hold national televised debates during elections have been refused by the state.[38] Allocating broadcasting space and time for opposition parties necessary to reach and inform the public of their respective political platforms have also virtually been non-existent in any of the networks. When opposition parties and members do make the news, the contents of their footage are usually portrayed negatively or taken out of context. This is not unexpected when major television networks, radio stations, and newspapers are either run by the state or indirectly owned by companies related to UMNO and other National Front component parties.

The incident at the Batu Burok parliamentary by-election in Terengganu state in 2007 exemplifies one of numerous biased reporting by the state-run media. A peaceful gathering of the opposition Islamic party PAS supporters and several independent journalists was confronted by the police, who then used force to disperse the crowd. In the tussle, two police officers fired live bullets into a group of people, seriously injuring two men. The media version of events, as claimed by National Front politicians and the police, pointed to officers defending themselves against a violent mob. No alternative explanation of the incident was reported or taken into account. According to a non-government coalition advocating for free and fair elections in Malaysia, Bersih, in their September 13, 2007, press release, there were credible witness accounts relating to plainclothes security personnel strategically placed in the gathering to instigate disturbances against the police. These men then moved in on the crowd on the pretext of quelling the "riot."[39] This report hardly reached the general public since none of the major newspapers or broadcasting networks ever published or aired them.

Despite increasingly vigorous campaigns for freer elections, the prospect for electoral changes in Malaysia is not expected to be forthcoming in the near future. In the 2008 federal elections, the National Front was surprised by the electoral gains made by the political opposition under the Pakatan coalition comprising of the People's Justice Party (PKR), Pan-Malayan Islamic Party (PAS), and Democratic Action Party (DAP), as well as the Malaysian Socialist Party. In a repeat of history, dissatisfaction among the urban Malay working and middle classes over their seemingly lack of economic progress and political freedom became a main factor behind fewer Malay votes for the UMNO-led National Front in these general elections.

Unlike in previous elections too, the opposition parties put up a strong concerted challenge against the National Front to deny the ruling incumbent its two-thirds parliamentary majority, which is essential for any amendment to the Federal Constitution. The opposition was also, for the first time, more ethnically diverse both in composition and in their voting pattern. Any substantial Malay and non-Malay support for the predominantly non-Malay parties of the MCA, Gerakan, and MIC within the National Front, also essentially disappeared in the 2008 elections. Likewise, a large number of Malay voters also came out in full support for non-Malay opposition candidates. In these elections, the Pakatan opposition coalition had made it a close contest by winning nearly 37 percent of total seats and nearly 48 percent of total votes (see table 7.1).

In order to put up a better performance in the next elections, the state has tightened its control of the electoral process through the EC. This was apparent in the various by-elections that have taken place since 2008, where despite several wins, the opposition parties still had to contend against the might of a well-oiled but heavily biased state-electoral machinery.

The deteriorating quality of Malaysia's electoral process, caused by its severe lack of neutrality and transparency, could be effectively remedied if the country had a strong and independent judiciary. This branch of government, however, has been virtually assaulted and subsequently placed under the effective scrutiny of the executive branch in recent years. The next section discusses this.

Taming the Judiciary

An independent and impartial judiciary is one of the hallmarks of a democratic society. Like Britain, the positions of leading judges in Malaysia are appointed by the King on the advice of the current Prime Minister. Although at one time an internationally admired body, Malaysia's judiciary has lost most of its reputable image in light of increased state intervention into its institutional autonomy.

The effective decline of the judiciary began in 1987, when incumbent UMNO president Dr. Mahathir Mohamad narrowly defeated an in-party challenge by Finance Minister Razaleigh Hamzah and his supporters, referred to as "UMNO Team B." Following a recount, it was discovered that there had been major abnormalities in the status of several party branches, whose votes went in favor of Mahathir's "Team A." A lawsuit by the losing side was brought to the High Court, where Judge Harun Hashim declared that "ramifications arising from the discrepancies found in the registration of these branches under the Societies Act have inevitably caused UMNO to become an unlawful society."[40]

The National Front had been reeling from recent national scandals surrounding the insolvencies and eventual bankruptcies of UMNO-linked Bumiputera Malaysia Finance and the MCA-owned Pan-Electric Industries. UMNO's dissolution would have been the final death blow to the Mahathir administration. At stake was billions of ringgits' worth of capital investments as well as debt tied to party-related projects. Furthermore, with the mid-1980s recession deepening, Malaysia's capitalist development would have potentially come to a standstill if the political crisis went unresolved. Mahathir and UMNO were now in their most vulnerable position and in danger of losing their political power, legitimacy, and influence if the decision to annul UMNO did not change in the state's favor.

The High Court decision angered Mahathir. The prime minister obdurately remained in office, claiming that only a "no-confidence" vote could dislodge him from the premiership. He made use of the state's Registrar of Societies to form a new party, called UMNO Baru (New UMNO), into which the party's leadership, comprising of "Team A" members, quickly transferred the party's vast assets. They also, quite unlawfully, restored the old UMNO name to the new party thereafter.[41] Having revived UMNO back from the dead, Mahathir consolidated his position and went on to make disparaging remarks about some of the country's top judges, specifically accusing them of attempting to elevate the constitutional power of the judiciary above the executive. The Lord President of the Supreme Court, Salleh Abas, who had remained firm in advising the state to follow proper procedures of appeal, was perturbed by the executive branch's public statements against the judiciary. In response, he and several Supreme Court judges wrote a formal letter to the King complaining about the prime minister's actions. This action was exploited and publicly portrayed by the Mahathir administration as a gross misconduct on the part of the judiciary, after which a state-endorsed tribunal was set up that hastened the suspension and eventual removal of Salleh and five of the nine Supreme Court judges from the bench.[42]

The beginning of the decline of the country's judicial system was set in motion from thereon. The crisis was followed by a 1988 constitutional change that downgraded the position of the Lord President slightly below that of the executive. The source of power of the courts that had previously been derived from the Constitution was transferred to the parliament, thereby relegating the status of the judiciary below that of the legislature. Later in 1994, to further reduce the prestige of the judiciary, the state urged parliament to amend the Constitution in order to rename the Supreme Court as the Federal Court. The Lord President's title was also changed to Chief Justice of the Federal Court, while designations of the Chief Justices of Malaya and Borneo were changed to "Chief Judge" of each of the respective regions.

Appointments and promotions of judges to the various positions in the judiciary have been exercised with punctilious screening to detect and monitor potentially "rebellious" judges. Those with a record of going against UMNO interests have been publicly reproved by the state and also slow in moving up the bench. This has been the case for appellate judge Hishamuddin Yunus, who ordered for the immediate release of state political detainees in 2001. Meanwhile, Justice Muhammad Kamil Awang, who ignored instructions to sway a major court case involving 1999 by-election results in Sabah in favor of the National Front, had been left exposed to verbal attacks by state politicians as well as others within the judicial system.[43]

The state has also been known to intimidate judges. The same Justice Muhammad was confronted by anonymous threats in relation to the Sabah by-election case from sources believed to be working for the ruling party. Others have been known to be subjected to intense pressuring, even bullying. This was confirmed in *The Star* newspaper article dated June 11, 2008, in which a High Court judge, Ian Chin, publicly revealed several threats made by the state against selected members of the judiciary, many of whom were also sent to a special "boot camp" for indoctrination sessions.[44]

If a judge attempted to uncover any defect in the legal system or any misdeed of its officers, he would be subjected to scorn by the judicial upper echelon. This happened to High Court judge Syed Aidid, who resigned from office in 1996 after he had whistle-blown on thirty-nine incidents of corruption, twenty-one cases of abuse of power, and fifty-two acts of judicial misconduct.[45] One of these involved a defamation lawsuit by MCA crony capitalist Vincent Tan against journalist M.G.G. Pillai, resulting in RM10 million (US$ 2.6 million) in damages awarded to the former. It was later revealed that Tan's counsel, V. K. Lingam had sponsored holiday trips to Italy and New Zealand for Eusoffe Chin, the presiding judge who later became Chief Justice of Malaysia. Although the charges were never really pursued against the judges, the High Court judge who lodged the complaints was instead, investigated for libel.

Control of the country's judicial bodies has also enabled the ruling elite to indirectly suppress the political opposition whenever its power is threatened. In 1998, another UMNO in-party conflict between Mahathir and his popular deputy Anwar Ibrahim ultimately led to the latter's imprisonment on trumped-up charges of corruption and forced sodomy. Directives from the Attorney-General's department to influence the proceedings of the court were discernibly obeyed by the presiding judge Augustine Paul, who among other things, threatened the defense team with contempt and arbitrarily expunged vital evidence from court records. An international coalition of independent lawyers raised their concerns regarding this trial in a report entitled *Justice in Jeopardy.*

They drew conclusively in their observations that the increased miscarriages of justice and transgressions of rule of law in Malaysia was clearly rooted in the subordination of the judiciary to the executive.[46]

However, the most sensational case to date involved the murder case of a Mongolian model, Altantuya Sharibuu. It was originally claimed that Ms. Sharibuu had been an "interpreter" on behalf of Malaysian company Perimekar, ran by UMNO crony Razak Baginda, in the RM6.7 million purchase of *Scorpene* submarines from French firm DCNS. It turned out that she was Baginda's mistress who had full access to transactional information, particularly with regards to the €114 million Perimekar received as commission for the submarines' delivery to the Royal Malaysian Navy. It was reported that the exasperated Sharibuu confronted and threatened Baginda at his home for her share of commission, only to be whisked away in an unmarked car. She was eventually found murdered, and her body blown up with C-2 explosives by two personal police bodyguards working for then Defense Minister Najib Razak.[47]

Razak Baginda was originally charged with abetting the murder but was eventually acquitted without his defense being called in 2008, leaving the two policemen with death penalty convictions.[48] Throughout the shoddy trial, the state prosecutor and the high court judge consistently deflected attempts to expose the "who and why" behind the order for the murder. Defense lawyers and attorneys holding brief for the deceased also repeatedly asked for Najib Razak to be summoned as a witness. That never happened. The trial's impact on Najib's image, if any, did not prevent him from becoming the next UMNO president. By virtue of his party position and the resignation of incumbent Abdullah Badawi, he eventually assumed office as Malaysia's sixth Prime Minister in 2009.[49]

There had been some optimism regarding possible reclamation of judicial autonomy with the arrival of a dynamic new chief justice in 2001. However, the fact that Malaysia's judicial institution has strongly remained a state-controlled apparatus since the mid-1980s clearly shows its inability to free itself from the stranglehold of the executive, no matter how hard it tries. The ruling elites' systemic influence over the strongest of existing Malaysian institutions extends even to the Malay monarchy, which has also not been spared the intrusive arm of the executive.

Bribing the Monarchy: Neocolonial Version

Since independence, the Federal Constitution had established the King as the supreme head of state of the federation. The ceremonial office of the *Yang Di Pertuan Agong* is rotated among the rulers of the various Malaysian states for a term of five years each. As a legacy of colonialism, the status of each individual sultan has been reduced to a mere sovereign and is officially devoid of any effective political power. Although the constitution confers paramount power to the King on a variety of functions, such power can only be exercised based on advice of the prime minister or cabinet of ministers. The same goes for each of the sultan or ruler in the states within the federation, where prior consultation with the chief minister or state executive council becomes a constitutional prerequisite for formal decrees and pronouncements.[50]

Despite the loss of political power, the Malay rulers have continued to enjoy the adulation and reverence of Malays, especially when the royal institutions stand to provide evidence of Malay cultural and historical indigenousness to the country. After the British left, UMNO has made full use of the sultans to solicit and sustain its monopoly of Malay electoral support. In return, the various sultans have been endowed with unparalleled royal privileges, allowing them to pursue extravagances beyond the imagination of ordinary citizens. Since only a handful of Malaysia's royal families are highly-educated, many have depended almost entirely on almost unlimited access to state money, land, and business concessions for their economic well-being. Several of them have even outdone their royal privileges by living out the lives of medieval rulers.

In 1981, the Sultan of Pahang and some members of his family had allegedly gambled away massive amounts of taxpayer money within days of an outing at an overseas casino. When the state government refused to settle the debt, the state's chief minister, Rahim Bakar, was forced to resign from office.[51] UMNO resolved the issue by officially replacing the minister with a more amenable candidate, who expeditiously helped in clearing the sultan's gambling dues. In return, the sultan has remained a strong and loyal advocate of UMNO, especially during elections.

The Sultan of Pahang at the time could not have personally been liable for any loss of public money because sultans and their immediate family members had, for a long time, enjoyed constitutional immunity from court convictions and civil proceedings. In this regard, the case of the late Sultan Iskandar of Johor (who also reigned as King of Malaysia from 1984 to 1989) would appear most vividly in the minds of many Malaysians. Notorious for his physical assaults on civilians, the late sultan was most well-known however, for a manslaughter conviction during his reign as the state's royal regent. Iskandar never served time for his guilty verdict primarily because he had been granted official pardon by his father during his regency.[52] Later, when he assumed the throne as King of Malaysia, he was said to have clubbed a caddy to death after a bad game of golf. No charges were brought forth because nothing in the way of official police report had been initiated. It would not have mattered anyway since his royal immunity status was protected by the Constitution.[53]

It was only in 1993 that the Malaysian state finally pulled the brakes on the lawless behavior of some of the Malay sultans by coaxing parliament to remove the Constitutional article on royal immunity with regards to both criminal and civil cases.[54] This sudden move followed an incident in which the late Sultan of Johor, again, had assaulted a hockey coach over a lost match in 1992. Sensing general Malay discomfort by such incidents, the state quickly acted. After a series of unprecedented media frenzy serving partly to expose past and current misdeeds of the various sultans, the state managed to generate public support for the proposed constitutional restrictions. This was promptly followed by parliament's rescinding of the rulers' immunity.

The show of force by UMNO left no one in doubt with regards to the party's omnipotent powers, which extended even into the most highly-regarded cultural institution in the country. It certainly served as a future reminder to the royal families with regards to who has the ultimate authority in Malaysia and of the consequences of failing to accommodate the political masters' directives and interests. The full control of the monarchy may be justified in view of the wayward behavior of several of its members. However, the real aim here was to ensure that the Malay royalty continued to serve a political function in preserving Malay electoral support for UMNO.

For the royals, the reward for subservience to the party would also sustain the continued enjoyment of unsurpassed advantages derived from being among the country's privileged classes. Several members of the Malay royalty, in fact, have found their way into UMNO's circle of crony entrepreneurs. While many have made huge fortunes, the general similarities with other Malay crony capitalists unfortunately do not end there. Many royalty-run businesses have resulted in numerous bankruptcies and financial catastrophes.[55] However, as long as the Malay rulers remained staunch UMNO supporters, they would be assured that their businesses stayed operational and are given access to lucrative commercial ventures.

Since many royal households have been dependent on close relations with UMNO, it is not surprising then to find some of the sultans publicly generating support for UMNO or admonishing those who have been critical of the party. One recent example can be captured in the relationship between UMNO and the present Sultan of Selangor, whose state had come under Pakatan coalition rule after the 2008 elections. At the time of writing, it was reported in a *Malaysiakini* article dated July 8, 2011, that His Highness, citing public safety concerns, had sternly warned members of the public against participating in a planned anti-UMNO demonstration for free and fair elections.[56] It was without dispute that the Sultan in this case had intervened on behalf of UMNO on matters considered outside his constitutional purview. This was also one of among other preceding public statements made by him that seemed to have placed him firmly on the side of UMNO.

To date however, the most controversial case involving the royal house concerns the National Front's sensational takeover of the Perak state government in 2009. In the 2008 elections, the Pakatan opposition alliance had succeeded in winning over the Perak state government albeit with a narrow 31-28 electoral margin. Under highly suspicious circumstances however, three of their state assemblymen pulled out of the coalition to become independents the following year.[57] Initially, there had been claims that the three had resigned and vacated their seats, which they later denied. Their jumping outside of the Pakatan coalition resulted in both the Pakatan and National Front deadlocked with 28 state representatives each in the state assembly. At the same time, the three "hoppers" remained as independents, but individually pledged their support for the National Front.

To resolve the crisis, Perak chief minister Nizar Jamaluddin of PAS sought an audience with the Sultan of Perak, Azlan Shah, for permission to dissolve the assembly in order to clear the way for state re-elections. However, after a closed door meeting with the then Malaysian deputy prime minister Najib Razak of UMNO, the Sultan decided on the unthinkable. Although constitutionally bound to remain free from politics, he surprisingly removed the chief minister along with his cabinet, and appointed an UMNO chief minister to form a National Front-led Perak government. The official reason given was that the Pakatan government no longer enjoyed the confidence of the majority of the state assembly.

Needless to say, many Malaysians were appalled. The Sultan, who once held the position of the Lord President of the Supreme Court, had been admired by the people as the most highly-educated among all the rulers. A year before, a *Bernama* news article dated November 7, 2008, captured the keynote address by the Regent of Perak, representing the Sultan, on National Integrity Day, which among other things mentioned: "Generally, the Rulers act based on the advice by government leaders elected by the people. Nevertheless, the Rulers cannot accede to acts which do not symbolise (sic) justice or sanction moves which do not mirror truth."[58]

To many, neither the interest of justice nor "truth" appeared to be the primary factor behind the sultan's action. Convinced of possible collusion between the royal house and UMNO, angry Pakatan supporters, mostly from PAS, swiftly organized a rally outside the royal mosque demanding the dissolution of the state assembly and the pursuit of fresh mandate through re-elections. So livid was the crowd that several people attempted to stop the royal convoy from returning to the palace after the Friday prayer. The demonstration was gradually suppressed by anti-riot police, and the crisis was brought to the High Court, which ruled that the Sultan had no jurisdiction to dismiss the chief minister. This decision, however, was overturned by the Court of Appeals, paving the way for a formal National Front takeover of Perak.[59]

As part of the country's elite circle, it is not unexpected that Malaysia's royal families have been inclined to constantly side with UMNO, especially when the rewards of collaboration have not only ensured their economic survival but are often irresistible. The Sultan of Perak's eldest daughter Eleena, for example, had profited immensely from her relationship with the country's ruling elite. As a major controlling shareholder of Gamuda, an UMNO-linked construction company, she was also among Malaysia's top 40 millionaires in 2011.[60] This has provided reasonable grounds for Malaysians to speculate on the connection between the Sultan of Perak's family fortunes and his willingness to circumvent the rule of law in order to dislodge the Pakatan government in Perak on behalf of UMNO.

The use of the Malay monarchy to advance the interests of UMNO as well as to pre-empt any political challenge by Malays against the state is reminiscent of the way the British had used the sultans to subjugate the Malay masses during colonialism. Another legacy of British rule that has carried political utility for the county's ruling elites is found within the Royal Malaysian Police Force.

The Federal Police Force

The 120,000-strong *Polis Di Raja Malaysia* (Royal Malaysian Police Force or PDRM) has extensive federal jurisdiction. Unlike other branches of the civil services, none of the states within the federation maintains a separate police force. Although allegations of police corruption, torture, and brutality have become increasingly rampant in the past decade, another major concern among Malaysians with regards to the PDRM has been its role in helping suppress the country's political opposition.

One case that stands out has been police's role in fabricating and disposing evidence in the trial of Malaysia's opposition leader Anwar Ibrahim in 1998. While in custody, Anwar himself was brutally assaulted by none other than the country's top police chief.[61] Similar to the experiences of judges and court officials in the country, police officers who had proven their complicit worth in protecting and advancing state interests at the expense of justice are normally rewarded with promotions. As an example, the investigating officer in Anwar's "sodomy" trial, despite being junior in rank, was later able to leapfrog over many other senior officers to attain the position of Inspector-General of Police.

On the other hand, officers who have been resolute in conducting their investigations of top corporate and government figures suspected of corruption have instead been subjected to various punitive measures. An example of this can be captured in the case of police commercial crimes investigator Ramli Yusoff, who recommended several corporate figures, including the Chief Executive of MAS, Tajudin Ramly, be charged for corruption for their involvement in the national airline's financial scandal. An *Asia Sentinel* article dated August 24, 2010, reported that while the alleged suspects were never brought to court, the officer was instead hauled in for various "misconducts."[62]

The police have also been selective in investigating cases that involved high-profiled National-Front politicians. In 1998, DAP member of parliament Lim Guan Eng was imprisoned for seeking justice on behalf of one of his constituents, an underage Malay girl who was allegedly raped by the then chief minister of Malacca and Vice-President of UMNO.[63] The charge filed against Lim was based on the "accusatory nature" of his publicly-distributed pamphlet, which was deemed seditious by the court and liable for criminal conviction. While Lim was subsequently sent to prison, the Chief Minister's purported involvement in the sexual assault was never seriously pursued by the police, allowing him to escape criminal proceedings.

The power, confidence, and efficiency with which the police have been able to move in on the political opposition and help avert public challenges against the state have also been largely attributed to the sanctuary they receive under Malaysia's draconian "emergency" laws. Like other state control mechanisms in Malaysia, these regulations have been a legacy of colonial administrative functions passed down to the current Malaysian state in order to assist the ruling elites with the maintenance of their political power in the country.

Repressive "Emergency" Laws

As discussed in chapter 5, the British response to the Malayan communist insurrection came in the form of various "Emergency Regulations" that gave the police extensive powers of search, arrest, and detention of suspected communist terrorists for up to a year without trial. These regulations were lifted in 1960 after the end of the communist insurgency, but the Malaysian state passed the Internal Security Act (ISA) in the same year to continue preventive surveillance on potential terrorist activities.

The state was quick to assure its people that the Act was not meant to curb individual liberties or repress political opposition but, was instead aimed at ensuring the country's peace and stability. Although several amendments have been made to accommodate the civil rights of suspected detainees, certain major sections of the Act still provide the Home Minister and the police with wide discretionary powers on arrest and detention. The Human Rights Watch, in its September 2005 report, stated that between 1960 and 2005, there had been more than 10,000 individuals served with ISA orders in Malaysia.[64] Comprised of trade unionists, members of opposition groups, social activists, and even ordinary citizens, many of those arrested had not been known to commit any serious crime.

In any case, it has been the systematic tendency for the state to use the ISA and other such laws against those who have been critical of the government. It has been for such purpose for which these emergency laws have been most renowned. In 2007, a huge public demonstration calling for free and fair elections organized by non-government group Bersih resulted in scores of people arrested and detained under the various public order acts. The *Wall Street Journal* in its August 2, 2009, article quoted opposition leader Anwar Ibrahim, a two-time ISA detainee himself, as saying that the ISA "represents a powerful threat to anybody criticizing the government."[65]

In justifying its use of the ISA, the state often publicly links those it arrests with activities it considers subversive and politically destabilizing. In the infamous 1987 *Operasi Lalang* (Operation Weed-out), the state rounded up various politicians and activists, whom it alleged were inciting ethnic tensions, but who were actually political opponents that became increasingly vocal in their criticisms of state policies. Ten years later, amidst massive demonstrations calling for Prime Minister Dr. Mahathir to resign, the state sanctioned the use of violence in conjunction with the ISA to suppress anti-Mahathir rallies. The magazine *Asiaweek* reported in its August 17, 2001, edition that during the "clean up," the state also arrested six members of the opposition KeAdilan party (Justice Party), who were allegedly storing "caches of ammunitions."[66] Although the claim later turned out to be false, it was enough to damage the reputation of the party.

The state has also reminded Malaysians that civil unrests and disturbances are often likely to erupt into ethnic strife, thereby causing serious disruptions to Malaysia's industrialization plans. As such, police attacks on public gatherings as well as state detentions of activists under the ISA have thus frequently been cited as necessary "pre-emptive actions" against impending threats to national security. During the cold war, the use of the ISA had been linked to suppressing various "communist-inspired" activities. Then, the state was quick to assign blame for any instance or provocation of ethnic tension on communist "agents," regardless of whether it was able to produce any incriminating evidence. For decades, Malaysians were sold to the idea that critical expressions against the state were considered treacherous and associated with communist elements.

After September 11, 2001, a large portion of ISA detainees, some of whom have been in custody without trial for several years, have allegedly been linked to various Islamic movements. The Malaysian state has constantly defended the use of ISA as a national security measure, especially in cracking down on terrorist groups such as the elusive *Jemaah Islamiyah* (JI).[67] The JI and other movements have become a convenient excuse for the state to come down hard on Muslim activists, considering many political opponents in Malaysia have come from PAS or other Malay-Islamic groups. To this day, many still have doubts about these detainees' ties to fringe extremist groups, since no evidence has been produced to suggest any such associations. Others have simply questioned whether such a group as the JI even exists as a real organization.[68]

Interestingly, western governments have always adopted a reticent stand on the Malaysian state's use of the ISA on its own citizens. During the cold war, the United States and other western countries continued their investments in the country, and worked closely with the state in intelligence-sharing and even arms assistance despite the state's enforcement of anti-democratic regulations. Today, the post-9/11 war on terrorism has become the west's *raison d'etre* for sanctioning Malaysia's suppression of civil liberties, especially when it is equated with the prevention and elimination of "Islamist" activism. When Prime Minister Mahathir visited the United States in May 2002, the Americans remained muted on questions regarding the imprisonment of political leaders and suspected terrorists under the ISA. The then-US Ambassador to Malaysia even recommended that the United States continued its support for the authoritarian Dr. Mahathir over challenger Anwar Ibrahim during the 1999 political economic crisis because "Anwar lacked Mahathir's political clout in tackling Islamists."[69]

Diplomatic relations between Malaysia and the United States have since become increasingly warm.[70] The Americans have often solicited the Malaysian state for close cooperation and expert advice on effective counter-terrorism measures, which inspired Mahathir during his time in office to affectionately liken the ISA to the US Patriot Act. Among Malaysia's "accomplishments" in international counter-terrorism, which have earned the state accolades from the west, includes the capture and internment of Singaporean Mas Selamat in 2009. Selamat was allegedly linked to the JI and had earlier escaped from the republic's maximum security prison.[71]

As a blanket measure against anti-systemic groups and organizations in Malaysia, the Societies Act 1966, another remnant of the colonial era, also functions to restrict any potential challenge against UMNO and the National Front. This law requires that all organizations, clubs, and non-government groups be registered with the Registrar of Societies before they are allowed to be operational. Those organizations the Registrar deems as "harmful" would not be allowed registration privileges and are thus considered illegal if continued to exist. Considering the extensive discretionary powers the Registrar wields in political and administrative decision-making, the terms of tenure associated with this post have, since colonial times, remained within the authority and influence of the state.

There have been other major restrictive laws often used by the state in juxtaposition with the ISA, especially in the constraining of what it considers "excessive" freedoms of speech and information. These include the Official Secrets Act 1972 (amended 1986), or OSA, that mandates a one-year prison sentence regardless of the extent of offence for any purported leakage of state official documents and information. Opposition leaders have often accused the state of shoring up the merit and necessity of the OSA as a way to deliberately cover up various state misconducts and improprieties. This is particularly so when numerous opposition members and activists who were detained under this Act had taken in during the course of attempting to uncover or expose instances of government corruption and abuses of power.[72]

Freedom of expression has also been further curtailed by the 1984 Printing Presses and Publications Act, which requires domestic and foreign publications annually apply for printing permits. Such permits would always take into consideration the political nature and orientation of the particular media organ in its propensity to criticize the state and its policies. An amendment in 1987 expanded the state's power over licensing renewal by inserting the clause prohibiting court challenges against state suspensions or revocations of permits.

The impact of this Act was felt in the aftermath of the 1999 elections. Loss of confidence in the mainstream print media had resulted in massive boycott of the state-owned newspapers and simultaneous increases in the limited subscription of opposition-owned publications. With the readership of PAS's news organ *Harakah* escalating from 75,000 to 369,000 in a matter of days, the Act was used by the state to curtail its circulation on a fortnightly basis. National news agency *Bernama* reported in January 13, 2000, that the paper's editor and chief publisher were also later arrested under the Sedition Act 1970, purportedly for allowing false reporting, thus making them liable for prison time.[73] Through the years, the OSA, Printing Act, and Sedition Act have shaped a mainstream journalistic culture in Malaysia that has generally been un-aggressive and bland in both approach and character. In many ways it also reinforced the political apathy of many Malaysians and their unwillingness to undertake public action.

Laws that have also encouraged political passivity in the country mainly deal with the proscription of public assemblies and demonstrations. This includes the Police Act 1988 (Amendment), which stipulates that any planned public gathering would require prior permission from the police. As a remnant of colonial-inspired legislation, this Act confers the PDRM extensive discretionary powers on whether or not to grant such authorizations. In most cases however, permissions have been denied approval, especially when the gatherings tend to involve one way or another, members of the political opposition.

Restriction on freedom can also be found in the University and University Colleges Act 1975, which specifically targets university students and prevents them from participating in any form of political activity, on or off campus. Students the world over are known to be among the most passionate and energetic in expressing opinions on political issues, and with this awareness, the state in Malaysia seeks to ascertain that college students confine their activities to the lessons they receive in the classrooms. Despite past incidents where students had either been suspended from their institutions or arrested by the police for participating or leading public demonstrations, there seemed to be a steady rise in campus protests over the last few years.

The latest came on January 1, 2012. A *New Straits Times* newspaper report mentioned that 17 students were arrested when police broke up a student rally at the campus of the Sultan Idris University in Tanjung Malim, Perak. The demonstration had apparently been organized to demand the repeal of the University Act in support for a student leader earlier detained by the police in Kuala Lumpur for "insulting" the Prime Minister.[74] In relation to this incident, a *Harakah Daily* article dated January 1, 2012, reported that despite the gathering being relatively peaceful, anti-riot police were called in to forcibly remove the students, resulting in several of them suffering serious injuries.[75]

Throughout Malaysia's capitalist development, these "emergency" laws have undoubtedly equipped the police with wide prerogative powers and have been successful in preventing civil society movements from mounting effective grassroots protests against the state. In a surprising turn however, Prime Minister Najib Razak announced in November 2011 that the state would soon consider repealing the ISA, along with several other regulations that allow detentions without trials, including the Police Act. Nevertheless, critics are unconvinced of the Minister's sincerity, pointing the proposal instead as a ploy to recoup his declining popularity, particularly after the poor handling of the second public demonstration for free and fair elections earlier in July.[76]

If Malaysians ever wondered if the ruling elite would deliver its promises of a freer and more progressive society, they did not have to wait too long. No sooner than having publicly announced its proposed repeal, the ISA was used by the Malaysian police in the arrest and detention of 13 suspected "Islamists" in the eastern state of Sabah. A report in *The Star*, dated November 11, 2011, mentioned that the detainees were alleged members of the JI who "posed a serious threat to the nation's security."[77]

Weeks after announcing the proposed repeal, the state surprised the country again when the National Front-dominated parliament rushed through to approve the Peaceful Assembly Act 2011. The state claimed that this law would allow "peaceful" gatherings of more than five persons as long as prior *notification* is given to the police.[78] The assumption embedded in the Act was that the police would permit such assemblies if organizers intended them to be mere gatherings.

However, members of the political opposition and scores of human rights lawyers and academicians promptly dismissed this assumption as misleading, and retorted that the new Act actually appeared more restrictive than the current Police Act. This was in view of the numerous restrictions placed on the proposed locations and purposes of such "assemblies." More significantly, it was obvious to many that the Act aimed clearly to impose an outright ban on street protests.[79] The powers of the police to freely determine the nature of the assembly would likely remain under this legislation, thereby undermining the so-called waiving of police permission as highlighted by the state with regards to this new Act. Since the police usually perform at the behest of the state, it would only be a foregone conclusion that the PDRM would decide its actions along the expectations and dictates of the ruling elites.

Control of Mainstream Media

The control of the media by the country's major ruling parties and their crony capitalists has furnished the state with the capacity to screen, manipulate and conceal controversial news contents relating to state actions and policies. Malaysia's primary broadcasting network Radio-Television Malaysia (RTM), whose news and programs often carry deifying commentaries of UMNO and its leaders, is run as a full government agency. The RTM has also, among other things, served as the propagation apparatus for the state's economic nationalism ideologies such as the *Wawasan 2020* and *Malaysia Boleh*.

Meanwhile, almost all private TV networks, radio stations, and leading newspapers in Malaysia have been fully-owned by Media Prima, a company with close links to the UMNO. Among the most important media assets acquired by the company were the country's main English and Malay-language newspapers, the *New Straits Times* and *Utusan Malaysia*.[80] With a daily average readership of about 71,000, *Utusan* has practically functioned as the official mouthpiece of UMNO. This paper has focused heavily on readership among the rural Malay populations, with its informational contents often carrying articles and editorials that not only have been supportive of UMNO and its policies, but that have also aggressively vilified the political opposition. Despite declining sales as of late, *Utusan*'s continuing utility and effectiveness as an indoctrinating vehicle among the rural electorate has sustained its role as UMNO's "jewel in the media."

The MCA meanwhile, has owned the country's second leading English daily, *The Star*, which it recently bought from its investment arm Huaren for RM1.28 billion. According to the *My Sinchew.Com* news report dated September 24, 2010, Huaren had also sold its equity in one of its larger conglomerates, Chinese Media International, but has still retained substantial influence in Malaysia's principal Chinese language newspapers *China Press*, *Nanyang Siang Pau*, and *Sin Chew Daily*.[81]

The excessively pro-National Front biases in many of the country's mainstream news reporting, helped by the absence of public space for major debates on political issues, have contributed to the decline in public confidence toward the Malaysian media. State control of the country's presses, through both self-censorship and the ownership of major media outlets, has also held back any optimism of Malaysia's transformation into a progressive and democratic country by 2020. In its annual 2010 survey report, the international organization Freedom House categorized Malaysia's press as "not free," ranking it 142 out of 195 countries. The main reason for this low standing was explained by, among other things, the existing impediments to a free press in the use of "emergency" laws to restrict freedom of expression, as well as an absence of any legislative policy prohibiting or limiting the control of media by the state.[82]

More critical has been the state's use of the media to destabilize ethnic relations. As of late, *Utusan* has also been singled out by critics for advertently seeking to incite ethnic and religious hostility against non-Malays.[83] It has not been uncommon anymore to come across front-page *Utusan* columns or RTM prime time national news segments subtly fermenting ethnic antagonisms solely for purposes of ensuring unity of Malay political support behind UMNO. Often, statements made by non-Malay opposition members involving issues surrounding the Malay language, Islam, or Malay "special rights" have often been inaccurately reported or misrepresented by the mainstream media and portrayed as these individuals' advertent disregard for Malay culture and Islam. Chinese and English readers, on the other hand, have been constantly fed with editorials and news about the impending submission of non-Muslims to Islamic *sharia* laws if they continued to support the Pakatan opposition coalition, of which PAS has been an integral member. The success of these strategies may have generally declined over the years, but they have continued to provide comparative advantages for the National Front, especially during elections when ethnic relations are most delicate and susceptible to exploitation.

Increasingly, the deliberate stoking of ethnic and religious tensions among Malaysians and the frequent disparaging of political opponents carried in the presses to divide oppositional forces in the country have cost the Malaysian media more than its credibility in journalism. It has placed the Malaysian ruling elites in the same unenviable category with some of the worst authoritarian regimes in the world. Ironically, the ruling elites' extensive media control has contradicted the state's own effort in promoting Malaysia as an international media hub. In the mid-1990s, Malaysia launched its *Multimedia Super Corridor*, an "intelligent" industrial zone stretching from the world-famous Petronas Twin Towers in Kuala Lumpur to the new administrative capital in Putrajaya, that housed world-class cyber-technology services and multimedia research for leading information-based firms.[84] However, in the same breath, the state has refused to relinquish its control over the media, and instead, continued to filter and frame the information coming out from the country's largest news organizations for its own political ends.

"Flawed" Democracy

Measurements of a country's political freedoms have, in recent times, taken on a more comprehensive, scientific, and comparative approach. The Economist Intelligence Unit (EIU) of *The Economist* magazine evaluates and compares each country on several indicators of democracy, namely its electoral process, transparency in governance, citizen participation in politics, culture of democracy, and practice in civil liberties. Quantifying these assessments in scores ranging between "1" (least freedom and openness) and "10" (maximum freedom and openness), each country's level of democracy can be appraised and contrasted relative to that of other countries in terms of these criteria.

In its analysis of democracy for 2011, the EIU scored Malaysia in the 5 and 6 ranges for most of these indicators, totaling up an average score of 6.19 (out of 10). Malaysia was ranked at number 71 among 167 countries, which was a downgrade from its previous rank of 68 in 2008.[85] Although Malaysia's overall scores and ranking were much better than neighboring Singapore (ranked 81), they however, lagged behind that of Indonesia (ranked 60). The results also placed Malaysia in the category of countries that the EIU labeled as a "flawed democracy."[86] This system describes countries which possessed the formal mechanisms for basic political freedoms, usually in the form of regular elections and a functioning legislative assembly, but where significant weaknesses exist in various operational aspects of a genuine democratic process. These inadequacies include an absence of government transparency, insufficient provision of full political participation for citizens, and substantial lack of prioritization given to individual civil liberties.[87]

Another 2011 survey conducted by the renowned organization Freedom House also revealed similar conclusions. The methodology of research was mainly premised on scores measuring the degree of political rights in each country by looking at its electoral process, citizen political participation, and effective functioning of government. It also rated a country's level of civil liberties in terms of, among other things, freedom of expression and belief, associational rights, and observance of the rule of law. On a range of scores from 1 (most free) to 7 (least free), Malaysia received a rating of "4" on each of these indicators, placing it in the category of "partly free" countries.[88]

Malaysia's mediocre scores in these international surveys generally reflect its inability to overcome the structural barriers to full democratization in the shape of state repressive laws, media control, and the manipulation of the judicial as well as electoral processes. These statistics convey some evidence that rapid capitalist development in Malaysia has not coincided with a proportionate growth in political liberalization in the country. They also support the assertion that there has been a continuing unwillingness on the part of the ruling elite to introduce wider and more effective steps toward greater democratic governance in Malaysia. Leaders within the National Front, especially in UMNO, have implicitly acknowledged this and have consistently remained unapologetic about their reluctance to institute or facilitate further democratization in Malaysia. In fact, they have often defended the state's "supervised" approach to democratic processes in the country, suggesting that full-fledged western-type liberal systems are irrelevant and disruptive to the needs of Malaysia's multiethnic structure. This is especially so, they fervently claim, when instabilities to the political order arising from ethnic conflicts would adversely affect the country's path toward full industrial development.[89]

Here, the ruling elites have taken to articulate their own discourse on democracy, and in the process mislead their audience by placing the relationship between full democracy and political economic stability as two mutually exclusive and opposing categories. Such an assertion often entails the belief that national economic development and stability could only be attained if political restraints are placed on the country's democratic process. Related to this is another foundational erroneous assumption—that Malaysians are generally unprepared for or have yet to achieve the level of political maturity needed in handling the responsibilities and challenges of a fully democratic society. Given the country's fragile multicultural structure and history, the state has often argued, unrestricted freedom of expressions pertaining to ethnic-related issues could easily be exploited by irresponsible individuals and groups to inflame ethnic tensions into full-blown civil wars. The state seemed to imply that democracy without political patronage was not only unsuitable for Malaysia but also perilous for its multiethnic coexistence.[90] Conveniently, the state has never admitted its recklessness and irresponsibility in inciting a large share of these ethnic and religious tensions, which on many occasions could have easily resulted into serious unrests.

It has become quite obvious thus far that the disinclination on the part of the ruling elite to expand democracy in Malaysia, evident in its emphatic perpetuation of economic nationalism and systemic control of the country's social-political institutions, has been heavily associated with its fear of a unified and cohesive challenge from a broad multiethnic coalition of civil society movements. The fear of anti-systemic uprisings has become all the more acute for UMNO, owing to the fact that outward defiance against the state has increasingly come not from non-Malays, who may be understandingly disgruntled with discriminatory state policies, but from a significant segment of the Malay population, whose political, economic, and cultural interests the state purportedly has claimed to protect in the name of *ketuanan Melayu*. As will be discussed further in the next chapter, this steady challenge of Malays against UMNO has become more prevalent among the younger and more-educated generations. This group has no longer accepted prolonged unemployment, rising costs of living, and increased social disparity gaps as natural accompanying features of development. Viewing these problems as by-products of state-corporate nepotism, young urbanized Malays would welcome any alternative structure or system that would accord a wider range of political economic opportunities and participation, even if they required the total dismantling of the present system.

With increased economic globalization, UMNO will find its primary role and legitimacy as an exclusive Malay ethnonational party and its broader pursuit of attaining the country's beloved *Wawasan 2020* goals to become increasingly incongruent. Malaysia's marginal position in the capitalist world economy would continue to constrain the country's ability to acquire much-needed techno-manufacturing bases for high-end products and services. The country's current exports and investments too, have been highly sensitive to the unpredictable rhythms of global market fluctuations and foreign investor stipulations. Consequently, the social and political costs of prolonged peripheral development may entail unpopular cutbacks on internal public spending, which in Malaysia's case will affect programs for the poor as well as those related to Malay affirmative-action initiatives. In view of these, the road to full industrialized status by 2020 has become more precarious and uncertain.

As the country's ruling elites strive to maintain their power through continued suppressions of civil liberties and political freedoms in the country, the struggle for greater democracy in Malaysia has also become more intense. This is attributed to the emergence of civil society groups and organizations able to efficiently mobilize support through the help of instantaneous and rapid global communication flows that, among other things, have provided alternative forums for political discussions. In the face of an increasingly restless and more sophisticated social activism, the state will find its capabilities in overcoming the complexity of an increasingly globalized world to be exceptionally arduous. This will be the analyses of the last chapter on this book.

Summary

Rapid industrialization has served as a source of immeasurable national pride for Malaysians, and in this, the Malaysian state has taken full acclaim for the country's economic performance. Economic nationalism has continuously been used by the state to unite Malaysians behind its state-led industrialization efforts while simultaneously serving to distract public attention away from the accumulating problems associated with dependent development. These include widespread corruption, state abuses of power, unremitting social disparities, and increased state suppression of civil freedoms. While periods of rapid economic growth have greatly helped the state affirm its legitimacy through the provision of economic benefits, the limitations of such growths, manifested in declining investments and exports during economic slowdowns, have placed serious doubts, even among Malaysians, concerning the state's capacity to achieve full industrialization by the year 2020.

More problematic for the ruling elites has been the dire need to attract more investments into a country whose marginal location in the world economy has subjected it to intense competition with other countries in the region for the provision of low manufacturing and labor costs. Malaysia's competitiveness could be enhanced if it instituted greater economic liberalization and major market-based reforms, including removing subsidization for its Malay-based industries and programs. Already, the ruling elites in UMNO have been confronted with serious criticisms from right-wing factions of the Malay political community with regards to the party's effort in attempting to pursue these reforms at the expense of possibly narrowing or lessening the scope of Malay-Bumiputera preferential policies. The escalating intensity in state power consolidation over the years has often reflected the ruling elites' response to these rising contradictions, which have considerably tarnished the state's legitimacy and authority.

In many ways, the present suppression of civil freedoms through direct and indirect controls of political and social institutions in Malaysia has resembled a rather similar approach used by the old colonial state in governing Malaya. The availing of the monarchy, the police force, and civil services as well as the manipulation of both the legislature and judiciary for the benefit of upholding state and ruling class interests have been among the indistinguishable features that the present Malaysian state shares with its colonial predecessors. Most disreputably of course, has been the unwarranted application of emergency laws, which in the case of the modern Malaysian state, has been additionally used to shelter the ruling elites from grassroots challenges as well as from the transparency of state decision-making. Like the colonial state, the modern Malaysian state may also find its repressive policies tested by the perseverance of civil society groups in seeking reforms. The results of the 2008 elections may have served as a preliminary but optimistic insight into such a possible scenario, indicating that multiethnic and justice-oriented goals may soon outlive the logic of ethnic-based politics.

This is partly because increased authoritarianism in Malaysia, upon which the ruling elites have moved toward increasingly, has turned into a double-edged sword. While an elite-driven or state-managed democratic process have hindered effective public actions by civil society organizations and the political opposition, such severe restrictions on freedoms and justice would only serve to aggravate the continuing tensions within the country. This could ultimately lead to the mobilization of collective and perhaps violent forces against the state as a desperate political alternative—an event many would desire to avoid. As the world becomes intricately connected through vast networks of sophisticated communications media however, these forces may find a new and effective ally in the mobilization of such actions against the state. This will be discussed in the next chapter.

Notes

1. Ishak Shari and Rugayah Mat Zin, "Patterns and Trends of Income Distribution in Malaysia, 1970-87," *Singapore Economic Review* 25, no. 4 (April 1990): 120-21.

2. Ozay Mehmet, *Development in Malaysia: Poverty, Wealth and Trusteeship* (Kent: Crom-Helm, 1986), 123. Although state scholarships were initially available to Malays and Bumiputeras, gradually a greater numbers of non-Malay students were also eligible to obtain full-funding from government-sponsored agencies such as the Ministry of Education and the Public Service Department.

3. NEAC, *New Economic Model for Malaysia* (Kuala Lumpur: Percetakan Nasional Malaysia, 2010), 60.

4. The measurement of the Gini coefficient in income inequality index ranges from 0 to 1. A coefficient of 1 displays perfect inequality, while a coefficient of 0 shows no inequality or perfect equality in a society. Data taken from Department of Statistics, *Yearbook of Statistics* (Kuala Lumpur: Government Printers, 2011), 185-86.

5. Data taken and calculated from Department of Statistics Malaysia, *Yearbook of Statistics* (Kuala Lumpur: Government Printers, 2011).

6. Average incomes relative to the national mean with ratios higher than 1.0 often indicate the bulk of the group located around the middle classes or higher. Data taken from Mat Zin, Rugayah, "Income Distribution in Malaysia: Old Issues New Approaches" (paper presented at the Eleventh International Convention of the East Asian Economic Association, Manila, The Philippines, November 2008), 11.

7. Faridah Jamaluddin, "Malaysia's New Economic Policy: Has It Been a Success?" in *Boundaries of Clan and Color: Transnational Comparison of Inter-Group Disparity*, ed. William Darity Jr. and Ashwini Deshpande (New York: Routledge, 2003), 159.

8. Wong Chin Huat, "UMNO's Unholy Trinity," *The Malaysian Bar* 2009, www.malaysianbar.org.my/general/umnos_unholy_treaty.html (accessed January 12, 2010).

9. Asan Ali Golam Hassan, *Growth, Structural Change, and Regional Inequality in Malaysia* (London: Ashgate, 2004), 64.

10. Leo Suryadinata, *Nationalism and Globalism; East and West* (Singapore: Institute of Southeast Asian Studies, 2000), 147-48.

11. For extensive reading on the *Wawasan 2020*, read Mahathir Mohamad, *The Way Forward* (London: Weidenfeld & Nicolson, 1998).

12. Gavin Stamp, "Malaysia Focused on Vision 2020." *BBC News Online* 2006, news.bbc.co.uk/2/hi/5020794.stm (accessed July 2, 2010).

13. K. S. Nathan, *Economic Slowdown and Domestic Politics: Malaysia Boleh*? Singapore: ISEAS, 1-18.

14. It was reported in *The Star* newspaper that one of the "firsts" of achievements by the Malaysian astronaut was to play Malay traditional games while in space. Read *The Star*, "Malaysia's Astronaut To Do What No One in Space Has Ever Done Before," *Star Online* 2006, thestar.com.my.news/story.asp?file=2006/11/05/nation20061115181546&sec=nation (accessed January 29, 2010).

15. Loh Kok Wah and Khoo Boo Teik, "Introduction," in *Democracy in Malaysia: Discourses and Practices,* ed. Francis Loh Kok Wah and Khoo Boo Teik (Richmond, UK: Curzon Press. 2002), 3-5.

16. Wan A. Manan, "A Nation in Distress: Human Rights, Authoritarianism, and Asian Values in Malaysia," *Journal of Social Issues in Southeast Asia* 14, no. 2 (October 1999): 360-61.

17. Robert E. B. Lucas and Donald Verry, *Restructuring the Malaysian Economy* (New York: St. Martin's Press, 1999), 264.

18. Joel Kahn, "Growth, Economic Transformation, Culture and the Middle Classes in Malaysia," in *The New Rich in Asia: Mobile Phones, McDonald's and Middle Class Revolution*, ed. Richard Robison and David S. G. Goodman (New York: Routledge, 1996), 50-51.

19. Nina Merchant Vega and Herizal Hazri, "Malaysia's Middle Income Trap." *In Asia* 2011, asiafoundation.org/in-asia/2011/01/26/malaysia's.html (accessed January 31, 2011).

20. For more information read NEAC, "NEM Class for Clusters of SMEs," *NEAC 2010* www.neac.gov.my/news&views.php?subcategory=news%20reporsts&ID1&title=nem%calls&for&cluster&smes (accessed January 30, 2010).

21. Michael O'Shannassy, "Malaysia in 2010: Between a Rock and a Hard Place," *Asian Survey* 51, no. 1(January 2010): 173-76.

22. Shazwan Mustafa Kamal, "Pakatan: Limp Reforms Fuelling Brain Drain." *Malaysian Insider* 2011, www.themalaysianinsider.com/malaysia/article/pakatan-limp-reforms-fuelling-brain-drain.html (accessed June 12, 2011).

23. Asrul Sani Abdullah, "Perkasa Complements UMNO, Say MPs," *Malaysian Insider* 2010, www.malaysianinsider.com/mobile/Malaysia/article/Perkasa-complements-UMNO-say-MPs.html (accessed June 10, 2011).

24. T. T. Tay, "A Power Struggle in the Offing," *Sin Chew Online* 2010, www,mysinchew.com/node/44818.html (accessed March 13, 2010).

25. Sue-Lyn Boo, "Pua Asks if NEM Already Dead?" *Malaysian Insider* 2010, www.themalaysianinsider.com/malaysia/article/pua-asks-if-nem-already-dead (accessed August 7, 2010).

26. *The Star*, "Malays May Lose Political Power, Warns Muhyiddon," *Star Online* 2010, thestar.com.my/news/story/2010/7/6/nation/20100706100848.html (accessed July 19, 2010).

27. Within the federation, Penang and Malacca, which were formerly states under the British Straits Settlements, along with Sarawak and Sabah, do not have a sultan, but a federally-appointed Governor or Head of State (*Yang di Pertuan Negeri)*.

28. Kamal Sadiq, "When Being Native is Not Enough: Citizens as Foreigners in Malaysia." *Asian Perspective* 33, No.1 (January 2009): 8-9.

29. Andreas Ufen, "The 2008 Elections in Malaysia: Uncertainties of Electoral Authoritarianism," *Taiwan Journal of Democracy* 4, No. 1 (July 2008): 164.

30. Mohamed Ariff, "Islam and the Private Sector: Southeast Asian Perspectives," in *The Muslim Private Sector in Southeast Asia,* ed. Mohamed Ariff (Singapore: ISEAS, 1991), 255.

31. Zuhrin Ahmad, "No Funds for Opposition MPs," *The Star* 2010, www.thestar.com.my/news/story.asp?file=/2010/12/10/nation/7/7593679.html (accessed January 21 2011).

32. Bernama, "Kelantan Government to Take Oil Royalty Issue to Court," *Malay Mail* 2010, www.malaymail.com.my/33886 (accessed January 12, 2011).

33. Sue-Lyn Boo, "Kelantan Claims RM800 Million per Annum Oil Royalty," *Malaysian Insider* 2010, www.themalaysianinsider.com/monile/Malaysia/article/kelantan-claims-rm800-per-annum-oil-royalty.html (accessed January 22, 2011).

34. Paul Tennant, "The Decline of Elective Local Government in Malaysia," *Asian Survey* 13, no. 4 (April 1973): 351-52.

35. The Election Commission was created through Article 114 of the Federal Constitution.

36. *Asia Sentinel*, "Zaid Ibrahim Blasts Elections Irregularities in Malaysia." *Asia Sentinel* 2010, www.asiasentinel.com/index.php?html (accessed December 3, 2010).

37. *Malaysian Insider*, "EC Passes Buck to MACC over Sibu Offer," *Malaysian Insider* 2010, www.themalaysianinsider.com/Malaysia/article/ec-passes-buck-macc-over-pms-sibu-offer.html (accessed August 31 2010).

38. An inaugural televised debate between opposition leader Anwar Ibrahim and Minister of Information Shabery Cheek did take place in July 2008, after the elections. The topic focused mainly on fuel prices, with discussions of contentious issues surrounding freedom of speech, the Internal Security Act, cronyism, not included in the debate.

39. Bersih, "Memorandum to Suhakam on Batu Burok," *Bersih.Org* 2007 bersih.org/?p=23 (accessed January 31, 2010).

40. Diane Mauzy, "Malaysia in 1987: Decline of the Malay Way." *Asian Survey* 28, No. 2 (February 1988): 213-15.

41. The internal dispute split party members into "Team A" and "Team B" camps. The latter, which made up of politicians opposed to Dr. Mahathir, supported the leadership of Razaleigh Hamzah, and went on to found the *Semangat 46* (Spirit of 46) party. *Semangat 46* managed to broker two loose coalitions with DAP and PAS in order to challenge the National Front in the 1990 elections. These coalitions could hardly be considered a united front, given the philosophical disagreements between the DAP and PAS, which forced Semangat 46 to establish separate unilateral alliances with PAS in the form of the *Angkatan Perpaduan Ummah*, and with the DAP and other smaller parties under the *Gagasan Rakyat.* In the 1990 elections, these alliances co-contested in the rural and urban areas respectively. Although yielding a much stronger showing than previous years, the political opposition still lacked of the unity and resources to unseat the National Front in that elections.

42. The Tribunal comprised of several local and carefully selected Commonwealth judges, headed by Malaysia's Chief Justice Abdul Hamid Omar, who would eventually take over as Lord President of the Supreme Court following Salleh Abas's removal.

43. Thomas Fuller, "Judge Nullifies Election of Ex-Minister in Malaysia," *International Herald Tribune* 2001, groups.yahoo.com/group/beritamalaysia/3565.html (accessed January 24, 2011).

44. *The Star*, "Justice Chin Tells of Threats and Indoctrination Attempts," *Star Online* 2008, thestar.com.my/news/story.asp?file=2008/6/11/nation/21512634&sec.html (accessed September 12, 2010).

45. *New Straits Times*, "No More the Broken Man," *NST Online* 2006, www.nst.com.my/Current_News/nst/Sunday/Frontpage/20060611175120/Article/index_html (accessed August 3, 2009).

46. International Bar Association, *Justice in Jeopardy, Malaysia 2000* (London: IBA, 2000), 55-59.

47. Wong Choon Mei, "French Probe: New Names Emerge, Focus Perimekar, Altantuya," *Malaysian Chronicle* 2010, www.malaysia- chronicle.com/2010/07/ french-probe-focus-on-perimekar-also.html (accessed December 13, 2010).

48. Chelsea Ng and Hurbaiti Hamdar, "Altantuya Case: Razak Acquitted," *Star Online* 2008, thestar.com.my/news/story.asp?file=/2008/10/31/nation/20082031084658.html (accessed February 12, 2010).

49. Najib Razak is the eldest son of Malaysia's second Prime Minister Tun Abdul Razak, who died in office in 1977.

50. For matters relating to the King's and each of the sultan's powers, refer respectively to Article 32 and Article 71 of the Malaysian Federal Constitution.

51. John Berthelesen, "Asia Sentinel Correspondent Accused of Insulting Sultans," *Asia Sentinel* 2009, www.asiasentinel.com/index.phpoption=com_content&task_view&id1723.html (accessed January 24, 2010).

52. Michael Sheridan, "Blog War over Sultan Mahmud Iskandar," *Sunday Times Online* 2010, www.timesonline.co.uk/tol/nes/world/asia/article7017953.ece.html (accessed.html. (accessed July 18, 2010).

53. The shooting incident of a trespasser that came too close to the Sultan's helicopter ended up in a manslaughter conviction. *Asia Sentinel*, "Perceptions and Royal Reality in Malaysia," *Asia Sentinel* 2010, www.asiasentinel.com/index.php?2262.html (accessed March 24, 2011).

54. For extensive reading on the Malaysian constitutional crisis in 1993, read: Books LLC, *1993 in Malaysia: 1993 Constitutional Amendments to the Constitution of Malaysia* (Memphis TN: LLC Books).

55. M. Mageswari, "Negri Ruler Tuanku Ja'afar Ordered to Pay Bank US$1m." *Star* 2008, thestar.com.my/news /story.asp?file=2008/10/15/nation/200810151107&sec.nation (accessed October 20, 2010).

56. *Malaysiakini*, "Selangor Sultan: Stay Away from Rally," *Malaysiakini* 2011, malaysiakinicom1.wordpress.com/2001/07/08/selangor-sultan-stay-away-from-rally.html (accessed September 12, 2011).

57. The three independents, two formerly from the Justice Party and one a former DAP member were suspected of taking huge bribes. The two Justice Party members had also been taken to court earlier for corruption before they left the PR. For more information, read *The Star*, "Perak State Assembly Calls for Dissolution, Polls," *Star Online* 2009, thestar.com.my/news/story.asp?sec=nation&file=1009/3/3/nation/20090308 5400sec=nation (accessed April 16, 2010).

58. This quote was taken from the Regent's speech on National Integrity Day, held in Kuching, Sarawak on November 5, 2008. Among other things, the Regent "reminded" Malaysians that part of the Malay rulers' role is to "strengthen the democratic system." Further details can be read at Malaysian Bar, "Rulers May Disagree with Government Leaders," Malaysian Bar Council 2008, www.malaysianbar.org.my/general_news/rulers_may_disagree_with_government_leaders_raja_nazrin.html (accessed September 1, 2011).

59. Lisa Goh and Yeng Ai Chun, "Court Rules Zambry is Valid MB," *Star Online* 2009, thestar.com.my/news/story.asp?file=/2009/5/23/3968185&sec=nation (accessed June 24, 2011).

60. Raja Eleena Azlan Shah has been in the Directorship of the UMNO-connected Gamuda Corporation since 1992, and owns about 7 percent of total shares. Eleena sits at number 33 of the top richest individuals in Malaysia for the year 2011. The Forbes list can be retrieved at www.forbes.com/lists/2011/84/Malaysia-billionaires-11_Eleena-Azlan-Shah_MDRG.html (accessed October 15, 2011).

61. For brief but incisive chronology of events, read BBC, "A Crisis Unfolds: Timeline," *BBC News Online* 1998, news.bbc.co.uk/2/hi/special_report/1998/10/98/malaysia_crisis/204632.stm (accessed March 15, 2010).

62. *Asia Sentinel*, "A Saga of Corruption Ignored: Tajudin Escapes, not His Accusers," *Asia Sentinel* 2010, www.asiasentinel.com/index.php?option=com_content&task=view&id=2658&Itemid=229 (accessed September 1, 2010).

63. In-Won Hwang, *Personalized Politics: The Malaysian State under Mahathir* (Singapore; ISEAS, 2003), 319.

64. *Human Rights Watch*, "Malaysia: ISA Detainees Beaten and Humiliated," *Human Rights Watch* 2005, www.hrw.org/en/news/2005/09/26/malaysia-isa-detainees-beaten-and-humiliated (accessed August 10, 2009).

65. James Hookway and Celine Fernandez, "Malaysian Protestors Clash with Riot Police," *Asian Wall Street Journal* 2009, online.wsj.com/article/SB124912276548999015.html (accessed January 24, 2010).

66. *Asiaweek*, "Tightening the Screws," *Asiaweek* 2006, www.pathfinder.com/asiaweek/magazine/Dateline/08782179522.html (accessed January 24, 2010).

67. James Hookway, "Terror Suspects Detained in Malaysia," *Asian Wall Street Journal* 2010, online.wsj.com/article/SB10001424052748704194504575030640380748702.html (accessed May 1, 2010).

68. Matthew Moore, "Challenge to the US: Prove JI Exists," *Sydney Morning Herald* 2003, www.smh.com.au/articles/2003/09/08/1062902001 91.html (accessed May 9, 2009). The origins of the Jemaah Islamiyah have been unclear. It was first highlighted by a so-called analyst and conservative terrorism expert Rohan Gunaratna, a Sri Lankan national working at the Nanyang Technologial Institute in Singapore. Gunaratna's reputation has come under question with charges of fraudulent research in many of his books. For further reading, see Gary Hughes, "Analyse This," *The Age* 2003, www.theage.com.au/articles/2003/07/20/1058545648013.html (accessed May 1, 2010).

69. K. Kabilan, "Anwar Lacked Dr. M's Clout in Tackling Islam," *Free Malaysia Today* 2011, www.freemalaysiatoday.com/2011/05/27html (accessed May 30, 2011).

70. Narayanan Ganesan, "Malaysia in 2002: Political Consolidation amid Change?" *Asian Survey* 43, no. 1 (January 2002): 151-55.

71. Anne Barrowclough, "Terror Suspect Mas Selamat Kastari Recaptured after Year on the Run." *Sunday Times* 2009 www.timesonline.co.uk/tol/news/world/asia/article6246307.ece.html (accessed January 31, 2010).

72. Anne Munro-Kua, *Authoritarian Populism in Malaysia* (New York: St. Martin's Press, 1996), 124-25.

73. Bernama, "Another Opposition Politician Arrested," *Bernama News* 2000, news.catcha.com/cgibin/news/bernamanews/gc1201_23html (accessed May 2, 2010).

74. Bernama, "17 Students Arrested in UPSI Crackdown, One Injured," *New Straits Times* 2012, www.nst.com.my/top-news/12-students-arrested-in-upsi-crackdown-one-injured-1.26336 (accessed January 1, 2012). A leader of a progressive student association, Adam Adli, had symbolically removed a flag bearing the Prime Minister's portrait flown in front of the UMNO headquarters, and replaced it with a flag protesting against the University and University Colleges Act, which many from the party equated with humiliating the Prime Minister.

75. *Harakahdaily*, "Outrage as Police Brutality Unleashed on Students," *Harakahdaily/En* 2012, enharakahdaily.net/index.php/headline/4098-outrage-as-polic-unleash-brutality-on-students.html (accessed January 1, 2012).

76. Shannon Teoh, "Najib Announces Repeal of ISA," *The Malaysian Insider* 2011, www.themalaysianinsider.com/Malaysia/article/najib-announces-repeal-of-isa-three-emergency-declarations.html (accessed September 30, 2011). In events leading up to the rally, the Prime Minister had promised to allow the gathering to take place in a stadium. He later reneged on this promise and consequently allowed the police to arrest around

1,600 of the tens of thousands of participants who chose to ignore police warnings to stay away from the protests.

77. Rashitha Hamid, "IGP: 13 Suspected JI Members Arrested under ISA in Tawau," *Star Online* 2011, thestar.com.my/news/story.asp?file-/2011/11/17/nation/20111117802O1&sec=nation (accessed December 1, 2011).

78. It is possible that the state would gradually replace the Police Act with the Peaceful Assembly Act. The state asserts that the difference between this Act and the Police Act is that this Act does not require any police permits for the organizing of "peaceful assemblies," while the former does.

79. Liz Gooch. "Bill Limiting Street Protests Moves Ahead in Malaysia," *New York Times* 2011, www.nytimes.com/2011/11/30/world/asia/30iht.malaysia30.html (accessed November 30, 2011). The prior Police Act did not specifically mention the ban on street protests, although it required police permission to organize such protests.

80. For information on UMNO's direct involvement in decisions regarding the operations of Media Prima can be retrieved at *The Star*, "No Decisions Yet on Merger," *Star Online* 2006, thestar.com.my/news/story/.asp?file=2007/1/9/nation/16512082&sec=nation(accessed February 7, 2009).

81. *My Sinchew*, "MCA's Huaren Holdings Sells Stakes in MCIL," *My Sinchew.Com* 2010, www.musinchew.com/node/45446 (accessed January 25, 2011).

82. Data taken from the website Freedom House, *Freedom of the Press 2010 Survey* 2010, freedomhouseorg/template.cfm?page=251&=2010 (accessed August 12, 2011).

83. Stephanie Sta. Maria, "Utusan Malaysia: Behind the Print," *Free Malaysia Today* 2011, www.freemalaysiatoday.com/2011/05/11/Utusan (accessed December 1, 2011).

84. For more information on Malaysia's Multimedia Super Corridor, go to its website at www.malaysia.gov.my/EN/Relevant%20Topics/IndustryInMalaysia/Business/ICT/MSC/Pages/MSC.aspx.

85. Economist Intelligence Unit, *Democracy Index 2010: Democracy in Retreat* (London. Economist Publishing, 2010), 3-8.

86. Economist. *Democracy*, 7-10.

87. Economist, *Democracy*, 28.

88. Freedom House, "Freedom in the World 2011: The Authoritarian Challenge to Democracy," *Selected Data from Annual Survey of Political Rights and Civil Liberties* 2011, freedomhouse.org.images/file/flw/FLW_2011_Booklet.pdf (accessed November 21, 2011).

89. Meredith Weiss and Saliha Hassan, "From Moral Communities to NGOs," *Social Movements in Malaysia: From Moral Communities to NGOs,* edited by Meredith Weiss and Saliha Hassan (London: RoutledgeCurzon, 2003), 6.

90. Weiss and Hassan, "From Moral Communities," 5.

Chapter 8
Communications Globalization and Prospects for Political Change in Malaysia, 1990-2011

The merging of computer and telecommunications technology in the late 1980s paved the way for a system of global information superhighways penetrating into the far reaches of the planet. As we enter the new millennium, this global information network has enabled the rapid sharing of ideas and information between different peoples across continents, enabling the fusions of cultures and paradigms in the process. For previously "closed" and marginalized societies, the ability to obtain direct and instantaneous information from almost anywhere around the globe has given them a new sense of empowerment—a collective awareness of their problems and the propensity for public action.

The "wiring" of Malaysia too has provided Malaysians with the expedience of connecting to alternative sources of information not usually carried by local mainstream media. The introduction of various types of social media in particular, has turned cyberspace communications into significant civic forums for political discourse, thereby facilitating informational exchanges between previously disparate organizations and groups seeking political reform. A new spirit of activism against the state has emerged, ushering in an unprecedented phase in the struggle for democracy in Malaysia.

Cyber Media Technology and Politics

One of the primary reasons behind the Malaysian ruling elites' ability to sustain their hold on political power has been owed to their ability in preserving the primordial character of Malaysian politics. As long as political mobilization, membership, and support for agendas have been organized along parochial lines, the effort to build a cohesive and multiethnic challenge against the present consociational structure has and will remain problematic.

Since 1998 however, UMNO's support from the Malay community has relatively weakened. The Malay lower classes and rural households bore the worst of the 1997 Asian financial crisis, while many from the middle classes experienced vulnerability to the lowering of their quality of life. It became obvious to many that there had been no hesitance on the part of the National Front government to institute numerous fiscal and macro-structural measures in order to save the country's largest banks, corporations, and crony capitalists, at a time when ordinary Malaysians were left struggling to survive the economic quagmire.[1] The entailing job losses and diminishing incomes among the middle and working classes also revealed in a major way, the country's general lack of resolve in providing safety nets for those in the lower rungs of the economic hierarchy, which still comprised large numbers of Malays.[2]

In picking up the concerns of the urban Malays, the then Deputy Prime Minister, Anwar Ibrahim, who also held the Finance Minister portfolio, aired his caution against the unrestrained use of state money for corporate bailouts. This led him into serious disagreements with Prime Minister Dr. Mahathir, which resulted in his prompt removal from his ministerial post and eventual dismissal from the party in 1998. Anwar, a charismatic politician often associated with representing the "common person," responded by organizing cross-country political tours to expose the various misdeeds of the Mahathir administration. Through these rallies, he also attempted to generate public support for political reform and change. The largest of these took place at the National Mosque in Kuala Lumpur on September 2, 1998. On the same night however, Anwar was arrested and taken into custody under the ISA for allegedly inciting civil unrest. The following year, he was tried and imprisoned for corruption and sodomy.[3]

Intent on exploring the details of the Anwar-Mahathir dispute, and mindful of mainstream media bias, many Malaysians began leaning toward alternative sources of information on the internet. This was made easy by the fact that many homes, especially in urban areas, had already been plugged into the country's provider network—a product, ironically, of the state's effort to encourage information literacy among Malaysians in the early 1990s. During this time, the state was embarking on its Multimedia Super Corridor project to attract foreign corporate investors for the country's information industry. To successfully achieve this, the Malaysian state had agreed to refrain from censoring any type of cyber-information flowing into the country. The Communications and Multimedia Act 1998 was an outcome of this, and by 1999, nearly half a million households had formal subscriptions to the internet.[4]

Through the internet, many Malaysians were now able to immediately follow events and news that otherwise would have remained buried under state censorship. In Anwar's case, Malaysians were able to view in delayed time, the brutal arrest of the country's former deputy prime minister in his home by police commandos. They also saw videos of his appearance in court with a bruised eye as a result of the beating he received while under police custody. Public curiosity would turn into dismay and concern. Scores of pro-Anwar websites began sprouting throughout cyberspace, many demanding his release, while others called for Mahathir's resignation. Others popped up merely to take advantage of the new-found freedom to discuss and exchange political opinions, particularly on possible systemic reforms.

A year earlier in 1997, access to satellite television and internet news had already allowed Malaysians to witness the chanting of *reformasi* (political reform) by Indonesian students and civil society activists in the streets of Jakarta, the capital of Indonesia. These protests eventually culminated in the toppling of the country's long-time dictator General Suharto. Malaysians were particularly impressed by the way ordinary people used e-mail, cell phones, and text messages to mobilize public protests against the powerful state machinery. From these civil uprisings, Malaysians were quick to notice the utility of cyberspace as a shaper and carrier of public opinion, made especially viable by the absence of state intrusion on its usage.[5]

It did not take long for Malaysian activists to emulate their Indonesian counterparts. The Social Justice Movement of Malaysia (GERAK) was established in 1998 and *reformasi* became its official call of struggle. Many were willing to overcome risks of reprisals by the police force in taking to the streets to express their displeasure with the state. Many more vented their frustrations in cyberspace through popular websites such as *Laman Reformasi* and *Mahafiraun* (abbreviated satire translated as *Mahathir the Ultimate Pharaoh*), which also carried critical commentaries against Mahathir and UMNO.[6] Since this movement grew out of the support for Anwar, it was not surprising that the majority of people who were associated with *reformasi* was largely Malays. For many urban Malays especially, the unraveling events associated with the treatment of Anwar lent to dispel their long-held beliefs about UMNO as a reputable Malay-Islamic organization.

Nevertheless, Anwar had insisted before his arrest that the struggle for *reformasi* had to be truly Malaysian, and therefore required the substantial participation of non-Malays. A year would pass before GERAK fully transitioned into a multiethnic political party—the National Justice Party or KeAdilan.[7] Contesting on the platform of cultural diversity, democratic governance, and social justice, KeAdilan, led by Anwar's wife Dr. Wan Azizah Ismail, attracted several more activists from outside the Malay community. In preparation for the 1999 general elections, KeAdilan also managed to pull together a coalition with the Chinese-dominated DAP party and the Malay-dominated Islamic party PAS in the form of the Barisan Alternatif (Alternative Front or BA). Representing Malaysia's first formal opposition alliance since independence, the BA was a mix of progressive democrats, socialists, Islamic scholars, and NGO activists, reminiscent of the brief AMCJA-PUTERA alliance of the 1940s.

With the momentum of *reformasi* swinging in its favor, the opposition through the BA pushed for an impressive showing in the 1999 elections, much better than it did four years before. Although the National Front still won by a comfortable 148-45 seat margin, UMNO registered an 8 percent drop in popular (mostly Malay) votes with a 20 percent reduction in parliamentary seats than the last elections. PAS, on the other hand, profited most by winning 18 percent more popular votes (majority Malays) and capturing an additional 20 parliamentary and 65 state seats from the 1995 elections. It also controlled two states—

Kelantan and Trengganu. Political analyst and scholar Maznah Mohamad, in her article in the newsmagazine *Aliran* later that year, asserted that a significant number of Malays had not been taken in by UMNO's demonizing of Anwar nor succumbed to its boasts of protecting Malay interests during the 1999 elections.[8] In fact, many came out to the polls to rebuke the party for its pretensions.

On the other hand however, the 1999 elections also confirmed that the full embrace of *reformasi* as a political agenda had largely been confined to the Malay-Muslim population; non-Malays were still cautious of any notion of reform associated with Malay or Muslim grassroots activism. The *reformasi* concept had also been too broad and blurry to begin with, and it sorely lacked operational effectiveness as well as specific political structure or design. The ethnic Chinese in particular, had been exceptionally worried about the DAP's partnership with the Islamic party PAS under the BA. Many believed, quite falsely, that if the BA overthrew the National Front government from power, *reformasi* might buckle under the weight of Islamic radicalism and the eventual establishment of an Islamic state in Malaysia.

The National Front had been well aware of the Islamophobic tendencies amongst large sections of the ethnic Chinese community, and fully exploited them to spook Chinese voters into abandoning the DAP. Obviously, the effort was highly effective. Although the DAP did not perform any worse in Chinese-majority areas, ethnic Chinese votes in multiethnic constituencies however, generally went to the ruling parties.[9] This also showed that a considerable number of non-Malays, especially, the middle classes, still preferred the stability of the National Front to that of an untested opposition government. Regretting its alliance with PAS, the DAP opted out of the BA after the elections.

By the time the 2004 general elections came around, *reformasi* was no longer the same force that inspired masses of citizens to the streets calling for change. This was largely due to the Malaysian economy recovering remarkably well and Dr. Mahathir retiring from office in 2003. In his place was Abdullah Badawi, whom many held in high regard for his contrasting persona to his former boss. Popularly known as "Mr. Nice Guy," Abdullah began quite promisingly on his political tenure by putting on hold and even canceling what many in the country considered to be the previous administration's wasteful "mega-projects." These included the proposed construction of the controversial Bakun Dam in Sarawak and of a third bridge linking the southern bustling city of Johor Baru with Singapore.[10]

It was also during Abdullah's time in office that the sodomy charge against Anwar Ibrahim was dropped, releasing him from prison. This certainly strengthened Abdullah's reputation and stature as a progressive leader then. In order to close the political divide within the Malay community through Islam, his administration also introduced *Islam Hadhari*, a state-prescribed concept in moderate Islamic practices for all Muslims, but whose wider aim was to alienate and label the PAS brand of Islam as "extremist."[11] Malaysians were discreetly impressed and hopeful of real changes, resulting in a resounding National Front victory at the 2004 polls.

Cyberspace as Civic Space

After its 2004 electoral victory however, the National Front did little to follow up on its pledge for major social and political changes. Instead, state-business nepotisms that had underscored the country's economic woes in the past years continued unabated. Unlike before however, state failures and weaknesses could no longer be kept secret or veiled behind censorships. To keep track of the country's political economic events, Malaysians turned again to the reliability of information carried by alternative news portals, blog postings, and foreign media on the internet rather than that of the local newspapers and television stations.

Through the alternative media, various accounts of government corruption, scandals, and abuses of power became more readily accessible to tens of thousands of internet subscribers, turning Malaysia's cyberspace once again into a discursive forum for reform-minded groups and individuals. A 2010 study conducted by the National University of Malaysia revealed that a substantial majority of local blogs and internet news sites using both Malay and English between December 2007 and April 2008 contained exchanges and commentaries that were highly critical of the National Front.[12]

The state had no effective response to these developments other than attempting to bring private bloggers and website editors to court for defamation or sedition. With the state fast losing its credibility, it also became apparent to many Malaysians that Abdullah's administration was not going to deliver any policy reform nor was it to able to tackle the country's massive corruption and cronyism problems. To bolster the National Front's waning image, and confident that Malaysia's electoral structure would ensure another convincing win for the ruling coalition, Abdullah called for general elections in 2008.

This turned out to be a near disaster for the National Front. In 2007, a non-government conglomeration of groups advocating for free and fair elections in Malaysia, known by its acronym Bersih (which in Malay translates into "clean"), organized a rally in the capital city that drew nearly 40,000 people. The efficiency with which the Bersih participants organized themselves was primarily owed to their expert usage of various social media, especially internet blogs, websites, and mass e-mails, now carried through hand-held devices and cell phones. Exchanges of instantaneous information through these media allowed for smooth and invaluable coordination between various civil society groups and opposition parties throughout the planning stages.

For the first time since Malaysian independence, a well-coordinated rally involving various civil society groups from all over the country was able to march down the streets of the capital city only to be brutally dispersed by riot police. The impact of both this demonstration and the crackdown however, would turn the political tide in favor of the opposition. Internet penetration, now at nearly 60 percent rate with nearly 14 million subscribers, allowed Malaysians to witness the state's mishandling of the rally.[13] World satellite network *Al Jazeera,* accessible in Malaysia, even carried out a dialogue with UMNO officials with regards to the state's response to the demonstration, with one unforgettable segment capturing a live phone interview with the Information Minister denying any mistreatments of protestors amidst police beating and tear-gassing of participants in the background.[14]

Many Malaysians were shocked. Already frustrated over a multitude of increasing national problems, ranging from high-level political scandals to re-emergent ethnic discords, urban voters irrespective of ethnicity, began to express their anger against the ruling National Front through the ballot box.[15] The return of Anwar into the political scene, and the resurgence of a collaborative political opposition in the formation of the Pakatan Rakyat (Pakatan or People's Alliance), replacing the defunct BA, presented itself as the primary challenger against the National Front.[16] This Pakatan, comprising the People's Justice Party (PKR—the new name for KeAdilan) and PAS, was also now bolstered by the return of the DAP to the opposition coalition.

The internet was again extensively used throughout the 2008 elections by Pakatan supporters as a means to channel critical information for public debate and action. Making the most of anti-state sentiments circulating throughout cyberspace, the opposition was able to carefully plan its election strategies, especially in terms of voter mobilization. Pakatan campaign workers began sending out live feeds of public rallies and party agendas on the internet, and in areas without fiber optic networks, they diligently coordinated the distribution of DVDs containing various opposition party speeches.[17]

Pakatan's use of the cyber media for its logistical planning was so successful that it was able to penetrate its campaigns into traditional National Front areas ahead of the elections. The efforts certainly bore fruition by the time the elections came. Despite extensive claims of widespread voting fraud and gross procedural irregularities favoring the ruling parties, the opposition still managed to achieve unprecedented gains, especially in capturing the states of Selangor, Penang, Perak, and Kedah, while strongly retaining Kelantan. If not for Sabah, Sarawak, and the major rural constituencies in Pahang and Johor, the National Front would have faced the end of their long reign that year.

On the state's side, frustrations over Abdullah's reluctance to continue with the preceding regime's policies had earned him the ire of many within the ruling elite, namely his predecessor Dr. Mahathir, who still wielded power and influence despite quitting UMNO in protest after his retirement from office.[18] Several prominent figures within the business circle were also anxious that the Abdullah administration's policy direction had not been in alignment with their own corporate goals and interests. Attacked from all sides, Abdullah was personally held responsible for the National Front's dismal outing in the 2008 elections, ungraciously forcing him into early retirement the following year.

Few in UMNO would have predicted however, that much of the anger directed at the party, and not Abdullah personally, would come back to haunt it in these elections. As in the past, UMNO has seemed oblivious to or been in deliberate denial of some of the glaring reasons behind the heightened public indignation against the party and its leaders, especially its continued nurturing and incessant use of the *ketuanan Melayu* vitriol to sustain its political weight. UMNO has yet to seriously realize the self-detriments of its rightist ethnonational stratagem, especially its impact on the non-Malay electorate. A case in point was the infamous incident involving former UMNO Youth President and Malaysian Home Minister Hishammudin Hussein. During a speech at the party's 2005 general assembly, the high-ranking politician unbecomingly unsheathed and kissed a *keris* (Malay traditional dagger), signifying UMNO's battle-readiness to defend and uphold Malay political hegemony against an implicated non-Malay "enemy."[19] Many in the non-Malay community were naturally upset at the minister's action, which it considered belligerent, unnecessary, and even racist. Although Hishammudin eventually apologized for the incident, photos and videos of his unceremonious gesture were already circulating through various internet websites, exacerbating the already tenuous relations between the non-Malay community and UMNO. The minister's antic was not readily forgotten among non-Malays during the 2008 elections. Some politicians within UMNO too, were convinced that this incident partly contributed to the National Front's poor showing, and thereby demanded the immediate resignation of the minister.[20]

Outside of UMNO, a substantial portion of the Malay community was already repulsed by the party's use of the *ketuanan Melayu* demagoguery for political mileage. As urban Malays became increasingly connected to the globalized world economy either through their jobs or social media interactions, many have begun to prioritize economic issues as well as problems relating to corruption, social inequality, and lack of political empowerment as their main areas of concern. In fact, many Malays perceive the Malay hegemony doctrine as irrelevant to their own political economic interests, since they have become all too aware that benefits derived from such hegemony have primarily been confined to the closed circle of UMNO elite and its business cronies.[21]

Importantly, there has also been eroding confidence among urban Malays with regards to the party's ability or willingness in solving the multitude of social problems besetting the Malay community such as poverty, drug-addiction, teen pregnancy, and crime. Helped by instant accessibility to cyber-media sources, many urban Malays also find greater identification with the political struggles and proposals of other predominantly Malay parties such as PKR and PAS than they do with UMNO. Political analyst Bridget Welsh in a *Channel News Asia* article dated January 17, 2009, affirmed that the monopoly of Malay support for UMNO has increasingly withered as a result.[22] The growing number of Malay political allegiances gravitating toward PKR and PAS since 2005 has now substantially split Malay votes in three different directions, one to UMNO and two others going toward the opposition.

Naturally, UMNO finds this trend particularly disquieting since such political divisions among Malays tend to chip away at the very heart of the party's support base. Desperate, the party has even reached out to PAS for talks related to "Malay unity" and possible alliance, to which the latter has consistently rejected.[23] The party's support has practically been left with its rural constituencies, whose gullibility to the dooming scenario of impending Malay disenfranchisement is reiteratively preyed upon by the state through hard-lined rabble-rousing rhetoric. Through its *Utusan Malaysia* Malay-language newspaper, the party has frequently posited the hypothesis that if the PKR and PAS took over the country's leadership from UMNO through collaboration with the Chinese-based DAP, Malays would ultimately suffer the same fate as their oppressed counterparts in Singapore.[24] The primary message conveyed to rural Malays was that Malay political leadership in Malaysia can only be permanently secured through the cohesive unity of all Malays under the single banner of UMNO.[25]

Nevertheless, UMNO has had to work harder at recouping the loss of support among Malay urbanites. Since the "Malay unity" initiative has not adequately impressed the Malay middle class, the party has extended its ethnic fear-mongering into the realm of religion. In May 2011, an *Utusan Malaysia* newspaper article reported on a dinner organized by a conglomeration of Christian churches honoring DAP Member of Parliament and Penang Chief Minister Lim Guan Eng. Based on information provided by a pro-UMNO blog site titled "Islam under Siege," the article publicized the event as a covert gathering to discuss the undermining of Islam as the official religion of the country.[26] The president of Malaysian Christian Federation, who attended the event, denied the claims of the article, as did the Chief Minister. However, despite condemnations from various civil society organizations and opposition parties, including PAS, over *Utusan*'s fanning of ethnic hatred—a crime punishable under the ISA—the newspaper received a mere reprimand from the Home Ministry. In fact, according to *The Star* dated May 7, 2011, the Home Affairs Minister initially defended the *Utusan* article, and even considered the agenda behind the event, but not the breach of journalistic ethics, as "serious."[27]

With possible general elections looming in the horizon, the underlying platform of UMNO's campaigns has been premised on the party's veracity and resoluteness in confronting and eliminating "external threats" to Malay political hegemony. However, UMNO and the National Front may find their ethnic scare tactics self-defeating in the long run. The stories being spun from the UMNO-controlled press to instill fear on Malays or deface the political opposition have become increasingly unconvincing to the point that they have appeared to ridicule the general aptitude of Malays.[28] More working and middle class Malays have become increasingly perturbed by UMNO's use of alarmist tactics, especially when cyberspace news sites have benefited them with more accurate views and comments on a varying range of social problems. Furthermore, the world of the twenty-first century is a stark contrast to the decolonization and cold war era, under which UMNO had emerged. The expanding worldviews of the Malay community on current political events and issues have increasingly rendered the discourse of ethnonational exclusiveness to be irrelevant for the more informed Malay.

Hence, in a world where progressivism has increasingly become the political norm even in many developing countries, UMNO's current approach to politics has gone against the political idealisms that normally attract legitimacy and support for governments in multiethnic societies. In today's electronically-networked and human rights-centered world especially, a country's political civility and state legitimacy have been observably and unequivocally measured by various dimensions of tolerance and inclusion. While the use of right-wing ethnic rhetoric to rationalize unequal and unjust polices may have not totally disappeared in many parts of the world, it has nevertheless, become increasingly outmoded in societies that call themselves developed and civilized. If UMNO insists on riling up ethnic sentiments as a way to gain political legitimacy and electoral success, it will only be a matter of time before such ideological bankruptcy would lead it to its own political obsolescence.

By contrast, Malaysian opposition parties have displayed more creativity and commitment in advancing multiculturalism and ethnic tolerance as major themes of their official mission and identity. This in part has been attributed to these parties' close cooperative relationships with a vast network of local human rights-based civil society organizations, who themselves have successfully generated a political following with their tireless promotion for multicultural democracy in Malaysia. Through the new media revolution, local civil society organizations have also established close contacts with international civil rights bodies such as Amnesty International and Human Rights Watch, which lends much-needed credibility and resources to these local organizations.

Indeed, the alliances between political opposition parties and civil society groups have come a long way in Malaysia. Prior to the new millennium, most reform-based non-government organizations (NGOs) in the country often replicated their political counterparts by catering to specific cultural agendas.[29] For NGOs that appeal to the English-educated circles of Malaysians such as Aliran (Malay acronym for National Awareness Movement), the Bar Council of Malaysia, and Suaram (Malay acronym for Citizens' Voice of Malaysia), their secular leanings and equal rights agenda were often depicted by the UMNO-dominated media as challenging the position of Malays and Islam.[30] This partly explains why there had been little support for these organizations among the Malay masses in the past. At the same time, NGOs operating on Islamic social justice themes such as the Malaysian Islamic Youth Movement (ABIM) and *Jamaah Islah Malaysia* (Malaysian Community for Reform) rarely captured the interests of non-Malays, or even urban Malays for that matter, since these organizations were usually communal in scope, and often portrayed by the state as promoting religious extremism.

Through the years however, many NGOs have begun to converge their organizational interests toward shared grievances against excessive state power, particularly in the discretionary use of repressive laws such as the ISA to detain activists. Closer collaboration and networking between these previously distinct civic organizations has been facilitated by technological breakthroughs in communications that have made it possible for these groups to work in close partnerships with each other as well as with numerous political opposition parties that advanced similar political objectives.

Through news portals and websites, the public too has been able to instantly access discussions and narratives on various aspects of social justice, ethnic equality, and multiethnic cooperation. These intense political dialogues have in turn enabled the successful shaping of public opinion toward a more inclusive political discourse, initiating a critical foundational step toward the attainment of a full multicultural democracy. Here, the role of the alternative media through cyber technology has been an important contributor to the rapid development of an increasingly diverse and multiethnic character of civil society organizations, compared to the past when efforts by human-rights NGOs to appeal to a cross-ethnic following had often been hampered by the intimidating presence of the state media and the various "emergency" laws.

Today, portals such as *Malaysiakini*, *Malaysia Today*, and *Harakahdaily* constitute some of the major alternative news sites that have enjoyed extensive following in the country. Known for their investigative style reporting on state abuses of power and other political excesses, these online media regularly feature columns by human rights activists and members of opposition parties, who promote and utilize contentious journalism as a means to further extend their political struggles into the electorate.[31] In the process, there have emerged considerable linkages of support across a community of journalists and various reform-oriented NGOs through alliances such as the Charter 2000 and the Centre of Independent Journalism that seek to advance press freedom and media reform in Malaysia.[32]

Thus when Malaysian police raided and briefly suspended *Malaysiakini* under the Seditions Act in 2003 for "false reporting," the news portal instantly generated moral and financial support from both domestic and international journalists as well as NGOs. Some contributed vast amount of money while others cautioned the state that Malaysia's image would suffer if the news site was not allowed to go back online.[33] Despite currently being forced to accept customer-paid subscription as a condition to run its website, the multilingual on-line newsmagazine has continued to attract individual memberships and grants from the public as well as various NGOs. The acclaim that *Malaysiakini* has acquired for its journalistic efforts has been captured by the numerous local and international awards it has received, such as the International Press Freedom Award in 2000 and the Reporters without Borders award in 2004, for its editor Steven Gan and reporter Fathi Omar.

While not as sophisticated in appearance and flair, *Malaysia Today* has gained immense popularity and reputation for its active blog reports in Malaysia. Its founder, Raja Petra Kamaruddin, living in self-exile in London at the time of writing, revealed that many of the site's accurate and reliable data have come from multiple sources. They have included members of the opposition, various NGOs, and even "insiders" working within the state.[34] The site's remarkable ability in publishing exclusive and privileged information relating to state corruption and abuses of power have amazed its readers, who not too long ago were confined to receiving state-filtered versions of news and events.

Harakahdaily is another of Malaysia's popular on-line news site. Unrivaled among the alternative media in terms of financial support and organizational efficiency, it is also the voice of PAS. In recent times, thematic discussions centering on the obligation of Muslims to ensure incorruptible governance and the compatible relations between religion, multiculturalism, and democracy, have increasingly resonated throughout its editorials and columns. Available in both Malay and English, it has also begun to attract substantial numbers of non-Muslim following. This is an important development, and one that has emerged from "the battle for Malays and Islam" between UMNO and PAS.

UMNO-PAS Rivalry: The Battle for Malays and Islam

The origins of the intense rivalry between UMNO and PAS for dominance among Malay and Muslim-Malaysians can be traced to the global Islamic resurgence that followed the 1979 Iranian Revolution. This event inspired and emboldened many Muslims in Malaysia, of whom Malays constitute the majority, to question the morality as well as validity of the Malaysian capitalist state that seemed to excessively pander to western economic interests. The impact of this world Islamic revival on the vast majority of Malays is easily seen in their increased religiosity, which have become especially more prominent among the youth population.[35]

Throughout the previous decades, PAS and UMNO have engaged in a war of attrition with regards to which political party best served the genuine interest of Malays and Islam in Malaysia. PAS has claimed that because it is the only Islamic party in Malaysia, it is therefore the organization that is unconditionally qualified and committed to pursuing Islamic social justice goals for Muslims in the country.[36] For much of its early history however, PAS rook on a traditionally narrow and provincial following. Support for the party had been especially popular in the northern Malay heartland that once constituted the least developed Un-federated Malay States (UFMS) during British colonialism. Until the 1970s, the politics in these states had been particularly unwelcoming toward UMNO and its English-educated leadership. Instead, Islam has always provided a strong backdrop not only in terms of religion but also in combating the hedonism and materialism associated with the capitalism system, which many saw to be visibly embodied within UMNO's concept of economic progress.[37] It is not surprising then that many here have comfortably identified with the politics of PAS, who in turn has worked diligently in protecting these communities' interests against the political economic encroachment of the federal government. Currently, Kedah and Kelantan are administered by PAS while Terengganu had been under PAS governance for five years following the 1999 elections.

In turn, UMNO has always attempted to sell its so-called tempered approach to religion as the correct form of Islam. In past years however, the impacting force of Islamic revivalism has strongly compelled the party to win over the more conservative Muslim population in the country with its own religious-oriented policies. This can be captured in the considerable presence of Islam in areas of education, media, and the civil service, where extensive Islamic values, attire, and traditions have been imbibed and adopted. In 2007, the state even claimed that Malaysia under UMNO was already an "Islamic state" since its approach to governance had always been premised on Islamic principles.[38]

The UMNO-led government has also strengthened the country's parallel but separate state-level *Shariah* court systems that administer and apply Islamic laws solely on Muslims. Today, each state's system of Islamic courts possess jurisdiction over a host of civil and family-related matters including divorce, marriage, and public conduct. Many of these courts have also been upgraded and professionalized, both in terms of management and personnel, in line with the country's secular courts.

Increasingly, the various state religious departments have been manned by very conservative leaderships that work closely with the ruling party. The effect of this "bureaucratization" of Islam has been to ultimately confer political authority and power to state-appointed officials over the definition and management of Islam in Malaysia.[39] This has made it easier for the state to officially impose upon Muslims, strict conformity to what it views as its "correct" version of Islam. Any fringe or sectarian branches of the religion, including the various strains of the Shiite school, have often been designated as "deviants" or "cults," and have therefore been formally outlawed in Malaysia. Many adherents to such groups have found their way to the country's detention centers under the ISA.

In contrast, despite being demonized by UMNO as "fundamentalist," PAS has increasingly appeared in many ways to be the more moderate and progressive political force. For example, the party has frequently asserted its opposition to state NEP-type programs, proclaiming any element of ethnic or religious preferences in public policy to be unjust and un-Islamic. Instead, PAS has officially advocated for the establishment of an equitable and far-reaching health and educational system for all Malaysians, specifically to assist poor and disadvantaged groups.

The increased attractiveness as well as confidence in PAS when compared to UMNO has also rested on the public image of its leaders. The PAS leadership, unlike that of UMNO, has rarely, if ever, been associated with any political scandal or outward ostentation in conduct. Through the alternative media, viewers have been able to follow the daily routines of its members of parliament and state representatives, as well as admire their simplicity in life and perseverance in political struggles. The Kelantan state chief minister, Nik Aziz Mat, in particular, has developed a venerable standing among Malaysians of all backgrounds, not only for his integrity as a political leader but also for his progressivism and humility as an individual.

That a wind of change has indeed moved the party away from its previously one-dimensional approach to national politics was confirmed at its June 2011 *muktamar* (general assembly and elections). At this summit, delegates soundly displayed their overwhelming preference for a more secular direction for the party with the election of professional politicians in the various leadership posts in place of the traditional *ulamas* (religious scholars). Importantly, throughout the proceedings, the party's customary "Islamic state" agenda had been noticeably de-emphasized, if not totally absent. What emerged instead was the party's official call for a struggle toward the establishment of a welfare-oriented multicultural society.[40]

Much of this new approach in political philosophy comes from the party's recent acknowledgement that the concept of an Islamic state does not actually exist in Quranic scripture. Instead, genuine interpretations of Islamic teachings have placed more emphasis and value on social tolerance and harmony within *majmuk* (pluralist) societies. As such, the party has obligated itself to realign its political struggles with the realities of a multiethnic democracy in Malaysia.[41] It was not surprising, therefore, to find PAS at the forefront in defending the rights of non-Muslims and Christians in the country. A particular example pertained to PAS's criticism of the state's impoundment of Malay-language Bibles that used the word "Allah" when referring to God.[42] The confiscation was done in response to an earlier outrage by right-wing UMNO politicians and NGOs who asserted that using the term "Allah" instead of *tuhan* (Malay for God) had been a deliberate attempt by local church authorities to endear and proselytize Malays to Christianity. PAS, on the other hand, supported for the rights of Malaysians to be allowed accessibility to these Bibles in the name of religious freedom.[43]

Much of PAS's success in projecting its progressive politics as well as broad class appeal has been accredited to the availability of the alternative media. The effective use of cyberspace as a mode of political conveyance by an increasing number of highly-educated, and blog-savvy PAS politicians had begun long before UMNO was able to effectively put together its own website through the internet. More recently, PAS's ability to reach out to all Malaysians has increasingly attracted a new generation of non-Muslims, who have been captivated by its reform-based agenda. This has culminated in the founding of a popular PAS Non-Muslim supporters' club in 2004. In a *Malay Mail* article dated October 18, 2009, PAS president Hadi Awang mentioned that because the party was committed to the establishment of a multicultural democracy, there have been plans to eventually turn the club into a party wing for purposes of possibly fielding non-Muslim electoral candidates in the next elections.[44]

While this may sound trivial to western audience, it marked a dramatic step forward for the previously closed political party, especially in Malaysia where religion and ethnicity still fall under a single and mutually inclusive category for Malays. This new direction for PAS was even more remarkable when compared to UMNO, whose political platform remained entrenched in racist rhetoric and whose membership requires the qualification of one's Malay-Bumiputera ethnicity.

Weak Political Mobilization in East Malaysia

The use of cyber technology for political mobilization in the eastern Malaysian states of Sabah and Sarawak has not been as intense as in the western part of the country mainly due to their relatively slower pace of economic development. The digital divide between this region and the rest of Malaysia has been evident with internet use still mainly limited to the relatively few middle class homes in the urban areas. This partly explained the inability of the political opposition to make successful inroads into the region during the 2008 elections.

Geographical-ethnic barriers, continuous poverty, and illiteracy have long prevented any unified mobilization against state abuses of power, particularly in Sabah. Public issues affecting Sabahans such as widespread environmental degradation, continued underdevelopment, and state cronyism have not been extensively discussed among the people due to lack of cyber-informational infrastructure and literacy. As long as underdevelopment remains a key feature of the state's economy, the likelihood for an effective civil society to emerge through cyber-mobilization would remote or non-existent.

The same goes for Sarawak. Chief Minister Taib Mahmud, a National Front politician from the *Parti Pesaka Bumiputera Bersatu Sarawak* (United Bumiputera Party of Sarawak), has been in office for more than thirty years. The almost absolute power he has wielded in Sarawak, which unofficially earned him the title "Brown Rajah," is reminiscent of the colonial rule under the Brooke dynasty. The outcome of recent state elections in April 2011 also showed minimal success in opposition voter mobilization, which was primarily confined to mainly urban areas where the DAP and PKR have taken a greater share of state assembly seats. In contrast, the well-run state machinery and media have successfully exploited the apathy and seclusion of local Bumiputera populations in the rural areas to ensure that Taib kept his reign in the state. A report by the NGO Aliran dated May 28, 2011, mentioned that prior to the elections, there had been open and rampant instances of state officials offering inducements and "assistances" to local populations in return for votes. The report also mentioned that there had been well-coordinated cyber attacks on popular pro-opposition websites throughout the elections, which it said were obviously aimed "to deny the electorate access to alternative non-mainstream news."[45]

For the past thirty years, state media in both Sarawak and Kuala Lumpur have been careful not to discredit the state's ruling family in any way. Despite this however, some public information have surfaced through the internet regarding the details of the Sarawak first family's excessive wealth. The *Sarawak Report* is one of the major websites dedicated to tracking the exploits of the Taib family and their numerous acquisitions of overseas assets worth billions in US currency. The site has repeatedly attributed the ease with which the Chief Minister has been able to accumulate his vast fortune primarily to his undisputed political power in the state and his unrestricted access to Sarawak's lucrative timber industry.[46] This is the same industry that throughout the decades, has spurred on the reckless felling of trees, causing massive depletions of forests and irreplaceable fauna in Sarawak. More importantly, wanton logging has given rise to the displacement of hundreds of indigenous people in a state that is paradoxically the richest in natural resources but poorest in economic ranking.

The plight of native peoples affected by federal and state economic projects in Sarawak has so often been taken lightly by both the federal and state authorities. Ongoing constructions of a series of hydroelectric dams that started nearly two decades ago, have over the years, displaced and forcibly resettled tens of thousands of indigenous Penans, forcing them to forsake their centuries-old horticultural lifestyle. This, however, has nowhere neared in comparison to the maltreatment of some members of that community by people involved in the timber industry. Several civil society organizations under the Penan Support Group published a report claiming a surge in the sexual exploitation of Penan women and young girls by men involved in logging activity. In response to the report, the Deputy Minister for Women, Family, and Community Development, Hang Seai Kie, flatly denied that there had been any sexual assaults. Echoing this, Land Development Minister Dr. James Masing, when asked by a BBC reporter about the rape of young girls, remarked that the Penans were "good storytellers," implying that any sexual activity involving the girls could have been merely consensual.[47] Consequently, *The Star* newspaper in its article dated July 7, 2010, also mentioned that the Attorney-General's office, after looking through the report, recommended that no further investigation be pursued for "lack of evidence."[48]

Sarawak's disenfranchised communities may not have yet received the justice they deserve. A more positive outlook however, lies in the increased interest and coverage on Sarawak's environmental problems by the world's major NGOs and media agencies. With increased global exposure on Sarawak and wider internet usage within the state, there would inevitably surface greater pressure on the current leadership to finally concede to the will of its citizens for political change and social reforms.

Conclusion: Prospects for Multicultural Democracy in Malaysia

Many observers saw that the fall of the Berlin Wall in 1989 and the ensuing "victory" of capitalism over of communism in Europe in the early 1990s as having closed the chapter on global power struggles for good. Some predicted that the remaining conflicts at the world level would be intensively confined to "civilizational" confrontations between western democracies and eastern-Islamic societies. There is a presumptuous notion by many in the west that European values of freedom, democracy, and individual liberties are not universally appreciated outside of the western world. As a result of these "irrevocable" cultural-ideological differences, many political commentators have forecasted tremendous ongoing resistance by predominantly Muslim countries against the incorporation of modern values in governance and democracy into their political framework.[49] Furthermore, the argument follows, if institutionalization of democracy was ever going to be attempted in eastern societies, it had to come from strong western pressures on these governments since their masses of people are culturally too passive and thereby lacked the necessary will and ambition to bring about substantial changes toward political liberalization.

These assumptions, of course, are weak and have been proven flawed in several ways. This includes the fact that much political suppression occurring in the developing world has been indirectly tied to both European colonialism and continuing western support for undemocratic systems in the protection of capitalist interests in those regions. Also, there have been major inconsistencies in the practice of capitalist democratic governance in western societies as well. These could be easily observed in the prevalent misalignments in western countries between their economic and labor policies and the social justice goals and values the democratic system was supposed to espouse. The unrestrained structural disparities and increased political disenfranchisements afflicting weaker social groups in many western countries are some resultant examples of the contradictions found in western capitalist democracies.

More significantly, the growth and proliferation of grassroots civil disobediences for greater democracy throughout the Arab world, and before that, in Indonesia and Malaysia since the late 1990s, is testimony to the inaccuracy of an important premise of this "clash of civilization" theory that postulates Muslim societies as having no serious propensity for democratic change. On the contrary, these uprisings have revealed that among the fiercest proponents of greater civil liberties and human rights in these predominantly Muslim countries have come from the various Muslim-based cultural and political organizations. These events have clearly shown that public action for political change has re-merged with greater vigor and efficiency than before, not only in the Middle-East but throughout the world. With the arrival of new social media and communications technology, a more intense pace in democratization has been seen to transverse throughout diverse nationalities, religions, and cultures.

Era of Public Action

In the wake of increased public action for reforms throughout the Middle East, Europe and the various "occupy" movements in US cities, *Time* magazine has honored "the protestor" as the person of the year for 2011.[50] The outcome of these protests have been varied. In Tunisia, Egypt, and Libya, it came in the form of removing long-time dictators and their *anciens regimes*. In the United States, there emerged extensive awareness of issues relating to the blatant social, economic, and political injustices imposed upon the majority of Americans by an all-powerful "one percent" economic elite. In any case, these protests did not occur in a vacuum. They were the culmination of widespread consciousness of the escalating problems associated with the current political economic conditions. More importantly, the groundwork for and organization of these protests were successfully carried out through the use and availability of various social media networks penetrating into nearly every corner of the world.

The same trend has begun in Malaysia. Traditionally, opposition parties in the country had provided the main institutional force in challenging the state for political change and reform. However, the ruling elites' ability to manage and control the country's democratic process had effectively impaired any prospect of a successful outcome. It became more and more apparent that any systemic transition toward a multicultural democracy in Malaysia required the combined efforts of other social forces, namely the various civil society organizations. Here, twenty-first century information technology has undoubtedly lifted such a struggle onto an unprecedented level by providing the much-needed springboard for greater democratization in the country. This process has been seen to occur in several ways. One, instantaneous information flows and exchanges have allowed civil society groups to generate a vibrant and open political discourse on multiculturalism and democratic reforms in the country. For the most part, this is to ensure that all citizens, or at least a good majority of them, would be fully consensual with the idea of a freer and more just multicultural society.

Additionally, the reachable presence of the alternative media, various local websites, and foreign news agencies has served to circumvent the traditional censoring of information by the state that for decades had successfully shielded the ruling elites from public criticisms, while impeding citizen mobilization for political change. As more Malaysians became better informed and able to see the inherent weaknesses within the consociational system, especially its inability to fulfill their social economic aspirations, they have begun to seek alternative political sources with which they could identify and lend support for reforms. The current advances in information technology in this case, have provided Malaysian political consumers the linkages to wider choices of civil society groups, opposition parties, and other interest-based associations championing similar goals for social and political changes.

This largely explains why, in recent times, the utility and effectiveness of "emergency" laws in deterring public protests or in silencing an increasingly vociferous discontentment in Malaysia has lessened. There seemed to be new-found valor on the part of those critical of the system to cross the limits of fear of the state and become more vocal and active in their political struggles, especially when knowledge of support from other citizens is made possible by the new communications technology. Aware that one is not alone in the cause of justice, and enticed by the prospective benefits of a freer system, groups and individuals have become more willing to directly involve themselves in outward anti-systemic action. In the process, they inspire others to publicly act, either on the streets or at the polls.

Such public actions have indeed brought about significant consequences in the struggle for democratization in Malaysia. As mentioned earlier, the first large rally for electoral reform organized by civil society group Bersih in 2007 contributed considerably to the opposition parties' improved showing in the 2008 elections. The state media had tried to play down the massive turnout at the rally, but the availability of the alternative and social media made it possible for a huge portion of the public to follow the event via the internet, broadband, and other forms of wireless telecommunications. It was not surprising then that the state and its ruling elites had been duly worried in the months leading to the second rally for free and fair elections that took place on July 9, 2011. This time, a larger conglomeration of civil society groups had pledged to overcome their fear of police brutality and arrest to attend the organized demonstration. Despite roadblocks at major entry points into the city on the day of the rally, some 25,000 protestors and activists managed to sneak into the capital and headed toward the historic Merdeka Stadium, where the assembly was planned. Along the way, around 1,600 others were arrested, while many more were forcibly dispersed by the targeted spraying of police water cannons and tear gas, causing dozens of injuries, including one death.[51]

Despite the failure to complete the march to the stadium, several promising developments became evident as far as the struggle for democratic reform was concerned. One was that the broadcast of the event had been followed much more extensively by other Malaysians through uploads of thousands of private twitters, cell phone cameras, and text messages. Another notable feature had been the greater presence of non-Malay participants in the rally. Although the majority remained Malays, the 2011 event was much more diverse in terms of class, ethnicity, and even age, than the earlier one that took place in 2007. This was truly extraordinary considering the country had not previously seen any political event of similar magnitude where diverse groups of people walked shoulder to shoulder toward a common political cause.

Another positive outcome of this rally was the worldwide attention and outcry from the international community with regards to the state's mistreatment of the peaceful marchers. Indeed, international media coverage of this event would not have been as significant had it not been for the state's heavy-handedness in crushing the rally. The *Human Rights Watch* organization, in its July 13, 2011, commentary, stated that "when basic liberties compete with the entrenched power of the (Malaysian) state, the government is quick to throw respect for human rights out the window."[52] Some of Malaysia's neighbors in ASEAN were also dismayed. After an editorial of *The Jakarta Post* had described Malaysia as a country that is "rich but not free" in reference to the state's reaction to the incident, UMNO attempted to undertake damage control by sending a delegation to Indonesia to explain the state's use of force during the demonstrations.[53] A major reason, the state astoundingly claimed, was that the Bersih rally had been an attempt by left-wing and Islamist groups to propel an overthrow of the National Front government. Prime Minister Najib Razak in further justifying the heavy clamping down of the rally, was quoted in the July

14, 2011, edition of the *New York Times* as saying "if we allow for street demonstrations, there's no end to it, there will be another group that wants to demonstrate."[54] Najib's statements sounded eerily similar to those made by Mubarak in his first public address after the Tahrir Square riots in Cairo.[55]

One may be forgiven for wondering whether such remarks from the Prime Minister signaled his subliminal awareness of an affinity between the National Front's hold on power and Hosni Mubarak's 30-year tyrannical rule in Egypt. After all, there had been parallels between the two countries. Although there had been relatively less freedom in Egypt, both countries shared the presence of a formidable but corrupt state catering to the interests of the ruling class and business elites. Both these states had also instilled a culture of fear embodied in an imminent "political instability" as justification for managing and repressing their countries' democratic institutions and civil liberties, which for too long have aided the state in its monopoly of political power.

This is where information-driven globalization has transformed the relationship between the state, the media, and citizens in both countries. Increased information flows into the homes of ordinary people have provided citizens with unimpeded access to information and knowledge of various political opinions and debates. In both Egypt and Malaysia, people have been able to analyze and link the causes for the widening of social disparities, high unemployment, and rising food prices to the ravaging of the national economy by state-business cronyism and foreign economic interests. The wastage of public funds to enrich the ruling elites and other well-connected groups has been recognized by many in both these countries' middle classes as a major source of their respective countries' prolonged economic inertia. Significantly, much of the public anger that has spilled onto the streets in Cairo and Kuala Lumpur emanated from accumulated frustrations over the absence of any political avenue under the existing system, through which issues relating to the political economic excesses of the ruling elites could be addressed.

It must be noted however that the significance of these street protests, even when successful in toppling dictatorial systems, lies not within its certainty to immediately introduce genuine democracy. Rather, it lies in the new-found capacity of previously helpless groups of citizens to organize and initiate demands for a freer and more equal society. In Malaysia, as in Egypt, this has inarguably been the case. The mobilization of support for civil society movements and their call for protest participation was clearly expedited by instantaneous and rapid social media communications, whose provision and accessibility have been within the reach of almost every middle class family in the urban areas. In the course of public action itself, broadband services furnished by the various alternative media and foreign news sources, and social media in the form of Facebook, Twitter, and text messaging capabilities have allowed grassroots movements and protest groups to effectively arm themselves with updated information in the face of state-police hostility.

However, it is true that uncontrolled and prolonged public action could transition into spiraling civil unrests that are just as harmful and divisive for proponents of democracy within the country. The degree to which grassroots anti-systemic energy could be channeled toward realizing a truly functioning and peaceful multicultural democratic society would heavily depend on the relational strategy taken by the Malaysian alternative media, various human rights-based civil society organizations, and progressive-minded politicians in shaping a culture of ethnic tolerance, democracy, and social justice within the struggle for democracy. Such mobilization requires the disciplined convergence of the various groups' struggles, missions, and experiences, toward achieving multicultural democratic goals. This is made more possible today by the new communications technology.

Civil Society as Agents of Change

That the current information technology revolution has provided a critical accessory to the democratization process in various parts of the world is a welcoming development for many. Not least for those who have invested great confidence in the power of discursive communication to stimulate successful dialogues on democracy and social-political reforms.[56]

Throughout the decades, the consociational system has been publicized by Malaysia's ruling elites as the most rational and stable method in maintaining the country's multicultural coexistence. However, the kind of multiculturalism that the state has endorsed all this while has not only sustained a system of rigid identity politics in the country, but has also served as a vehicle through which the ruling elites have managed to justify their own political power in the name of so-called national stability.

The ruling elites, particularly in UMNO, have thus far achieved this by outwardly reiterating its so-called ethnonational obligation to protect, at all costs, Malay political interests and constitutional privileges. In persistently advocating its ethno-survivalist ideology, UMNO has become confident in securing its Malay electoral support, even at the expense of heightening ethnic discords between Malays and non-Malays. In doing this however, it has also become noticeably clear that the state has failed to effectively construct a common identity to which Malaysians could collaboratively subscribe; to date, the current system has yet to forge any meaningful concept of national unity or sense of belonging among Malaysians. Over time, there is possibility that the porosity of Malaysia's consociational rule to the flows of recurring historical prejudices and antagonisms between ethnic groups could permanently disentangle whatever is left of the country's fragile multicultural reality.

For a truly effective and just multicultural democracy to emerge in Malaysia, its ethnic politics must gradually be abandoned for the cultivation of a new political culture based on deeper understanding of ethnic-cultural relations in the country. Such efforts are meaningless without an accompanying system that provides equal opportunity for all groups to voice their political concerns as well as participate in the proposals for solutions to problems. Resolving ethnic problems in Malaysia, in other words, must be equated by honest attempts in addressing grievances and apprehensions on all sides. Discussions can be commenced by apportioning equal weight to genuine Malay concerns about being politically and economically subsumed by the more prosperous non-Malay communities as well as to the legitimate frustrations of non-Malays regarding their second-class political status in the country. In such discussions, it is imperative that exchanges and suggestions be framed objectively but managed with cultural sensitivities, mutual respect, and historical understanding. Unjustifiable discursive rhetoric aimed at ostracizing or subjugating any group would only aggravate existing ethnic prejudices and hostilities.

Hence, civil society organizations incorporating scholars, politicians, and the alternative media must therefore be responsible for putting forth a new and all-inclusive political dialogue for Malaysians—different from the agenda that had accompanied the country's struggle against colonial rule, which had mostly benefited the present elites. Here, all reform-minded NGOs and political groups should use the alternative media and other cyber sites to remind Malaysians that the political health of every ethnic, cultural, and religious group is contingent upon the stability of a socially just and politically equal multicultural co-existence. It is equally critical to countervail the divisive and inflammatory approach of the current National Front with a political discourse emphasizing responsible multiculturalism and civic integration. In this, there must be consistent as well as cogent efforts in establishing forums that seek to foster genuine and sincere inter-ethnic interaction and understanding through the prioritization of civility and social justice among all groups.

Professionalism and careful discretion must also be used in highlighting constructive commentaries as well as isolating belligerent voices which seek to cause hostilities against others. This new direction requires that each ethnic group departs from strategies that serve to mainly and solely consolidate one's own political economic advantages, and also from any attempt to adjudge ethnic compromises in terms of xenophobic and zero-sum responses. Past events in Malaysia have shown that when there are minimal ethnocentrisms involved or when larger collective goals are given focus, cross-ethnic collaborations for social and political reform tend to be more effective and successful.

One of the most important features of this new direction also involves addressing the sources of continuing ethnic divisions and inequalities in the country. This means that dialogues carried out within the alternative media must also seek and uncover the larger aims of a multicultural democracy as a remedy to narrow disparity gaps along ethnic and class lines. The emerging political discourse thereby should be expanded to include class-related contexts of ethnic problems rather than singling out particular ethnic groups as oppressors and others as victims. Malaysians must eventually acknowledge that the source of social inequality in Malaysia has never been due to a scarcity in resources but rather to their unequal and unjust distribution by the powerful and privileged.

This brings us to the larger framework for the analyses of all social problems in Malaysia—capitalism as a potentially exploitative and highly susceptible system that has easily been used to disproportionately reward the powerful and penalize the weak in society. Advocates of an alternative and progressive form of capitalism must reiterate that the system can only function beneficially if its excesses are tempered by mechanisms that protect the rights of the vulnerable in society as well as provide a more equal starting point for future Malaysian citizens in their quest to fulfill their life ambitions and goals. Here, human rights-based civil society organizations must incorporate in their missions, the importance of equal and fair provisions of basic services such as quality education, housing, and healthcare as a means to guarantee the wellbeing of all Malaysians regardless of ethnicity, class, or gender. In other words, a multicultural democracy in Malaysia will function most effectively if it is able to safeguard and facilitate social and economic progress for all of its citizens—men, women, the young, the old, the disabled.

Interestingly, efforts toward a multicultural democracy must also involve the parallel pursuits of national integration and cultural autonomy. Although the freedom and liberty to preserve each ethnic group's cultural history and vernacular traditions forms the quintessential feature of a democratic society, a national integrative identity would nevertheless give Malaysians a feeling of national belonging crucial to the long-term social and political stability of the country. For Malaysia, the best form of social-political integration remains in the widespread use of the national language. As an official language, the use of Malay is not only simple but also serves to carry on the historical legacy of the Malay Archipelago, where it had facilitated the region's thriving and vibrant economy. Unfortunately, the effort to give equal focus on the Malay language alongside English by ordinary Malaysians and the alternative media has not been widespread.[57]

While Indonesia has successfully adopted the Malay language to unite its vast republic, in Malaysia, it has been almost pathetic that this language has not been extensively spoken outside of the Malay-Bumiputera community. There remain deep ethnocentrisms among non-Malays, especially the Chinese, in their unwillingness to acknowledge the constitutional importance of the Malay language. A clear example of this was a debate organized by a local Chinese TV network in February 2012 between a DAP politician and the president of the MCA, which was conducted in Mandarin instead of the national language.[58] It was astounding that a national level event such as this seemed to exclude the rest of the country as though they did not exist. Even among Malays, the correct and standardized version of the language has rarely been used, preferring instead the colloquialisms of their own local provinces.[59] A more widespread use of Malay among all Malaysians is crucial not only for respecting the role of the national language as a unifying vehicle, but also for the inclusion of the largely mono-lingual Malay rural peasantry into the fold of progressive political discourse.

Additionally, both Malays and non-Malays must understand that the obsession to prioritize their respective cultural preferences at the expense of the spirit of national unity and peaceful co-existence would also likely reinforce the sources of instabilities that ultimately affect the future interests of every group in Malaysia. Thus while it is important that the Malay language remains as one of the country's critical integrative vehicle, deeper efforts in inter-cultural diffusion should be accelerated to structure in a unique national character that would realistically symbolize Malaysia as a nation that is united, multiethnic, and free. In order to constructively foster true multiculturalism as well as effective integration in Malaysia, inter-ethnic encounters and interactions through schools, businesses, and social events as well as through inter-faith councils and neighborhood associations must therefore be highly encouraged, and where possible, mandated.

The development of a transcendent Malaysian identity in the long term would hopefully render the obsolescence of ethnic-based groups, which prey on the hardships of particular segments of their community to further the political interests of their own leaderships. Organizations such as the Malay right-wing Perkasa and the ultra-conservative ethnic Indian Hindu Rights Action Force, which seek to "defend" the rights and interests of ethnic Malays and Hindus respectively, not only encourage ethnic exclusiveness in politics but also serve to sustain the persistence of an indefinable and superficial multicultural co-existence. The same goes for ethno-cultural organizations, whose primordialist agendas effectively hinder efforts toward the emergence of a multiculturalism based on mutual tolerance and appreciation. In this respect, organizations such as the Chinese educationists *Dong Jiao Zong* as well as political parties such as UMNO, MCA, and MIC, truly represent themselves as major obstacles to achieving both an integrative national identity and a peaceful multiethnic co-existence; the faster the demise of these organizations, the better it would be for the realization of a genuine multicultural democracy.

Importantly, civil society organizations in Malaysia must also advocate and engender a *secular* political system based on the rule of law. While religious practices and traditions should be allowed to flourish, they must nevertheless be kept separate from national political life as much as possible in order to prevent the abuse of the system by groups bent on the pursuits of ethno-religious objectives. Above all, a secular political system, supported by primacy in the rule of law, would serve best in respecting as well as allowing the freedom and sensitivities of each particular religion and culture to exist in harmony with others. Additionally, it would also protect the religio-cultural interests of every ethnic group from being oppressed by others, politically or economically.

In the larger context, real and genuine political changes toward social justice can only be said to have been achieved when democratic actions and processes could themselves be seen and felt by citizens. The critical importance placed on the institutional protection of civil liberties through the state, the courts, and the legislative assemblies, hugely lies in the guaranteed and transparent provision of avenues through which individuals and groups are able to prevent, challenge, and seek redress from discrimination and mistreatments committed against them by any party.

Finally, the key to developing and sustaining a multicultural democracy in Malaysia currently rests with a responsible civil society; as long as civic organizations and political opposition are divided and continue to persist along either cultural lines or pursue self-serving goals, the chances for attaining a full democracy in Malaysia will remain elusive. The extent to which civil society in Malaysia has reached this required level of multicultural consciousness can be readily tested in the upcoming thirteenth general elections, which at the time of writing had not been officially called. If by then, a substantially united and vocal civil society could visibly emerge to provide strong advocacy and conviction for a progressive multicultural democratic system, the prospects for greater democratization in Malaysia may well be encouraging and bright.

Civil Society and Sustainable Development

Malaysian civil society groups can also effect changes toward a socially just and stable multicultural democracy by ensuring that the country's industrial development rewards its citizens fairly and equitably. Despite experiencing industrial growth, Malaysia's development remains heavily dependent on the decisive and self-profiting economic actions of the powerful global north, who seek to safeguard its own production, exports, and marketing interests throughout the world. Constrained by the lack of high-end manufacturing capabilities as well as deprived of any ownership of technology by international patent right laws, Malaysia has perpetually been imprisoned within a highly vulnerable "middle-income" economy. As the book has shown, this dependent-type development, since colonial times, has also been a principal contributive source to Malaysia's widening social divisions, ongoing corruption, and increased state control of the country's democratic institutions and processes.

Considering that the peripheral location of Malaysia in the capitalist world economy has been the primary basis for the country's serious structural limitations in development, efforts to ameliorate the inequities of the system may seem insurmountable. Nevertheless, an effective way through which Malaysia's civil society would be able to embark on initial steps toward better economic terms of development for the country is through the coordinative alliances with other regional and world NGOs seeking fair international and global trade practices. In this age of globalization, such relationships are readily forged and maintained through the utilization of cyberspace as an efficient form of civic space. Through the close support and collaboration with major fair trade-based international NGOs, who have been active in sending their own delegations of protestors and media correspondents to elite capitalist events such as the World Trade Organisation (WTO) talks, G-8 summits, and World Economic Forum meetings, Malaysian civil society organizations would do well to converge world economic justice issues with the struggle for democratization at home.

This is especially worth considering since both the pursuit of multicultural democracy in Malaysia and the larger struggle for global economic justice are virtually two sides of the same coin. The reason why Malaysia's ruling elites have been insistent on maintaining the consociational ruling structure as well as their elite-driven industrialization has partly to do with the fact that these partnering arrangements have bestowed upon them the privileges of the modern capitalist system. There is good reason to believe that any major change in the current global political economic order toward a fairer system would almost likely lead to a more equitable system in Malaysia as well. This would leave the elites' absolute hold on the country's power and resources susceptible to greater and more formidable challenges from the people.

Furthermore, in today's globalizing world, critical assessments against the conventional materialist approach to economic growth have become more valid and justifiable, and thus widely supported by an increasing number of people across the planet. There has been accumulating evidence presented thus far, that explains the serious environmental decline, excessive waste, and perpetual inequities in resource distribution and political power as inevitable products of unrestrained capitalist growth. As a result, issues of democratization and social justice have been successfully acknowledged to be intricately tied to a larger and comprehensive human rights discourse seeking to advance the quality of life for the world's future generations through an environmentally sustainable, fair, and equitable political economic path.[60]

In this respect, civil society groups in Malaysia must intensify their efforts to counter and discredit the present system by supporting a new paradigm in development, premised on the promotion of social equality, political freedom, and environmental sustainability for all communities. Here, Malaysia's civil society organizations, with the support of the progressive alternative media, must be able to endorse a communal and ecological-based development strategy that de-emphasizes the anthropocentrism, materialism, and individualism inherent in the present version of economic growth. Such efforts may seem daunting against the might of the state and other political forces seeking to preserve the status quo, but they are nevertheless, not impossible to achieve. This is because the present world economic arrangement is as good only as the various ruling and economic elites are able to maintain their hegemony over society.

As it stands today, the impact of the wastefulness and inequities of global capitalism on citizens have already manifested in the system's increased vulnerability to popular contestations, as evidenced by the recent series of protests taking place across continents. A paradigmatic shift toward a more sustainable society begins with exposing the irrelevant and exploitative aspects of the current system, through what environmental sociologist Michael M. Bell describes as "phenomenological rupture."[61] Here, citizens must be made to realize the damaging effects that come with continued subscription to the current approach of the capitalist system on their personal and occupational lives. Simultaneously, it must be made critically known that the benefits of an alternative and highly sustainable economic system with a more responsible and equitable dimension to economic prosperity would entail greater profitability in both material and communitarian terms. When Malaysians begin to appreciate the potential rewards of a sustainable economic growth fully facilitative of extensive social-environmental benefits, there should follow a responsive desire for such reforms of the present system, which all this while has enabled disproportionate material accumulations for a privileged few at the detriment and harm of others. Here, communications technology has begun and will continue to aid the progressive civil society sector in Malaysia in its struggle for greater democratization against the state and the present system by empowering it with greater informational resources and effective mobilization strategies.

Summary: A Theoretical Model

The summarization of discussions in this chapter and their connection to the findings from previous chapters are encapsulated in figure 8.1 on the opposite page. This "open system" diagram illustrates the theoretical framework of this research hinging on two major historical processes of the current world economy—capitalist development and communications-driven globalization.

Malaysia's capitalist development has been historically shaped by its peripheral position within the capitalist world economy. The decolonization process had helped eased into power an elite-driven capitalist democracy of the present consociational system, which has been highly accommodative to western capitalist interests, and at the same time, preventive of internal challenges to the ruling elites' political power. The persisting yet unequal relationship between the world's major economic players and developing countries has also significantly placed a near impenetrable ceiling for Malaysia to reach full industrialization. This will remain so as long as the scope and nature of Malaysia's economic growth continues to be heavily reliant on as well as facilitative of the needs of the world's major industrialized countries and their TNCs operating within the global economy. Inherited from British colonialism and sustained by dependent capitalist development, the elite-driven democracy in Malaysia is represented in figure 8.1 by the top left solid-lined box.

The book has explained that Malaysia's own elites have profited from the consociational system in the same way the British elites have acquired tremendous local power under the imperial system. Through the years, the country's elite-driven democracy has enabled its privileged classes to preserve their political economic interests and legitimacy, illustrated by the set of solid lines and boxes flowing on the left side of the model in figure 8.1. Following this portion of the diagram, and starting with the box on the furthest left, the model explains that the elitist democratic system has also allowed Malaysia's ruling elites to successfully maintain their hegemony and legitimacy primarily through its intricate relationship with the state.

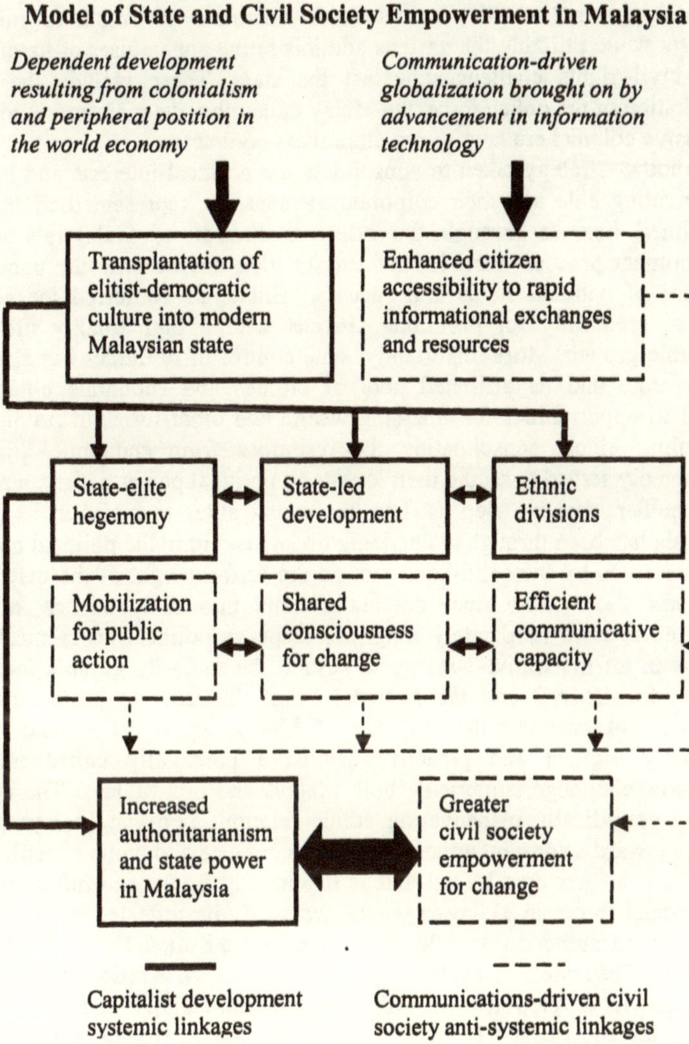

Figure 8.1: Impact of world transformational changes in the form of dependent capitalist development and communication-driven globalization on Malaysia's democratization process, 1824-2011.

As discussed in the book, a major strategy in maintaining ruling elite hegemony involves the efficient propagandizing of economic nationalism and the overextension of state administrative powers into the country's major social and political institutions. These are evidenced by increased state usurpation of the legislature and judiciary, which has successfully restricted their functioning as autonomous bodies. The state has also effectively manipulated the country's electoral process in order to determine outcomes favorable to ruling elite interests while utilizing the various administrative apparatuses at its disposal to stifle civil rights challenges against the state. These include the use and exploitation of the police force, the Malay monarchy, the mainstream media, and repressive colonial era laws to pre-empt mass civil action.

Another strategy taken to consolidate the political interests and legitimacy of the ruling elite and their corporate mercenaries, represented by the middle solid-lined box, is through the effective control of Malaysia's economic development process. State-led industrialization has become the unquestioned measure of national status and success, which has conferred the state with political credibility for providing citizens with a high quality life through economic growth. More importantly, state control of resources has also availed to the state and its affiliated pool of cronies and economic elites, almost unlimited opportunities for amassing wealth and other forms of privileges. For the ruling elites, consolidating the resources from economic growth has undoubtedly served to secure their long-term political power in the country.

Another effective step used by the ruling elites to maintain its power in Malaysia has been through maintaining divisions within the political opposition, as represented by the solid-lined box on the furthest right of the diagram. The book has shown how since colonialism and into independence, Malaysia's ruling elites have desperately sought to dispense political economic favors to Malays in an imperative strategy to sustain the majority group's ineffaceable support for UMNO and the National Front. In order to protect its pivotal advantage of carrying the majority of Malay support, the state has been constantly vigilant and proactive against a potentially united multiethnic grassroots challenge comprising both Malays and non-Malays. The state does this by periodically maneuvering ethnic relations between Malays and non-Malays toward a constant atmosphere of discordance and mutual hostility.

The strategies used by the state to maintain its power and influence over all other social forces in Malaysia would eventually be reflected in the increasing trend toward authoritarian rule, represented by the model's left-bottom solid-lined box. The state's escalation of power becomes more rationalized and urgent as capitalist development in Malaysia consequentially produces widening inequalities and marked by almost unbridled state corruption among its elites. All these have made the promises of industrialization and developed country status by the year 2020 to become increasingly distant and non-forthcoming. On their part, the ruling elites, through the state, have employed every means possible to suppress or conceal information related to the country's political economic problems from any public discussion or contestation.

However, another major historical process within the capitalist world economy, which has increasingly become an effective force in weakening the state's capability in controlling information, has emerged. Since the beginning of the new millennium, revolutionary advancements in information technology have helped enhance communication channels between groups of people worldwide, enabling them to acquire knowledge of current events as well as share and circulate opinions on various options to political reform. While it is true that digital and cyber-communications have made economic transactions much faster and more efficient for the benefit of capitalists, they have also increasingly empowered Malaysia's civil society in terms of direct and instantaneous informational exchanges and accessibility. In figure 8.1, this is represented by the broken-lined box on the top right.

Following the diagram in figure 8.1, the influence of advanced communicative technology on civil society empowerment in Malaysia is illustrated along the right side of the model, represented by the flow of broken lines and boxes. These anti-systemic linkages appear in the form of strategies currently employed by the civil society in Malaysia to enhance its ability in challenging the state. Starting with the broken-lined box on the furthest right, such strategies have involved the use of instantaneous information to establish expeditious communicative relationships between and among civil society groups and their members. The book has shown that an important impact of this has been the forging of a collective citizen consciousness for political change (middle broken-lined box), thereby mobilizing support for social justice-based public action against the state (farthest left broken-lined box).

Hence, an unprecedented form of civic space in Malaysia has been established by the new communications technology for the dissemination and discussion of justice-related issues. To date, the alternative media, private *blogospheres*, and NGO websites have helped provide rapid communications exchanges between citizens and other members of the public who have been gravely concerned about as well needing a platform for addressing problems relating to the lack of democratization in the country. More importantly, rapid developments in communications technology have also successfully unraveled the ability of the state to use traditionally media outlets to censor or filter critical information and news regarding the misuse of resources, breach of trusts, and other forms of misconducts carried out by the ruling elites and their cronies.

Once these alternative communication networks become well-established, civil society organizations and proponents of multicultural democracy are able to shape and strengthen a new collective consciousness among citizens with regards to the injustices of state policies and actions, and in providing possible options for solutions to current problems. These solutions should converge upon the demand for an alternative system based on high-level inter-cultural respect, equality of opportunities, and pursuit of social justice goals for all citizens. The attractiveness of political reforms and the desire for social changes, spurred on by plurality of support and conviction, would gradually emerge and become reinforced. In Malaysia, these processes have shown to help empower civil society and other advocates of greater freedom in their quest for political change. More significantly, they have provided alternative avenues for political dissent not available before the new century.

As political sentiments swing toward greater democratization, civil society organizations and advocates of multicultural democracy would become more confident in organizing concerted public actions for real effective changes. The most suitable approach for political change, of course, is through the ballot box. However, since the electoral process has yet to be completely autonomous, this must either be supplemented or preceded by citizens' show of force in the form of large peaceful assemblies and civil disobediences. In the diagram, this is represented by the right bottom broken-lined box along the communications-driven civil society anti-systemic linkages.

The outcome of political contestation between the forces associated with state-capitalist development systemic linkages and those linked to civil society anti-systemic linkages would be determined by the stronger of the two. Those on the side of civil society for change would have to survive and overcome the formidable nature of the current system in order to be able to dismantle it under the weight and pressures of democratization. But once successful, it would be more than likely that the democratic system would prevail for future political contestations to take place between opposing parties and groups.

To conclude, it must be stated that it is not the aim of this book to propose any type of universal theory on the relationship between capitalist development and democracy in all developing countries. The book, as explained in the first chapter, analyzes the historical and dynamic relations between capitalist development and the growth of democracy in Malaysia as products of the country's subordinate position within the capitalist world economy. It is hoped however, that this research would invaluably contribute toward or inspire further investigations of social issues and problems surrounding state and civil society relations in the rest of the developing world, particularly those that affect the process of democratization.

Notes

1. Assif Shameen and Tim Healy, "Seeking a Middle Course," *Asiaweek* 25, no. 7 (January 1999): 24-28.

2. UNDP, *Mitigating the Human Impact of the Asian Financial Crisis: The Role of the UNDP* (New York: OUP, 1999), 29-30.

3. Many political analysts believe that the sodomy charge was aimed at tarnishing Anwar's Islamic credibility and reputation, especially among the religious Malays who consider such commission as unbecoming of a Muslim leader. Although sodomy is a crime even under Malaysia's secular laws, the country's courts have rarely charged anyone with homosexuality since it is rather prevalent and generally tolerated.

4. The Multimedia Super Corridor began as one of many pet projects of the Mahathir administration designed to bring Malaysia closer toward developed country status. It is a Silicon Valley-type complex that stretches from the Twin Towers in Kuala Lumpur to the International Airport, housing smart schools, a university, an industrial research center, and other high-tech and information-based facilities. Read more from its website at www.malaysia.gov.my/EN/Relevant%20Topics/IndustryInMalaysia/Business/ICT/MSC/Pages/MSC.aspx.

5. Meryna Lim, "Lost in Transition? The Internet and Reformasi in Indonesia," in *Formatting Politics: Information Technology and Global Civil Society*, ed. Jodi Dean, Jon W. Anderson, and Geert Lovink (New York: Routledge, 2006), 92-95.

6. Chen May Yee, "Mahathir Vexed by His Own Internet Policy," *Asian Wall Street Journal Weekly Edition*, March 30, 1999, 14.

7. BBC, "Anwar's Wife Launches Reform Group," *BBC World News Online* 1998, news.bbc.co.uk/2/hi/asia-pacific/232513.stm (accessed March 30, 2008).

8. Maznah Mohamad, "UMNO and its Partners in the New Malaysia: Doing It Not in the Shy Way," *Aliran* 1999, www.aliran.com/oldsite/high9912.html (accessed June 1, 2008).

9. K. S. Nathan, "Outcome for the Barisan Nasional Coalition" (paper presented at Trends in Malaysia Seminar, Singapore, December 3, 1999), 22-29.

10. Vejai Balasubramaniam, "The Politics of Locality and Temporality in the 2004 Malaysian Parliamentary Elections," *Contemporary Southeast Asia: Journal of International & Strategic Affairs* 27, no.1 (April 2005): 44-46.

11. For more information on *Islam Hadhari*, read Abdullah Ahmad Badawai, *Islam Hadhari: Towards A Progressive Islamic Civilization* (Kuala Lumpur: JAKIM).

12. Ali Salman and Mohd Safar Hasim, "New Media and Democracy: The New Political Landscape in Malaysia," *Akedemika* 81, no.1 (January 2011): 16.

13. S. L. Lee, "Cyberspace is Now the New Frontline," *New Straits Times*, March 12, 2008, 25.

14. The *Al Jazeera* news caption can be accessed through *YouTube* video at www.youtube.com/watch?v=jfpYZ4IGenY.

15. Abdul Rashid Moten, "The 2004 and 2008 General Elections in Malaysia: Towards a Multicultural, Bi-party Political System?" *Asian Journal of Political Science* 17, no. 2 (August 2009): 175–6.

16. The National Justice Party (KeAdilan) was renamed the National Justice Party or PKR following its merger with the Malaysian People's Party.

17. Salman and Hasim, "New," 17-19.

18. Dr. Mahathir rejoined UMNO after Abdullah resigned.

19. In traditional Malay culture, this powerful ritual symbolizes a warrior's offer of sacrifice and martyrdom as well as his readiness to shed blood in the name of ruler and kingdom.

20. Hamdan Abdullah, "Hishammuddin Urged to Quit over Keris Issue." *Star Online* 2008, thestar.com.my/news/story.asp?file=/2008/4/27/ (accessed June 11, 2009).

21. Mariam Mokhtar, "Muhyiddin Makes a Mockery of Democracy," *Malaysian Mirror* 2011, www.Malaysianmirror.com/media-buzz-detail/41-opinion/55765-muhyid din-makes-a mockery-of-democracy (accessed December 1, 2011).

22. Channel News Asia, "Malaysia's Opposition Wins Critical By-Election in Kuala Terengganu," *Channel News Asia Online* 2009, www.channelnewsasia.com/stories/afp _asiapacific/view/403139/1/.html (accessed January 21, 2010).

23. Alyaa Alhadjri, "PAS Says it Again: No to Unity Talks," *The Sun Daily* 2011, www/thesundaily.my/news/239171 (accessed December 20, 2011).

24. The ethnic Malay population in Singapore makes up the poorest community in that republic. The ethnic Chinese, which are the largest in terms of population, are also the politically dominant ethnic group and the most economically prosperous. There is evidence that the policies of the ruling PAP party have been more favorable to the dominant group in terms of political economic opportunities as well as power distribution. For further reading on this subject, read Christopher Tremewan, *Political Economy of Social Control in Singapore* (New York: St. Martins Press); and Lily

Zubaidah Rahim, The Singapore Dilemma: *The Political and Educational Marginality of the Malay Community in Singapore* (New York: Oxford University Press).

25. Asrul Sani Abdullah, "Utusan's 1 Bumi 1 Melayu Movement a Personal Opinion Says PM," *Malaysian Insider* 2011, www.themalaysianinsider.com/malaysia/article/utusan/1Bumi.1Melayu.html (accessed June 8, 2011).

26. Debra Chong, "Interfaith Chief Says Utusan Report Fans Religious Divide," *Malaysia Insider* 2011, www.themalaysianinsider.com/malaysia/article/interfaith-chief-says-utusan-report-fans-religious-divide/ (Accessed May 31, 2011).

27. *The Star*, "Hishammuddin: Agenda to Make Christianity Official Religion Serious Matter," *Star Online* 2011, thestar.com.my/news/story/.asp?file=/2011/5/7/nation/201105077193559&sec=nation (accessed August 12, 2011).

28. Mariam Mokhtar, "Muhyiddin Makes a Mockery of Democracy," *Malaysian Mirror* 2011, www.Malaysianmirror.com/media-buzz-detail/41-opinion/55765-muhyiddin-makes-a mockery-of-democracy (accessed December 1, 2011).

29. Meredith Leigh Weiss, "History, Legal Framework, and Characteristics," in *Social Movements in Malaysia: From Moral Communities to NGOs,* ed. Meredith Weiss and Saliha Hassan (London: RoutledgeCurzon, 2003), 19-25.

30. The labeling of human-rights organizations as "anti-Islam" is still frequently used by UMNO as an effort to deter Malay support for these NGOs. The latest victim to this right-wing UMNO–affiliated rhetoric has been BERSIH, which has led public demonstrations for free and fair elections. Read Shannon Teoh, "Anti-Islam BERSIH Using Malays," *Malaysian Insider* 2011, www.themalaysianinsider.com.my/malaysia.articles/anti-islam-bersih-using-malays-says-zul-noordin/ (accessed December 1, 2001).

31. Cherian George, *Contentious Journalism and the Internet: Towards Democratic Discourse in Malaysia and Singapore* (Seattle: University of Washington Press, 2006), 172-3.

32. The Centre of Independent Journalism was started out by five journalists as a website during the upheaval of the 1998 *reformasi* protests. Official Website for the organization is available at: http://cijmalaysia.org/about-cij/.

33. George, *Contentious,* 174.

34. Raja Petra often refers to one of his important informational sources as "the deep throats of Bukit Aman." Bukit Aman is the location of Malaysia's Police Headquarters. Raja Petra's popular website is at Malaysia-today.net.

35. Steven E. Krauss, Azimi Hamzah, Turiman Suandi, Sidek Noah, Rumaya Juhari, Jamiah Manap, Khairul Mastor, Hasnan Kassa, and Azma Mahmood, "Exploring Regional Differences in Religiosity among Muslim Youths in Malaysia," *Review of Religious Research* 47, no. 3 (March 2006): 238-52.

36. Farish Noor, "PAS Post Fadzil Noor: Future Directions and Prospects" (Singapore: ISEAS, 2002), 14-15.

37. Patricia Martinez, "Democracy, the 'Islamic State,' and Embedded Realities in Malaysia," in *Religious Organizations and Democratization: Case Studies from Contemporary Asia*, ed. Tun Jeng-Cheng and Deborah A. Brown (New York: M.E. Sharpe, 2006), 263-64.

38. Bernama, "Furore over Najib's Malaysia Islamic State Remark," *The Malaysian Bar* 2007, www.malaysianbar.org.my/bar_news/berita_badan_peguam.html (accessed December 6, 2010).

39. Maznah Mohamad, "The Ascendance of Bureaucratic Islam and the Secularization of the Sharia in Malaysia," *Pacific Affairs* 83, no. 2 (September 2010): 522-23.

40. G. Manimaran and Latifah Kasmuri, "PAS Insists Welfare State Own Brainchild," *Malaysian Insider* 2011, my.news.yahoo.com/insists-welfare-state-own-brainchild-095527262.html. (accessed June 13, 2011).

41. Shazwan Mustapha Kamal, "PAS Looks to Fill PKR's Shoes," *Malaysian Insider* 2010, www.themalaysianinsider.com/malaysia/article/PAS-looks-to-fill-PKRs-shoes.html (accessed June 12, 2010).

42. The usage of the word "Allah" in the Bible has been a long-standing practice among Christians in Indonesia as well as the Middle-East. Most Christians in Malaysia who use the Malay-language Bible are from the various Bumiputera groups in Sabah and Sarawak, whose educational language is Malay. However, there has been constant concern among conservative Malays that the willful use of "Allah" instead of the Malay word *tuhan* (God) to describe Jesus might confuse many Muslim-Malays, if they happened to read the Bible. This however, has never been proven. Nevertheless, by presenting to the rural Malays that an external threat exists in the form of Christian proselytizing, UMNO seeks to maintain ethnic divisions between Malays and non-Malays as well as to exemplify the party's readiness in protecting Islam and Malays in the country. UMNO has had support from many right-wing groups and leaders, who believe that the Malay translations of the scriptures were a deliberate act on the part of non-Malays to "weaken" the unity and faith of Malays and Muslims. Partly as a result of this contentious debate, a new Malay Bible published in Anaheim, California has emerged, in which the term "Yahweh" is used in lieu of "Allah." Read Michael Kuang, "New Malay Bible Shows Up in Sabah Interior," *Free Malaysia Today* 2011, www.free malaysiatoday.com/2011/07/31/new-malay-bible-show-up-in-sabah-interior.html (accessed August 1, 2011).

43. PAS's stand on religious freedom has increasingly won them the accolades of many non-Malays. Read FMT Staff, "PAS's Stand on Malay Bibles Enlightening," *Free Malaysia Today* 2011, www.freemalaysiatoday.com/2011/03/19/pas-stand-on-malay-bible-enlightening (accessed August 1, 2011).

44. Bernama, "PAS To Turn Non-Muslim Supporters Club into Party Wing," *Malay Mail* 2009, www.mmail.com.my/content/16089-pas-turn-nonmuslim-supporters-club-party-wing. (accessed June 23, 2011).

45. Andrew Aeria, "PKR Succeeds against All Odds," *Aliran 2011*, aliran.com/5622.html (accessed August 4, 2011).

46. See *Sarawak Report*, "Billions Abroad! Questions over Taib's Contacts with Foreign Property Tycoons," *Sarawak Report* 2011, www.sarawakreport.org/2011/01 /billions-abroad-questions-over-taibs-contacts-with-foreign-property-tycoons/ (accessed June 24, 2011).

47. Angus Stickler, "Borneo Tribe Fights for Survival," *BBC News Online* 2010, www.bmf.ch/files/news/BBC_News_Today_Borneo_tribe_fights_for_survival_1.pdf. (a-ccessed December 20, 2010).

48. *The Star*, "More Penans Claim Rape," *Star Online* 2010, thestar.com.my/news/ story.asp?file=/2010/7/7/nation/6616414&sec=nation (accessed June 2, 2011).

49. For more information on this topic, read Samuel Huntington, *Clash of Civilizations and the Remaking of the World Order* (New York: Simon and Schuster); Francis Fukuyama, "Democracy's Future: The Primacy of Culture," *Journal of Democracy* 6, no. 1 (January 1995): 3-15.

50. Rick Stengel, "2011 Person of the Year," *Time Magazine*, December 26 2011, 52-60.

51. Liz Gooch, "Thousands of Malaysians Rally for Changes to Elections," *New York Times* 2011, www.nytimes.com/2011/07/10/world/asia/10malaysia.html (accessed July 10, 2011).

52. *Human Rights Watch*, "Malaysia: Investigate Crackdown on Pro-Democracy March," *Human Rights Watch* 2011, www.hrw.org/en/news/2011/07/13/malaysia-investigate-crackdown-pro-democracy-march (accessed July 15, 2011).

53. The *Jakarta Post* Editorial, "Malaysia: Rich Not Free," *Jakarta Post* 2011, www.thejakartapost.com/2011/07/11/editorial-malaysia-rich-not-free.html (accessed December 1, 2011).

54. Mathew Saltmarsh and Liz Gooch, "Malaysian Prime Minster Defends Muzzling of Protests," *New York Times*, 2011, www.nytimes.com/2011/07/15/world/asia/15iht-malaysia15.html?_r=1&pagewanted=all (accessed July 15, 2011).

55. Mubarak's speech on February 11, 2011, was carried out worldwide through various major networks. A Fox News caption titled "Egyptian Tyrant Speaks to People," can be followed at www.youtube.com/watch?v=GWH628fFetI (accessed June 21,2011).

56. Manuel Castells, *Communication Power* (New York: Oxford University Press, 2009), 414-15.

57. One can observe the general pattern of non-Malays publicly delivering their personal opinions or organizational information in English or Chinese, rather than in Malay. Part of this may be attributed to serious weakness on the part of these individuals in articulating their thoughts in the national language, while some have been known to disregard the use of the Malay language for reason that they considered it to be a non imperative.

58. The debate, titled "Malaysian Chinese at a Political Crossroads," can be followed on Youtube at www.youtube.com/watch?v=FolvdWVMV84&feature=related (accessed February 19 2012).

59. Jacobson Rodolfo, "In Search of Status: Bahasa Malaysia as a Language for National Unification," in *Status Change of Languages*, ed. Ulrich Ammon and Marlis Hellinger (Berlin: De Gruyter, 1991), 219-20.

60. Michael M. Bell, *Invitation to Environmental Sociology* (Thousand Oaks, CA: Pine Forge Press, 2012), 255-72.

61. Michael M. Bell, *Farming for All of Us: Practical Agriculture and the Cultivation of Sustainability, College Station* (PA: Penn State University Press, 2004), 220-21.

Bibliography

Abas, Marhalim. "Government Need Not Reveal Syabas Deal: Appeals Court." *Malay Mail*. 2011. www.mmail.com.my/content/64939 (accessed April 2, 2011).

———. "MACC to Meet MAS to Discuss Tajudin Case." *Malay Mail*. 2010. www.mmail.com.my/content/47639 (accessed September 12, 2010).

Abdul Khalid, Abdullah Azmi. *The Trade of Malaya with Special Reference to the Federated Malay States*. Sydney: University of Sydney, 1981.

Abdullah, Asrul Sani. "Utusan's 1 Bumi 1 Melayu Movement a Personal Opinion Says PM." *Malaysian Insider*. 2011. www.themalaysianinsider.com/malaysia/article/utusan/1Bumi.1Melayu.html (accessed June 8, 2011).

———. "Perkasa Complements UMNO, Say MPs," *Malaysian Insider*. 2010. www.malaysianinsider.com/mobile/Malaysia/article/Perkasa-complements- UMNO-say-MPs.html (accessed June 10, 2011).

Abdulllah, Firdaus. *Radical Malay Politics: Its Origins and Early Development*. Petaling Jaya, Malaysia: Pelanduk, 1985.

Abdullah, Hamdan. "Hishammuddin Urged to Quit over Keris Issue." *Star Online*. 2008. thestar.com.my/news/story.asp?file=/2008/4/27/ (accessed June 11, 2009).

Abdullah, Nabir. *Maahad Illhya Assyarif, Gunung Semanggol 1934–1959*. Bangi: National University of Malaysia, 1976.

Abdullah, Taufik. *Schools and Politics: The Kaum Muda Movement in West Sumatra 1927-1933*. Singapore: Equinox, 2009.

Ahmad, Abu Talib. "The Malay Community and Memory of the Japanese Occupation." In *War and Memory in Malaysia and Singapore*, edited by Patricia Pui Huen Lim and Diana Wong, 45-90. Singapore: Institute of Southeast Asian Studies, 2000.

Ahmad, Sharifah Suhanah. *Malaysian Legal System*. Kuala Lumpur: Malayan Law Journal, 2007.

Ahmad, Zuhrin. "No Funds for Opposition MPs." *Star Online*. 2010. www.thestar.com.my/news/story.asp?file=/ 2010/12/10/nation/7/7593679 (accessed January 21 2011).

Akashi, Yoji. "Japanese Policy towards Malayan Chinese." In *Japan and Southeast Asia: From the Meiji Restoration to 1945*, edited by Wolf Mendl, 275-312. London: Routledge, 2001.

Alagappa, Muthiah. "The Bases of Legitimacy." *Political Legitimacy in Southeast Asia*. Stanford, CA: Stanford University Press, 1995.

Alatas, Syed Hussein. *The Myth of the Lazy Natives*. New York: Frank Cass, 1977.

———. "Collective Representations and Economic Development." In *Modernization and Social Change: Studies in Modernization, Religion, Social Changes and Development in South-East Asia*. Sydney: Angus and Robertson, 1972, 53-64.

Alavi, Rokiah. *Industrialisation in Malaysia: Import Substitution and Infant Industry Performance.* London: Routledge, 1996.

Alhadjri, Alyaa. "PAS Says it Again: No to Unity Talks." *The Sun Daily.* 2011. www/thesundaily.my/news/239171 (accessed December 20, 2011).

Allen, James de Veere, A.J. Stockwell, and L. R. Wright, eds. *A Collection of Treaties and Other Documents Affecting the States of Malaysia 1761-1963.* London: Oceana Publications, 1981.

Amin, Mohammed, and Malcolm Caldwell. *Malaya: The Making of a Neo-Colony.* Nottingham, England: Russell Press, 1977.

Amin, Samir. "Crisis, Nationalism, and Socialism." In *Dynamics of Global Crisis,* edited by Samir Amin, Giovanni Arrighi, Andre Gunder Frank, and Immanuel Wallerstein, 167-232. New York: Monthly Review Press, 1982.

———. *Unequal Development.* New York: Monthly Review Press, 1976.

Ammarrel, Gene. "Bugis Migration and Modes of Adaptation to Local Cultures." In *Ethnology* 41, no.1 (Winter 2001): 51-67.

Andaya, Barbara Watson, and Leonard Andaya. *A History of Malaysia.* New York: St. Martin's Press, 2001.

Anderson, Benedict. *Imagined Communities: Reflections on the Origins and Spread of Nationalism.* London: Verso, 1983.

Arasaratnam, Sinnapiah. "Malaysian Indians: The Formation of Incipient Society." In *Indian Communities in Southeast Asia,* edited by Kernial Singh Sandhu and A. Mani, 190-210. Singapore: Institute of Southeast Asian Studies, 2006.

———. *Indians in Malaysia and Singapore.* Kuala Lumpur: Oxford University Press, 1980.

Ariff, Mohamed. "Islam and the Private Sector: Southeast Asian Perspectives." In *The Muslim Private Sector in Southeast Asia,* edited by Mohamed Ariff, 245-60. Singapore: ISEAS, 1991.

Asia Sentinel. "Perceptions and Royal Reality in Malaysia." *Asia Sentinel.* 2010. www.asiasentinel.com/index.php?option=2262.html (accessed March 24, 2011).

———. "Zaid Ibrahim Blasts Elections Irregularities in Malaysia." *Asia Sentinel.* 2010. www.asiasentinel.com/index.php?option=246.html (accessed December 3, 2010).

———. "Bailout Alert in Malaysia." *Asia Sentinel.* 2007. www.asiasentinel.com/index.php?option=510.html (accessed June 12, 2009).

Auerbach, Sascha. *Race, Law, and the Chinese Puzzle in Imperial Britain.* New York: Palgrave Macmillan, 2009.

Badie, Bertrand, and Pierre Birnbaum. *The Sociology of the State.* Chicago: University of Chicago Press, 1983.

Badiozaman, Raja Mohar. "Foreign Investment: The Malaysian Experience." Paper presented at the *Annual Lecture of the Malaysian Economic Association,* Kuala Lumpur, Malaysia, November 1976.

Balasubramaniam, Vejai. "The Politics of Locality and Temporality in the 2004 Malaysian Parliamentary Elections." *Contemporary Southeast Asia: A Journal of International & Strategic Affairs* 27, no.1 (April 2005): 44-63.

Barrowclough, Anne. "Terror Suspect Mas Selamat Kastari Recaptured after Year on the Run." *Sunday Times.* 2009. www.timesonline.co.uk/tol/news/world/asia/article6246-307.ece.html (accessed January 31, 2010).

Bayly, Christopher, and Tim Harper. *Forgotten Wars: Freedom and Revolution in Southeast Asia.* Cambridge MA: Harvard University Press, 2007.

BBC. "Anwar's Wife Launches Reform Group." *BBC World News Online.* 1998. news.bbc.co.uk/2/hi/asia-pacific/232513.stm (accessed March 30, 2008).

Bedlington, Stanley S. *Malaysia and Singapore: The Building of New States*. Ithaca, NY: Cornell University Press, 1978.

Behdad, Ali. *Belated Travelers: Orientalism in the Age of Colonial Dissolution (Post-Contemporary Interventions)*. Durham, NC: Duke University Press, 1999.

Bell, Michael M. *An Invitation to Environmental Sociology*. Thousand Oaks, CA: Pine Forge Press, 2012.

———. *Farming for All of Us: Practical Agriculture and the Cultivation of Sustainability*. College Station, PA: Penn State University Press, 2004.

Bergere, Marie-Claire. *Sun Yat-Sen*. Translated by Janet Lloyd. Stanford CA: Stanford University Press, 1998.

Bernama. "Kelantan Government to Take Oil Royalty Issue to Court." *Malay Mail*. 2010. www.malaymail.com.my/33886 (accessed January 12, 2011).

———. "Furore over Najib's Malaysia Islamic State Remark." *The Malaysian Bar*. 2007. www.malaysianbar.org.my/bar_news/berita_badan_peguam.html (accessed December 6, 2010.)

Bernard, Mitchell, and John Ravenhill. "Beyond Product Cycles and Flying Geese: Regionalization, Hierarchy, and the Industrialization of East Asia." *World Politics* 47, no.2 (January 1995): 171-209.

Berthelsen, John. "Asia Sentinel Correspondent Accused of Insulting Sultans." *Asia Sentinel*. 2009. www.asiasentinel.com/index.phpoption=com_content&task=view&id-1723.html (accessed January 24, 2010).

Bhagwati, Jagdish. *Wind of the Hundred Days: How Washington Mismanaged Globalization*. Boston, MA: MIT Press, 2001.

Boestamam, Ahmad. *Merintis Jalan ke Punchak*. Kuala Lumpur: Kejora, 1972.

Bollen, Kenneth. "World-System Position, Dependency, and Democracy: The Cross-National Evidence." *American Sociological Review* 48, no.4 (August 1983): 468-479.

Boo, Sue-Lyn. "Kelantan Claims RM800 Million per Annum Oil Royalty." *Malaysian Insider*. 2010. www.themalaysianinsider.com/monile/Malaysia/article/kelantan-claims-rm800-per-annum-oil-royalty.html (accessed January 22, 2011).

———. "Pua Asks if NEM Already Dead?" *Malaysian Insider*. 2010. www.themalaysianinsider.com/Malaysia/article/pua-asks-if-nem-already-dead.html (accessed August 7, 2010).

Borrus, Michael. "Left for Dead: Asian Production Networks and the Revival of US Electronics." Working Paper No. 100 presented at Berkeley Roundtable on the International Economy, San Francisco, CA, September 1997.

Bowie, Alasdair. *Crossing the National Divide: State, Society and the Politics of Economic Transformation in Malaysia*. New York: Columbia University Press, 1991.

Braudel, Fernand. *Perspectives of the World. Vol. 3, Civilization and Capitalism 15th - 18th Century*. New York: Harper & Row, 1984.

Brown, C. C. *The Malay Annals*. Kuala Lumpur: Oxford University Press, 1976.

Brown, Rajeswary. "The Contemporary Indian Elites in Malaysia." In *Indian Communities in Southeast Asia*, edited by K.S. Sandhu and A. Mani, 237-265. Singapore: ISEAS, 2006.

Bruton, Roy. *Farewell to Democracy*. Devon, UK: Merlin Books, 1993.

Burridge, Kenelm O.L. "Racial Relations in Johore." *The Australian Journal of Politics and History* 2, no.2 (May 1957): 151-168.

Butcher, John. *The British in Malaya 1880-1941: The Social History of a European Community in Colonial Southeast Asia*. Kuala Lumpur: OUP, 1979.

Butcher, John, Howard Dick, and Nathan Dick, eds. *The Rise and Fall of Revenue Farming Elites and the Emergence of the Modern State in Malaya.* New York: St. Martin's Press, 1993.

Carstens, Sharon A. *Histories, Cultures, Identities: Studies in Malaysian Chinese Worlds.* Singapore: Singapore University Press, 2006.

Caso, Martha. *Invisible and Voiceless.* Bloomington, IN: Universe, 2011.

Castells, Manuel. *Communication Power.* New York: Oxford University Press, 2009.

Chan Kok Eng and Tey Nai Peng. "Demographic Processes and Changes." In *The Chinese in Malaysia,* edited by K.H. Lee and C.B. Tan, 71-90. Kuala Lumpur: Oxford University Press, 2000.

Chase-Dunn, Christopher. "The World System since 1950: What Has Really Changed?" In *Labor in the Capitalist World Economy,* edited by Charles Bergquist, 75-104. Beverly Hills, CA: Sage, 1984.

Che Man, Wan Kamaruddin. *Muslim Separatism: The Moros in Southern Philippines and Malays of Southern Thailand.* Singapore: Oxford University Press, 1990.

Cheah Boon Kheng. *Red Star over Malaya: Resistance and Social Conflict During and After the Japanese Occupation of Malaya, 1941-1946.* Singapore: NUS Press, 2003.

———. *Malaysia: The Making of a Nation.* Singapore: Institute of Southeast Asian Studies, 2002.

———. "Erosions of Ideological Hegemony and Royal Power and the Rise of Post-war Malay Nationalism." *Journal of South East Asian Studies* 19, no. 1 (March 1988): 1-27.

Chen May Yee. "Mahathir Vexed by His Own Internet Policy," *Asian Wall Street Journal Weekly Edition,* March 30, 1999, 14.

Cheong, Sally. *Bumiputera Controlled Companies in the KLSE.* Petaling Jaya: Corporate Research Services Sdn. Bhd, 1993.

Chilcote, Ronald. *Theories of Comparative Political Economy: New Paradigms.* Boulder, CO: Westview Press, 2000.

Chin, C. C., and Karl Hack. *Dialogues with Chin Peng: New Light on the Malayan Communist Party.* Singapore: NUS Press, 2005.

Chin, Christine B. N. *In Service and Servitude.* New York: Columbia University Press, 1998.

Chong, Debra. "Interfaith Chief Says Utusan Report Fans Religious Divide." *Malaysia Insider.* 2011. www.themalaysianinsider.com/malaysia/article/interfaith-chief-says-utusan-report-fans-religious-divide/ (Accessed May 31, 2011).

Choo, Chi Sek. "Accelerated Industrialization and Employment Opportunities in Malaysia." *Geoforum* 13, no. 1 (January 1982): 11-18.

Clifford, Hugh. "Life in the Malay Peninsula: As it Was and Is." In *Honourable Intentions: Talks on the British Empire in Southeast Asia, Delivered at the Royal Colonial Institute 1874-1928,* edited by Paul Kratoska, 224-48. Singapore: ISEAS, 1983.

———. *Stories by Hugh Clifford.* Introduced by William R. Roff. Kuala Lumpur: Oxford University Press, 1967.

Clutterbuck, Richard. *Conflict and Violence in Singapore and Malaysia 1945-1983.* Boulder, CO: Westview Press, 1985.

Collins, Alan. "Securitization, Frankenstein's Monster, and Malaysian Education." *Pacific Review* 18, no. 4 (December 2005): 567-588.

Comber, Leon. *Malaya's Secret Police 1945-60: The Role of the Special Branch in the Malayan Emergency.* Singapore: ISEAS, 2008.

———. "The Malayan Security Service (1945–1948)." *Intelligence and National Security* 18, no.3 (Autumn 2003): 128–153.

Connor, Walker. *Ethnonationalism: The Quest for Understanding*. Princeton, NJ: Princeton University Press, 1994.

Crouch, Harold. *Government and Society in Malaysia*. Sydney: Allen & Unwin, 1996.

Cruickshank, Charles. *SOE in the Far East*. Oxford: Oxford University Press, 1983.

Darwin, John, and Frederick Madden. *The Dependent Empire: 1900-1948, Colonies, Protectorates, and the Mandate*. London: Greenwood Press, 1991.

De Jong, P. E. "The Character of the Malay Annals." In *Malayan and Indonesian Studies*, edited by John Bastin and R. Roolvink, 235-241. London: Oxford University Press, 1964.

De Oliveira, Miguel Darcy. "Deepening Democracy in Latin America." In *Global Civil Society 2007/8: Communicative Power and Democracy*, edited by Martin Albrow, Helmut Anheier, Marlies Glasius, Monroe Price, Mary Kaldor, 120-21. London: Sage, 2008.

Defty, Andrew. *Britain, America and Anti-Communist Propaganda, 1945-1958: The Information Research Department*. London: Routledge, 2004.

Del Tufo, M. V. *Malaya: A Report on the 1947 Census of Population*. Singapore: Government Press, 1949.

Department of Statistics Malaysia. *Yearbook of Statistics*. Kuala Lumpur: Government Printers, 2011.

Donnelly, Jack. "Human Rights, Globalizing Flows, and State Power." In *Globalization and Human Rights*, edited by Alison Brysk, 226-241. Los Angeles: University of California Press, 2002.

Doolittle, Amity. *Property & Politics in Sabah, Malaysia: Native Struggles over Land Rights*. Seattle: University of Washington Press, 2005.

Douglas, Mary. "Traditional Culture: Let's Hear No More about It." In *Culture and Public Action*, edited by Vijayendra Rao and Michael Walton, 85-109. Stanford, CA; Stanford University Press, 2004.

Drabble, John H. *An Economic History of Malaysia, c.1800-1990: The Transition to Modern Economic Growth*. New York: St. Martin's Press, 2000.

Duvall, Raymond, and John Freeman. "The State and Dependent Capitalism." In *World Systems Structure*, edited by W. Ladd Hollist and James Rosenau, 223-242. W. Beverly Hills, CA: Sage, 1981.

Easter, David. "Keep the Indonesian Pot Boiling: Western Covert Intervention in Indonesia, October 1965-March 1966." *Cold War History* 5, no. 1 (February 2005): 55-73.

———. *Britain and the Confrontation with Indonesia 1960-66*. New York: St. Martin's Press, 2004.

Easterly, William. *The White Man's Burden: Why the West's Efforts to Aid the Rest Have Done So Much Ill and So Little Good*. New York: Penguin Books, 2006.

Economist Intelligence Unit. *Democracy Index 2010: Democracy in Retreat*. London. Economist Publishing, 2010.

Emerson, Rupert. *Malaysia: A Study in Indirect and Direct Rule*. Kuala Lumpur: Oxford University Press, 1974.

Emmanuel, Mark. "Viewspapers: The Malay Press of the 1930s." *Journal of Southeast Asian Studies* 41, no.1 (February 2010): 1-20.

Esman, Milton. J. *Ethnic Conflict*. Cambridge, UK: Polity Press, 2004.

Evers, Hans-Dieter. "On the Evolution of Urban Society in Malaysia." In *Melaka: The Transformation of Malay Capital, c.1400-1980*, edited by Kernail S. Sandhu and Paul Wheatly, 324-350. Kuala Lumpur: Oxford University Press, 1983.

Feagin, Joe. *The White Racial Frame: Centuries of Racial Framing and Counter Framing*. New York: Routledge, 2010.

Fisk, Ernest Kelvin and H. Osman-Rani, eds. *The Political Economy of Malaysia*. Kuala Lumpur: Oxford University Press, 1982.

Frank, Andre Gunder. *Crisis in the Third World*. New York: Holmes and Meier, 1981.

Freedman, Amy. *Political Participation and Ethnic Minorities: Chinese Overseas in Malaysia, Indonesia, and the United States*. New York: Routledge, 2000.

Fukuyama, Francis. "Democracy's Future: The Primacy of Culture." *Journal of Democracy* 6, no. 1 (January 1995): 3-15.

Fuller, Thomas. "Judge Nullifies Election of Ex-Minister in Malaysia." *International Herald Tribune*. 2001. groups.yahoo.com/group/beritamalaysia/message/3565.html (accessed January 24, 2011).

Funston, John. "Writings on May 13." Paper presented at Seminar Aliran Kini dalam Sains Kemasysrakatan dan Kemanusiaan, National University of Malaysia, Bangi, Malaysia October, 1974.

Ganesan, Narayanan. "Malaysia in 2002: Political Consolidation amid Change?" *Asian Survey* 43, no. 1 (January 2002): 147-155.

Garrett, Peter. "Meanings of Globalization: East and West." In *The Handbook of Language and Globalization,* edited by Nikolas Coupland, 447-475. Singapore: Wiley-Blackwell, 2010.

Gellner, Ernest. "Civil Society in Historical Context." *International Social Science Journal* 43, no. 3 (August 1991): 495-510.

George, Cherian. *Contentious Journalism and the Internet: Towards Democratic Discourse in Malaysia and Singapore*. Seattle: University of Washington Press, 2006.

Gereffi, Gary. "Commodity Chains and Regional Divisions of Labor in East Asia." In *The Four Asian Tigers: Economic Development and the Global Political Economy*, edited by Eun Mee Kim, 93-124. San Diego, CA: Academic Press, 1998.

Goh, Daniel. "Imperialism and Medieval Natives: The Malay Image in Anglo-American Travelogues and Colonialism in Malaya and the Philippines." *International Journal of Cultural Studies* 10, no. 3 (September 2007): 323-341.

Goh, Lisa, and Yeng Ai Chun. "Court Rules Zambry is Valid MB." *Star Online*. 2009. thestar.com.my/news/story.asp?file=/2009/5/23/3968185&sec=nation.html (accessed June 24, 2011).

Gomez, Terence Edmund, and K.S. Jomo. *Malaysia's Political Economy: Politics, Patronage, and Profits*. Cambridge, England: Cambridge University Press, 1997.

Gooch, Liz. "Bill Limiting Street Protests Moves Ahead in Malaysia." *New York Times* 2011. www.nytimes.com/2011/11/30/world/asia/30iht.malaysia30.html (accessed November 30, 2011).

———. "Thousands of Malaysians Rally for Changes to Elections." *New York Times*. 2011. www.nytimes.com/2011/07/10/world/asia/10malaysia.html (accessed July 10, 2011).

Gould, Stephen Jay. *The Mismeasure of Man*. New York: Norton, 1996.

Government of Federated Malay States. *Annual Report on the Federated Malay States 1920*. Kuala Lumpur: Government Printers, 1920.

Government of Malaya. *Census of Malaya 1957*. Kuala Lumpur: Government Printers, 1959.

Grey, Jeff. *Military History of Australia*. Cambridge, UK: Cambridge University Press, 2008.

Hack, Karl. "Theories and Approaches to British Decolonization in Southeast Asia." In *The Transformation of Southeast Asia: International Perspectives on Decoloniza-*

tion, edited by Marc Frey, Ronald W. Pruessen, and Tai Yong Tan, 105-136. New York: M.E. Sharpe, 2004.

———. *Defence and Decolonisation in Southeast Asia: Britain, Malaya and Singapore, 1941-1968*. London, Routledge, 2001.

Haggard, Stephan. *The Political Economy of Asian Financial Crisis*. Washington D.C.: Institute for International Economics, 2000.

Hall, D. G. E. *History of Southeast Asia*. London: Macmillan, 1964.

Hara, Fujio. "Malaysia's New Economic Policy and the Chinese Business Community." *The Developing Economies* 19, no. 4 (December 1991.): 340-370.

Harper, T. N. *The End of Empire and the Making of Malaya*. Cambridge, UK: Cambridge University Press, 1999.

Harun Abdul Majid. *Rebellion in Brunei: The 1962 Revolt, Imperialism, Confrontation, and Oil*. New York: Palgrave Macmillan, 2007

Hashim, Muhammad Yusoff. *The Malay Sultanate of Malacca: A Study of Various Aspects of Malacca in the Fifteenth and Sixteenth Centuries in Malaysian History*. Kuala Lumpur: University of Malaya Press, 1992.

Hashim, Shireen. "The NEP and Changes in Poverty and Income Distribution." In *Sustaining Growth, Enhancing Distribution: The NEP and NDP Revisited*, edited by J. Yahaya, N.P. Tey and K.K. Yeoh, 1-15. Kuala Lumpur: CEDER, 2003.

———. *Income Inequality and Poverty in Malaysia*. Lanham, MD: Rowman and Littlefield, 1998.

Hassan, Asan Ali Golam. *Growth, Structural Change, and Regional Inequality in Malaysia*. London: Ashgate, 2004.

Haynes, Jeff, ed. *Democracy and Political Changes in the Third World*. New York: Routledge, 2006.

Heng Pek Koon. "The Chinese Business Elite in Malaysia." In *Southeast Asian Capitalists*, edited by Ruth Thomas McVey, 127-144. Ithaca, NY: Cornell Southeast Asia Program Publications, 1997.

———. *Chinese Politics in Malaysia: A History of the Malaysian Chinese Association*. Singapore: University of Singapore Press, 1988.

Hill, R. D. *Rice in Malaya: A Study in Historical Geography*. Kuala Lumpur: Oxford University Press, 1977.

Hirschman, Charles. "The Making of Race in Colonial Malaya: Political Economy and Racial Discourse." *Sociological Forum* 1, no. 2 (Spring 1986): 331-362.

Hoffman, Lutz, and Tan Tew Nee. "Pattern of Growth and Structural Change in West Malaysia's Manufacturing Industry 1959-68." In *Readings on Malaysian Economic Development*, edited by David Lim, Chapter 6. Kuala Lumpur: Oxford University Press, 1975.

Hong, Caroline. "Investments Outflows Spark Debate in Malaysia." *Straits Times* 2010. www.asianewsnet.net/home/news.php.html (accessed September 12, 2010).

Hoogvelt, Ankie. *Globalisation and the Postcolonial World: The New Political Economy of Development*. Baltimore: John Hopkins University Press, 2001.

Hookway, James. "Terror Suspects Detained in Malaysia." *Asian Wall Street Journal*. 2010. online.wsj.com/article/SB10001424052748704194504575030640380748702.html (accessed May 1, 2010).

Hookway, James, and Celine Fernandez. "Malaysian Protestors Clash with Riot Police." *Asian Wall Street Journal*. 2009, online.wsj.com/article/SB124912276548999015.html (accessed January 24, 2010).

Hopkins, Terence, Immanuel Wallerstein, Robert Bach, Christopher Chase-Dunn, and R. Mukherjee. "Patterns of Development in the World System." In *World-System Analysis: Theory and Methodology,* edited by Terence Hopkins. Beverly Hills, CA: Sage, 1982.

Hoyt, Sarnia Hayes. *Old Malacca*. Singapore: Oxford University Press, 1993.

Hua Wu Yin. *Class and Communalism in Malaysia: Politics in a Dependent Capitalist State*. London: ZED, 1982.

Huff, W. G. *The Economic Growth of Singapore: Trade and Development in the Twentieth Century*. Cambridge, UK: Cambridge University Press, 1997.

Hughes, Gary. "Analyse This." *The Age*. 2003. www.theage.com.au/articles/2003/07/20/1058545648013.html (accessed May 1, 2010).

Hussain, Mustapha, Insun Mustapha, and K.S. Jomo. *Malay Nationalism before UMNO: The Memoirs of Mustapha Hussain*. Kuala Lumpur: Utusan Press, 2005.

Hwang, In-Won. *Personalized Politics: The Malaysian State under Mahathir*. Singapore; ISEAS, 2003.

Hyam, Ronald. *Britain's Declining Empire: The Road to Decolonisation 1918-1968*. Cambridge, UK: Cambridge University Press, 2006.

Inglehart, Ronald. *Modernization and Postmodernization: Cultural, Economic, and Political Change in 43 Societies*. Princeton, NJ: Princeton University Press, 1997.

Inglehart, Ronald, and Christian Welzel. *Modernization, Cultural Change, and Democracy: The Human Development Sequence*. New York: Cambridge University Press, 2005.

International Bar Association. *Justice in Jeopardy, Malaysia 2000*. London: IBA, 2000.

Ishkanian, Armine. "Democracy Promotion and Civil Society." In *Global Civil Society 2007/8: Communicative Power and Democracy,* edited by Martin Albrow, Helmut Anheier, Marlies Glasius, Monre Price, Mary Kaldor, 58-86. London: Sage, 2008.

Jackson, J.C. *Planters and Speculators: Chinese and European Enterprise in Malaya: 1786-1921*. Kuala Lumpur: University of Malaya Press, 1968.

Jacobs, Els M. *Merchant in Asia: The Trade of the Dutch East India Company during the Eighteenth Century*. Amsterdam: CNWS, 2006.

Jamaluddin, Faridah. "Malaysia's New Economic Policy: Has It Been a Success?" In *Boundaries of Clan and Color: Transnational Comparison of Inter-Group Disparity*, edited by William Darity Jr. and Ashwini Deshpande, 152-173. New York: Routledge, 2003.

Jessop, Bob. *The Capitalist State: Marxist Theories and Methods*. New York: New York University Press, 1982.

Jesudason, J. V. *Ethnicity and the Economy: The State, Chinese Business and Multinationals in Malaysia*. Singapore: Oxford University Press, 1989.

Jomo, K. S. "Plantation Capital and Indian Labour in Colonial Malaya." In *Indian Communities in Southeast Asia*, edited by K.S. Sandhu and A. Mani, 288-313. Singapore: ISEAS, 2006.

———. ed. *Japan and Malaysian Development: In the Shadow of the Rising Sun*. New York: Routledge, 2001.

———. "Malaysia Props up Crony Capitalists." *Asian Wall Street Journal,* December 21, 1998, A6.

______. *Growth and Structural Change in the Malaysian Economy*. London: Macmillan Press, 1990.

———. *A Question of Class: Capital, the State, and Uneven Development in Malaya*. Singapore: University of Singapore Press, 1986.

Kabilan, K. "Anwar Lacked Dr. M's Clout in Tackling Islam." *Free Malaysia Today*, 2011. www.freemalaysiatoday.com/2011/05/27html (accessed May 30, 2011).

Kahn, Joel. "Growth, Economic Transformation, Culture and the Middle Classes in Malaysia." In *The New Rich in Asia: Mobile Phones, McDonald's and Middle Class Revolution*, edited by Richard Robison and David S. G. Goodman, 49-75. New York: Routledge, 1996.

Kaldor, Mary, and Denise Kostovicova. "Global Civil society and Illiberal Regimes." In *Global Civil Society 2007/8: Communicative Power and Democracy*, edited by in Martin Albrow, Helmut Anheier, Marlies Glasius, Monre Price, Mary Kaldor, 86-113. London: Sage, 2008.

Kamal, Shazwan Mustafa, "Pakatan: Limp Reforms Fuelling Brain Drain." *Malaysian Insider*. 2011. www.themalaysianinsider.com/malaysia/article.html (accessed June 12, 2011).

———. "PAS Looks to Fill PKR's Shoes." *Malaysian Insider*. 2010. www.themalaysianinsider.com/Malaysia/article/PAS-looks-to-fill-PKSs-shoes.html (accessed June 12, 2010).

Kathirithamby-Wells, Jeyamalar. "Political Authority and the Orang Kaya in the Western Archipelago circa 1500-1800." *Journal of Southeast Asian History* 17, no. 2 (September 1986): 256-67.

Kaur, Amarjit. *Wage Labour in Southeast Asia since 1840*. New York: Palgrave-Macmillan, 2004.

———. *Economic Change in East Malaysia: Sabah and Sarawak since 1850*. London: Macmillan, 1998.

———. *Bridge and Barrier: Transport and Communication in Colonial Malaya, 1870-1957*. Kuala Lumpur: Oxford University Press, 1985.

Kazancigil, Ali. *The State in Global Perspective*. Paris: Gower-UNESCO, 1986.

Kedit, P.M. *Modernization among the Iban of Sarawak*. Kuala Lumpur: Dewan Bahasa Pustaka, 1980.

Khor, Kok Peng. *The Malaysian Economy: Structures and Dependence*. Kuala Lumpur: Marican Press, 1983.

Kloby, Jerry. *Inequality, Power, and Development: Issues in Political Sociology*. New York: Humanity Books, 2004.

Kratoska, Paul. "The Peripatetic Peasant and Land Tenure in British Malaya." *Journal of Southeast Asian Studies* 16, no. 1 (January 1985): 16-45.

———. *The Chettiar and the Yeoman: British Cultural Categories and Rural Indebtedness in Malaya*. Singapore: Institute of Southeast Asian Studies, 1975.

Krauss, Steven. E., Azmi Hamzah, Turiman Suandi, Sidek Noah, Rumaya Juhari, Jamiah Manap, Khairul Mastor, Hasnan Kassa, and Azma Mahmood. "Exploring Regional Differences in Religiosity among Muslim Youths in Malaysia." *Review of Religious Research* 47, no. 3 (March 2006): 238-252.

Krugman, Paul. *The Return of Depression Economics*. New York: W.W. Norton & Company, 1999.

Larrain, Jorge. *Theories of Development*. Cambridge: Polity Press, 1989.

Lee Boon Thong. "A Historical Analysis of Formative Settlement Patterning: A Background to the Klang Valley Dominance." *Malayan Journal of Tropical Geography* 25, no.2 (December 1994): 102-114.

Lee, S.L. "Cyberspace is Now the New Frontline," *New Straits Times*, March 12, 2008, 25.

Lee Sheng Yi. *Monetary and Banking System of Malaysia and Singapore*. Singapore: Singapore University Press, 1990.

Leigh, Michael B. *The Rising Moon: Political Change in Sarawak*. Sydney: Sydney University Press, 1974.

Lijphart, Arendt. *Thinking about Democracy: Power Sharing and Majority Rule in Theory and Practice*. New York: Routledge, 2008.

Lim Chong Yah. *Southeast Asia: The Long Road Ahead*. Singapore: World Scientific Publications, 2009.

———. *Economic Development of Modern Malaya*. Kuala Lumpur: Oxford University Press, 1967.

Lim, Meryna. "Lost in Transition? The Internet and Reformasi in Indonesia." In *Formatting Politics: Information Technology and Global Civil Society*, edited by Jodi Dean, Jon W. Anderson, and Geert Lovink, 85-106. New York: Routledge, 2006.

Lim, T.G. *Peasants and their Agricultural Economy in Colonial Malaya 1874-1941*. Kuala Lumpur: Oxford University Press, 1977.

Lipset, Seymour Martin, and Jason M. Lakin. *Democratic Century*, Norman, OK: University of Oklahoma Press, 2004.

Loh Kok Wah, Francis. "Dr. Mahathir and the BN's Hegemony." *Aliran Monthly*. 2003. aliran.com/archives/monthly/2003a/8f.html (accessed May 12, 2009).

Loh Kok Wah, and Khoo Boo Teik. "Introduction." In *Democracy in Malaysia: Discourses and Practices*, edited by Francis Loh Kok Wah and Kho Bo Teik, 1-19. Richmond, UK: Curzon Press, 2002.

Loh, Philip. *Seeds of Separatism: Educational Policy in Malaya 1874-1940*. Kuala Lumpur: Oxford University Press, 1975.

———. *The Malay States 1877-1895 Political Change and Social Policy*. Kuala Lumpur: Oxford University Press, 1969.

Lomperis, Timothy. *From People's War to People's Rule: Insurgency, Intervention, and Lessons from Vietnam*, Chapel Hill, NC: UNC Press, 1996.

Loo Seng Piew. "Schooling in Malaysia." In *Going to School in East Asia*, edited by Gerard Postiglione and Jason Tan, 207-232. London: Greenwood Publishing, 2008.

Lucas, Robert E. B., and Donald Verry. *Restructuring the Malaysian Economy*. New York: St. Martin's Press, 1999.

Luxemburg, Rosa. *The National Question*. New York: Monthly Press Review, 1983.

Magdoff, Harry. "Third World Debt: Past and Present." *Monthly Review* 37, no. 9 (July 1996): 1-10.

Mageswari, M. "Negri Ruler Tuanku Ja'afar Ordered to Pay Bank US$1m." *Star Online*. 2008. thestar.com.my/news/story.asp?file=/2008/10/15/nation/200810151107&sec.nation (accessed October 20, 2010).

Mahathir Mohamad. *The Way Forward*. London: Weidenfeld & Nicolson, 1998.

Mak Lau Fong. *The Sociology of Secret Societies: A Study of Chinese Secret Societies in Singapore and Peninsular Malaysia*. Kuala Lumpur: Oxford University Press, 1981.

Malaysian Bar. "Rulers May Disagree with Government Leaders." *Malaysian Bar Council*. 2008. www.malaysianbar.org.my/general_news/rulers_may_disagree_with_government_leaders_raja_nazrin.html (accessed September 1, 2011).

Manan, Wan A. "A Nation in Distress: Human Rights, Authoritarianism, and Asian Values in Malaysia." *Journal of Social Issues in Southeast Asia* 14, no. 2 (October 1999): 359-381.

Mani, A. "Indians in Singapore Society." In *Indian Communities in Southeast Asia*, edited by, K.S. Sandhu and A. Mani, 788-809. Singapore: ISEAS, 2006.

Manimaran, G., and Latifah Kasmuri. "PAS Insists Welfare State Own Brainchild." *Malaysian Insider*. 2011. my.news.yahoo.com/insists-welfare-state-own-brainchild-095527262.html. (accessed June 13, 2011).

Marimuthu, T. "The Plantation School As an Agent of Social Reproduction." In *Indian Communities in Southeast Asia*, edited by K.S. Sandhu and A. Mani, 465-483. Singapore: ISEAS, 2006.

Martinez, Patricia. "Democracy, the 'Islamic State,' and Embedded Realities in Malaysia." In *Religious Organizations and Democratization: Case Studies from Contemporary Asia*, edited by Tun Jeng-Cheng and Deborah A. Brown, 242-266. New York: M.E. Sharpe, 2006.

Mat Zin, Rugayah. "Income Distribution in Malaysia: Old Issues New Approaches." Paper presented at the Eleventh International Convention of the East Asian Economic Association, Manila, The Philippines, November 2008.

Mauzy, Diane. "From Malay Nationalism to Malaysian Nation?" In *After Independence: Making and Protecting the Nation in Postcolonial and Post-Communist States*, edited by Lowell Barrington, 45-70. Ann Arbor, MI: University of Michigan Press, 2006.

———. "Malaysia in 1987: Decline of the Malay Way." *Asian Survey* 28, no. 2 (February 1988): 213-222.

———. "Language and Language Policy in Malaysia." In *Language Policy and National Unity*, edited by William R. Beer and James E. Jacob, 151-177. Totowa, NJ: Rowman and Littlefield, 1985.

McClelland, David. "Business-Drive and National Achievement." In *Social Change*, edited by Amitai Etzioni and Eva Etzioni, 165-178. New York: Basic Books, 1964.

McRoberts, R. "A Study of Growth: An Economic History of Melaka 1400-1510." *Journal of Malaysian Branch of the Royal Asiatic Society* 64, no. 2 (December 1991): 47-79.

Means, Gordon P. "Soft Authoritarianism in Malaysia and Singapore." *Journal of Democracy* 7, no. 4 (October 1996): 103-117.

Mehmet, Ozay. *Development in Malaysia: Poverty, Wealth and Trusteeship*. Kent, UK: Crom-Helm, 1986.

Mills, C. Wright. *The Sociological Imagination*. New York: Oxford University Press, 2000.

Milne, R. S., and Diane K. Mauzy. *Malaysian Politics under Mahathir*. London: Routledge, 1999.

Milne, R. S., and K.J. Ratnam. *Malaysia: New States in a New Nation*. London: Frank Cass, 1974.

Mohamad, Maznah. "The Ascendance of Bureaucratic Islam and the Secularization of the Sharia in Malaysia." *Pacific Affairs* 83, no. 2 (September 2010): 505-524.

Mohamad, Mustapa. "The Case of Malaysia after the Financial Crisis and the Way Ahead." Paper presented at the Forum for Economic Transition and Change, Northern University of Malaysia, Sintok, Malaysia, October 2001.

Mohamed, Rugayah. "Public Enterprises." In *Privatising Malaysia: Rents, Rhetoric, Realities*, edited by K.S. Jomo, 63-80. London: Westview, 1995.

Mokhtar, Mariam. "Muhyiddin Makes a Mockery of Democracy." *Malaysian Mirror*. 2011. www.Malaysianmirror.com/media-buzz-detail/41-opinion/55765-muyiddin-makes-a mockery-of-democracy (accessed December 1, 2011).

Moore, Matthew. "Challenge to the US: Prove JI Exists." *Sydney Morning Herald*. 2003. www.smh.com.au/articles/2003/09/08/106290200191.html (accessed May 9, 2009).

Morgan, Michael. "The Rise and Fall of Trade Unionism, 1945-1950." In *Malaya: The Making of a Neo-Colony*, edited by Mohamed Amin and Malcolm Caldwell, 150-198. Nottingham, UK: Russell Press, 1977.

Morrison, Ian. "The Communist Uprising in Malaya." In *Southeast Asia, A Colonial History: Peaceful Transitions to Independence*, edited by Paul Kratoska, 180-189. London: Routledge, 2004.

Moten, Abdul Rashid. "The 2004 and 2008 General Elections in Malaysia: Towards a Multicultural, Bi-party Political System?" *Asian Journal of Political Science* 17, no. 2 (August 2009): 173-194.

Mukherjee, Wendy. "Kaum Muda and Kaum Tua in West Java." In *Islam: Essays on Scripture, Thought, and Society: A Festschrift in Honour of Anthony H. Johns*, edited by Peter G. Riddell and Tony Street, 309-323. London: BRILL, 1997.

Munro-Kua, Anne. *Authoritarian Populism in Malaysia*. New York: St. Martin's Press, 1996.

Muzaffar, Chandra. "Political Marginalization in Malaysia." In *Indian Communities in Southeast Asia*, edited by K.S. Sandhu and A. Mani, 211-236. Singapore: ISEAS, 2006.

My Sinchew. "Ling Applies to Transfer Case to High Court." *My Sinchew.Com*. 2010. www.mysinchew.com/node/44378 (accessed January 12, 2011).

Nagl, John. *Counterinsurgency Lessons from Malaya and Vietnam: Learning to Eat Soup with a Knife*. New York: Praeger. 2002.

Nathan, K.S. *Economic Slowdown and Domestic Politics: Malaysia Boleh?* Singapore: ISEAS, 2001.

———. "Outcome for the Barisan Nasional Coalition." Paper presented at Trends in Malaysia Seminar, Singapore, December 3, 1999.

NEAC. *New Economic Model for Malaysia*. Kuala Lumpur: Percetakan Nasional Malaysia, 2010.

Netto, Anil. "Bumpy Road for Proton." *Asia Times*. 2005. www.atimes/atimes/Southeast Asia/GG30Ac01html (accessed March 20, 2008).

New York Times. "Malaysia Takes Control of No.2 Bank Company." *New York Times*. 1998. www.nytimes.com/1998/12/01/business (accessed December 2, 2010).

Ng, Chelsea, and Hurbaiti Hamdar. "Altantuya Case: Razak Acquitted." *Star Online*. 2008. thestar.com.my/news/story.asp?file=/2008/10/31/nation/20081031084658.html (Accessed February 12, 2010).

NOC. *May 13 Tragedy*. Kuala Lumpur: Government Printers, 1969.

Nonini, Donald. *British Colonial Rule and the Resistance of the Malay Peasantry, 1900-1957*. New Haven, CT: Yale University Press, 1992.

Noor, Farish. "PAS Post Fadzil Noor: Future Directions and Prospects." Singapore: ISEAS, 2002.

Numazaki, Ichiro. "The Export-oriented Industrialization of Pacific Rim Countries and their Presence in the Global Market." In *The Four Asian Tigers: Economic Development and the Global political Economy*, edited by Eun Mee Kim, 64-87. San Diego: Academic Press, 1998.

O'Shannassy, Michael. "Malaysia in 2010: Between a Rock and a Hard Place." *Asian Survey* 51, no. 1 (January 2010.): 173-185.

Omar, Ariffin. *Bangsa Melayu: Malay Concepts of Democracy and Community, 1945-50*. Kuala Lumpur: University of Malaya Press, 1993.

Ongkili, James P. *Nation-Building in Malaysia, 1946-1974*. Singapore: Oxford University Press, 1985.

Oorjitham, Susan. "Urban Working-Class Indians in Malaysia." In *Indian Communities in Southeast Asia*, edited by K.S. Sandhu and A. Mani, 504-512. Singapore: ISEAS, 2006.

Othman, Muhammad Reduan. *Islam dan Masyarakat Melayu. Peranan dan Pengaruh Timur Tengah*. Kuala Lumpur: University of Malaya Press, 2005.

Palmore, J.A., Ramesh Chander, and Dorothy Fernandez. "The Demographic Situation in Malaysia." In *Population and Development in Southeast Asia,* edited by J.F. Kantner and L. McCaffrey, 57-82. Lexington, MA: Lexington Books, 1975.

Pang Eng Fong. "Race, Income Distributions, and Development in Malaysia and Singapore." In *The Chinese in Southeast Asia, Ethnicity and Economic Activity,* edited by in Linda Lim and L. A. Gossling, 316-335. Singapore: Maruzen Press, 1983.

Parmer, J. N. *Colonial Labour Policy and Administration: A History of Labor in the Rubber Plantation Industry in Malaya c. 1910-1941*. Locust Valley, NY: J.J. Augustin, 1960.

Perumal, Muniappan. "Economic Growth and Income Inequality in Malaysia 1957-1987." *Singapore Economic Review* 34, no. 2 (October 1989): 33-46.

Pillai, Shanthini. *Colonial Visions, Postcolonial Revisions: Images of the Indian Diaspora in Malaysia*. Newcastle, UK: Cambridge Scholars Publishing, 2007.

Poulantzas, Nicos. *State, Power, Socialism*. Translated by Peter Camiller. London: Verso, 2001.

Purcell, Victor. *The Chinese in Southeast Asia*. London: Oxford University Press, 1965.

Pye, Lucian C., and Mary W. Pye. *Asian Power and Politics: The Cultural Dimensions of Authority*. Cambridge, MA: Harvard University Press, 1985.

Rabushka, Alvin. *Race and Politics in Urban Malaya*. Washington D.C.: Hoover Press, 1973.

Rajakrishnan, R. "Social Change and Group Identity among Sri Lankan Tamils." In *Indian Communities in Southeast Asia*, edited by K.S. Sandhu and A. Mani, 541-557. Singapore: ISEAS, 2006.

Ramakrishna, Kumar. "Making Malaya Safe for Decolonization: The Rural Chinese Factor in the Counterinsurgency Campaign." In *The Transformation of Southeast Asia: International Perspectives*, edited by Marc Frey, Ronald W. Pruessen, and Tai Yong Tan, 161-179. New York: M.E. Sharpe, 2003.

Ramasamy, P. "Social Economic Transformation of Indian Plantation Workers." In *Indian Communities in Southeast Asia*, edited by K.S. Sandhu and A. Mani, 314-322. Singapore: ISEAS, 2006.

Reece, Bob. *The White Rajahs of Sarawak, a Borneo Dynasty*. Singapore: Archipelago Press, 2004.

Robinson, William. *Promoting Polyarchy: Globalization, US Intervention, and Hegemony*. New York: Cambridge University Press, 1996.

Rodolfo, Jacobson. "In Search of Status: Bahasa Malaysia as a Language for National Unification." In *Status Change of Languages*, edited by Ulrich Ammon and Marlis Hellinger, 200-228. Berlin: De Gruyter, 1991.

Roff, William. *The Origins of Malay Nationalism*. Kuala Lumpur: Oxford University Press, 1995.

Rostow, Walt Whitman. *Stages of Economic Growth*. Cambridge, UK: Cambridge University Press, 1970.

Rueschemeyer, Deitrich, Evelyn Stephens, and John Stephens. *Capitalist Development and Democracy*. Cambridge, England: Polity Press, 1992.

Ryan, N. J. *A History of Malaysia and Singapore*. Kuala Lumpur: Oxford University Press, 1976.

Sadiq, Kamal. "When Being Native is Not Enough: Citizens as Foreigners in Malaysia." *Asian Perspective* 33, no.1 (January 2009): 5-32.

Sadka, Emily. *The Protected Malay States, 1874-1895*. Kuala Lumpur: University of Malaya Press, 1968.

Said, Edward. *Culture and Imperialism*. New York: First Vintage Books, 1994.

Said, Muhammad Ikmal. "Ethnic Perspectives of the Left." In *Fragmented Vision*, edited by Joel S. Kahn and Francis Loh, 254-281. Honolulu, HI: University of Hawaii Press, 1992.

Salih, Kamal, and Zainal Aznam Yusof. "Overview of the NEP and Framework for a Post-1990 National Economic Policy: Options." *Malaysian Economic Review* 24, no. 2 (March 1989): 13-61.

Salleh, Hashim. "Globalization and the Challenges to Malay Nationalism as the Essence of Malaysian Nationalism." In *Nationalism and Globalization: East and West*, edited by Leo Suryadinata, 132-174. Singapore: ISEAS, 2000.

Salleh, M. Zainuddin, and Zulkifly Osman."The Economic Structure." In *Political Economy of Malaysia*, edited by E. K. Fisk and H. Osman-Rani, 141-147. Kuala Lumpur: Oxford University Press, 1982.

Salman, Ali, and Mohd Safar Hasim. "New Media and Democracy: The New Political Landscape in Malaysia." *Akedemika* 81, no.1 (January 2011): 15-21.

Sandhu, Kernail Singh. *Indians in Malaya: Some Aspects of their Immigration and Settlement (1786–1957)*. Cambridge: University Press, 2010.

———. "The Coming of the Indians to Malaysia." In *Indian Communities in Southeast Asia*, edited by K.S. Sandhu and A. Mani, 151-189. Singapore: ISEAS, 2006.

———. "Sikhs in Malaysia: A Society in Transition." In *Indian Communities in Southeast Asia*, edited by K.S. Sandhu and A. Mani, 558-567. Singapore: ISEAS, 2006.

Sani, Mohammad Azizudin. "Freedom of Speech and Democracy in Malaysia." *Asian Journal of Political Science* 16, no.1 (April 2008): 85-104.

Saruwatari, Keiko. "Malaysia's Localisation Policy and its Impact on British-Owned Enterprises," *Developing Economies* 29, no. 4 (December 1991): 371-385.

Saunders, Graham E. *History of Brunei*. New York: Routledge, 2002.

Saw Swee Hock. *The Population of Malaysia and Singapore*. Singapore: Institute of Southeast Asian Studies, 2007.

Scalapino, Robert. "National Political Institutions and Leadership in Asia." *Washington Quarterly* 15, no.4 (Winter 1992): 152-172.

Scott, James. C. *Weapons of the Weak: Every Day Forms of Peasant Resistance*. New Haven: Yale University Press, 1985.

Seabrook, Jeremy. *Victims of Development: Resistance and Alternatives*. London: Verso, 1993.

Shameen, Assif, and Tim Healy. "Seeking a Middle Course." *Asiaweek* 25, no. 7 (January 1999): 24-28.

Shamsul Amri Baharuddin. *From British to Bumiputera Rule: Local Politics and Rural Development in Peninsular Malaysia*. Singapore: Institute of Southeast Asian Studies, 2004.

———."The Economic Dimension of Malay Nationalism." *Developing Economies* 35, no. 3 (September 1997): 240-261.

———. "The Battle Royal: The UMNO Elections of 1987." In *Southeast Asian Affairs*, edited by Mohammed Ayoob and Ng Chee Yuen, 170-188. Singapore: Institute of Southeast Asian Studies, 1988.

Shannon, Thomas. R. *An Introduction to the World-System Perspective.* Boulder, CO: Westview Press, 1996.

Shari, Ishak, and Rugayah Mat Zin. "Patterns and Trends of Income Distribution in Malaysia, 1970-87." *Singapore Economic Review* 25, no. 4 (April 1990): 102-123.

Sharif, Kamaruddin. "The Demographic Structure." In *The Political Economy of Malaysia*, edited by E.K. Fisk and H. Osman-Rani, 66-87. Kuala Lumpur: Oxford University Press, 1982.

Shennan, Margaret. *Out in the Midday Sun: The British in Malaya 1880-1960.* London: John Murray, 2000.

Sheridan, Michael. "Blog War over Sultan Mahmud Iskandar." *Sunday Times Online.* 2010. www.timesonline.co.uk/tol/nes/world/asia/article7017953.ece.html. (accessed July 18, 2010).

Shin, Kwang-Yeong. "The Political Economy of Economic Growth in East Asia: South Korea and Taiwan." In *The Four Asian Tigers: Economic Development and the Global political Economy*, edited by Eun Mee Kim, 3-32. San Diego, CA: Academic Press, 1998.

Short, Anthony. *The Communist Insurrection in Malaya 1948-1960.* London: Oxford University Press, 1976.

Sidhu, J. "Decentralization of the Federated Malay States 1930-34." *Peninjau Sejarah* 1, no.66 (1966):17-28.

Silcock, T.H. "Approximate Racial Division of National Income." In *Political Economy of Independent Malaya*, edited by T.H Silcock and and E.K. Fisk, 276-282. Berkeley: University of California Press, 1963.

Smith, Jackie. *Social Movements for Global Democracy.* Baltimore, MD: Johns Hopkins Press, 2008.

Smith, Simon. *British Relations with the Malay Rulers from Decentralization to Malay Independence.* Kuala Lumpur: Oxford University Press, 1995.

So, Alvin Y., and Stephen K. Chui. "Modern East Asia in World–Systems Analysis." In *A World Systems Reader: New Perspectives on Gender, Urbanism, Cultures, Indigenous Peoples and Ecology*, edited by Thomas D. Hall, 271-283. Lanham, MD: Rowman & Littlefield, 2000.

Sta. Maria, Stephanie. "Utusan Malaysia: Behind the Print." *Free Malaysia Today.* 2011. www.freemalaysiatoday.com/2011/05/11/utusan-behind-the-print (accessed December 1, 2011).

Stamp, Gavin. "Malaysia Focused on Vision 2020." *BBC News Online.* 2006. news.bbc.co.uk/2/hi/5020794.stm (accessed July 2, 2010).

Stengel, Rick. "2011 Person of the Year," *Time Magazine*, December 26, 2011, 52-60.

Stenson, M.R. *Class, Race and Colonialism in West Malaysia: The Indian Case.* St. Lucia: University of Queensland Press, 1980.

———. *Industrial Conflict in Malaya.* London: Oxford University Press, 1970.

Stevenson, Rex. *Cultivators and Administrators: British Policy toward Malays 1875-1906.* Oxford, UK: Oxford University Press, 1975.

Stickler, Angus. "Borneo Tribe Fights for Survival." *BBC News Online.* 2010. www.bmf.ch/files/news/BBC_News_Today_Borneo_tribe_fights_for_survival_1.pdf (accessed December 20, 2010).

Stockwell, A. J. "British Imperial Policy and Decolonization in Malaya, 1942-52." In *Southeast Asia: Colonial History Volume 5*, edited by Paul Kratoska, 210-231. London: Routledge, 2001.

———. *British Policy and Malay Politics during the Malayan Union Experiment, 1945-1948*. Kuala Lumpur: Oxford University Press, 1979.
Strand, David. "Community, Society, and History in Sun Yat Sen's Sanmin Zhuyi." In *Culture and State in Chinese History,* edited by Theodore Huters, R.B. Wong, and Pauline Yu, 326-345. Stanford, CA: Stanford University Press, 2002.
Strange, Susan. "The Declining Authority of States." In *The Globalization Reader*, edited by Frank Lechner and John Boli, 219-225. Malden, MA: Blackwell Publishing, 2007.
Suny, Ronald Grigor. "Don't Paint Nationalism Red! National Revolution and Socialist Anti-imperialism." In *Decolonization: Perspectives from Now and Then*, edited by Prasenjit Duara, 176-198. New York: Routledge, 2004.
Suryadinata, Leo. *Nationalism and Globalism; East and West*. Singapore: Institute of Southeast Asian Studies, 2000.
Swettenham, Frank. *A Nocturne and Other Malayan Stories and Sketches*. Introduced by William R. Roff. Kuala Lumpur: Oxford University Press, 1993.
Tai Yuen. *Labour Unrest in Colonial Malaya*. Penang, Malaysia: Universiti Sains Malaysia Publications, 1999.
Talib, Shaharil. *After Its own Image: The Terengganu Experience 1881-1941*. Kuala Lumpur: Oxford University Press, 1984.
Tan Chee Beng. *Chinese Overseas: Comparative Cultural Issues*. Hong Kong: Hong Kong University Press, 2004.
Tan Cheng Lock. "One Country, One People, One Government." Speech delivered at the *Presidential Address at Meeting of General Committee of the MCA*, Penang, October 30, 1949.
Tan Eng Teik. *The Rhetoric of Bangsa and Minzu: Community and Nation in Tension, the Malay Peninsula, 1900-1955*. Sydney: Monash Asia Institute, 1988.
Tan Liok Ee. "Baggage from the Past, Eyes on the Future: Chinese Education in Malaysia Today." In *Ethnic Chinese in Singapore and Malaysia: A Dialogue between Tradition and Modernity,* edited by Leo Suryadinata, 155-171. Singapore: Time Academic Press, 2002.
Tan Tai Yong. *Creating Greater Malaysia: Decolonization and the Politics of Merger*. Singapore: ISEAS, 2008.
Tan, Jeff. *Privatization in Malaysia: Regulation, Rent-seeking, and Policy Failure*. London: Routledge, 2008.
Tarling, Nicholas. *Imperialism in Southeast Asia* London: Routledge, 1999.
———. *The Cambridge History of Southeast Asia: From World War Two to the Present*. Cambridge, UK: Cambridge University Press, 1999.
———. "Brooke Rule in Sarawak and Its Principles." *Journal of the Malaysian Branch of the Royal Asiatic Society* 65, no.1 (1992): 15-26.
Tate, D. J. M. *The Lake Club 1890-1990: In Pursuit of Excellence*, Kuala Lumpur: Oxford University Press, 1990.
Tay, T. Y. "A Power Struggle in the Offing." *Sin Chew Online*. 2010. www.mysinchew.com/node/44818.html (accessed March 13 2010).
Tennant, Paul. "The Decline of Elective Local Government in Malaysia." *Asian Survey* 13, no. 4 (April 1973): 347-365.
Teoh, Shannon. "Najib Announces Repeal of ISA, Three Emergency Declarations." *The Malaysian Insider*. 2011. www.themalaysianinsider.com/Malaysia/article/najib-announces-repeal-of-isa-three-emergency-declaration.html (accessed September 30, 2011).

Tham Seong Chee. "Ideology, Politics and Economic Modernization: The Case of the Malays in Malaysia." *Southeast Asian Journal of Social Science* 1, no. 1 (August 1973): 41-59.

Thornton, A. P. *The Imperial Idea and Its Enemies.* London: MacMillan, 1985.

Tregonning, K.G. *History of Modern Sabah (North Borneo 1881-1963).* Kuala Lumpur: University of Malaya Press, 1965.

———. *Papers on Malayan History.* Singapore: University of Malay Press, 1962.

Trocki, Carl. *Opium and Empire: Chinese Society in Colonial Singapore, 1800-1910.* Ithaca, NY: Cornell University Press, 1990.

Turnbull, C.M. *A Short History of Malaysia, Singapore, and Brunei.* Winchester, MA: Allen and Unwin, 1989.

Ufen, Andreas. "The 2008 Elections in Malaysia: Uncertainties of Electoral Authoritarianism." *Taiwan Journal of Democracy* 4, No. 1 (July 2008): 155-169.

UNCTAD. *World Investment Report 2007: Transnational Corporations, Extractive Industries, and Development.* Geneva: United Nations Publications, 2007.

UNDP. *Mitigating the Human Impact of the Asian Financial Crisis: The Role of the UNDP.* New York: OUP, 1999.

Vega, Nina Merchant, and Herizal Hazri. "Malaysia's Middle Income Trap." In *Asia.* 2011. asiafoundation.org/in-asia/2011/01/26/malaysia's.html (accessed January 31, 2011).

Verma, Vidhu. *Malaysia: The State and Civil Society in Transition.* Boulder CO: Lynne Rienner, 2002.

Vinod; G. "DAP Calls for New IPP-TNB Deal," *Free Malaysia Today.* 2011. www.freemalaysiatoday.com/2011/05/31/dap-calls-for-new-tnb-ipp-deal. (accessed June 31 2011).

Von Vorys, Karl. *Democracy without Consensus.* Princeton, NJ: Princeton University Press, 1975.

Voon Phin Keong. *Western Rubber Planting Enterprise in Southeast Asia 1876-1921.* Kuala Lumpur: University of Malaya Press, 1976.

Wadley, Reed. "Punitive Expeditions and Divine Revenge: Oral and Colonial Histories of Rebellion and Pacification in Western Borneo, 1886-1902." *Ethnohistory* 51, no. 3 (Summer 2004): 609-636.

Walker, John Henry. *Power and Prowess: The Origins of Brooke Kinship.* Honolulu: University of Hawaii Press, 2002.

Wallerstein, Immanuel. *World System Analysis: An Introduction.* Durham NC: Duke University Press, 2004.

———. *The Capitalist World Economy.* Cambridge UK: Cambridge University Press, 1997.

———. *Geopolitics and Geoculture.* New York: Cambridge University Press, 1991.

Webster, Anthony. *Gentlemen Capitalists: British Imperialism in Southeast Asia 1770-1890.* New York: St. Martin's Press, 1998.

Weiss, Meredith Leigh. *Protests and Possibilities: Civil Society and Coalitions for Political Change in Malaysia.* Stanford, CA; Stanford University Press, 2006.

———. "History, Legal Framework, and Characteristics." In *Social Movements in Malaysia: From Moral Communities to NGOs,* edited by Meredith Weiss and Saliha Hassan, 17-44. London: RoutledgeCurzon, 2003.

Weiss, Meredith Leigh, and Saliha Hassan. "From Moral Communities to NGOs." *Social Movements in Malaysia: From Moral Communities to NGOs,* edited by Meredith Weiss and Saliha Hassan, 1-15. London: RoutledgeCurzon, 2003.

Whitmeyer, Joseph. "Elites and Popular Nationalism," *British Journal of Sociology* 53, no. 3 (September 2002): 321-341.

Wild, Anthony. *The East India Company: Trade and Conquest from 1600*. London: Harper-Collins, 2000.

Wong Chin Huat. "UMNO's Unholy Trinity." *Malaysian Bar*. 2009. www.malaysianbar.org.my/general_comments/umnos_unholy_treaty.html (accessed January 12, 2010).

Wong Choon Mei. "French Probe: New Names Emerge, Focus Perimekar, Altantuya." *Malaysian Chronicle*. 2010. www.malaysia- chronicle.com/2010/07// french-probe-focus-on-perimekar-also.html (accessed December 13, 2010).

Wong, Danny Tze Ken. *Historical Sabah: Community and Society*. Kota Kinabalu: Natural History Publications, 2004.

Wong, Joseph. "The Adaptive Developmental State in Asia." *Journal of Southeast Asian Studies* 4, no. 3 (September 2004): 345-362.

Wong, Raphael. "Eric Chia Acquitted of CBT." *Star Online*. 2007. thestar.com.my/news /story.asp?file=2007/6/27/nation (accessed June 11, 2009).

Woolley, George Cathcart. *The Timogun Muruts of Sabah*. Kota Kinabalu: Kota Kinabalu Natural History Publications, 2004.

Worcester, D. E. *The Philippines, Past and Present*. New York: Macmillan, 1930.

World Bank. *World Development Report 1993*. New York: Oxford University Press, 1994.

Wright, L. R. *The Origins of British Borneo*. Hong Kong: Hong Kong University Press, 1970.

Yasuda, Nokuyuki. "Malaysia's New Economic Policy and the Industrial Co-Ordination Act." *Developing Economics* 39, no. 4 (December 1991): 330-349.

Yen Ching-Hwang. *The Chinese in Southeast Asia and Beyond: Socieconomic Dimensions and Beyond*. Singapore: World Scientific Publishing, 2008.

———. "Historical Background." In *The Chinese in Malaysia,* edited by Lee Kam Hing and Tan Chee-Beng, 1-36. Kuala Lumpur: Oxford University Press, 2002.

———. *A Social History of Chinese in Singapore and Malaya 1800-1911*. Singapore: Oxford University Press, 1987.

———. "Overseas Chinese Nationalism in Singapore and Malaya 1877-1912." *Modern Asian Studies* 16, no. 3 (1982): 397-425.

Yeo Kim Wah. *The Political Development in Singapore 1945-1955*. Singapore: Singapore University Press, 1973.

Yeoh, Brenda. *Contesting Space in Singapore: Power Relations and the Urban Built Environment*. Singapore: NUS Publishing, 2003.

Yeung, Henry W. C. "The Internationalization of Ethnic Chinese Business Firms from Southeast Asia: Strategies, Processes and Competitive Advantage." *International Journal of Urban and Regional Research* 23, no. 1 (March 1999): 103-127.

Yong, C. F. "The Origins and Development of the Malayan Communist Movement, 1919-1930." *Modern Asian Studies* 25, no. 4 (October 1991): 625-648.

Zakaria Ahmad. "The 1999 General Elections: A Preliminary Review." Paper presented at Trends in Malaysia Seminar, Singapore, December 1999.

———. "The Political Structure." In *The Political Economy of Malaysia*, edited by E. K. Fisk and H. Osman-Rani, 94-110. Kuala Lumpur: Oxford University Press, 1982.

Zakaria Ahmad, and Sharifah Alatas. "Malaysia: In an Uncertain Mode." In *Driven by Growth*, edited by Paul Morley, 176-196. New York: M.E. Sharpe, 1999.

Zakaria, Fareed. *The Future of Freedom: Illiberal Democracy at Home and Abroad*. New York: W.W. Norton, 2007.

Index

About the Author

Dr. Azlan Tajuddin is associate professor and chair of the Sociology Department at La Roche College in Pittsburgh, Pennsylvania. A graduate of political science and international relations from the University of Minnesota, he went on to obtain a doctorate in sociology from the University of Tennessee. Prior to his involvement in the collegiate world, Dr. Tajuddin had worked in various lower and middle management positions in both business and government. His experiences took him to numerous places around the world, and introduced him to different peoples and cultures in the various countries visited. As an academician, Dr. Tajuddin is trained as a political economist. He has presented papers and published several works in the area of development, ethnic relations, educational sociology, and even management. As an instructor, he considers himself a general sociologist and teaches a variety of courses within the discipline including the environment, sports, stratification, ethnic conflict, religion, political sociology, urbanization, migration, social movements, global problems, and cultural anthropology.

www.ingramcontent.com/pod-product-compliance
Lightning Source LLC
Chambersburg PA
CBHW051253200926
51612CB00001B/35
* 9 7 8 0 7 3 9 1 7 1 9 6 7 *